CW01338352

IN-HOUSE LAWYERS' ETHICS

This book provides an empirically grounded, in-depth investigation of the ethical dimensions to in-house practice and how legal risk is defined and managed by in-house lawyers and others. The growing significance and status of the role of General Counsel has been accompanied by growth in legal risk as a phenomenon of importance. In-house lawyers are regularly exhorted to be more commercial, proactive and strategic, to be business leaders and not (mere) lawyers, but they are increasingly exposed for their roles in organisational scandals. This book poses the question: how far does going beyond being a lawyer conflict with or entail being more ethical? It explores the role of in-housers by calling on three key pieces of empirical research: two tranches of interviews with senior in-house lawyers and senior compliance staff; and an unparalleled large survey of in-house lawyers. On the basis of this evidence, the authors explore how ideas about in-house roles shape professional logics; how far professional notions such as independence play a role in those logics; and the ways in which ethical infrastructure are managed or are absent from in-house practice. It concludes with a discussion of whether and how in-house lawyers and their regulators need to take professionalism and professional ethicality more seriously.

In-House Lawyers' Ethics

Institutional Logics, Legal Risk and the Tournament of Influence

Richard Moorhead
Steven Vaughan
and
Cristina Godinho

•HART•
OXFORD • LONDON • NEW YORK • NEW DELHI • SYDNEY

HART PUBLISHING

Bloomsbury Publishing Plc

Kemp House, Chawley Park, Cumnor Hill, Oxford, OX2 9PH, UK

HART PUBLISHING, the Hart/Stag logo, BLOOMSBURY and the Diana logo are
trademarks of Bloomsbury Publishing Plc

First published in Great Britain 2019

Reprinted 2019

Copyright © Richard Moorhead, Steven Vaughan and Cristina Godinho, 2019

Richard Moorhead, Steven Vaughan and Cristina Godinho have asserted their right under the Copyright,
Designs and Patents Act 1988 to be identified as Authors of this work.

All rights reserved. No part of this publication may be reproduced or transmitted in any form or
by any means, electronic or mechanical, including photocopying, recording, or any information storage
or retrieval system, without prior permission in writing from the publishers.

While every care has been taken to ensure the accuracy of this work, no responsibility for
loss or damage occasioned to any person acting or refraining from action as a result
of any statement in it can be accepted by the authors, editors or publishers.

All UK Government legislation and other public sector information used in the work is
Crown Copyright ©. All House of Lords and House of Commons information used in the
work is Parliamentary Copyright ©. This information is reused under the terms of the
Open Government Licence v3.0 (http://www.nationalarchives.gov.uk/doc/
open-government-licence/version/3) except where otherwise stated.

All Eur-lex material used in the work is © European Union,
http://eur-lex.europa.eu/, 1998–2019.

A catalogue record for this book is available from the British Library.

Library of Congress Cataloging-in-Publication data

Names: Moorhead, Richard, author. | Vaughan, Steven, author. | Godinho, Cristina, author.

Title: In-house lawyers' ethics : institutional logics, legal risk and the tournament of influence /
Richard Moorhead, Steven Vaughan and Cristina Godinho.

Description: Oxford, UK ; Portland, Oregon : Hart Publishing, 2019.

Identifiers: LCCN 2018029511 (print) | LCCN 2018030726 (ebook) |
ISBN 9781509905935 (Epub) | ISBN 9781509905942 (hardback : alk. paper)

Subjects: LCSH: Corporate legal departments—Great Britain. | Legal ethics—Great Britain.

Classification: LCC KD472.I5 (ebook) | LCC KD472.I5 M66 2018 (print) | DDC 174/.30941—dc23

LC record available at https://lccn.loc.gov/2018029511

ISBN: HB: 978-1-50990-594-2
ePDF: 978-1-50990-592-8
ePub: 978-1-50990-593-5

Typeset by Compuscript Ltd, Shannon
Printed and bound in Great Britain by TJ International Ltd, Padstow, Cornwall

To find out more about our authors and books visit www.hartpublishing.co.uk.
Here you will find extracts, author information, details of forthcoming events
and the option to sign up for our newsletters.

For our Mums
They knew when and how to say, 'No'.

Acknowledgements

WE HAVE BEEN working on this book, in one form or another, since 2013. Over that time, a number of people have been generous enough to contribute to our data and to our thinking. We are indebted to the many in-house lawyers we spoke to as part of the process of designing the research, considering its findings and, most importantly, to those who made time available for us to interview them and who attended the seminars which helped clarify our thinking. They must remain anonymous. A number of organisations assisted with the distribution of our survey. Here, we would like to thank the Solicitors Regulation Authority, the Bar Association for Commerce and Industry, the GC100, LBC Wise Counsel, and *Legal Business* magazine. Julie Ball provided considerable research assistance with the conduct of the legal risk part of our work, for which we are very grateful. Tom Kilroy, (then) Chief of Staff at Misys, helped us design the ethical case studies we have used in this research, and Stephen Mayson provided important thoughts on our research instruments and results. Paul Gilbert, of LBC Wise Counsel, assisted us in facilitating the initial meetings and provided expert assistance as the research has progressed. His enthusiasm drove our decision to conduct the survey that is the backbone for this work.

A number of academics, regulators and practitioners kindly provided comments on earlier drafts. We are indebted for feedback from Julia Black, Iris Chiu, James Faulconbridge, John Flood, Hazel Genn, Robert W Gordon, Chris Hanretty, Sung Hui Kim, Renee Knake, Joan Loughrey, Tim Livesley, Bruce Macmillan, Suzanne le Mire, Jonathan Montgomery, Christine Parker, Mitt Regan, Deborah L Rhode, Mari Sako, William H Simon, Leo Staub, Eli Wald, Julian Webb, and David B Wilkins. Emily Braggins and Sinead Moloney at Hart Publishing have been (overly) patient with us. We are very grateful, and hope what follows was worth the wait. Our families have also been supportive during this project, and understanding of when time on the book has taken time away from them. Steven is, in particular, grateful to Richard's wife Leanne for taking his side (and not Richard's) in all arguments grammatical.

We are grateful too to the Centre for Ethics and Law at UCL's Faculty of Laws for supporting this work. The Centre was, during the life of this project, supported by BAE Systems, Carillion plc, HSBC, and Norton Rose Fulbright. Their sponsorship part-funded this work but has been run entirely independently of them. It is the same for the Economic and Social Research Council, whose grant to Steven part-funded his time on this project (grant reference ES/K00834X/1). Steven was also lucky enough to spend time as a visiting fellow at the universities of Melbourne, Michigan State, and Stanford, where he was able to road-test some of the ideas in this book. The same holds true for papers given by Richard at Melbourne, Leeds, Fordham, Vrijje Amsterdam and (with Steven) at NYU for an Ethical Systems event. Elements of the work were also road-tested at practitioner conferences run by the Law Society, the Scottish Law Society, the *Economist*, the Dutch Bar, the NDPB Lawyers' Group, Legal Business, LBC Wise Counsel and at many in-house legal team training days. In-house lawyers have been, almost without exception, a brilliant community to engage with. They are an enormously talented and open group of individuals.

Finally, while we would like to blame any errors or omissions in this book on some distant chief executive who either made us do it, or created a culture which inevitably led to failings for which we can in no sense be held responsible, those errors and omissions are sadly our own.

Contents

Acknowledgements .... *vii*

1. Introduction 1
   Context 2
   Professionalism 5
   Ethics and Lawyers' Ethics 11
   Legal Risk 15
   Institutional Logics and Regulation 20
   The Structure of this Book and Our Conclusions 23

2. Methods 26
   The First Set of Interviews 29
   The Second Set of Interviews 31
   The Survey 32
   Mapping Indicators of In-House Practice 34
       In-House Role Identity 34
       Professional Orientation 38
   Conduct of the Survey and Responses 40
   A Note on Terminology 44
   Conclusions 44

3. The In-House Lawyer and Their Place in Networks 46
   Understanding In-House Lawyers' Place in the Profession 47
   The Move In-House 47
   The Evolution of the In-House Role 50
   The Balancing of Roles 52
   Structural Predictors and Mediators 54
   Presence on the Board 58
   Employer–Employee Relations and the Role of the In-House Lawyer 60
      (i)   Component 1 – The Existence of Sometimes Negative
           Relationships with the Business 61
      (ii) Component 2 – An Understanding of Independence and Role 62
      (iii) Component 3 – The Existence of Uneven Relationships with
           the Organisation 62
   Ethical Pressure 64
   Conclusion 68

x Contents

4. The Tournament of Influence: Saying 'No' and The Independent In-House Lawyer 70
   The Tournament of Influence 70
   The Tournament of Influence 73
   Saying 'No' 78
   Who Says 'No' (and When and How)? 79
   Getting Comfortable 86
   Conclusion 89

5. Competing Logics – A Look at Risk 95
   Risk and Risk Management Logics: An Overview 96
   Risk Appetite 98
      Risk Appetite: Defined and Undefined, Dependent or Independent 99
      Risk Conservatives 101
      Risk Accepters 102
      Risk Facilitators 103
   Who Owns 'Legal' Risk? 104
      The Broad Approach 105
      The Narrower Approach 106
      A Broader, Broad Approach 108
      Are More Focused Definitions of Risk Necessary? 109
   Looking Beyond Risk Appetite and Risk Definition – A Vignette ... 111
   Legal Risk Management Processes 114
   Experiential vs Systems Approaches 114
   Risk Mitigation 118
   Risk as a System of Understanding and Influence within the Company 120
   Narrow and Broad Framing: Some Examples from the Vignettes 122
   Conclusions 123

6. Ethics and Legal Risk Management 124
   Ethics and Risk 126
   Red Lines 128
   Utility, Socialisation and Biases: The Network of Influence 132
   Vignette – The Network Influence 135
   Vignette – Dealing with Breaches 137
   What Influences Reporting Up or Out 138
   An Ethical Space in Legal Risk Assessment? 139
   Vignette – Misuse of the Legal Function 143
   Conclusions 144

7.	**Striking the Balance: Identity and Orientation**	147
	The Distinctiveness of the In-House Lawyer	149
	Role Conception	151
	Commercial Orientation	154
	Exploiting Uncertainties Orientation	157
	Neutral Advisor Orientation	160
	Ethical Orientation	163
	Independence Orientation	165
	A Closer Look at the Orientations	167
	In-House Lawyer Team Orientations	170
	Conclusions: Identity, Orientations and the Tournament of Influence	172
8.	**Mapping the Moral Compass: Orientations, Infrastructure and Ethical Inclination**	176
	Professional Orientation	176
	Do Employers Understand Professional Obligations?	183
	Professional Ethical Infrastructure	184
	Metrics for the Moral Compass	188
	Moral Attentiveness	190
	Moral Disengagement	190
	Which Orientations are Independently Associated with Ethicality?	192
	Cluster Analysis – Inclination to Ethicality	194
	Characterisation of the Clusters	195
	Conclusions	198
9.	**The Ecologies of In-House Ethicality**	201
	Social Trusteeship	202
	Ecological Approach	205
	Teasing out Institutional Logics	208
	The Place of In-Housers in the Network of Influences	211
	Independence	214
	A Blend of Commercial and Legal Thinking – Risk	216
	Broader Influences	218
	Law and other Influences	222
	Professional Influences	225
	Some Final Thoughts	228
Appendix A: Interview Schedules		231
Index		239

1
Introduction

> General Counsel have failed as guardians.
> Ben W Heineman, Jr[1]

THE MAIN AIM of this book is to examine, in-depth, qualitatively and quantitatively, the professionalism of in-house lawyers: how they balance client and public interests, or, in the words of Heineman, how they balance their partner and guardian roles.[2] We explore the status, role and, most importantly, ethicality of in-house lawyers. To do this, we interviewed 67 in-house lawyers and senior compliance personnel and surveyed 400 lawyers working in-house in business, for the government, and in the third sector. We look at the in-house role in general and within specific contexts.

Our work builds on the existing literature in two main ways. First we quantify concepts previously examined qualitatively, teasing out fresh understandings of role-orientation and contextualising these with similarly new quantitative explorations of professional orientation, organisational pressure, and other contextual factors (such as reporting arrangements and ethical infrastructure). We complete our quantitative analysis by testing for relationships between these orientations and more general indicators of ethical inclination, mapping, in a reductive but important way, the normative implications of in-house logics.

Secondly, we aim to deepen and enrich contextual understandings of in-house lawyering through extensive use of interview data. In particular, we take an emergent 'commercial' discipline, legal risk management, and consider how in-house lawyers conceptualise that discipline as professionals; how they define and how they manage risk. We see legal risk management as an instantiation of professional logics in the decision-making apparatus of organisations, thereby examining how the tensions between organisational imperatives, independence, and legality are manifest and resolved. Our survey and interview data help us understand not only the emergent discipline of legal risk management, but also general concepts relevant to understanding in-house lawyers: commerciality, professionalism, and ethics. Through our exploration, we hope to deepen

---

[1] Ben W Heineman Jr, 'Caught in the Middle' *Corporate Counsel* (April 2007).
[2] Ben W Heineman Jr, *The Inside Counsel Revolution: Resolving the Partner-Guardian Tension* (Ankerwycke, 2016).

2 Introduction

understanding of in-house ethics and explore a key area of in-house practice not adequately captured by existing paradigms.

We agree also with Kirkland's observation that it is necessary to understand ethical problems, such as the independence of in-house lawyers, within specific contexts.[3] As a result, we push our analysis further by asking lawyers to respond to specific vignettes (realistic case studies) of risk problems. Through this multi-layered approach – from the general (professional and occupational concepts) to the specific (legal risk management) to the particular (legal risk cases) – we explore the terrain of in-house ethicality in significant depth and with particular regard to context, critically examining what would otherwise risk being abstract or nebulous. Drawing on institutional theory, we examine how in-house lawyers construct ideas of risk and ethicality, individually and institutionally.[4] We assess the way the logics interact with each other and with broader notions of right and wrong. Through this detailed, and mixed methods approach, we hope to offer fresh insights on the in-house lawyer. Whilst it provides evidence relevant to the traditional question of whether in-house lawyers really are 'professionals' or mere employees, we think the more important contribution is to inform debate on how to make in-house lawyers *more* ethical. Improvement, not judgement, is the ultimate aim here.

We are incredibly grateful to the in-house lawyers who participated in the research and gave us the enormously rich data that enable us to explore ideas about professionalism. Our hope is that this book will speak to multiple audiences: in-house lawyers and those who employ them; those in private practice; regulators; academics interested in professionalism, in organisational dynamics and change, in lawyering, and in ethics; and those more generally interested in organisations and how they manage and respond to complexity. As far as we are aware, this work represents the most detailed profiling of in-house lawyers undertaken anywhere. What unfolds in the following eight chapters uniquely links data on organisations, individuals, individual and team identities, and approaches to professional principles to externally validated proxy measures of ethical inclination. In this way, we map the moral compass of in-house lawyers. Also uniquely, we are able to map out a diversity of identity and understandings about the in-house role and evidence likely links between those understandings and the ethicality of in-house lawyers.

CONTEXT

There are two main sets of stories about in-house lawyers – those lawyers who work for, and are employed by, corporations, public bodies, and/or the

---

[3] Kimberly Kirkland, 'Ethics in Large Law Firms: The Principle of Pragmatism' (2005) 35 *University of Memphis Law Review* 631.

[4] Patricia H Thornton, William Ocasio and Michael Lounsbury, *The Institutional Logics Perspective: A New Approach to Culture, Structure, and Process* (Oxford University Press, 2012).

third sector, rather than working on their own account or in law firms. Those two sets of stories are mainly about in-house lawyers working in the corporate sphere. The first set of stories is of occupational success. In-housers are increasingly well-paid, high-status, powerful individuals within both their organisations and the wider legal profession.[5] The growth of in-house lawyer roles has been dramatic; they constitute a fifth of the entire current population of solicitors in England & Wales.[6] Once the 'forgotten men' of the legal profession,[7] women are now firmly in the majority in-house. Pivotal to the evolution of commercial legal services,[8] in-housers are equally crucial to government legal functions.[9] Even law firms have a cadre of their own General Counsel.[10] General Counsel (GCs) increasingly take leadership positions in their host organisations, with each board-level GC appointment seen as a badge of honour for the in-house community. Importantly, the roles of in-house lawyers are increasingly defined widely to encompass business, law, and strategy. As purchasers of legal services, they exert powerful economic and cultural influence over their colleagues in private practice.[11] In-housers increasingly demand fee discounts, alternative billing, and 'added-value' services such as training and secondments from the firms they instruct.[12] In these ways, in-house lawyers have, or aspire to, *influence*. That influence is built partly on notions of in-house lawyers as value-adders, and partly on the notion that business, especially international business, is subject to increasing, and increasingly complex, regulation where they need inside help. As partners of their organisations, in-house lawyers are a success.

The second set of stories suggests that the in-house role is an ethically compromised endeavour. Some in-house lawyers have been shown to manage illegality through secrecy, to offload risk onto unwitting third parties, covering dubious conduct in the cloak of absolute legality, and otherwise aiding and abetting harmful conduct.[13] General Motors' ignition-switch scandal was related

---

[5] Ben W Heineman Jr, 'The General Counsel as Lawyer-Statesman' (Harvard Law School Program on the Legal Profession Blue Paper, 2010).
[6] Law Society, 'Annual Statistical Report 2016' (Law Society, 2017).
[7] Karl Mackie, *Lawyers in Business: And the Law Business* (Springer, 1989).
[8] David Wilkins, 'Team of Rivals? Toward a New Model of the Corporate Attorney-Client Relationship' (2010) 78 *Fordham Law Review* 2067; John P Heinz and others, *Urban Lawyers: The New Social Structure of the Bar* (The University of Chicago Press, 2005) 297.
[9] Ben Yong, 'Government Lawyers and the Provision of Legal Advice within Whitehall' (The Constitution Society and The Constitution Unit Report, 2013).
[10] Elizabeth Chambliss, 'The Professionalization of Law Firm In-House Counsel' (2005) 84 *North Carolina Law Review* 1515; Jonathan Kembery, 'The Evolution of the Lawyer's Lawyer' (2016) 19 *Legal Ethics* 112.
[11] On the potential for in-house lawyers to shape the ethics of the private practice law firms they engage, see Suzanne Le Mire and Christine Parker, 'Keeping It In-House: Ethics in the Relationship between Large Law Firm Lawyers and Their Corporate Clients through the Eyes of In-House Counsel' (2008) 11 *Legal Ethics* 201.
[12] Steven Vaughan and Claire Coe, 'Independence, Representation and Risk: An Empirical Exploration of the Management of Client Relationships by Large Law Firms' (Solicitors Regulation Authority Report, October 2016).
[13] See further Chapter 3 of Deborah L Rhode, *Cheating: Ethics in Everyday Life* (Oxford University Press, 2018).

4   Introduction

to a culture hidebound by "a pattern of incompetence and neglect" significantly bolstered by the inadequacies of their in-house lawyers.[14] An Enron GC was criticised for failing to inquire genuinely into fraudulent accounting transactions partly responsible for the company's spectacular collapse.[15] In-house lawyers at Arthur Andersen were rebuked for reminding colleagues of document retention policies (effectively encouraging documents to be shredded), when it was helpful to Arthur Andersen to have allegedly incriminating documents destroyed.[16] An in-house lawyer at Apple was fired amidst investigations for acquiescing in the backdating of managerial stock options.[17] An Energy Solutions in-house lawyer was criticised by a High Court judge for not resisting plans for paying employee witnesses bonuses if the company was successful in litigation. Those employees then appeared as witnesses.[18] The GC at Tyco was accused but acquitted of improperly receiving and concealing unauthorised compensation and loans from the company, helping the former Tyco chairman and chief executive officer conceal thefts from the company.[19] Within Siemens, about 2,000 bogus business-consulting agreements were created to hide, 'more than $1.4 billion in bribes to officials in 65 nations all across the globe'.[20] Casualties in the clear-out of staff that followed included the GC and head of the audit and compliance functions.[21] Two former Barclays GCs have been interviewed in the UK under caution and many have been moved on.[22] Two lawyers at Uber lost their jobs for their role in the company's cover-up of a major security breach.[23] There is a raft of other examples, some of which we discuss later in this book. Government lawyers are not immune: two famous examples being from the US (John Yoo's advice as regards the legality of the so-called 'torture memos' in the Iraq War)[24] and the UK (Lord Goldsmith's advice about the legality of the invasion of Iraq).[25]

[14] Heineman (n 2) 1755–72.
[15] Sung Hui Kim, 'Inside Lawyers: Friends or Gatekeepers?' (2016) 84 *Fordham Law Review* 1867, 1884; 'USATODAY.Com – Unindicted, yet under a Shadow', http://usatoday30.usatoday.com/money/industries/energy/2006-01-29-enron-unindicted-usat_x.htm, accessed 11 July 2016.
[16] Yuri Mikulka and John M Horan, 'General Counsel Under Attack: Criminal and Enforcement Proceedings, Investigations, and the Travails of In-House Counsel' (Committee on Corporate Counsel Report, American Bar Association, 17 October 2007).
[17] Kim, 'Inside Lawyers' (n 15) 1886; Mikulka and Horan (n 16).
[18] *Energysolutions EU Ltd v Nuclear Decommissioning Authority* [2015] EWCA Civ 1262.
[19] Sung Hui Kim, 'The Banality of Fraud: Re-Situating the Inside Counsel as Gatekeeper' (2005) 74 *Fordham Law Review* 983, 990–91.
[20] Heineman (n 2) 1791.
[21] ibid 1810.
[22] Caroline Binham, 'Ex-Barclays Bankers to Give Evidence to Fraud Agency' *Financial Times* (London, 24 September 2014).
[23] Eric Newcomer, 'Uber Paid Hackers to Delete Stolen Data on 57 Million People' Bloomberg (21 November 2017), www.bloomberg.com/news/articles/2017-11-21/uber-concealed-cyberattack-that-exposed-57-million-people-s-data, accessed 17 April 2018.
[24] See, for example, W Bradley Wendel, 'Legal Ethics and the Separation of Law and Morals' (2005) 91 *Cornell Law Review* 67.
[25] Richard Moorhead, 'Independence Play – Chilcot on the Legal Process | Lawyer Watch', https://lawyerwatch.wordpress.com/2016/07/07/independence-play-chilcot-on-the-legal-process/, accessed 17 April 2018.

Despite these stories, away from the media's gaze, in-house lawyers can also prevent wrongdoing, investigate and respond to human rights abuses, ensure products and services are advertised and sold in legal and reputable ways, and – for listed companies and heavily regulated companies – can play a key role in ensuring companies deal fairly with markets and regulators. Whilst in-house lawyers are rightly scrutinised for their independence and their position as ethically risky insiders, there are also ethical opportunities to being an insider.[26] These opportunities exist where in-house lawyers have greater information; where they have greater and earlier influence on management decisions (to nip problems in the bud or shape decisions for the better); and where they are able to lead and proactively manage an organisation's legal functions in ways which strengthen the ethicality and legality of the organisation. Although we must also bear in mind that any claims by in-house leaders to be advancing ethical sophistication in their organisations is playing to a particular audience which demands an improvement in corporate culture.[27]

PROFESSIONALISM

That organisational misconduct can be perpetrated and enabled, but also inhibited or prevented, by in-house lawyers is dependent on their embeddedness within organisations. Embeddedness makes egregious conduct both more and less likely. The impact of this embeddedness is contingent on how in-house lawyers themselves, and the organisations they work for, see their role. And central to our interest is the question of whether and how their role as professionals impacts on that contingency. What does being professional mean in such embedded in-house contexts? And how does being professional influence in-house lawyers, and their organisations, towards or away from misconduct?

Professions are traditionally seen as being distinct from occupations, and are granted status and privileges by the State as a result, garnering status, economic rewards, and regulatory advantages over 'mere' occupations.[28] But for professions to be given these privileges, professions must serve a useful purpose for society. A key question is: what *is* that purpose? One answer is that professions are created to ensure that a particular body of esoteric knowledge is used for the *public* good, rather than lawyers' self-interests, or the interests of government,

---

[26] Kim suggests in-house lawyers have a greater 'capacity to monitor' and possibly a greater 'capacity to interdict' in relation to unethical conduct, but this does not mean they have a greater willingness to interdict. See Sung Hui Kim, 'Gatekeepers Inside Out' (2008) 21 *Georgetown Journal of Legal Ethics* 411.

[27] See, for example, Martin Arnold and Banking Editor, 'Banking Standards Report Has More Questions than Answers' *Financial Times* (8 March 2016), www.ft.com/cms/s/0/61cb8166-e483-11e5-a09b-1f8b0d268c39.html#axzz4HZrbk4JZ, accessed 17 April 2018.

[28] Alan A Paterson, 'Professionalism and the Legal Services Market' (1996) 3 *International Journal of the Legal Profession* 137.

or for private interests such as powerful clients.[29] As a result, professions are interposed between market and state promising to put other interests before their own; typically, the interests of their client and of society.[30] So, for example, lawyers are obliged to protect the rule of law and the administration of justice as well as the best interests of their clients.[31] When advising or implementing the client's legal plans, lawyers perform a balancing of individual and collective rights. They ensure, as far as possible, that a client is free to organise their affairs in the way which suits them best; that the client properly takes account of what the law requires of them; and the lawyer, when working for the client, behaves with integrity and in accordance with their professional obligations. As such, organisations are free to do business or implement policy in ways of their choosing, but with proper respect for the law.

In this way, professions traditionally claim a public-interest function. How is one to work out whether professionals really do perform that public-interest function? One way is to consider the traits of the professional group under consideration. If (in our case) in-house lawyers are properly qualified as lawyers, work to standards set by their profession, abide by rules of ethics and practice set by the profession; and manage their own work (because only they really understand that work), then on the face of it they are properly regarded as professionals.[32]

Trait-based approaches have a number of weaknesses. Of primary interest to the debate about in-house lawyers is the increasing complexity of the environments within which professions work;[33] the diminishing role for self-regulation;[34] and the increasing influence of commercial forces that make traditional professional theories less descriptively accurate.[35] To some, these indicate the end of professionalism, or a new species, or renegotiation, of professionalism.[36] But

---

[29] See: Magali Safratti Larson, *The Rise of Professionalism – A Sociological Analysis* (University of California Press, 1977); Eliot Freidson, *Professionalism, the Third Logic: On the Practice of Knowledge* (University of Chicago Press, 2001).

[30] Freidson (n 31).

[31] We come back to this below, but the regulatory codes of conduct for both solicitors and barristers in England & Wales place the public interest at the heart of professional obligations.

[32] See, for example, Julia Evetts, 'A New Professionalism? Challenges and Opportunities' (2011) 59 *Current Sociology* 406; Roy Suddaby and Daniel Muzio, 'Theoretical Perspectives on the Professions' in Laura Empson, Daniel Muzio, Joseph Broschak and Bob Hinings (eds) *The Oxford Handbook of Professional Service Firms* (Oxford University Press, 2015).

[33] Hilary Sommerlad and others, *The Futures of Legal Education and the Legal Profession* (Hart, 2015).

[34] Andrew Boon, 'Professionalism under the Legal Services Act 2007' (2010) 17 *International Journal of the Legal Profession* 195.

[35] Hilary Sommerlad, 'The Commercialisation of Law and the Enterprising Legal Practitioner: Continuity and Change' (2011) 18 *International Journal of the Legal Profession* 73; Gerard Hanlon, 'Professionalism as Enterprise: Service Class Politics and the Redefinition of Professionalism' (1998) 32 *Sociology* 43.

[36] Evetts (n 32); Herbert M Kritzer, 'The Professions Are Dead, Long Live the Professions: Legal Practice in a Postprofessional World' [1999] 33 *Law and Society Review* 713–59; Paterson (n 28).

to us they indicate the need to focus more acutely on the actual balancing of individual and collective interests that professionals undertake with a greater sensitivity to the context.[37]

We adopt Abbott's idea of professional ecology and see in-house lawyers as part of a system of linked sub-systems that are, 'neither fully constrained nor fully independent',[38] that have their own ways of thinking of, and acting on, problems but that are influenced by other social sub-systems.[39] The task then is to examine whether in-house lawyers are distinct, different from their host organisations, and whether their distinctiveness is, in a meaningful way, professional.

Abbott's approach would suggest that in-house lawyers constitute a sub-system nested within the broader systems of their profession and their host organisations, where they compete for job satisfaction, influence and status. Each system and interaction between systems brings to bear ways of thinking relevant to the interaction (the piece of advice, the deal, the reputational mishap). These ways of thinking and acting can derive from the in-house lawyers as professionals, as lawyers, or more specifically as in-house lawyers; or from their organisations or industries (say as policy formulators or commercial actors). Through examining this interplay of ideas, it is tempting to get lost in the complexity; yet we think we can explore what it means to be an in-house lawyer and still maintain a strong focus on the normative dimensions to those ways of thinking. And, in exploring 'risk', we explore how a concept originating in organisational and scientific thinking is adapted to the language and intellectual architecture of lawyers.

The growing influence of in-house lawyers is an occupational success story; in-house lawyers are increasingly important parts of the social system that makes up their organisations and the business of law. But we need to go further if we are to ask whether that success-story is a professional one. The relationship with 'clients' is particularly interesting.[40] In-house lawyers are both part of and serve that client. They are dependent and constituent; servant and agent. Further, the more senior those in-house lawyers are in the organisation the more they become an important part of the client's directing mind. This mixed servant-agent role does not fit well with the historical archetype that one professional served many individual clients (and thus retained

---

[37] Lynn Mather and Leslie C Levin, *Lawyers in Practice: Ethical Decision Making in Context* (University of Chicago Press 2012).

[38] Andrew Abbott, 'Linked Ecologies: States and Universities as Environments for Professions' (2005) 23 *Sociological Theory* 245.

[39] ibid.

[40] For example, Simon is one of many suggesting in-housers conflate the interests of the organisation with the goals of its incumbent management. William H Simon, 'Whom (or What) Does the Organization's Lawyer Represent?: An Anatomy of Intraclient Conflict' [2003] *California Law Review* 57.

their independence).[41] A collapsing of the client–professional divide negates claims to professionalism if the professional simply emulates what the client wants without regard to the public interests the profession protects.

For a while this meant in-house lawyers were seen as professionally inferior. The tendency of lawyers to elide the eliteness of one's clients with high professional status,[42] and the growing corporatisation of legal practice, now makes in-house practice look less incongruous. Outside practice has itself become more dependent.[43] Furthermore, the growing power of in-house lawyers as agents of clients over private practice has bolstered the professional status of in-house lawyers in spite of, but also because of, that dependency.[44] In the profession's everyday discourse, this building of professional reputation is most often framed in terms of advancing status and influence: values of self-interest rather than public interest. It does not really speak to professionalism in the terms we mean it. One could insinuate that in-house power and status manifests in their acceptance and promotion of client power not professionalism. Indeed, contrary to the idea that professionals resist 'vulgar' markets and bureaucracy,[45] in-housers are heavily influenced, as we will see, by commerciality and bureaucratic hierarchy. Nor does the conventional interpretation of professional power as exercised by expert lawyers over inexpert, atomised clients generally apply,[46] with some suggesting in-house lawyers are better seen as isolated, marginalised, or swamped by the cognitive and economic influence of an organised client.[47]

We should pause here and note that the literature on in-house lawyers has tended to concentrate on public interest, rather than client interest, concerns.[48] The work often assumes or does not concern itself with the idea that in-house lawyers are able and willing to deliver on an organisation's needs. This relative silence is an interesting contrast to one of the pre-eminent debates in the commercial world and government legal sector about lawyers not being sufficiently commercially aware or client-focused.[49] Our emphasis in this book is similarly on tensions between lawyers and the public interest, but we do seek

---

[41] Although compare with patronage, and see Terence J Johnson, *Professions and Power* (Macmillan, 1972).

[42] John P Heinz and others, 'The Constituencies of Elite Urban Lawyers' (1997) 31 *Law & Society Review* 441; Heinz and others (n 8); Steven Brint, *In an Age of Experts: The Changing Role of Professionals in Politics and Public Life* (Princeton University Press, 1996).

[43] Robert L Nelson, *Partners with Power: The Social Transformation of the Large Law Firm* (University of California Press, 1988); Vaughan and Coe (n 12).

[44] Vaughan and Coe (n 12); Christopher J Whelan and Neta Ziv, 'Privatizing Professionalism: Client Control of Lawyers' Ethics' (2011) 80 *Fordham Law Review* 2577.

[45] Talcott Parsons, *The Social System* (Psychology Press, 1991). The caveat here, of course, is that large law firms have become, over time, increasingly bureaucratic organisations and one of many forms of 'professional service firms'.

[46] Johnson (n 41).

[47] Pam Jenoff, 'Going Native: Incentive, Identity, and the Inherent Ethical Problem of In-House Counsel' (2011) 114 *West Virginia Law Review* 725.

[48] For an exception, see Heineman (n 2).

[49] See, for example, Gillian K Hadfield, *Rules for a Flat World: Why Humans Invented Law and How to Reinvent It for a Complex Global Economy* (Oxford University Press, 2016).

to address in part the potential failure of lawyers to meet their organisations' needs. Indeed, one of the reasons for focusing on legal risk management is that it is an emergent discipline within legal practice, where lawyer competency may sometimes be described, as we will see in Chapter 5, as embryonic.

Should we also pause before taking the rising status and influence of in-house lawyers as a signal of professional vacuity? Are in-house legal professionals the useful idiots, or amoral adjutants, of their organisations? Or is something more interesting going on? Often the focus on public interest questions assumes a 'professional conflict' model: that public and business interests regularly conflict and that lawyers as 'professionals' should side with the public interest but as entrepreneurial employees would side with the business. A number of ideas about in-house lawyers have developed as a result of fearing the latter. One is that in-housers may have a different occupational identity to conventional private practice lawyers, more aligned with the ideology of business than of profession.[50] Nelson and Nielsen's were anxious about lawyer entrepreneurialism.[51] Gunz and Gunz suspected that in-house lawyers did not generally feel a conflict between organisational and professional roles because they prioritised their organisational view.[52] Jenoff, Kim, and others suggest cognitive and economic forces neutralise more professional instincts.[53] Mastenbroek and Peeters Weem suggest legislative drafters conform to the political imperatives when faced with professional-occupational conflicts.[54]

This public interest gaze has a tendency too to focus on one role of the in-house lawyer: that of the lawyer as gatekeeper who exists to stop illegal conduct within the organisations in which they work.[55] The willingness of in-house lawyers to say 'No', when faced with proposals that their employer wants to do something illegal, is seen as a role which is essential to in-house professionalism and one which some in-house lawyers may be reluctant to

---

[50] See, for example, our discussion of Gunz and Gunz's work in Chapter 2.

[51] Robert L Nelson and Laura Beth Nielsen, 'Cops, Counsel, and Entrepreneurs: Constructing the Role of inside Counsel in Large Corporations' [2000] *Law and Society Review* 457.

[52] Hugh P Gunz and Sally P Gunz, 'The Lawyer's Response to Organizational Professional Conflict: An Empirical Study of the Ethical Decision Making of in-House Counsel' (2002) 39 *American Business Law Journal* 241.

[53] Jenoff (n 47); Kim, 'Banality of Fraud' (n 19); Kim 'Gatekeepers Inside Out' (n 26).

[54] Ellen Mastenbroek and Tanja Peeters Weem, 'In Spagaat Tussen Brussel En Den Haag: De Europeanisering van Het Wetgevingsvak' ['Balancing between Brussels and The Hague: The Europeanization of Legal Drafting'] (Nijmegen, Radboud University Report, 2009); discussed in Berry Tholen and Ellen Mastenbroek, 'Guardians of the Law or Loyal Administrators?: Toward a Refined Administrative Ethos for Legislative Drafters' (2013) 35 *Administrative Theory & Praxis* 487.

[55] On gatekeeping, see: Reinier H Kraakman, 'Corporate Liability Strategies and the Costs of Legal Controls' (1984) 93 *The Yale Law Journal* 857; Reinier H Kraakman, 'Gatekeepers: The Anatomy of a Third-Party Enforcement Strategy' (1986) 2 *Journal of Law, Economics, & Organization* 53; John C Coffee, *Gatekeepers: The Professions and Corporate Governance* (Oxford University Press, 2006); Christine Parker, Suzanne Le Mire and Anita MacKay, 'Lawyers, Confidentiality and Whistleblowing: Lessons from the McCabe Tobacco Litigation' (2017) 40 *Melbourne University Law Review* 999.

adopt.[56] Whether this is in fact the case is contested. Rostain provides a suite of reasons, and some pilot evidence, for thinking that general counsel in the US are 'strong gatekeepers'.[57] Our evidence is more extensive, looks at a larger number, and wider range of in-house lawyers including GCs, and shows that some in-house lawyers plainly are unwilling to ever say 'No' to their employers, and that this is a problem.

Yet we seek to make a wider point. The desire to focus on binaries – are in-house lawyers independent? Are they good gatekeepers? Do they say 'No' to their clients? Are they lawyers or business people? – is something of a normative simplification.[58] To be clear, we do not think it is wrong to focus significantly on such concepts. If looking at issues such as independence were a failing, we would be as guilty as others. But we should not reduce professionalism to a test of these binaries. It is important to contextualise as fully as possible; to understand whether in-house lawyers are willing to say 'No', but also to understand *when* and *how* they do so. It is also important to understand how independence is manifested, managed and delivered other than, or in addition to, saying 'No'; as well as the ways in which independence is compromised without a 'Yes'/'No' question being put. And some generalisations – for instance, that in-house lawyers are less ethical than private practitioners – are founded on a thinly evidenced set of assumptions about private practitioners which fail to take account of the very different roles that such lawyers often play on the ground.[59]

Much socio-legal work on the professions generally, and on in-housers more specifically, recognises the importance of context and the contingencies that make up ethical practice,[60] but we think it is possible to go further. Nelson and Nielsen's characterisation of in-house lawyers as cops, counsellors and entrepreneurs,[61] for example, is vivid and nuanced but elides ideas which we would argue are conceptually distinct. Their entrepreneurs liked to do work of high commercial value to their organisations (like deals); concentrated on getting practical results (like business-people); and used uncertainty in the law for business advantage, for example exploiting loopholes in the law (like regulatory entrepreneurs).[62] In tying this cluster of ideas together, they mixed positive

[56] A classic discussion of this is Robert Jackall, *Moral Mazes: The World of Corporate Managers* (Oxford University Press, 2010).

[57] Tanina Rostain, 'General Counsel in the Age of Compliance: Preliminary Findings and New Research Questions' (2008) 21 *Georgetown Journal of Legal Ethics* 465.

[58] Rosen was well ahead of us in arguing for a more nuanced framing of the role of in-house lawyers. See Robert Eli Rosen, 'The Sociological Imagination and Legal Ethics' (2016) 19 *Legal Ethics* 97; Robert E Rosen, *Lawyers in Corporate Decision-Making* (Quid Pro Quo Books, 2015); Robert Eli Rosen, 'The Inside Counsel Movement, Professional Judgement and Organizational Representation' (1988) 64 *Indiana Law Journal* 479.

[59] See, by way of contrast, Vaughan and Coe (n 12); Richard Moorhead and Victoria Hinchly, 'Professional Minimalism? The Ethical Consciousness of Commercial Lawyers' (2015) 42 *Journal of Law and Society* 387.

[60] Mather and Levin (n 37).

[61] Nelson and Nielsen (n 43).

[62] For example Doreen McBarnet, 'Legal Creativity: Law, Capital and Legal Avoidance' in Maureen Cain and Christine Harrington (eds), *Lawyers in a Postmodern World: Translation and Transgression* (Open University Press, 1994).

and negative potentialities, portraying the overall implications of an entrepreneurial role with ambivalence and scepticism from a public-interest perspective. Our work builds on and disentangles these separate ideas, through identifying in-house role orientations: a commercial orientation; an advisory orientation; an orientation around the exploitation of uncertainty; an ethical orientation; and an independence orientation. We articulate and test the presence of these orientations in survey work with in-house lawyers and examine their normative dimensions through looking at the relationships between these role orientations and ethical inclination.

One benefit of this approach is that we can probe Nelson and Nielsen's uncertainty about whether the three characterisations were types (individuals gravitated towards being one of the three) or dispositions (which most in-house lawyers could draw upon depending on the context of any problem they were trying to solve). This is an important distinction. Seeing characterisations of in-house role as dispositions suggests greater flexibility; a repertoire of options that in-house lawyers can draw upon (they can be entrepreneurial when a situation demands it, say). It also serves as a reminder that the context of a task or an organisation might significantly influence individuals towards one or other approach and also towards what that approach 'meant'.

If shifting between dispositions is important, then we need to redouble our attention to context. Independence needs to be called upon when there are conflicts between organisational values and professional ones. Yet Gunz and Gunz found a lack of such conflict in lawyers who had gone in-house. They wondered what explained the absence of such conflict: were professionals working within 'good' businesses? Was their professional identity too weak to recognise or be worried by such conflicts that did arise? Or were organisational and professional values harmfully aligned?[63] To better model the importance of context, we explore the tensions in host organisations between legal and other parts of the organisation and the existence of ethical pressure (the pressure to do things that are unlawful or unethical). We then relate these pressures to occupational and professional identity and so can explore the questions of alignment and professional identity. Unlike Gunz and Gunz, we *do* evidence conflict between professional and organisational values, getting a clearer understanding of the different responses to such pressure that are possible, and what supports an ethical response as a result. We also show that conflict can be associated with stronger, public-interest ideas about professional orientation.

ETHICS AND LAWYERS' ETHICS

Our understanding of professionalism depends on a balancing of individual and collective interests in the public interest; and seeing that balancing as being

---

[63] Gunz and Gunz (n 52).

influenced by the ecologies of profession, organisation, and beyond. How lawyers conduct that balancing raises the question of ethics and requires us to define what we mean when we speak of in-house lawyers' ethics in this book. We see two elements. Primarily, we mean the ethicality of the in-house lawyer *as lawyer*: acting in accordance with professional rules and principles. Independence, integrity, and protectiveness of clients' interests and of the rule of law are professional obligations that require balancing. Note the interests of individuals (the client, the lawyer's integrity), and the collective (through the rule of law). Whether, when, and how in-house lawyers are well placed to understand and implement their professional obligations is the primary concern of our analysis.

The second definition of ethics is broader, important, but less central to the role of in-house lawyers *as* lawyers. This 'general' ethicality is something that lawyers are often more sceptical of,[64] but that organisations and some lawyers are increasingly interested in: namely, taking account of and acting in accordance with widely held social norms. Professional and general ethicality are not necessarily absolutely distinct. Behaving with professional integrity or behaving in a way that maintains public trust overlaps with general ethical concepts,[65] albeit integrity to one's role might also sometimes conflict with those concepts. It is also possible for general ethicality to influence professional roles ecologically: a client's reputation, and therefore their best interests, may be served by not engaging in aggressive lawyering either because it prompts regulatory scrutiny or a public backlash. So, whilst we are less interested in ethics in this general sense, we do not exclude it from view; and we are mainly concerned with general ethics' influence on the lawyer's role *as* lawyer.

Ideally, to understand the ethicality of in-house lawyers, one would like to be able to examine their professional inclinations, relate those inclinations to actual behaviour, and examine that behaviour to assess its ethicality against general and professional standards. In the context of our quantitative work that was not practical. What we were able to do was to use established measures of general ethical inclination as proxies for evaluating likely behaviour. Measuring ethicality is of course both difficult and multi-dimensional, but measures of ethical inclination – moral attentiveness and moral disengagement – have been shown to be predictive of ethical misconduct (such as lying and cheating) and less prone to social response bias than other approaches.[66] These general ethical measures provide a normative perspective on the organisational and professional orientations we explore as defining the in-house role. As such, we are able to explore

---

[64] Steven Vaughan and Emma Oakley, '"Gorilla Exceptions" and the Ethically Apathetic Corporate Lawyer' (2016) 19 *Legal Ethics* 50.

[65] See, for example *Wingate v Solicitors Regulation Authority* [2018] EWCA Civ 366.

[66] Scott J Reynolds, 'Moral Attentiveness: Who Pays Attention to the Moral Aspects of Life?' (2008) 93 *Journal of Applied Psychology* 1027; James R Detert and others, 'Moral Disengagement in Ethical Decision Making: A Study of Antecedents and Outcomes.' (2008) 93 *Journal of Applied Psychology* 374.

the extent to which, for example, being commercially oriented relates to general ethicality. And because professional ethicality generally requires one not to lie and cheat, for instance, we also see these measures as useful, if incomplete, indicators of professional ethicality.

The incompleteness of the indicators leads us onto another important part of the discussion. In general, empirical work on in-house lawyers focuses on role orientations. We go further, developing measures of professional orientation alongside role orientations.[67] We also examine, qualitatively, in-housers' own, often rather modest, understandings of their professional obligations through interviews and the vignettes of legal risk problems. We see often basic and quite intuitive understandings of their professional rules, and a hierarchy of professional principles which treats the client's interests as paramount. There are, however, important variations: some in-housers emphasise one set of interests – the client's needs; others emphasise two sets – ethics as a matter of integrity (their own) and the client's needs; and the third group emphasises three sets of interests – the client's needs, the needs of the lawyer to behave with integrity, and also the need to take account of broader concerns such as the interests of justice. In this way, we see a range of approaches within our cohort progressing from simpler to more complex professional ethical models.

We discovered that few of our in-house lawyers were influenced *only* by the client's interests, and that many had something of a justice-oriented view that extended beyond the client and their own integrity. But our recognition of this is tempered by finding also that it was not known to many that, under their code of conduct, *all* solicitors *are obliged* to recognise interests other than those of their client. This code is also clear that where there is a conflict between principles, the client's interest is *not* paramount unless it aligns with the public interest.[68] Further, we are able to identify a minority of lawyers in our sample who do seem to view client interests as paramount, even to the extent of allowing commerce to trump legality. In-house professional models are thus varied and generally out of line with professional rules. For some, that misalignment is serious enough to be critical.

Whilst the quantitative modelling of professional orientations is a distinctive feature of our research, we should emphasise it is a simplification. In particular, philosophically oriented readers will want to complicate or challenge the notion that lawyers must act in the public interest to be properly professional. The so-called 'standard conception' of lawyer's ethics suggests client primacy is in the public interest; it sees lawyers as having, 'special duties to the

---

[67] See: www.sra.org.uk/solicitors/handbook/handbookprinciples/content.page, accessed 17 April 2018. Very similar principles exist for barristers too as 'Core Duties'. These can be found here: www.barstandardsboard.org.uk/regulatory-requirements/bsb-handbook/, accessed 17 April 2018.

[68] See para 2.2. of the SRA Principles: www.sra.org.uk/solicitors/handbook/handbookprinciples/content.page, accessed 17 April 2018. The position is the same for barristers in England & Wales. See Core Duty 1 and guidance C1, Bar Code of Conduct: www.barstandardsboard.org.uk/media/1918141/bsb_handbook_1_february_2018.pdf, accessed 17 April 2018.

client that allow and perhaps even require conduct that would otherwise be morally reprehensible'.[69] A defence of the lawyers who treat their client's interests as paramount would begin with such theories. Such a view is no defence to lawyers allowing commerciality to trump legality, however. And, in any event, the in-house lawyers we surveyed and spoke to did not conform to the 'standard conception' view of the lawyer as amoral agent. Often a strong client orientation sat alongside a purportedly strong ethical orientation. Our analysis of risk shows this ethical orientation emerges rather fitfully. We see resistance and sometimes acquiescence to requests for in-housers to advise or assist with unlawful or unethical action, and we see interestingly diverse attitudes to the autonomy of the client (an essential characteristic of the standard conception).[70] In particular, the idea that lawyers are 'mere' advisors, whilst the client decides, is an orientation which is strong but not dominant in our in-house lawyers. In-house lawyers may tend towards 'civil obedience' to their client's definitions of what they want, why and how, but that obedience is not total and there are opportunities to shape the object of their obedience because they are part of the client themselves and because of the uncertainties inherent in the facts and laws with which they work.[71]

Equally, through notions of ethical orientation, through understanding that in-house attitudes to exploiting uncertainty in law are critical, and through our detailed exploration of risk management, we see how some in-house lawyers make contextual, discretionary judgements about 'justice' (where justice is used to mean the legal – and not moral – merits of any given case). This could be argued to be broadly consistent with some jurisprudential approaches to legal ethics.[72] And some in-housers draw upon common morality (what ordinary individuals would think of as right and wrong) to guide their actions in situations of uncertainty.[73] This is not to offer up 'idealized portraits of the moral [lawyer] agent.'[74] Rather, we would suggest that many of our in-house lawyers

---

[69] Tim Dare, 'Mere-Zeal, Hyper-Zeal and the Ethical Obligations of Lawyers' (2004) 7 *Legal Ethics* 24.

[70] Stephen L Pepper, 'The Lawyer's Amoral Ethical Role: A Defense, a Problem, and Some Possibilities' (1986) *American Bar Foundation Research Journal* 24. Schneyer also writes of the importance of respect for a client's autonomy. See Ted Schneyer, 'Moral Philosophy's Standard Misconception of Legal Ethics' [1984] *Wisconsin Law Review* 1529.

[71] Alice Woolley and W Bradley Wendel, 'Legal Ethics and Moral Character' (2010) 23 *Georgetown Journal of Legal Ethics* 1065. Wendel argues that, 'the law supercedes societal controversy and provides a moderately stable, provisional framework for cooperation, notwithstanding normative and empirical disagreement.' See W Bradley Wendel, 'Legal Ethics Is about the Law, Not Morality or Justice: A Reply to Critics' (Social Science Research Network Paper 2011) and W Bradley Wendel, *Lawyers and Fidelity to Law* (Reprint edition, Princeton University Press, 2012).

[72] William H Simon, *The Practice of Justice: A Theory of Legal Ethics* (Harvard University Press, 1998) 138.

[73] David Luban, *Lawyers and Justice: An Ethical Study* (Princeton University Press, 1988). See further, on the morally activist lawyer, Robert K Vischer, 'Legal Advice as Moral Perspective' (2006) 19 *Geo J Legal Ethics* 225.

[74] Woolley and Wendel (n 71).

were generally loyal in the standard conception sense, but sometimes justice-seeking, and moral too: their approaches straddle the three classical schools of thought on how lawyers should do ethics. Justice-seeking and, especially, moral agency are applied more tentatively though.

We do not say that in-house lawyers choose the approach best-suited to the problem before them, or that our analysis shows the standard conception (say) to be wrong, but we do think our data show the importance of focusing on what lawyers actually *do* when thinking about how lawyers should *be*.[75] We get some sense of the ethical risk posed by being exploitative of uncertainty, or in seeing one's role as the non-accountable adviser, both ideas associated with the zealous lawyer, but that is not to disprove the standard conception. It does, however, emphasise the behavioural dimensions to ethics: the orientations of lawyers – which may derive from an intellectual understanding of their role or a practical working-up of the role in an organisation – are important.[76] This nuance may be more important than more artificial debates about hypothetical notions of zeal. What lawyers ought to do must begin with a clear understanding of how lawyers actually behave in situ, and how this relates to their specific practice contexts, as well as wider organisational, social and economic conditions of their work. Professional ethics needs to be both practical and normative.[77]

LEGAL RISK

In thinking ecologically about in-house practice we also ask how different systems (law, business, bureaucracy) interact to contest and solve problems.[78] The middle section of this book focuses on one such interaction: a relatively new and under-studied element of in-house lawyers' work, risk management. We see risk management as a paradigm example of the means by which in-house lawyers have gained greater status as managers within organisations, and as an important example of the embedding of in-house lawyers in the management of organisations.[79]

---

[75] See: Deborah L Rhode, *In the Interests of Justice: Reforming the Legal Profession* (Oxford University Press, 2003); Sharon Dolovich, 'Ethical Lawyering and the Possibility of Integrity' (2001) 70 *Fordham L Rev* 1629; Wendel, 'Lawyers and Fidelity to Law' (n 71) 3.

[76] Jennifer K Robbennolt, 'Behavioral Ethics Meets Legal Ethics' (2015) 11 *Annual Review of Law and Social Science* 75; Andrew M Perlman, 'A Behavioral Theory of Legal Ethics' (2015) 90 *Indiana Law Journal* 1639.

[77] Alice Woolley, 'The Problem of Disagreement in Legal Ethics Theory' (2013) 26 *Canadian Journal of Law & Jurisprudence* 181; Christine Parker, 'A Critical Morality for Lawyers: Four Approaches to Lawyers' Ethics' (2004) 30 *Monash University Law Review* 49.

[78] Andrew Abbott, *The System of Professions: An Essay on the Division of Expert Labor* (University of Chicago Press, 1988).

[79] KPMG, 'Beyond the Law, KPMG's Global Study of How General Counsel Are Turning Risk to Advantage' (General Counsel Survey, 2012); Roger McCormick, *Legal Risk in the Financial Markets* (Oxford University Press, 2010); Stuart Weinstein and Charles Wild, *Legal Risk Management, Governance and Compliance: A Guide to Best Practice from Leading Experts* (Globe Law and

Risk is typically defined as the likelihood of harm and the likely impact of that harm from a given hazard or set of hazards. Seen in negative terms, and associated with anxiety and undesirability,[80] Beck famously argued that risk went hand-in-hand with high technological innovation, scientific development, and the inability to fully know the dangers we face.[81] Risk is thus elided with uncertainty and randomness;[82] with rendering the future less uncertain whilst essentially unknown.[83] Equally, progress often entails risk: faster travel, better health interventions, improved financial instruments may all require the balancing of pros and cons, the weighing of risks and benefits, the pondering of unknowns. Similarly, risk is now a core organising principle for organisations and governments; much, some argue all,[84] regulatory activity is being defined or reconstituted in terms of risk. The nature and existence of a risk will depend on human behaviour, and the acceptability of risk is dependent upon cultural context.[85] And how organisations respond to and manage risk is becoming an important element of good governance.[86] Risk management is important too because it provides strategic focus. It enables, or purports to enable, managers to 'see' complex organisations and 'target' the risks that are revealed by focusing on the most 'material' potential harms.[87]

For our purposes, the basic idea behind *legal* risk management is that the in-house lawyer helps their organisation decide which legal risks the organisation takes, or – and this is an important difference – the risks that the in-house legal team generates, and how the organisation can mitigate, avoid or otherwise minimise and protect itself against such risks. Risk management is a messy task: in fashioning systems measuring and governing risk, 'knowledge claims [are made] ... both somewhat arbitrary and sincerely advanced'.[88] The application of expert rules, norms, and beliefs may often be symbolic.[89] Systems are established because management or regulators demand them, but the substantive quality of

---

Business, 2013); Deloitte, 'Deloitte Global General Counsel Report 2011: How the Game Is Changing' (London, 2011).

[80] Nikolas Rose, *Powers of Freedom* (Cambridge University Press, 1999) 160.

[81] Ulrich Beck, *Risk Society: Towards a New Modernity* (Sage, 1992).

[82] There are those who argue that true uncertainty is wholly separate from risk, as risk requires that the likelihood of harm be capable of assessment. This is not a debate with which we need to concern ourselves here.

[83] Julia Black, 'The Role of Risk in Regulatory Processes' in Robert Baldwin, Martin Cave and Martin Lodge (eds) *The Oxford Handbook of Regulation* (Oxford University Press, 2010) 317.

[84] Elizabeth Fisher, *Risk Regulation and Administrative Constitutionalism* (Hart Publishing, 2007).

[85] ibid 8.

[86] Michael Power, *Organized Uncertainty: Designing a World of Risk Management* (Oxford University Press, 2007).

[87] Geoffrey P Miller, *The Law of Governance, Risk Management and Compliance* (Wolters Kluwer Law & Business, 2014) 544.

[88] Richard W Scott, 'Lords of the dance: Professionals as institutional agents' (2008) 29 *Organization Studies* 219, 221.

[89] ibid 222.

those systems is necessarily uncertain.[90] In Chapters 5 and 6, we explore how lawyers see risk as an opportunity to demonstrate value, through a systemisation and quantification of risk that enables organisations to take on legal risk as well as reduce it.

The interpenetration of logics is important: legal risk hybridises bureaucratic, legal, and commercial ideas, but to what end? It is not at all clear to us how robust the processes of systemisation and quantification are. Such hybrids call into question what skills and expertise are needed to engage successfully in quantified risk management. Yet, in-housers' evidence of the success of risk management relied mainly on their experience rather than data.

Similarly, we explore how legal risk management is shaped for, or by, social forces in what we call the tournament of influence. Being able to lead on and manage legal risk can be a basis for claiming managerial status, because it makes the legal function relevant in pan-organisational and strategic terms. It is a way of in-house lawyers talking the language of management. As we will see in this book, the conceptualisation and management of legal risk poses a series of questions about independence, about the quality of decision-making, and about the ability of professional lawyers to both promote their organisation's interests and protect the rule of law and the administration of justice.

More positively, in-houser proactivity emerges as being of central importance to evolving approaches in risk management. This proactivity is not a virtue we see as originating *from* professionalism. It is a response to external stimuli. Risk has shifted from something which is a 'fact of life', to something which must be anticipated, controlled (and perhaps accepted) or minimised. Organisations that lay claim to the benefits of modernity and markets are treated as responsible for the risks that arise from their actions (and inactions).[91] This responsibilisation takes place through law, markets, and reputation. The dishonesty and cynicism exposed by corporate scandals means the public has recalculated the extent to which risks created by large corporates are tolerated as accidental. And because concern about legal risk is also reputational, it extends beyond the boundaries of legal questions: being perceived as doing something that is unlawful can be as harmful as actually doing something that is unlawful.

Uncertainty and reputation open up the need to look beyond the letter of the law to how the law *might* be interpreted or how it *might* develop or be reformed by legislatures. Uncertainty provides a practical reason for looking to develop standards which are in accordance with the spirit of laws, or which conform to the highest international standards. Whilst standard-raising arguments

---

[90] Kim Pernell, Jiwook Jung and Frank Dobbin, 'The Hazards of Expert Control: Chief Risk Officers and Risky Derivatives' (2017) 82 *American Sociological Review* 511.

[91] Oberdiek states: 'modern life is distinctively risky. It is so both because risk permeates modern societies and because these ubiquitous risk are, in the main, morally cognizable'. See John Oberdiek, 'Risk' in Dennis Paterson (ed), *A Companion to Philosophy of Law and Legal Theory*, 2nd edn (Wiley-Blackwell, 2010).

are not supreme, some articulate them as an essential tool of integrity-based management.[92]

The importance of legal risk is ratcheted up as regulatory institutions have begun to enlist organisations and professionals as regulatory surrogates, in particular giving them responsibilities for preventing and/or reporting bribery, money laundering, and terrorism (sometimes with extraterritorial effect).[93] Human rights obligations are increasingly relevant to business.[94] As a result, organisations have responded through systemising the, 'way of dealing with hazards and insecurities induced and introduced by modernization itself'.[95] As organisations claim to manage the risk society, their sense of control may be exaggerated.[96] And the fluidity of legal risk, via uncertainty in law, may provide opportunities for creative compliance, sharp lawyering, and regulatory arbitrage. The definition, measurement, and control of risk may aid in the management of risk, but may also lead to box-ticking and complacency.[97] It may desensitise corporate actors to risk. It may window-dress the harms it is designed to address, or lay the risks off on those least able to understand and protect against them. Some claim legal risk management de-ethicalises those organisations that engage in it.[98] This raises an interesting set of questions about whether legal risk management is understood by in-house lawyers as a compliance issue (reducing the liabilities of the organisation) or whether in-housers see themselves as the guardians of legal/ethical imperatives, pushing back against corruption and terrorism, and promoting human rights.

Whether risk management really desensitises organisations or not depends in part on the approach of in-house lawyers, as we aim to show in this book. We saw a range of strategic responses in our data: there were late responders and expert opportunists. There were also different kinds of underpinning order: those who saw the in-house legal function and the organisation as separate; those who saw the natural order of the market as dictating what was done; those who saw risk as part of the constructed order of reputation; and those who sought an ethical order of authenticity in their approach to risk. Similarly, when our respondents discussed ethical problems in our vignettes, we saw those who took a defensive approach to problems ('What evidence exists that will harm us?'; 'Are there plausible defences to allegations of wrongdoing?'); those who took a more active approach (understanding what really happened, rather than

---

[92] Heineman (n 2).
[93] On regulatory surrogates, see Carolyn Abbot, 'Bridging the Gap – Non-State Actors and the Challenges of Regulating New Technology' (2012) 39 *Journal of Law and Society* 329.
[94] John Gerard Ruggie, *Just Business: Multinational Corporations and Human Rights* (WW Norton & Company, 2013).
[95] Beck (n 81) 31.
[96] Jenny Steele, *Risks and Legal Theory, Legal Theory Today* (Hart Publishing, 2004) 48–49.
[97] Winmark, 'The Legal World on Its Future, The Winmark Looking Glass Report' (Thomson Reuters, 2012); Ernst & Young, 'Turn Risks and Opportunities into Results' (Global Report, 2012).
[98] Anthony V Alfieri, 'The Fall of Legal Ethics and the Rise of Risk Management' (2005) 94 *Georgetown Law Journal* 1909.

what damaging evidence exists and whether any defences are meaningful and of good quality); and those who took a more proactive approach ('Does wrongdoing signal a broader underlying problem?'; 'What are the best responses to tackling the immediate allegation of wrongdoing and any broader problem?'). In this way, different commercial, managerial and professional ideologies were at play: commercially driven or zealous advocate type lawyers might incline to a narrow, defensive approach; whereas those inclined to see a broader notion of ethicality as important to their role might look to behave in a different fashion. Personal inclinations were also shaped by the risk appetite and culture within in-houser's host organisations.

We seek to capture how these institutional logics are conditioned or moderated by professional reflexivity. It is rare, we would say, for in-house lawyers to challenge themselves via reflection based around their professional identity as lawyers, but they often claimed a more folksy ethicality. That 'doing the right thing' helped minimise legal and reputational risk because it decreased the likelihood of that thing being prohibited. We generally see varied, minimalistic, and poorly articulated notions of when professional obligations require restraint on managerial risk-taking. Their professional contribution to the ecologies within which they work was primarily seen as technical-rational knowledge. Wise counsel (or 'judgement') may provide a space which allows for some ethical influence, but it is a space which is pragmatic, results-oriented, and consequentialist, rather than professionally ethical in a more principled sense. The ethics that inhabit this space are more organisational or business ethics in nature than professional.

Being embedded in their organisations, external influences may shape the balancing of public and organisational interests at the heart of any hybrid notion of professionalism more strongly than professional ones.[99] Legal and regulatory frameworks may be more important than professional ones. In the US, the Securities and Exchange Commission, the Sarbanes-Oxley Act (SOX), the Foreign Corrupt Practices Act (FCPA), the Alien Tort Claims Act, a significantly stronger culture of prosecutor scrutiny of lawyers involved in corporate scandals, and higher levels of academic scrutiny are all seen as having a significant impact on the outlook of in-house lawyers.[100] There is the increasingly

---

[99] For a discussion of various forms of lawyer regulation, see: Renee Newman Knake, 'The Commercialisation of Legal Ethics' (2016) 29(3) *Georgetown Journal of Legal Ethics* 715.

[100] On which, see Daniel P Ashe, 'The Lengthening Anti-Bribery Lasso of the United States: The Recent Extraterritorial Application of the US Foreign Corrupt Practices Act.' (2004) 73 *Fordham Law Review* 2897; David C Weiss, 'The Foreign Corrupt Practices Act, SEC disgorgement of profits, and the evolving international bribery regime: Weighing proportionality, retribution, and deterrence' (2008) 30 *Michigan Journal of International Law* 471; Courtney Shaw, 'Uncertain justice: liability of multinationals under the Alien Tort Claims Act.' (2002) *Stanford Law Review* 1359; David D Christensen, 'Corporate Liability for Overseas Human Rights Abuses: The Alien Tort Statute After *Sosa v. Alvarez-Machain*.' (2005) 62 Wash & Lee L Rev 1219; Roger C Cramton and others, 'Legal and ethical duties of lawyers after Sarbanes-Oxley' (2004) 49 Vill L Rev 725; and Leonard M Baynes, 'Just Pucker and Blow: An analysis of corporate whistleblowers, the duty of care, the duty of loyalty, and the Sarbanes-Oxley Act' (2002) 76 John's L Rev 875.

20 Introduction

prevalent practice (which began in the US, but is now reportedly adopted by the UK's Serious Fraud Office), of certain prosecutors requiring the waiver of legal professional privilege as a demonstration of cooperation with that prosecutor when seeking a deferred prosecution agreement.[101] In the UK, the Bribery Act and the Financial Conduct Authority's proposed changes to the Senior Managers Regime are two examples of a more responsibility-led approach to regulation likely to contribute to the evolving role of the in-house lawyer.

INSTITUTIONAL LOGICS AND REGULATION

In examining legal risk more minutely, we seek to demonstrate how particular institutional logics sometimes act 'as carriers of normative, coercive, and mimetic pressures.'[102] Understanding institutional logics pushes us to articulate what 'categories, principles, and conceptual tools' lawyers use to define and frame their ethicality in particular.[103] And we must locate those in the complexities of context. Remuneration and status may be more tied towards risky behaviour.[104] Lawyers are prone to client-loyalty biases which compromise their assessments of risk.[105] Ethical fading, the ability to behave self-interestedly and allowing ethicality to fade whilst still believing oneself to be moral,[106] is a problem to which lawyers, with their training in seeing both sides of the same story and the separation of law and morals, may be particularly prone,[107] especially if they are most interested in law and business.[108] Behavioural science findings on framing, priming, biases and the like provide a number of clues as to how different social systems influence behaviour, sometimes sub-consciously. This is one reason why the orientations we explore throughout this book are important: frames of this kind limit or facilitate our inclination to think ethically.[109]

---

[101] See Paul J Larkin Jr and John Michael Seibler, 'All Stick and No Carrot: The Yates Memorandum and Corporate Criminal Liability' (2016) 46 Stetson L Rev 7; and Julie O'Sullivan, 'How Prosecutors Apply the Federal Prosecutions of Corporations Charging Policy in the Era of Deferred Prosecutions, and What That Means for the Purposes of the Federal Criminal Sanction' (2014) 51 Am Crim L Rev 29.

[102] Daniel Muzio, David M Brock and Roy Suddaby, 'Professions and Institutional Change: Towards an Institutionalist Sociology of the Professions' (2013) 50 *Journal of Management Studies* 699, 700.

[103] ibid.

[104] Donald C Langevoort, 'Getting (Too) Comfortable: In-House Lawyers, Enterprise Risk, and the Financial Crisis' (2012) Wis L Rev 495.

[105] See the discussion in Perlman (n 76).

[106] Ann E Tenbrunsel and David M Messick, 'Ethical Fading: The Role of Self-Deception in Unethical Behavior' (2004) 17 *Social Justice Research* 223.

[107] Elizabeth Mertz, *The Language of Law School: Learning to 'Think Like a Lawyer'* (Oxford University Press, 2007).

[108] Richard Moorhead and others, 'The Ethical Identity of Law Students' (2016) 23 *International Journal of the Legal Profession* 235.

[109] Maryam Kouchaki and others, 'Seeing Green: Mere Exposure to Money Triggers a Business Decision Frame and Unethical Outcomes' (2013) 121 *Organizational Behavior and Human Decision Processes* 53; Francesca Gino and Dan Ariely, 'The Dark Side of Creativity: Original Thinkers Can Be

In the last chapter of the book we develop these ideas of institutional logics and examine what we see as having the most important influences on in-house lawyers. We draw on our data from in-house lawyers working in a variety of organisational settings: from the largest multi-national financial services organisations with more than a thousand in-housers, to the sole in-house lawyer working for a small charity. The lawyers we engaged with mostly worked in England & Wales. This is not to say that this book will not speak to those outside the jurisdiction. Indeed, many of the logics shaping in-house practice are not tied to a given jurisdiction. What will, however, differ from jurisdiction to jurisdiction is the underpinning regulatory framework governing the practices of in-house lawyers (and the extent to which those regulatory frameworks influence day-to-day professional practice).[110] We discuss the framework for solicitors in England and Wales as the one most relevant to our respondents.

We have sought to go further than previous work on in-house lawyers by more clearly and more comprehensively isolating the professional and organisational logics at work.[111] That is not to say our measures are comprehensive or perfect, but rather that we are able to provide a more comprehensive and more carefully specified insight into the tensions inherent in in-house lawyer practice, an insight which more fully relates those tensions to the contexts within which in-housers work. Through quantifying these logics we seek a sense of which carry the most weight, both descriptively and normatively.

It is the 'exploiting uncertainty' orientation that is the most normatively problematic of the role orientations we explore. The commercial orientation, a focus of much concern in the literature to date, has a more nuanced relation to ethical inclination. And when we examine our interview data more closely, we begin see to how 'cops' might not simply stop illegality, but also police broader notions such as ethicality or reputation, and that much of the policing work is done through activity which falls short of, or is very different to, the act of saying 'No'. What is more, a far broader range of activities and approaches may be as or more important in constructing and delivering ideas of ethicality and legality within organisations, with proactivity and being organised being particularly important.

There was variation in how reflective in-house lawyers are about the institutional practices they design and apply, and how conscious, or protective, they

---

More Dishonest' (2012) 102 *Journal of Personality and Social Psychology* 445; Francesca Gino and Joshua D Margolis, 'Bringing Ethics into Focus: How Regulatory Focus and Risk Preferences Influence (Un)Ethical Behavior' (2011) 115 *Organizational Behavior and Human Decision Processes* 145.

[110] We note here that solicitors granted title by the SRA are regulated by the SRA wherever in the world that they work. This is similarly true for other lawyers granted title out of England & Wales but working in England & Wales. We do not get into the debate in this book about norm conflict or double regulation.

[111] Patricia H Thornton and William Ocasio, 'Institutional Logics and the Historical Contingency of Power in Organizations: Executive Succession in the Higher Education Publishing Industry, 1958–1990' (1999) 105 *American Journal of Sociology* 801.

are of their own agency in these processes. But generally, beyond situations of 'clear criminality', dealing with dissonance between the lawyer's and the organisation's view of legality is often seen as a personal rather than professional choice, part of intra-organisational human politics. Certainly, choices about legal risk and legality are highly embedded in the culture of the organisation. In adapting to organisational logics in this way, professionals are at risk of abandoning a more civic-minded morality (or 'social trusteeship').[112] A more positive interpretation can be attempted by seeing the behaviours as those of *hybrid* professionals managing institutional complexity. Hybrids interpret conflicting institutional logics 'to construct problems and solutions that [align] with all the logics at play.'[113] In this way, the balancing and interaction of logics is crucial to understanding whether *and when* a socially useful professional hybrid is being constructed.[114]

Our answer is that professionalism in-house *is* at risk of being diminished, but being commercially oriented is not as much of a problem as being committed to exploit uncertainty. More legality-oriented notions of professionalism mitigate ethical disinclination. Faulty or weaker professional logics are a significant part of the problem: it is not simply about client pressures overcoming virtuous professionals. Those in-housers who get the balance of competing logics wrong risk creating 'an inherent instability in the meaning of professionalism ... itself',[115] but those who get it right show us the conditions under which hybrids advance a positive ethic of in-house professionalism.

Thus our end-point is not whether the in-house legal role is generally or fundamentally compromised, but the circumstances and attitudes which make such compromise more or less likely.[116] Heineman suggests that an embedded professionalism can be established alongside strategic and entrepreneurial approaches to the role.[117] This depends on simultaneously managing in-house lawyers towards professionalism, meeting organisational goals, and being receptive to public interest goals as seen through the law and through reputational influences. Ethicality is not just about the willingness (or failure) to say 'No' when presented with an unlawful action, but also about the willingness and authenticity with which the legal function helps lead ethically in situations of

---

[112] Brint (n 42) 11, 103, 114.

[113] Maria Blomgren and Caroline Waks, 'Coping with Contradictions: Hybrid Professionals Managing Institutional Complexity' (2015) 2 *Journal of Professions and Organization* 78, 78.

[114] James Faulconbridge and Daniel Muzio, 'Organizational Professionalism in Globalizing Law Firms' (2008) 22 *Work, Employment & Society* 7; Aaron Cohen, *Multiple Commitments in the Workplace: An Integrative Approach* (Psychology Press, 2003); Crawford Spence and Chris Carter, 'An Exploration of the Professional Habitus in the Big 4 Accounting Firms' (2014) 28 *Work, Employment & Society* 946.

[115] Spence and Carter (n 114) 5.

[116] Graeme Currie, Nicola Burgess and Penelope Tuck, 'The (Un)Desirability of Hybrid Managers as "Controlled" Professionals: Comparative Cases of Tax and Healthcare Professionals' [2016] *Journal of Professions and Organization* 142.

[117] Heineman (n 2).

uncertainty; its resistance to loop-holing; and the way in which it helps set a tone of authentic 'spirit of the law', not 'letter of the law', compliance. Thus whilst seeing lawyers as 'cops' or 'counsellors' draws on traditional models of the lawyer–client dyad, our research shows a web of organisational influences which emphasise, when working well, support for legality through institutional practice, the building of ethicality, and the management of integrity. As we have set out, we emphasise not only negative agency (there are problems around a reluctance to say 'No') and polycentric agency (in-house lawyers operating in networks of influence and decision), but also positive agency (the capacity for in-house legal teams to lead on ethical issues falling within their purview). The importance of proactivity (in the management of risk) represents a positive manifestation of more positive agency, but so does a willingness to see uncertainty through a lens not of opportunism but of ethicality and leadership.

Such balancing is complex but is already part and parcel, to greater and lesser degrees, of the everyday lives of in-house lawyers who help construct social order within their organisations and, when dealing with third parties such as suppliers and regulators, beyond.[118] They construct such orders collaboratively, drawing on other resources if working in well-resourced and bureaucratically savvy organisations. They also do so with a clear eye on external frameworks. The professionalism of in-house lawyers is located in, and is influenced by, the choices made within their organisations, and those in turn are influenced by the regulatory frameworks and other environments influencing them.[119]

An important part of this relates not just to how in-house lawyers see their role, but also to how their *employers* see the in-house role. Ethical in-house practice is about individual understandings of the role; it is about the approach of in-house teams and about the organisations those teams work in; it is about understanding and drawing on all the obligations of professionalism; and it is about building a better infrastructure to manage the tensions within the role. We can but speculate on what corporate and governmental mishaps might have been avoided or managed better, with concomitant reduction in social and economic harm; or what stress could have been avoided, or how many careers could have been saved, by understanding and acting on this. We must recognise this complexity, and support the positive, as well as call out the negatives, if in-house lawyers are to influence their organisations legally, professionally, and ethically.

THE STRUCTURE OF THIS BOOK AND OUR CONCLUSIONS

The remainder of this book unfolds as follows. In Chapter 2, we set out our methods. Whilst it will be tempting for many readers to skip this chapter, it is

---

[118] Ruggie (n 94).
[119] Robert A Kagan, Neil Gunningham and Dorothy Thornton, 'Explaining Corporate Environmental Performance: How Does Regulation Matter?' (2003) 37 *Law & Society Review* 51.

important to understand the nature of our interview and survey cohorts and, we hope, it is also of interest to see how our measures of in-house identity and professional orientation are constructed from the survey data. In Chapter 3, we explore the place of in-house lawyers in organisational networks. Here, we set out some of the history of in-house roles, we explore our interviewees' reasons for starting their law careers in-house or moving in-house, how our interviewees perceived the changes to the role of the in-house lawyer, and their relationships with their employer organisation. We look at some of the day-to-day work of the in-houser and we finish by exploring the concept of ethical tension, which runs, in various forms, throughout this book.

Chapter 4 opens with a series of organisational scandals involving in-house lawyers, to show the potential significance of in-houser independence and saying 'No' to the organisation. We explore how organisational imperatives (in business, the commercial orientation) are always seen as legitimate; but that the influence of the in-house legal team has to be managed, protected, and sometimes fought for. We show how independence is relational, specific to the circumstances of each case, and – from the perspective of the in-house lawyers – best understood as having a temporal dimension, being part of a series of interventions and non-interventions on their part. And we show how saying 'No' is part of a continuum of context specific responses, and one requiring significant effort as well as internal human capital. An in-house lawyer may need to be both well-placed in the tournament of influence, but also resourceful and willing to organise alliances within the organisation, before they can say 'No'. 'No' is both decided and negotiated. It is also often avoidable if the in-house lawyer wants to avoid it.

Chapter 5 begins our look at legal risk management and how professional logics are instantiated in the decision-making apparatus of organisations. We do so first by showing how organisational imperatives and the technical and professional skills of lawyers are used to construct the notion of legal risk management. In notions of risk appetite, we see the balancing of organisational imperatives against more public-facing values. And in looking at how risk is defined and managed, we see instantiations of the legal role and influence of lawyers in their organisations. Chapter 6 raises the ethical dimensions to risk management. It asks whether approaches to risk diminish the ethicality of decision-making and what ethical issues are, or ought to be, raised. A particular interest is in whether in-house lawyers have redlines around risk-appetites and risk decisions, and what ideas shape those red lines.

Chapter 7 develops the idea of institutional logics by looking at in-house orientations, seeking to disentangle the multiple strands of thinking associated with in-house lawyers to examine the extent to which such ideas are prevalent in our sample of in-house lawyers, and at how that moves us beyond existing understandings. Chapter 8 seeks to evaluate these orientations normatively and link them to other dimensions of in-house practice: professional orientations, team orientations, relationships with the organisation, and ethical pressure. Here we see that commercial orientations (being business-focused or, outside of business contexts, client-focused) are ubiquitous; they are inescapable. To wish for a purer form of professionalism without such orientations would be to offer a false prospectus, but we can focus on the nature and meaning of the orientations and their relationship to measures of ethical inclination. We demonstrate that there are distinctive but common orientations to the in-house role (commercial, ethical, etc), that individuals emphasise these orientations differently, and that that those differences are associated with different ethical inclinations. For example, thinking of exploitation of uncertainty as part of the in-house role is associated with a weaker ethical inclination on all our indicators.

In Chapter 9, we speculate on the implications of our study. We see that, in the complex interactions between different value systems and the tournament of influence, there is a currently muted but important role for professional identity. We see significant weaknesses in the dominant approaches to professional identity, but we also show that where professional identity is stronger, then ethical inclination is *also* stronger. Furthermore, we show that ethical infrastructure is potentially important to generating a more resilient form of professionalism for in-house lawyers. Having sought to isolate the influences on in-house lawyer ethicality, we think about how those influences might be affected by regulation, both professional and beyond, and what in-housers might do for themselves.

2
Methods

As we set out in Chapter 1, the central aim of this book is to examine, in-depth, the professionalism of the in-house lawyer. We explore the status, role and, most importantly, the ethicality of in-house lawyers. Unusually, the work is one of mixed methods, seeking to explore both qualitatively *and* quantitatively the complexities of in-house role and ethicality. To do this, we interviewed 67 in-house lawyers and senior compliance personnel (who were often lawyers by training) and surveyed 400 lawyers working in-house in business, government and the third sector. We look at general concepts, understandings of professional ethics, thinking on roles and so on. We also examine those general concepts within specific contexts. In particular, we take the emergent discipline of legal risk management and consider how in-house lawyers instantiate that concept. This involves us looking at how in-housers define legal risk, how they manage it, and how they perceive and deal with the ethical issues that result. This helps us understand legal risk management but also provides a contextualisation for general concepts relevant to understanding in-house lawyers: commerciality, professionalism and ethics, for example. We deepen this contextualisation by asking lawyers to respond to specific vignettes. These realistic case studies of risk problems tell us more about how our respondents see risk and ethics than talking about abstract concepts and processes can on their own. Through this multi-layered approach – from the general (professional and occupational concepts), to the specific (legal risk management), to the particular (legal risk cases) – we explore the terrain of in-house ethicality in significant depth and with particular regard to context.

We aim to go further than previous work on in-house lawyers in two main respects. The first is to look in-depth at legal risk management. Legal risk management provided a perfect opportunity to consider how professional and organisational ideas (often commercial ideas, given that most in-house lawyers are hosted in businesses) interacted. As a relatively new phenomenon, we hoped we might see professional and organisational ideas contest ownership of the problem. The apparent conflation of bureaucratic systems and quantification of legal judgments in risk management combined elements which, we suspected, were a mixture of the familiar and the forbidding to in-house lawyers. We were especially interested in a sociological question: did risk represent a new way of thinking – an institutional logic – changing the way in-house lawyers thought about and conducted their role?[1] We were also interested in whether risk represented fresh challenges to the ethicality of lawyers or reproduced old ones. In this way, we see risk as an opportunity to consider in-depth the ethical and managerial challenges facing in-house lawyers. Risk management is, of course, not all that in-house lawyers do, but it is a significant part of what they do. The shift from in-house roles in general to risk management in particular is intended to recognise that one's actions and thoughts about role are likely shaped by circumstance.[2] In particular, it is one thing to say that a lawyer is generally inclined to be entrepreneurial in approach, but another to say they are entrepreneurial in their approach to a situation when that situation calls for more cop-like behaviour.[3] Similarly, the vignettes were a conscious response to the criticism that research on in-house lawyers' ethics needs to address how lawyer approaches adapt to specific circumstances.[4]

The second way in which our work goes further than previous studies is in seeking to examine quantitatively some of the phenomena explored to date in socio-legal work on in-house lawyers. As far as we are aware, this work represents the most detailed profiling of in-house lawyers undertaken anywhere. It provides detailed data on organisations, individuals, individual and team identities, and approaches to professional principles. Uniquely it links these to externally validated proxy measures of the inclination to behave ethically. As we were unable to measure ethical misconduct directly, these measures provide the next best alternative. They are validated proxies for ethical misconduct and as such provide a good indicator of ethical risk.[5] We use these general measures of ethical inclination to map the moral compass of in-house lawyers and examine how these relate to ideas about lawyer identity, role and context.

There is very little sociologically rich quantitative work on ideas about the role and behaviour of in-house lawyers.[6] Instead, ideas about role identity have

---

[1] Patricia H Thornton and William Ocasio, 'Institutional Logics and the Historical Contingency of Power in Organizations: Executive Succession in the Higher Education Publishing Industry, 1958–1990' (1999) 105 *American Journal of Sociology* 801.

[2] Leslie C Levin and Lynn Mather, *Lawyers in Practice: Ethical Decision Making in Context* (University of Chicago Press, 2012).

[3] We introduced the ideas of in-housers as cops, counsellors and entrepreneurs in Chapter 1. We continue this in Chapter 7.

[4] See, for example, Kimberly Kirkland, 'Ethics in Large Law Firms: The Principle of Pragmatism' (2005) 35 *University of Memphis Law Review* 631.

[5] See, for example, Scott J Reynolds and Jared A Miller, 'The recognition of moral issues: moral awareness, moral sensitivity and moral attentiveness' (2015) 6 *Current Opinion in Psychology* 114; Peter L Jennings, Marie S Mitchell and Sean T Hannah, 'The moral self: A review and integration of the literature' (2015) 36 *Journal of Organizational Behavior* 104; and David Light Shields, Christopher D Funk and Brenda Light Bredemeier, 'Predictors of moral disengagement in sport' (2015) 37(6) *Journal of Sport and Exercise Psychology* 646.

[6] Gunz and Gunz is a very honourable exception. In the main, otherwise, quantitative work generally emanates from management and accounting scholars and focuses on data from organisations not individuals. See Byungjin Kwak, Byung T Ro and Inho Suk, 'The Composition of Top

been developed qualitatively rather than quantitatively. Such research provides rich – if sometimes contradictory – ideas about such roles. In particular, Nelson and Nielson's identification of cops, counsellors and entrepreneurs is a rewarding starting point for thinking about in-house lawyers, but they are not able to say whether they identify types of people or the types of action people can take. In other words, do lawyers tend to adhere to a type? Are they more or less permanently cops or counsellors, or do they choose to be a cop or counsellor as befits the circumstances they find themselves in with any given problem?[7] In addition, whilst Nelson and Neilson hypothesise about ethical problems, they are not able to directly correlate ideas about role with ethicality. We begin that task, disentangling the bundle of ideas that make up ideal-types and examining their relationships to ethical inclination.

To give a specific example, Nelson and Neilson see entrepreneurialism as a bundle of positive and negative traits, but the overall tenor of their analysis is to see entrepreneurialism as ethically risky.[8] We hoped a more precise approach would begin to clarify matters. We wanted in particular to see if the role identities seen in the literature were coherent, manifest and measureable, and whether and how they related to ethicality. To do so, we saw the need to look across a range of factors.[9] Those factors are contextual and individual; professional and commercial. We have developed measures of context (ethical pressure, team culture, ethical infrastructure), individual attitudes (role orientation) and professional orientation. This provides a wide, if not comprehensive, approach to sketching the dimensions of the in-house lawyer role. Through our measures, we demonstrate links between in-house role orientation, professional orientation, team culture, ethical infrastructure and general ethical inclination. Seminal questions debated in the ethics literature are informed by this analysis. Is thinking commercially likely to inhibit ethicality? Are lawyers right to think of themselves as 'mere advisors'? What is it about entrepreneurialism that may be ethically problematic? And so too are practical questions, such as whether ethical infrastructure is important and whether lawyers should sit on the boards of their organisations.

Management with General Counsel and Voluntary Information Disclosure' (2012) 54 *Journal of Accounting and Economics* 19; Alan D Jagolinzer, David F Larcker and Daniel J Taylor, 'Corporate Governance and the Information Content of Insider Trades' (2011) 49(5) *Journal of Accounting Research* 1252; Jayanthi Krishnan, Yuan Wen and Wanli Zhao, 'Legal Expertise on Corporate Audit Committees and Financial Reporting Quality' (2011) 86(6) *The Accounting Review* 2099; Preeti Choudhary, Jason D Schloetzer and Jason D Sturgess, 'Boards, Auditors, Attorneys and Compliance with Mandatory SEC Disclosure Rules' (2013) 34 *Managerial and Decision Economics* 477; Justin J Hopkins, Edward L. Maydew and Mohan Venkatachalam, 'Corporate General Counsel and Financial Reporting Quality' (2015) 61(1) *Management Science* 129–45; and Beng Wee Goh, Jimmy Lee and Jeffrey Ng, 'The Inclusion of General Counsel in Top Management and Tax Avoidance' (Social Science Research Network Paper, 8 July 2015).

[7] Robert L Nelson and Laura Beth Nielsen, 'Cops, Counsel, and Entrepreneurs: Constructing the Role of inside Counsel in Large Corporations' [2000] *Law and Society Review* 457.

[8] ibid.

[9] Richard Moorhead and others, 'Designing Ethics Indicators for Legal Services Provision' (Legal Services Board Report, 2012).

Equally, our development of measures across this wide range has its limits. Our first attempts to develop measures of role and professional orientation for in-house lawyers can no doubt be improved. Similarly, our sample of interviewees is sizeable but it also has its limits. Inevitably, with any sample of practising lawyers recruited voluntarily to participate in research of this kind, the sample is not demonstrably representative of the entire population of in-house lawyers. The garnering of such samples with hard to reach professionals is difficult, in fact all but impossible, at the best of times. This is doubly true on a topic as sensitive as ethics. We combat this problem by comparing our sample to the general population and also through the rich contextualisation provided by our interview data.

Similarly, our quantitative research demonstrates relationships between ideas of interest, rather than causal links. In some ways, this does not matter: if we demonstrate that a particular attitude to uncertainty is associated with a weaker ethical inclination, this is an advance on previous knowledge and a clear signal that attitudes to uncertainty need scrutiny. It leaves open the question of whether particular attitudes to uncertainty lead to weaker ethicality or vice versa. Further work could look at these questions of causal direction and whether particular contexts or problems or ways of framing problems stimulate particular role and professional orientations. Finally, many ethics scholars will react against the simplicity of our metrics. Attitudes to uncertainty, to commerciality, to professionalism, and to ethical inclination are of course more complicated than psychometrics can capture. Again, we tackle this through the data provided in interviews. We hope through the combination of qualitative and quantitative data that we provide fresh insight and depth into the world of in-house lawyering.

THE FIRST SET OF INTERVIEWS

Our interviews took place in two distinct phases. The first set of interviews were conducted at the end of 2013. They explored how legal risk is defined, identified, predicted and managed within companies. In so doing, we provide a vehicle for exploring professional ethics and corporate governance arising from these issues and a space in which practitioners and academics can explore best practice and challenges in legal risk management.

Using interviews in this way is not designed to be representative of practice generally. The aim here is instead to explore differences and similarities in approach so as to generate ideas and questions about current practice. Interviewing elites (such as in-house lawyers and senior compliance personnel) can prove difficult.[10] They can be hard to locate and may be unwilling (for a variety of

---

[10] For an account of these challenges, and how they can be overcome, see Steven Vaughan, 'Elite and Elite-Lite Interviewing: Managing our Industrial Legacy' in Alex Franklin and Paul Blyton (eds), *Researching Sustainability: A Guide to Social Science Methods, Practice and Engagement* (Earthscan, 2011).

reasons) to participate in academic research.[11] For this first set of interviews, we developed a list of practitioners known to be interested in legal risk, drawn from our existing contacts and where practitioners had public profiles around legal risk (be it from writing or conference presentations on risk).[12] From that list, we snowball-sampled by asking these practitioners to suggest or introduce other practitioners from other organisations.[13] We also contacted FTSE 100 companies and asked the senior in-house lawyer or senior compliance person to participate, where their contact details were available. Senior compliance officers were particularly difficult to identify this way, having lower public profiles than General Counsel. Interviewees were recruited on the basis that their participation would be anonymous.[14] They agreed that interviews would be recorded and transcribed to assist in data analysis. In total, 34 practitioners were interviewed.

Of the 34 interviewees in this first phase, 23 were in-house lawyers (14 working for financial institutions; nine in other sections) and 11 were compliance personnel. In the book, we use 'IHL' to signify quotations from in-housers,[15] and 'Compliance' to signify quotes from compliance personnel.[16] So, for example, 'IHL12' denotes the twelfth in-house lawyer interviewee who took part. Twenty-two of the interviewees were men, 12 were women. Twenty-six of the practitioners were qualified solicitors and three had been called to the Bar (all of the latter worked in legal roles in the financial sector). Two had other professional qualifications, and three had no professional qualifications (they worked in compliance sector roles in non-financial services companies). The majority of our first set of interviewees had more than 25 years of post-qualification experience, most of which had been spent in-house.

Twenty-eight of the interviews were conducted over the telephone and six interviews were conducted in person. They averaged 50 minutes in length. The interviews were semi-structured, using interview schedules designed as a series of topic areas to guide and shape the conversation, rather than directed by means of closed questions.[17] These topic areas were developed based on a literature review, the project's aims, and the issues identified from an initial

---

[11] See, for example: David Richards, 'Elite interviewing: Approaches and pitfalls' (1996) 16(3) *Politics* 199; Jeffrey M Berry, 'Validity and reliability issues in elite interviewing' (2002) 35(4) *Political Science & Politics* 679; and William S Harvey, 'Strategies for conducting elite interviews' (2011) 11(4) *Qualitative Research* 431.

[12] Jane Ritchie, Jane, Jane Lewis and Gilliam Elam, 'Designing and Selecting Samples' in Carol McNaughton Nicholls and Rachel Ormston (eds), *Qualitative Research Practice: A Guide for Social Science Students and Researchers* (Sage, 2013).

[13] Patrick Biernacki and Dan Waldorf, 'Snowball sampling: Problems and techniques of chain referral sampling' (1981) 10(2) *Sociological Methods & Research* 141.

[14] For a discussion of the importance of anonymity in interviews like this, see Darren G Lilleker, 'Interviewing the political elite: Navigating a potential minefield' (2003) 23(3) *Politics* 207.

[15] This is for all interviews with in-housers, from this first set of interviews and from the second set discussed below.

[16] For example, 'IHL17' would signify a quotation from the seventeenth in-houser we spoke with.

[17] Steinar Kvale, *Doing Interviews* (Sage, 2008); and Kathryn Roulston, *Reflective Interviewing: A Guide to Theory and Practice* (Sage, 2010).

'think tank' seminar held at University College London with 12 in-house lawyers and compliance officers.[18] Coding of the interview data took place against the original interview schedule topic guide using NVivo software.[19]

Interviews on process and definition can become abstract or nebulous. And interviews on ethics face particular social response bias problems.[20] To counter these problems, we sought an opportunity to engage interviewees with specific factual scenarios about legal risk and see how responses to those scenarios differed. Using vignettes (case studies) has been suggested as a technique to deal with topics, 'where the participant may not feel comfortable discussing their personal situation and may conceal the truth about their own actions or beliefs.'[21] Three vignettes were included in the interview schedule which identified hypothetical situations that raise a legal, compliance and/or ethical issue for the practitioner. We discuss these later on in this book where they illuminate issues raised in relation to the interviews more generally.

THE SECOND SET OF INTERVIEWS

The second set of interviews took place in 2016. These built upon the results of the online survey we had undertaken in 2015, described below, and participants were recruited from among those who had completed the survey. We included an item at the end of the survey to be completed by those willing to be interviewed and to talk further about the project. Up to three emails were sent to those who had given their contact information (an initial email with details on the interviews, and then two follow-up chasers). Thirty-three interviews were completed as part of the survey follow-up: 11 with men, 22 with women. As with the first set of interviews, most of these participants had spent the majority of their working lives in-house. Twenty-nine had qualified as solicitors, two as barristers. Two had qualified in-house. We explore their careers in more depth in Chapter 3, looking in particular at drivers for the move in-house and for perceptions of differences between in-house and private practice work.

As with the first set of interviews, this second set were also semi-structured. The topic guide is set out in Appendix 1. Here, we were keen to explore, in more depth, some of the themes and issues coming out of our survey data: relationships between in-house lawyers and their employers; the nature of

---

[18] The interview guide is in Appendix 1.
[19] Patricia Bazeley and Kristi Jackson, *Qualitative Data Analysis with NVivo* (Sage, 2013).
[20] Donna M Randall and Maria F. Fernandes, 'The social desirability response bias in ethics research' (1991) 10 *Journal of Business Ethics* 805.
[21] Annabelle Gourlay and others, 'Using Vignettes in Qualitative Research to Explore Barriers and Facilitating Factors to the Uptake of Prevention of Mother-to-Child Transmission Services in Rural Tanzania: A Critical Analysis' (2014) 14 *BMC Medical Research Methodology* 21. See also Rhidian Hughes, 'Considering the Vignette Technique and Its Application to a Study of Drug Injecting and HIV Risk and Safer Behaviour' (1998) 20 *Sociology of Health & Illness* 381.

working in-house; the impacts of professional regulation; challenges to ethicality; the framing and shape of in-house ethical infrastructures etc.

All of these second set interviews were conducted by telephone.[22] Most lasted around 45 minutes. Again, and as with the first set, interviewees were recruited on the basis that their participation would be anonymous. They agreed that interviews would be recorded and professionally transcribed to assist in data analysis. These second set of interviews were analysed by hand by one of the authors (and without the aid of software). However, the underlying logic in coding data (whether via software or done manually) differed little.[23] With both sets of qualitative data, our aim, on the first pass of the data, was to look for first-order, manifest themes (those directly observable in the interview transcripts, tacking back to the themes and issues contained in the interview topic guides),[24] and to then, in a second pass of the data, look for second-order, latent themes which underlay what our interviews were saying to us (that is, to interpret the data to explore the response itself as well as what may have been inferred or implied by the response).[25] The data, once coded, were analysed for linking elements and interrelationships, what Miles and Huberman label 'causal networks'.[26] Throughout this book, we seek to compare these codes and causal networks against the results of the survey (discussed immediately below), both to triangulate the emerging themes and to be able to pinpoint areas of disagreement between the interview data and the survey data.[27]

THE SURVEY

Through the survey, we wanted to explore issues of identity, ethics and risk in a way that was both reasonably comprehensive and manageable. Aware that ethics indicators can relate to context, character and capacities, and of the ways these interact, we needed to prioritise pragmatically, based on our understandings of

---

[22] There are strengths and weaknesses in each of telephone and face-to-face interviewing. With elites, time is often a limited resource and telephone interviews can fit in well with a busy schedule. For more discussion of this, see Judith E Sturges and Kathleen J Hanrahan, 'Comparing telephone and face-to-face qualitative interviewing: a research note' (2004) 4(1) *Qualitative Research* 107.

[23] For a discussion of the pros and cons of each approach, see Amanda Coffee and Paul Atkinson, *Making Sense of Qualitative Data: Complimentary Research Strategies* (Sage, 1996); and Themia Basit, 'Manual or electronic? The role of coding in qualitative data analysis' (2003) 45(2) *Educational Research* 143.

[24] Richard E Boyatzis, *Transforming Qualitative Information: Thematic Analysis and Code Development* (Sage, 1998).

[25] Karsten Jonsen and Karen A Jehn, 'Using triangulation to validate themes in qualitative studies' (2009) 4(2) *Qualitative Research in Organizations and Management* 123.

[26] Matthew B Miles and Michael Huberman, *Qualitative Data Analysis: An Expanded Sourcebook* (Sage, 1994) 163.

[27] Charles Teddlie and Abbas Tashakkori, *Foundations of Mixed Methods Research: Integrating Quantitative and Qualitative Approaches in the Social and Behavioral Sciences* (Sage, 2009).

what the specific literature on in-house lawyers said to date (which emphasised context and role identity),[28] and what the general ethics literature said to date (where ethical infrastructure, in particular, emerged as an important area not much dealt with in the empirical literature on in-housers).[29] We also wanted to provide some key data on demographics and the organisational characteristics of organisations hosting in-house lawyers. We discussed our survey design with in-house lawyer contacts to ensure we reflected what they felt were their key concerns, whilst also developing the issues seen in the literature. As a result, we collected data on: (i) demographics and careers; (ii) the employer organisation; and (iii) in-house role structures (eg reporting lines).

Most importantly for our purposes, we have also used the survey data to develop composite measures of a number of individual and organisational characteristics:

- in-house role orientation;
- team orientation;
- relationships between the legal team and the wider organisation;
- ethical pressure;
- professional orientation; and
- ethical infrastructure.

With half an eye on how the results might be used to inform debates on regulation, we also collected data on attitudes to regulation of the in-house role.

Through these indicators, we hoped to explore whether it was possible to develop measures of these concepts and then to map differences within the in-house community. We also sought to see how such measures correlated with ethicality more broadly understood. As we set out in Chapter 1, measuring ethicality is of course both difficult and multi-dimensional. We settled upon two measures of ethical inclination as most appropriate to the task: a measure of moral attentiveness and a measure of moral disengagement. We explain these more fully below, but it is worth noting here they have been shown to be predictive of ethical misconduct and less prone to social response bias than other measures.[30]

---

[28] Moorhead and others (n 9).
[29] Ann E Tenbrunsel, Kristin Smith-Crowe and Elizabeth E Umphress, 'Building Houses on Rocks: The Role of the Ethical Infrastructure in Organizations' (2003) 16 *Social Justice Research* 285; although see Elizabeth Chambliss and David B Wilkins, 'Promoting Effective Ethical Infrastructure in Large Law Firms: A Call for Research and Reporting' (2001) 30 *Hofstra L Rev* 691; Kimberly Kirkland, 'Ethical Infrastructures and De Facto Ethical Norms at Work in Large US Law Firms: The Role of Ethics Counsel' (2008) 11 *Legal Ethics* 181; and Christine Parker and others, 'The Ethical Infrastructure of Legal Practice in Larger Law Firms: Values, Policy and Behaviour' (2008) 31 *UNSWLJ* 158, where ethical infrastructure is discussed.
[30] Reynolds and others (n 5); Jennings and others (n 5); and, Light Shields and others (n 5).

34 *Methods*

When examining statistical significance we employ a conventional alpha level of $p < .05$.

MAPPING INDICATORS OF IN-HOUSE PRACTICE

We use the survey to develop quantitative indicators of in-house identity, professional orientation, team orientation, ethical infrastructure and so on. We explain two of the more interesting of these indicators in some detail here, so that readers can get a sense of how the measures are constructed, and think critically about their validity. We have chosen the two we think will be of most interest, and perhaps most controversial, to readers: the measures of in-house identity and of professional orientation.

In-House Role Identity

In an attempt to 'measure' in-house lawyer role identity we produced a set of questions on the in-house lawyer role to be asked of our survey respondents. We began with 'What is your attitude to the following statements about the in-house lawyer role?', and then gave respondents 28 attitudinal statements with which they could agree or disagree on a Likert Scale. This list of questions was based on our analysis of the literature and on our first-stage interviews with in-house lawyers. We were especially interested in the entrepreneurial, cop, and counsellor in-houser role orientations described by Nelson and Neilson, and whether 'risk manager' might emerge as a distinctive type, but we were generally looking to identify the range of role orientations that emerged from the literature and our interviews and discussions with in-house lawyers as typifying in-house roles.

To build measures of this kind, one needs to assess their validity and reliability, ensuring that we have the appropriate number of dimensions (that is, that the measures we use identify distinct and separate elements of identity, professional orientation and so on), and that we reliably measure such dimensions.[31] In simple terms, what we do is analyse our questions for patterns of similarity, test the questions that are answered similarly to see if they appear to be measuring the same underlying construct, and test whether that construct is meaningful and reliably measured.

All the questions in the survey, including these role identity questions, were refined and tested for face validity by asking a cohort of in-house lawyers to complete and comment on pilot surveys. These lawyers were invited to comment on questions which did not make sense to them, on questions which they thought were not important or otherwise problematic, and to suggest areas of interest

---

[31] Mike Furr, *Scale Construction and Psychometrics for Social and Personality Psychology* (Sage, 2011) 4–15.

that we might have missed.[32] We refined the survey questionnaire in the light of such comments and tested the revised questions with in a similar way a second time. The coherence and meaningfulness of our measures have also been road-tested at a dozen or more seminars with in-house lawyers where the findings have been explored.

In creating these measures, we ran statistical analyses to identify the appropriate number of dimensions. To illustrate this, let us describe how we produced metrics for role orientation. We first reduced the 28 variables to a set of principal components. Principal component analysis (PCA) is an exploratory multivariate analysis technique that transforms a set of correlated variables into a subset of independent variables called "principal components". Thus, a PCA allows us to reduce the complexity of the data, summarising the information presented in correlated (and thus, to a certain extent, redundant) variables into independent variables which represent a large proportion of the information contained in the original variables. With PCA we are able to see structure in our data and pull out the concepts that best differentiate the responses to our survey questions. We use it here to reduce the number of variables included in the analyses, whilst retaining the analytic dimensions that underlie substantively different sets of variables. The data met key tests for performing a PCA,[33] with relevant testing conducted to ensure both that the number and nature of the components (or dimensions) were appropriate,[34] and that the variables contained within the components contributed significantly to that component.[35] As a result, we are

---

[32] For accounts of the importance of pre-testing in survey design, see Shelby D Hunt, Richard D Sparkman Jr and James B Wilcox, 'The pretest in survey research: Issues and preliminary findings' (1982) *Journal of Marketing Research* 269; Floyd Jackson Fowler Jr, 'How unclear terms affect survey data' (1992) 56(2) *Public Opinion Quarterly* 218; and Pamela Campanelli, 'Testing survey questions' (2008) *International Handbook of Survey Methodology* 176.

[33] Besides the input variables being numerical, and having at least five times more cases (ie, participants) than the number of variables, the input variables should be correlated in order to run a PCA. We have verified the correlation among input variables using the Kaiser-Meyer-Olkin (KMO) statistic, which varies between 0 and 1. The higher the KMO, the higher the correlation between input variables and thus, the more consistent should be the extracted principal components.

[34] For deciding how many components to extract and retain in the final solution, we have used the following criteria: 1) Kaiser criteria, retaining all components showing an eigenvalue higher than 1; and 2) Scree test, which involves examining the graphical representation of the eigenvalues and finding the natural bend or break point in the data where the curve flattens out. The number of factors to retain is usually the number of data points above the 'break' (ie, not including the point at which the break occurs). It is common to use rotation in order to simplify and clarify the data structure, making the extracted components easier to interpret. There are a number of possible rotation methods that can be used. Varimax is the most commonly used orthogonal method. Orthogonal methods produce factors that are uncorrelated; however, in social sciences it is reasonable to expect some correlation among factors, since cognitive and/or behavioural factors tend to be interdependent. Also, it has been verified that if factor correlations exceed .32 there is 10% (or more) overlap in variance among factors, which is enough variance to warrant oblique rotation. Thus, in those cases we have opted to use the Oblimin rotation method.

[35] It is also important to look at the commonalities, ie, part of variance of each original variable that is captured by the extracted components. Commonalities lower than .05 are considered to be low, indicating that the original variable is not well represented in the final solution of extracted components. In those cases we have considered deleting the variables showing low commonalities and running a new PCA without those variables.

satisfied both that our measures are coherent and meaningful indicators of the responses given by our in-house respondents, and that they capture underlying constructs.

You can get a better sense of what we mean by examining the components that were extracted from our PCA of the data. Each of the orientations indicates a group of questions which our respondents tended to answer in similar ways. A final test of the validity of the components (or 'orientations', as we will now refer to them) is to examine each group of questions and to consider whether it makes sense to say they are measuring one concept (i.e. whether they are sufficiently similar to say they sensibly measure the same overarching concept). The labels we have given each orientation represent our interpretation of the overarching concept that results. As we can see from Table 2.1, eight orientations were identified.

With perhaps one exception, each of these orientations appears to be coherent and meaningful. Not only are the statements of identity underneath each heading clearly related to each other statistically, they also make sense analytically. The potential exception is the 'troubled subservience' orientation. Seeing that an emphasis on commercial awareness sometimes inhibits the in-house lawyer in performing his or her role might be expected to be in tension with the apparent acceptance of subservience to commercial aims even where this may be inappropriate. Even so, there is quite a strong logic to the component.

Table 2.1 Orientations Summary

Commercial orientation (α = .78)	Independence orientation (α = .61)
• The commercial success of my organisation is important to me • Commercial awareness is vital to the function of in-house lawyers • Our advice goes beyond legal matters to consider business considerations • It is important for a legal adviser to add value to the business	• The organisation needs to understand that my view is independent • It is important to me that I can offer an independent opinion on the legality of business action
Exploitation of uncertainty orientation (α = .74)	Troubled subservience orientation (α = .56)
• Loopholes in the law should be identified that benefit the business • Where the law is uncertain, I help the business benefit from that uncertainty	• Saying 'no' to the organisation is to be avoided, even when there is no legally acceptable alternative to suggest

(continued)

Table 2.1 *(Continued)*

• My role is to exploit the law for commercial ends	• Where commercial desirability and legal professional judgement are in tension, commercial desirability is more important. • An emphasis on commercial awareness sometimes inhibits the in-house lawyer in performing his or her role • Others in the organisation are responsible for considering the ethics of its decisions; my role is to advise on the law
Advisory orientation ($\alpha = .72$)	**Risk management orientation** ($\alpha = .57$)
• My job is to advise on legal risk and the business decides how much risk it then wants to take • Where the law is uncertain, we advise and the business decides	• My job is to manage to a known risk appetite • My job is to help set appetite for risk within legal bounds
Ethical orientation ($\alpha = .66$)	**Legality orientation** ($\alpha = .28$)
• My advice goes beyond legal considerations to assess whether something is the right thing ethically to do • Where a proposed action is lawful, but I think it is nevertheless unethical, I will not hesitate to voice my concerns • Where the law is uncertain, I take a lead on what the right thing to do is	• Insisting something cannot be done within the law is sometimes necessary • Sometimes it's necessary to think less about the organisation's needs and more about what the law requires

As well as testing whether the components identified were distinct (in the sense that the PCA analysis suggests each of these orientations is distinct from the others and measured by the individual statements shown by the bullet points in Table 2.1),[36] we also tested whether the components reliably measure the concepts we identified by testing each component for internal consistency.[37]

---

[36] See the commentary in the previous two footnotes. KMO was acceptable (.79) and the eight components explained 56.7% variance. Communalities were below .50 for items 5, 16 and 20 and thus they were taken out from the analysis and the procedure was repeated. Items with factor loadings below |.50| or loading heavily in more than one factor were excluded.

[37] Using Cronbach's Alpha coefficient.

The Cronbach Alpha (α) scores in Table 2.1 give the measure of reliability. Five of these orientations are sufficiently reliable for us to use them in subsequent analysis: the commercial, ethical, independence, exploitation of uncertainty, and advisory orientations. Two of these five, however, had consistency ratings at the borderline of the conventional test of reliability (the ethical orientation and the independence orientation). We have included them here, given the early, experimental nature of this research and the importance, and face validity,[38] of the concepts and their individual dimensions.[39] Subsequent research should seek to increase the robustness of measures of the independence and ethical orientations. The remaining orientations also remain of interest, and might be capable of better definition and measurement in subsequent studies.

We discuss the five orientations in more detail in Chapter 8, but for now it is worth noting that what Nelson and Neilson might have identified as entrepreneurialism we identify as three separate orientations: a commercial orientation; an exploiting uncertainty orientation; and perhaps, subject to the concerns about reliability expressed above, a troubled subservience orientation. Because each of these orientations is distinct, it shows us that it is possible for in-house lawyers to have a commercial (or in non-commercial contexts, an organisational) orientation but to not see the exploitation of legal uncertainty for commercial/organisational ends (or to identify loopholes) as part of their role. Similarly, it is possible to be commercially and ethically oriented on these measures.

Essentially the same approach to isolating dimensions and testing their validity and reliability was applied to other elements of our survey. We discuss one more in detail.

Professional Orientation

As we set out in Chapter 1, a key question for in-house lawyers is the extent to which they are meaningfully 'professional' in their approach. To examine that, respondents were asked: 'To what extent do the following obligations have an important influence on you in practice?' The principles required under the regulatory Handbook of the Solicitors Regulation Authority (SRA) were then listed.[40] Survey respondents were asked to indicate their responses on a Likert

---

[38] The extent to which a test is subjectively viewed as covering the concept it purports to measure.
[39] Cronbach's Alpha coefficients were calculated. This is a test of internal consistency which indicates how closely the individual elements of a group of variables are related to each other. Conventionally, an α> .7 is seen as an acceptable level of reliability. Although .70 is the most conventionally used cut-off level for Cronbach alpha measure of reliability, there is no gold standard of acceptable or unacceptable level of α and in some cases conventionally low levels of α are still useful: N Schmitt, 'Uses and abuses of coefficient alpha' (1996) 8(4) *Psychological Assessment* 350–53. As this is the first study to look at in-house lawyer perceptions in this way we have included components with an α> .6 where the components make analytical sense.
[40] Most of our respondents were expected to be (and were) solicitors, hence we decided to use the solicitors' principles. Broadly similar duties are found in the code of conduct for barristers.

scale (very frequently, frequently, sometimes, rarely, and never). These principles bind solicitors at all times, in all things that they do. However, we did not label them as the SRA's professional principles to minimise response bias associated with being explicitly reminded these were mandatory.[41]

We did not have prior expectations about how these responses might cluster, but PCA suggested that there were three distinct groupings.[42] These are set out in Table 2.2.

Table 2.2 Professional Orientation

Independence and legality (α = .81)	Effectiveness and integrity (α = .71)
• Maintaining the trust the public places in you and in the provision of legal services • Upholding the rule of law and the proper administration of justice • Preventing my independence from being compromised • Dealing with your own regulators in an open, timely and co-operative manner • Complying with your own legal and regulatory obligations as a lawyer	• Carrying out your role in the organisation effectively and in accordance with proper governance and sound financial and risk management principles • Providing a proper standard of service to the business • Acting with integrity
\multicolumn{2}{c}{**Client's interests**[a]}
\multicolumn{2}{c}{• Acting in the best interests of the organisation}

[a] As this component has only one element, there is no internal consistency to test for.

In this way, in the top left of Table 2, we see a cluster of principles which respondents tended to treat similarly which are relevant to the lawyers' obligations other than to themselves and the client. An exception is independence. Independence can be identified via its negative referents (typically independence from the client and from the State) but to be meaningful as a professional concept independence ought also to have a positive referent. It might most properly be seen as being independent in the administration of justice (if one considers the best interests of the client are protected by other principles, as they are). Importantly, then,

---

[41] On this, see Donna M Randall and Maria F Fernandes, 'The social desirability response bias in ethics research' (1991) 10(11) *Journal of Business Ethics* 805.
[42] A principal component analyses was run for items assessing professional principles. KMO was good (.86). On the basis of two criteria – a) retaining components that have eigenvalues > 1; and b) scree test – three components were extracted. The three components explained 65.6% variance. Communalities were all above .50 (except for item 8, that was .48). Given that some of the correlations between the four components exceeded .32, oblique rotation (ie, Oblimin) was performed.

this analysis confirms a view that independence and the upholding of the rule of law and administrative justice are closely aligned in the minds of many of our respondents. As a result we think this cluster of principles is best described as a concern for 'independence and legality' (although independence and justice might serve equally well as a label, the inclusion of regulatory obligations suggests that legality is the better emphasis).

The second cluster (effectiveness and integrity) focuses on the role and effectiveness of the individual lawyer vis-à-vis their employer (or client). A concern for integrity might be seen as more personal than a connection with justice and legality as suggested by the independence and legality cluster. If integrity is construed more narrowly as honesty (see Chapter 7), it may also suggest this cluster of principles is narrower in terms of the kinds of relationship or values it calls into play.

The third element is a single principle: acting in the best interest of the client. If we see independence and legality as being concerned with collective interests, and effectiveness and integrity as being concerned about the relationship between the lawyer and the client, then this third component is concerned with the interests of the client only. Another way of describing the three clusters, albeit a simplification, is to see the three clusters as showing a concern with tri-, bi- and unilateral values (lawyer-client-public, lawyer-client, client interests). As we discuss later in the book, it is common for lawyers to emphasise the pre-eminence of client interests, in spite of this not being the position of their codes of conduct. It is interesting, therefore, to see this principle being seen as separate from the others as well as being the one most strongly supported by our respondents (see Chapter 8).

As well as role and professional orientations, we developed a suite of other indicators from our data in the same way. These include team orientation, organisational approaches to legal, ethical pressure and, ethical infrastructure. We describe them when discussing the results in the chapters that follow.

CONDUCT OF THE SURVEY AND RESPONSES

Our online survey was distributed by the Solicitors Regulation Authority to their list of registered in-house solicitors (either on the roll, or with practising certificates). The online link was further distributed by the Bar Association for Commerce, Finance and Industry (BACFI), by the Association of Corporate Counsel (ACC) to their members, and to the extensive in-house contacts of *Legal Business* magazine. We are very grateful to those organisations for their help.

Four hundred in-house lawyers completed the survey. Whilst this provides very useful data on the sample, and we explore below how representative of the general population of in-house lawyers this sample is, the data are of much less certain use in describing in-house lawyers as a whole. The response rate is low (we estimate as many as 27,000 in-house lawyers would have received a request to participate in the survey), and the risk of response bias is strong. We were able to examine this in our general data analysis, looking for indications that the data contained biases through the over-representation of extreme viewpoints, for example. As set out above, we also road-tested our findings on wide and varied audiences of in-house lawyers. Few doubted and many supported the broad thrust of the findings, but some were anxious that the picture presented was too pessimistic. We are confident that the survey represents a very useful and detailed analysis of a sample of mainstream in-house opinion as a result, but we do not claim it is representative of all in-house lawyers. We think, for instance, that the most ethically disengaged lawyers would have been unlikely to respond. We would thus caution against seeing the data here as measuring (say) the level of ethical problems in practice. There is good reason for thinking that our methods might under- or over-estimate such incidence; but our analysis provides a strong starting point for future analyses.

More importantly for us, the enables us to examine the relationships between different indicators in the dataset. We are able to explore and test relationships in a way that has not been done previously. In this way, we are engaged in theory generation more than testing with finality a definitive truth about in-house practice. So, we are able to deconstruct the concept of 'entrepreneurialism' with greater rigour and precision, for example, and examine the extent to which (say) a commercial orientation correlates with ethical inclination. Again, we cannot be sure such relationships are generalizable to all areas of in-house practice. We would expect that the respondents to our survey would be more interested in ethical practice than those who did not respond. The high levels of ethical orientation in our survey responses support this. Thus it might be that the relationships we see are in fact relationships which are only demonstrated amongst more ethically inclined groups. The discussions of our interview data, and some of the survey findings, would, however, serve to cast doubt on such an assumption. Our interviewees – many of whom participated in the survey also – showed a wide range of approaches to risk and in-house ethicality, for instance. We must nonetheless remain very alive to this possible limitation on the findings.

That said, in broad terms, our 400 survey respondents were fairly representative of the underlying population of in-house solicitors in England & Wales. There is a good range of experience in the sample: a quarter of respondents had been admitted eight years or less, half had 15 years or more experience, and a quarter had in excess of 24 years of post-qualification experience. Overall, about two-thirds had more than five years of experience of working in-house, and about 60 per cent of our sample had less than five years of experience of private practice. Our survey sample was marginally more experienced than the population of in-house lawyers from which they were drawn.[43] Women

---

[43] The SRA provided us with data on gender, date of qualification and work areas which we compared with the data from our survey respondents.

42 Methods

were somewhat under-represented in our survey, although not dramatically so (53 per cent in our survey were women, compared to 57 per cent in the population of solicitors in-house based on SRA data). Our survey respondents were typically General Counsel (GCs) (27 per cent of the sample) or in another senior in-house legal role (42 per cent).[44] Twenty-six per cent identified as in-house legal, and 5 per cent as 'other'.[45] Within our survey sample, proportionately more men were GCs than women were. This was a modest and not statistically significant gender difference.[46] Similarly, proportionately more men were working in the commercial sector, but again this was not a significant difference.[47] The men in our sample did tend to have been qualified for longer, and worked in bigger teams (both these differences were statistically significant). The men had also spent somewhat longer in-house and worked in bigger organisations on average (here the differences were not statistically significant). In terms of professional qualification, 12 per cent of our survey respondents had multiple professional qualifications. 95 per cent were qualified as solicitors; 6.5 per cent were qualified as barristers; and 2.7 per cent were qualified as legal executives.[48] Although 18 per cent had qualifications in more than one jurisdiction, respondents were principally qualified in England and Wales.[49]

We also collected data on the types of organisation in which our respondents work. Our survey grouped lawyers into three broad categories, which we compare against the SRA's categories.[50] We can see, in Table 2.3, that in-house lawyers working in business are more strongly represented in our survey, although again the difference is not dramatic.

Table 2.3 Categories of Workplace

	SRA Data (%)	Our Survey Sample (%)
Business	63.7	67.3
Charity/Social Enterprise	4.5	7.3
Public Sector	31.9	25.4

---

[44] In many companies of a certain size (usually multinationals) the term 'General Counsel' is often applied to the most senior lawyer in a country, business unit or division

[45] 'Other' roles included a variety of in-house legal or associated roles: from chief compliance officer to corporate paralegal, directors of ethics and various legal management roles.

[46] Chi-square was not significant. Of 211 women respondents, 23.7% were GCs. Of 187 men respondents, 28.9% were GCs.

[47] 70.4% of the men worked for a business (compared with 64.5% of women. 26.1% of women worked for a public sector organisation (compared with 24.7% of men) and 4.8% of men worked for a charity (compared with 9.5% of women).

[48] 9.5% held other qualifications, such as the New York Bar.

[49] 3.7% were qualified in Scotland, 0.7% in Northern Ireland, 3.2% in the rest of the EU, and 3.2% in the USA.

[50] The SRA have more detailed categories which we collapsed into business, public and third sectors.

We also collected more specific data on the type of business engaged in, based on UK Office of National Statistics categories.[51] This provides, in Table 2.4, an overview of the sectors within which the respondents work.

Table 2.4 Type of Business

	N	%
Financial	58	14.4
Public administration and compulsory social security	41	10.2
Manufacturing	32	8.0
Information and communication	32	8.0
Professional, scientific and technical activities	24	6.0
Construction	20	5.0
Education	16	4.0
Electricity, gas, steam and air conditioning supply	14	3.5
Real estate activities	14	3.5
Human health and social work activities	14	3.5
Wholesale and retail trade; repair of motor vehicles and motorcycles	13	3.2
Insurance	13	3.2
Arts, entertainment and recreation	10	2.5
Defence	8	2.0
Water supply; sewerage, waste management and remediation activities	6	1.5
Mining and quarrying	5	1.2
Administrative and support service activities	5	1.2
Transportation and storage	4	1.0
Accommodation and food service activities	4	1.0
Agriculture, forestry and fishing	2	0.5
Other service activities	64	15.9
Total valid responses to this question	399	99.3

Most of our respondents worked for organisations headquartered in England and Wales, although over a quarter had headquarters outside of the UK and many had offices all over the world. The size of organisation and the size of the team that our survey respondents worked within differed widely. Organisation size was generally high (half worked in organisations above 1,500 employees)

---

[51] ONS UK Standard Industrial Classification (SIC) 2007 Hierarchy categories, www.neighbourhood.statistics.gov.uk/HTMLDocs/SIC/ONS_SIC_hierarchy_view.html.

and, as one would expect, the size of in-house team was partly a function of the size of the organisation.[52] Half of our in-house lawyer survey respondents worked in teams of 13 or fewer. In fact: (i) a quarter were working in teams of five or fewer; (ii) 8 per cent were (in) teams of one person; and (iii) although the in-house legal teams are dominated by admitted lawyers, 14 per cent of our respondents had more than 50 per cent non-admitted staff working in their teams.

A NOTE ON TERMINOLOGY

Much of the other work on in-housers is on those working for corporations, and concerns business influences on those in-housers. As we have seen, our survey respondents and interviewees worked for a wide variety of employers, from large multinational corporations to small NGOs to UK government departments. In this book, we use the term 'organisation' to encompass the many employers for whom our in-housers work but use the phrase commercial orientation to refer to the interests of organisation. This last choice reflects the fact that commercial organisations dominate employment of in-house lawyers and organisational interests, even government, often had a commercial flavour to them. Where our conclusions speak solely (or more significantly) to those working in particular sectors, we make this clear.

CONCLUSIONS

This chapter has discussed our methods. Our aim has been to provide a rich, mixed method study of in-house lawyering. Our particular focus is on professionalism and how, more particularly still, in-house lawyers manage risk, conceive of their role, and think about their ethical responsibilities. We have developed measures of a number of relevant concepts at the individual level, such as role orientation and professional orientation, and at the organisational level, such as relationships with their host organisation and ethical pressure. These enable us to explore questions about professionalism quantitatively on a large sample of in-house lawyers. Furthermore, we are the first to demonstrate links between such concepts and recognised measures of ethical inclination. Such measures predict ethical misconduct and thus provide important evidence of how individual and organisational influences on professionalism matter.

Seminal questions debated in the ethics literature are informed by this analysis. Is thinking commercially likely to inhibit ethicality? Are lawyers right to think of themselves as 'mere advisors'? What is it about entrepreneurialism

---

[52] There was a statistically significant, moderate correlation, $r(388) = .474, p = .000$.

that may be ethically problematic? And so too are practical questions, such as whether ethical infrastructure is important and whether in-house lawyers should sit on boards. Through our interview data, we hope to provide also a rich picture of the complexity beyond these measures.

Having set out our approaches to data collection and analysis, we turn in the following chapter to use our data to consider the place of in-house lawyers in organisational networks: their place in the wider legal profession; the evolution and content of the in-house role; the structural precursors to a successful blending of professional and organisational imperatives (forms of remuneration, line management etc); and relationships between employee in-house lawyers and their employers.

3

The In-House Lawyer and Their Place in Networks

THE ACADEMIC LITERATURE tends to concentrate on organisational (especially business) influence as largely negative, and compromising of professionalism.[1] In-housers are seen as flawed gatekeepers, either inadequately protecting their organisations from deliberate illegality led by managers, or as too willing to be entrepreneurial in their approach to the in-house role.[2] It is an agent-heavy picture that focuses on in-house lawyers as agents failing in their choices, albeit choices shaped by context and structure. Another body of work suggests the potential for a positive blending of business and professional factors where the ethical agency of in-housers may influence organisations for the better, as partners. Such work has come from practitioner leaders, but also from economics and management-science, seeking to measure levels of regulatory compliance and wrongdoing.[3] Similarly, in sociological work, the idea of hybrid professionals suggests what we call later a blended professionalism. A third strand of work, similar to the first, but supported by economics and psychology, suggests that organisational ideas, structures and incentives shape in-house lawyers towards risk-taking. Here, professionals disguise, support, facilitate, fail to spot, or even lead riskier decisions the closer they are to management.[4]

Through the idea of blended professionalism, we suggest that professional hybrids, be they business-professional or bureaucratic-professional, might be capable of resolving logic conflicts successfully by blending organisational and professional norms. To give an example, a business that wants to innovate and succeed according to the law, might be more successfully governed with hybrid

---

[1] See, for example, Pam Jenoff, 'Going Native: Incentive, Identity, and the Inherent Ethical Problem of In-House Counsel' (2011) 114 *West Virginia Law Review* 725; Sung Hui Kim, 'Inside Lawyers: Friends or Gatekeepers?' (2016) 84 *Fordham Law Review* 1867; Sung Hui Kim, 'Naked Self-Interest? Why the Legal Profession Resists Gatekeeping' (2011) 63 *Florida Law Review* 129.

[2] Kim, 'Inside Lawyers' (n 1); Robert L Nelson and Laura Beth Nielsen, 'Cops, Counsel, and Entrepreneurs: Constructing the Role of inside Counsel in Large Corporations' [2000] *Law and Society Review* 457.

[3] For an example from a practitioner-leader, see Ben W Heineman Jr, *The Inside Counsel Revolution: Resolving the Partner-Guardian Tension* (Ankerwycke, 2016).

[4] See, for example, Donald C Langevoort, 'Getting (Too) Comfortable: In-House Lawyers, Enterprise Risk, and the Financial Crisis' (2012) *Wis L Rev* 495.

professionals in situ than without. To simplify, hybrid professionals provide an alternative to rapacious market-driven behaviour and the enforcement of clumsy, overly prescriptive regulation.

Each of these approaches suggests that a key question influencing our understanding of the professional identity of lawyers is their place in a variety of networks: professional networks (with other lawyers, with representative bodies etc); and, and in particular, organisational networks (what kinds of organisations they work for, what kinds of work they do within those networks etc). In this chapter, we outline key data on the place of in-house lawyers in organisational networks. We also bring in interview data about reasons for moving in-house (or starting a legal career in-house), how our interviewees perceived the role of the in-house lawyer had changed, and their relationships with their employers. We finish by exploring the ethical tensions related to these networks.

UNDERSTANDING IN-HOUSE LAWYERS' PLACE IN THE PROFESSION

We begin with a discussion of the basics of where in-house lawyers work and what they do. In England & Wales, in-house lawyers currently make up around one-fifth of all practising solicitors.[5] Of these, 60 per cent work for over 5,000 different employers in the private sector in the fields of commerce, industry or accountancy.[6] 32 per cent of the entire in-house population work in financial services: five FTSE 100 banks employ more than 200 in-house lawyers.[7] The largest in-house team (HSBC) employs over 1,000 lawyers.[8] If HSBC's in-house team were a private practice law firm, it would rank in the top 25 in England & Wales for size.[9] Not all in-house teams are so large, however. One survey found that 86 per cent of companies employed 10 or fewer solicitors in the UK.[10] Away from the business sector, in-housers work in the public sector, including for the Crown Prosecution Service, the Government Legal Department, local authorities, and for other bodies, with a modest number working in the third sector.[11]

THE MOVE IN-HOUSE

The growth in the in-house sector has been startling. What has prompted this move? For employers, it is the recognition that in-house lawyers may offer

---

[5] Data provided to us by the Solicitors Regulation Authority.
[6] Oxera, 'The Role of In-House Solicitors' (Report for the Solicitors Regulation Authority, 2014) 6.
[7] The Lawyer, 'LMI FTSE 100 2015' (The Lawyer Market Intelligence Reports, 2015) 4.
[8] ibid.
[9] The Lawyer, 'Top 200 2015' *The Lawyer* (London, 9 November 2015).
[10] Eversheds, 'Benchmarking the In-house Legal Department' (Eversheds Report, 2011) 2.
[11] Oxera (n 6). This report was based on data provided to Oxera by the SRA, an online survey of just over 2,000 solicitors and telephone interviews with 213 in-house lawyer employers.

significantly better value for money, might get closer to them and (through being more 'business focused') understand their needs better, and may be necessary to ensure compliance and legality. These three reasons (cheaper, better, more legal) are, as we will see, not always equally recognised by all employer organisations but it is important to hold all three of them in mind as potential influences on in-house roles and recruitment.[12]

How does the move in-house look from the perspective of those making that move? Working as an in-house lawyer has not always been a respected career path. Indeed, in some European jurisdictions, in-house lawyers are obliged to relinquish their membership of the local Bar,[13] because of concerns over a lack of independence from their client employer.[14] In the 1960s and 70s, in-housers were regarded with disdain by private practice lawyers, as those 'who couldn't make partner'.[15] Going in-house was once associated with reduced pay, poorer quality legal work, and increased administrative burdens.[16] For our older and more experienced interviewees, moving in-house was risky, something from which there was 'no route back' for people perceived as not 'up to the pressures and rigours of private practice' [IHL25], 'the career equivalent of "failed in London, try Hong Kong"!' [IHL35]. In-house was once spoken of patronisingly by private practitioners as 'a great place for women to go and work whilst they've got married and they're waiting to have babies' [IHL39].

Yet, it has become increasingly common to hear that this position as 'status-inferior' is shifting:[17] 'in the course of a generation, [in house lawyers'] prestige, status, compensation, power and position in the core of major transnational corporations has been transformed.'[18] Senior in-house lawyers can earn sizeable

---

[12] Wilkins and Khanna's analysis replicates our own; they speak of economic, substantive, and professional jusitifcations for the growth of the in-house movement. See, in David B Wilkins and Vikramaditya S Khanna, 'South by Southeast: Comparing the Development of In-House Legal Department in Brazil' in Luciana Gross Cunha and others (eds) *The Brazilian Legal Profession in the Age of Globalization: The Rise of the Corporate Legal Sector and its on Lawyers and Society* (Cambridge University Press, 2017). See also, Robert E Rosen, 'The Inside Counsel Movement, Professional Judgement and Organizational Representation' (1989) 64 *Indiana Law Journal* 479.

[13] For an overview, see Philippe Coen and Christophe Roquilly (eds) *Company Lawyer: Independent by Design* (LexisNexis, 2014). This is also true in India. See David B Wilkins and Vikramaditya S Khanna, 'Globalization and the Rise of the In-House Counsel Movement in India' in David B Wilkins, Vikramaditya S Khanna and David M Trubek (eds), *The Indian Legal Profession in the Age of Globalization: The Rise of the Corporate Legal Sector and its Impact on Lawyers and Society* (Cambridge University Press, 2017).

[14] See Case C-550/07 *Akzo Nobel Chems Ltd v Commission* [2010] ECR 11-03523.

[15] Carl D Liggio, 'A Look at the Role of Corporate Counsel: Back to the Future – Or is it the Past?' (2002) 44 *Arizona Law Review* 621.

[16] Eli Wald, 'In House Myths' (2012) *Wisconsin Law Review* 407, 408.

[17] Nelson and Nielson (n 2) 457–58. See further Erwin O Smigel, *The Wall Street lawyer, professional organization man?* (Midland Books, 1964); Jeffrey S Slovak, 'Working for Corporate Actors: Social Change and Elite Attorneys in Chicago' (1979) 4(3) *Law & Social Inquiry* 465; and Eve Spangler, *Lawyers for Hire* (Yale University Press, 1986).

[18] Ben W Heineman Jr, 'The General Counsel as Lawyer-Statesman' (Harvard Law School Program on the Legal Profession Blue Paper, 2010).

salaries (though normally lower than comparable fields in private practice, and bonuses).[19] These once 'forgotten men' of the legal profession are now seen as pivotal to the evolution of commercial legal services and central to legal risk, ethics, and compliance in large organisations.[20]

Our interviewees talked of a broad and growing regard for the role of the in-houser, a 'respect ... that probably you didn't [get] 20 or 30 years ago' [IHL35]. This is because the in-house role has expanded and changed, but also because private practice lawyers have come to realise that their own economic survival depends on having (or appearing to have) respect for the hands that feed them: 'they have to relate to in-house lawyers and work with them, whereas in the past they thought they could probably usurp them and deal direct with the leaders or the directors of the businesses' [IHL46].

Interviewee career trajectories helped explain what had prompted them to move in-house. Most had moved from private practice.[21] Some spoke of a 'high quality of life' [IHL28] and 'better diversity of work' [IHL27] in-house. Interestingly, the move in-house could be a resistance to specialisation: 'Everybody was becoming more specialist. I wanted to maintain a generalist approach and a generalist experience' [IHL54]. The oft-cited idea in the literature that going in-house brings the lawyer closer to their client was clearly important to some. Private practice was felt to be 'far removed from understanding the business and the drivers for the decisions that were being made' [IHL49]. A number pushed back (rather vehemently) against the idea of in-house life as a 'comfortable nine to five type job' [IHL46], emphasising, 'This is not the place for people who want that nine to five existence' [IHL38]. The implicit equation of working long hours with equivalent professional status that several interviewees made was striking.

The justifications so far are material and relational in nature: they focus on the technical, material, and status-oriented differences of the in-house role. Yet our interviewees also often explicitly rejected private practice values: its perceived 'moral bankruptcy' (IHL24); the 'schmoozing and entertaining' (IHL 26); and 'complete dissatisfaction with their environment' due to 'not being valued' (IHL 25). Some preferred not to work solely with other lawyers: 'in industry ... you come across a lot of people who are much better than they realise. Whereas most lawyers, if their ability matched their arrogance they would be world beaters' [IHL41].

Secondments had provided a gateway into in-house practice for some:

I had my eyes opened by the secondment ... [with in-house] lawyers who had stopped really thinking of themselves in relatively narrow specialisms and were a repository of knowledge, information, advice on a whole range of matters. And it was that breadth of work really that really appealed to me. [IHL30]

---

[19] See www.thelawyer.com/issues/5-september-2016/salary-survey-2016-pdf/, accessed 17 April 2018.
[20] Kark Mackie, *Lawyers in Business: and the Business of Law* (Springer, 1989).
[21] Three started as paralegals in-house and qualified there; the third starting his career as a company secretary and moving on from that position.

Other work has shown that secondments are increasingly expected by clients as part of an overall relationship package,[22] and law firms gain trainees and associates (on their return to the firm) with better knowledge of the firm's clients. However, such secondments also allow clients to see and assess potential future recruits and give the secondees an in-depth insight into the workings (and possible advantages) of working in-house. The flow to and from in-house practice may be, in part at least, cyclical. A number of interviewees spoke of the 1992 downturn or the post-2008 crash, when 'promotion prospects had suddenly taken a bit of a downturn' [IHL35] or 'It was the only place that offered me a job … in … the worst period for retention with firms [2011]' [IHL36]. Movement between private practice and in-house was not unidirectional: some of our interviewees had gone back to private practice before returning in-house, or were about to return there; some had taken sales or mainstream leadership roles. Part of this movement was prompted by promotion and advancement in-house being perceived as quite flat.

THE EVOLUTION OF THE IN-HOUSE ROLE

Interviewees perceived the role of the in-house lawyer as having changed over time. Three interconnected themes emerged: (i) an increasing importance of in-housers 'adding value' to their organisations; (ii) the increasing integration of in-house lawyers into the business; and, (iii) the changing nature of the job (away from 'pure' legal advice towards risk management and commercial input). In these three ways in-house lawyers did more than simply manage the legal budget of outside counsel:

> … in the 1990s there was still a sense that all the important stuff got moved to … a law firm it went to for legal advice as a Board and that the in-house Counsel … had a procedural responsibility for managing stuff rather than actually [being] a key advisor. [IHL24]

These three trends all speak to forms of organisational integration. They suggest the interpenetration of legal and organisational ways of seeing problems. Interviewees spoke of being 'positioned in the business' [IHL50], 'more central and even more core to the business' [IHL27]. This transition is from (a) manager of an external legal budget, to (b) legal advisor, to (c) commercial and risk advisor within an integrated decision-making process. But this is not a linear transition. Not all in-house lawyers operate, or operate at all times, at the integrated end of this spectrum. Yet integration was a common theme in the interviews: 'a journey from being a service provider to give advice and walk away, to actually being

---

[22] For an account of how secondment clauses work in outside counsel guidelines, see: Claire Coe and Steven Vaughan, 'Independence, Representation and Risk' (Report for the Solicitors Regulation Authority, October 2015).

much more part of the assurance and control frameworks' [IHL31]. Another lawyer who had been in-house since the early 1980s with a number of different employers said: 'over the last five to ten years, it has become much more a compliance-based and governance-based role' [IHL46].

The notion of 'adding value' (beyond managing the budget for external counsel and/or providing 'pure' legal advice) was seen as both a boon and a bane: in-houser value-adders are allowed a better place at the management table, but that place comes with a constant need to justify their existence in terms of value-added. More than one interviewee suggested in-house was 'better' than private practice because of this increasing influence:

> you get significantly more input into the outcomes because you are closer to the business ... you understand the issues much better and you're absolutely in control of how much information you have ... you get a lot more say and you get listened to ... any external lawyer only sees what the business decides they should, in terms of cases, in terms of information, in terms of aspects of the business. [IHL35]

And whilst value-add is a commercial concept, broader developments in regulation, with a stronger emphasis on governance and corporate responsibility, have also contributed to the evolving role of the in-house lawyer. Consumer protection legislation, and personal liability for directors meant, 'companies started to see that the in-house role could be more supportive, give more direction' [IHL25]. Regulatory schemes for 'data privacy, bribery, FCPA ... requires some legal knowledge and analysis to carry out proper investigation etc' [IHL47]. Equally, 'lessons learned and hopefully still being learned' from poor behaviour uncovered after the financial crash, meant 'there was the opportunity there to actually look at governance and compliance' [IHL41]. We return to the impact of external forces later in the book.

A common narrative was that in-housers had a stronger and more proactive role in corporate governance and anticipating regulators than those in private practice:

> being able to get things through the Board and get things through the Regulator ... that's not just a rubber stamp and an afterthought ... There is far more challenge now ... So the governance aspects of the role have become heightened ... you're listened to a bit more now and used more. [IHL38]

For all of our interviewees, the 'day job' was broad. For those more junior, the core of the role might be in contract negotiations, giving legal advice to the business, preparing for regulatory changes, and/or signing off what deal teams wanted to do. It was the more senior roles that had become more about governance and strategy. This long quote sets out well the various 'things' that senior in-house lawyers do, and the role of in-housers in the various networks of their organisations:

> Increasingly it's a management role. It's about delegating work, about making sure that people are doing things on time and to the right standard. Looking at ways

of organising the department differently. Looking at changing the processes that are used in the business. Speaking to people outside [the department] formally and informally ... Making sure that people are happy with the way that things are done, or making sure that they're aware of things that are going on in our department. Making sure that I'm aware of things that are going on elsewhere in the business. So I think that's increasingly the main part of my role ... I think a lot of the time I find that I'm not really advising on legal points but just on being sensible ... it's not about here's what the law says you should do, it's just about in my experience this is what's worked best in that situation. So giving that kind of advice over quite a broad range of areas probably. [IHL34]

THE BALANCING OF ROLES

We can see the three justifications for in-house lawyers – cheaper, better, and more legal in the accounts of our interviewees, but we cannot see much about how the three are balanced. Of course, many of our interviewee accounts are focused on what the job gives them ('better', richer, more-rounded, less-specialised work) but does it really lead to more ethical (or more law-abiding) organisations? There have been several studies that look at this question by examining the impact of appointing lawyers to senior executive positions in US listed companies. One study finds significantly reduced compliance breaches (related to accounting and insider trading) and monitoring breaches (general failures of legal risk management related to contract, antitrust, disclosure and so on) associated with senior lawyer appointments.[23] Another that companies with senior lawyers in the top management 'are more likely to issue forecasts, particularly bad news forecasts, than other firms.'[24] A third that that 'the presence (and proportion) of directors with legal backgrounds on the audit committee is associated with higher financial reporting quality.'[25] And that legal expertise and accountancy expertise each benefits from the presence of the other in this context.

Some evidence supports the idea that lawyers have an impact independent of board strategies to improve governance: the claim is that, 'individual lawyers matter'.[26] Attempts to measure the influence of individual lawyers appointed to seniority are necessarily general and difficult to disentangle from other possible influences on compliance. It is not possible to say, for instance, whether such data tell us something about lawyers in organisations generally, or lawyers in senior

---

[23] Adair Morse, Wei Wang and Serena Wu, 'Executive Lawyers: Gatekeepers or Strategic Officers?' (National Bureau of Economic Research 2016, Working Paper 22597).

[24] Byungjin Kwak, Byung T Ro and Inho Suk, 'The Composition of Top Management with General Counsel and Voluntary Information Disclosure' (2012) 54 *Journal of Accounting and Economics* 19, 19.

[25] Jayanthi Krishnan, Yuan Wen and Wanli Zhao, 'Legal Expertise on Corporate Audit Committees and Financial Reporting Quality' (2011) 86 *The Accounting Review* 2099, 2099.

[26] Morse, Wang and Wu (n 23).

roles in organisations. It follows that a more refined view may be necessary. Share price reaction to adverse disclosures made by listed companies with senior lawyers in top positions is stronger:[27] perhaps markets take disclosures from companies with lawyers more seriously, or perhaps these are companies to whom the markets already pay more attention? Credit risk analysts are also sensitive to gatekeeping risk; they think in-house legal teams become *less effective* gatekeepers as lawyers are promoted to senior management positions.[28] The apparent riskiness of corporate debt increased significantly in companies that promoted lawyers to their senior team.[29]

We would expect a range of conflicting findings in such a small group of studies. It may be that what is influencing behaviour is not seniority per se, or the presence of lawyers per se, but the way those roles are structured. Regulation, and corporate policies in response to regulation, can accentuate personal responsibility for gatekeeping functions. Jagolinzer et al look at corporate policies on insider trading, and find that where companies require General Counsel (GC) approval for potential insider trades this is associated with, 'a substantial reduction in informed trading by insiders.'[30] Their results also suggest that the Sarbanes-Oxley Act may have amplified the positive effects of legal expertise in this process. Similarly, the GC signing-off function was an important factor driving SEC compliance in Morse et al's results.[31]

Conversely, 'contracting of lawyers into strategic activities' (through higher levels of equity-based remuneration) can reduce that gatekeeping effort in relation to monitoring.[32] Morse et al estimate that 'on average the hiring of a [senior] lawyer implies a 31.4% reduction in securities fraud … [but] when the lawyer is hired with high equity incentives, she only reduces fraud by 6.6%.'[33] Similarly, Hopkins et al suggest gatekeeping behaviour is moderated by senior lawyer compensation structures: firms with highly compensated GCs had, 'lower financial reporting quality and more aggressive accounting practices' but also that, 'GCs play an important gatekeeping role in keeping the firm in compliance with generally accepted accounting principles.'[34] The implication they find is that 'GCs appear to tolerate moderately aggressive behaviour but constrain it such that it would not result in violation of securities laws and jeopardize their standing within the firm.'[35]

---

[27] Kwak, Ro and Suk (n 24) 19.
[28] Charles Ham and Kevin Koharki, 'The Association between Corporate General Counsel and Firm Credit Risk' (2016) 61 *Journal of Accounting and Economics* 274.
[29] ibid.
[30] Alan D Jagolinzer, David F Larcker and Daniel J Taylor, 'Corporate Governance and the Information Content of Insider Trades' (2011) 49 *Journal of Accounting Research* 1249, 1252.
[31] Morse, Wang and Wu (n 23).
[32] ibid.
[33] ibid.
[34] Justin J Hopkins, Edward L Maydew and Mohan Venkatachalam, 'Corporate General Counsel and Financial Reporting Quality' (2015) 61 *Management Science* 129, 129.
[35] ibid.

If this is right, the risk of regulators attributing compliance failures to in-housers personally is in tension with incentives, some of which may be reputational. Looked at in this way, Goh et al's finding that, 'the inclusion of general counsel in top management is associated with a firm's tax avoidance' looks less contradictory.[36] GCs do not need to certify tax compliance, the risks for tax policy can be more easily shared with external advisers, and the potential for significant commercial benefits from tax minimisation alter the reputational calculus.[37] The result? Where lawyers are part of the top management team those firms, 'have lower GAAP effective tax rate, more uncertain tax positions, a higher likelihood of engaging in tax shelter activities, and more tax haven countries in which the firm reports a significant subsidiary, relative to firms without a general counsel in top management.' Also, 'tax avoidance is greater when (1) the general counsel has tax-related expertise, (2) the firm hires an external auditor with tax expertise or purchases more tax services from its external auditor, and (3) the CEO has more power over the general counsel.'[38] Increases in tax avoidance are also shown to be related to certain GCs who move from one organisation to another (they appear to carry the strategy with them). The potential for diffusion of responsibility by engaging external consultants on matters of law is further emphasised by evidence that the retention of 'top-tier' outside lawyers reduced the completeness of SEC mandatory disclosures.[39]

STRUCTURAL PREDICTORS AND MEDIATORS

The studies just discussed mainly focus on remuneration to identify in-house lawyer seniority. Other structural indicators may be as or more important. For example, board membership for in-house lawyers is increasingly prevalent. It is interpreted as a badge of status and influence but also, by some, as a conflict of interest.[40] Heineman takes a subtler view: he favours presence on the board but not membership.[41] Similarly, the line manager of a General Counsel may have

---

[36] Beng Wee Goh, Jimmy Lee and Jeffrey Ng, 'The Inclusion of General Counsel in Top Management and Tax Avoidance' (Social Science Research Network 2015, SSRN Scholarly Paper ID 2538292).

[37] See, generally, Tanina Rostain and Milton C Regan, *Confidence Games: Lawyers, Accountants, and the Tax Shelter Industry* (MIT Press, 2014), although they are mainly concerned with tax practice by accountants and law firms.

[38] Goh, Lee and Ng (n 36).

[39] Preeti Choudhary, Jason Schloetzer and Jason Sturgess, 'Do Corporate Attorneys Influence Financial Disclosure' (Working Paper, Georgetown University, 2012); Preeti Choudhary, Jason D Schloetzer and Jason D Sturgess, 'Boards, Auditors, Attorneys and Compliance with Mandatory SEC Disclosure Rules' (2013) 34 *Managerial and Decision Economics* 471.

[40] John C Coates and others, 'Hiring Teams, Firms, and Lawyers: Evidence of the Evolving Relationships in the Corporate Legal Market' (2011) 36 *Law & Social Inquiry* 999.

[41] Heineman (n 3).

some impact on the nature of the GC's decision-making. There is little doubt that reporting to the CEO increases status and can allow for robust advice to be given to the CEO directly.[42] In-house lawyers who are managed by and report directly to the board are perceived by those in the organisation as having greater importance to the organisation than those in-house lawyers who report to someone lower down the chain.[43] As such, management and lines of reporting can speak to respect for, and importance of, the in-house legal function. Equally, having in-house lawyers report directly to the board has the potential to provide the board with a better insight into the legal risks faced by the business, and the ways those risks can be managed.[44] And lawyers who have direct relationships with the board may be better able to demonstrate the value of the legal team in environments where that team may otherwise simply be seen as a cost centre.[45] Yet Coffee writes: 'In the absence of independent professionals – auditors, attorneys and analysts – boards will predictably receive a stream of selectively edited information from corporate managers that presents the incumbent management in the most favourable light possible.'[46]

What do our data say about such structural issues? Table 3.1 explores line manager relationships from our survey data.

Table 3.1 Line Manager by Role

	Role				
Line Manager	GC or equivalent	Senior In-House Legal	In-house Legal	Other (please specify)	N
The chief executive officer (**CEO**)	52.9%	6.0%	1.0%	14.3%	69
The chief financial officer (**CFO**)	16.3%	1.2%	1.0%	4.8%	21
Another senior executive (board member)	9.6%	12.5%	5.7%	14.3%	40
Another employee of the business	3.8%	4.8%	6.7%	9.5%	21

(continued)

[42] Tanina Rostain, 'General Counsel in the Age of Compliance: Preliminary Findings and New Research Questions' (2008) 21 *Geo J Legal Ethics* 465, 473; Heineman (n 3) 1118.
[43] Prashant Dubey and Eva Kripalani, *The Generalist Counsel: How Leading General Counsel are Shaping Tomorrow's Companies* (Oxford University Press, 2013).
[44] ABA Task Force on Corporate Responsibility, 'Report of the American Bar Association Task Force on Corporate Responsibility' (2003) 59 *The Business Lawyer* 145, 161.
[45] Omari Scott Simmons and James D Dinnage, 'Innkeepers: A Unifying Theory of the In-House Counsel Role' (2011) 41 *Setton Hall Law Review* 77, 146.
[46] John Coffee, *Gatekeepers: The Role of the Professions and Corporate Governance* (Oxford University Press, 2006) 7.

Table 3.1 (Continued)

Line Manager	Role				
	GC or equivalent	Senior In-House Legal	In-house Legal	Other (please specify)	N
Another lawyer[47]	11.5%	72.6%	82.9%	57.1%	233
Another senior non-executive on the board	1.0%	2.4%	1.0%	0.0%	6
The chair of the Audit Committee	0.0%	0.0%	1.0%	0.0%	1
The chairman	4.8%	0.6%	1.0%	0.0%	7
N	104	168	105	21	398

About a third of our respondents were line-managed by a member of the executive board, whereas only 3.5 per cent were managed by a non-executive. The remainder were managed by other lawyers or employees. Given that many GCs see a reporting line to the chief executive officer (CEO) as an essential prerequisite of their role, for the 4.7 per cent that do not have that reporting line this raises interesting questions about their ability to have influence on their own needs and whether those GCs may be less effective in their roles than is ideal.

Equally though, it is possible to see board membership or participation as problematic. Direct access to the board may help to preserve the independence of the in-house lawyer from distorting influences elsewhere in the organisation, but engagement in decision-making at the board level may pose conflicts of interest for in-house lawyers and compromise – in subtle and not-so-subtle ways – their ability to advise independently. One of our interviewees captures the conflict neatly having switched from having a solid line to the business unit's CEO and a dotted line to the Group General Counsel. The switch 'made my life a lot easier actually, because I was under a certain amount of pressure to sign things off that I wouldn't have been comfortable signing off, and personally I took quite a lot of blows from reporting to the CEO' [IHL38]. Yet, the Group General Counsel reporting not to the CEO but to the chief operating officer was seen as less than ideal. 'I think really you should be reporting to the CEO, ideally, at the top of the tree.' [IHL38]

There is also a potential challenge in reporting to multiple people or to the wrong people. There was some concern from our interviewees about in-house lawyers having a hard reporting line to the chief financial officer (CFO):

> from an operational point of view ... the legal department is only seen as a cost of doing business. ... you're only the braking function; 'you're slowing us down; you

---

[47] It may seem strange to have GCs reporting to other lawyers, but some organisations have GCs for divisions/particular sectors of their organisation, regarded as GCs in their own right given the size of their team, independence etc.

have to be kept in check'. You're also seen as a cost so it's harder to get budget for things, and it's harder to show the value you bring when you go into things like budget fights. [IHL33]

IHL50 described a General Counsel reporting to both the finance director and the CEO as, 'stuck between a rock and a bloody hard place' with the CEO wanting action and the CFO not wanting to spend money on that action. Rostain also found reporting to the CFO problematic and risking independence.[48]

Heineman emphasises the need for in-housers to report directly to the CEO as well as, 'a direct, unfettered relationship with the board of directors.'[49] He further suggests GCs should report to the board and to committees charged with integrity functions (such as the audit or risk committees)[50] and that, 'the General Counsel should meet alone with the board as a whole or with the Audit or Risk Committee at least two times per year to discuss any issues of concern to the GC or to answer any questions from the directors.'[51] Hamermesh suggests encouraging direct access to the CEO, and, 'providing regular opportunities for the independent directors to consult with the general counsel' in 'executive session,' without the CEO and other senior managers and more informally.[52] Interestingly, GCs appear more conscious of their role as CEO adviser than they are of their role as board adviser.[53]

This body of other work should be borne in mind when interpreting the surprisingly low levels of line manager and reporting relationships with non-executive directors we see in our data. Non-executive reporting lines, of a formal or informal nature, only appeared to be in place for 18 per cent of our survey respondents.[54] Moreover, slightly less than half of those in-house lawyers line managed by CEOs in our survey also had reporting lines to non-executive board members. Only a third of those reporting to the CEO also had a line of reporting to the chairman (and still fewer had reporting lines to other non-executives). The position for those who were line-managed by the CFO or other senior executive was of even weaker reporting lines to the non-executive directors. This might be particularly important if the in-house lawyers were to exercise the significant gatekeeper or governance roles they described their roles as encompassing.

The absence of reporting lines to non-executive directors may thus give rise to particular concerns. As part of a shift towards better corporate governance, the numbers and importance of non-executive directors has grown. They are not corporate employees, almost exclusively sit part time, and act (in theory)

---

[48] Rostain (n 42) 473.
[49] Heineman (n 3) 1118–21.
[50] Heineman (n 3) 1453–55.
[51] Heineman (n 3) 1464-65.
[52] Lawrence A Hamermesh, 'Who Let You into the House?' (Social Science Research Network 2011, SSRN Scholarly Paper ID 1969065) 379ff.
[53] Rostain (n 42) 473; ACC, 'Skills for the 21st Century General Counsel' (Association of Corporate Counsel Survey, 2015) 13.
[54] 22% also reported to another lawyer, 15% also reported to the CEO, and 9% also to the CFO.

as wise counsellors and critics to the executive team. Non-executives are seen as holding the potential for important checks and balances on the exercise of powers by the executive, by bringing to the board a combination of expertise, independence and impartiality.[55] Having in-house lawyers report (either primarily or additionally) to non-executive directors may help to reinforce (for the lawyer, and the employer) that the organisation is the ultimate client and that its interests may, at times, conflict with those of senior executives, employees, and other constituencies.[56] As Weaver notes, 'the close working relationship between management and [in-house] corporate counsel may create confusion and uncertainty about the role of corporate counsel in the representation of the organization.'[57] As such, a number of scholars in the US have suggested that non-executive directors should have their own, wholly separate, in-house lawyers.[58]

PRESENCE ON THE BOARD

About 60 per cent of our survey respondents reported that at least one in-house lawyer attended or sat on their organisation's board.[59] Thirteen per cent of our sample attended the board (although often not as a member). Seven per cent reported a lawyer who was not a member of the in-house team attended the board. Sixty-five per cent of our survey respondents reported that at least one in-house lawyer attended or sat on the Executive Committee.

It may be challenging for an in-house lawyer who sits on the board of their organisation to manage the multiple, and possibly conflicting, duties they would owe: as a director; as an employee; and as a professional regulated by the relevant professional codes. Yet for many, there were positives in the status and influence that being on a board could bring: 'influence all the way down that hiring chain' [IHL26]; 'things get the attention that they deserve and you have a voice in the direction of the company' [IHL 33]. A board member is seen as:

> an equal of the people who sit on the board, people will ask me questions whereas before they would have seen me just as a resource or as a support service; whereas they are more inclined now to see me as a Counsel to them and to the board and to come and ask questions. [IHL50]

---

[55] Charlie Weir and David Laing, 'Governance structures, director independence and corporate performance in the UK' (2001) 13(2) *European Business Review* 86.

[56] Simmons and Dinnage (n 45) 112.

[57] Sally R Weaver, 'Ethical Dilemmas of Corporate Counsel: A Structural and Contextual Analysis' (1997) 46 *Emory Law Journal* 1023, 1028.

[58] See, for example: E Norman Veasey, 'Separate and Continuing Counsel for Independent Directors: An Idea Whose Time Has Not Come as a General Practice' (2004) 59 *The Business Lawyer* 1413; and Geoffrey C Hazard, Jr and Edward B Rock, 'A New Player in the Boardroom: The Emergence of the Independent Directors' Counsel' (2004) 59 *The Business Lawyer* 1389.

[59] See, also, Eversheds (n 10) 2.

Board membership was sometimes seen as a signal of the company's commitment to propriety, to doing the right thing: 'we have to have a lawyer as a director of each and every subsidiary within the Group ... [whose role is] to put it crudely, "you do the right thing or else"' [IHL53].

However, being on the board was not in and of itself seen as critical by our interviewees: it was instead the culture of the organisation which meant that an in-house lawyer sitting or not sitting on the board would (or could) make a difference. Whether the GC's input is valued by the board, for example, and how proactive and well-respected the GC is:

> I think it's a wee bit too simple to say, 'No, General Counsel should never be on the Board' because if you get a General Counsel who think they're there to do the Board's bidding all the time then it doesn't matter whether they're on the Board or whether they're not on the Board, you still don't necessarily get the right end result. [IHL31]

And the extent to which our interviewees thought lawyers should be on boards appeared to be tied (at least in part) into what they perceived the role and function of in-house lawyers to be. So, for example, this interviewee sees the role of the in-house lawyer in quite passive terms and was, in general, against in-housers sitting on boards:

> And to my mind as a legal counsel you are there to give counsel, not to enter into the debates that the directors are entering into and so obviously you speak up if there's a point that you need to raise from a legal point of view, you've noted a conflict or something like that, but generally you wouldn't be speaking up because you're not a member of the board. [IHL40]

Push-back against the idea of in-house lawyers on boards centred on a worry that such proximity will erode the independence of the in-house lawyer (which we discuss in the next chapter), and on a worry that sitting on a board brings with it multiple obligations that may well come into conflict: 'where you're also general counsel, I think you're compromised' [IHL27].

The potential for conflicting obligations may become even more acute in certain financial services firms where various people in those firms can owe duties to the relevant financial services regulators (in addition to other groups). One interviewee in particular had given the matter a lot of thought, and undertaken his own research, before accepting a board position on a subsidiary of the financial services company he worked for. As he sets out, there is a potentially wide number of differing, and different, obligations that a lawyer on such a board might owe. But, equally, he was confident he could navigate those potential tensions well:

> There is an argument to say that a director has conflicting obligations anyway in a regulated financial services firm, where for example if you're a Control Function 1 ... [with] obligations to the regulator, and they are obligated to clients of the firm, and when making decisions they should put the interests of the client first and they should be open and honest with the regulator. Second, as a [company] director you have

obligations under the Companies Act which says very clearly that your primary obligation is to the shareholders of the company ... Similar to that, as a lawyer you owe an obligation to advise the directors of the company, and you want to be able to give the fullest possible advice ... If you're Head of Compliance and you're CF10, another significant influence function [in financial services regulation], your obligation again is to the regulator and you're independent, and there are a lot of people in financial services' firms who are head of legal and compliance, so again you could argue there's a conflict there because on the one hand they owe an obligation to the directors of the company to advise them properly and to give them all of the options under legal privilege. But then on the other side they owe an obligation to the regulator to reveal information to the regulator about things that they think are unacceptable within the firm. So both for a director and for someone in that role those conflicts potentially exist ... I think as long as you give good advice to the company, and as long as you recognise that the interests of the business are bound up with the interests of clients, then I think it's quite easy to marry those different obligations together ... If you do your job properly I don't think there's a conflict. [IHL34]

Given the number of potentially differing roles and obligations highlighted by this quote, it was perhaps unsurprising that those of our interviewees working in financial services were those most likely to raise conflicts of interests as the reason for thinking hard about in-house lawyers being on the board.

EMPLOYER–EMPLOYEE RELATIONS AND THE ROLE OF THE IN-HOUSE LAWYER

The changing nature of the job may have an important influence on how in-house lawyers see their role and on how they behave. Being embedded in organisations, and being responsible to others higher in a hierarchy, may compromise in-house willingness to be independent of their employers.[60] Employment creates incentives to align with the business rather than employing independent judgement. Even so, the subservience of being an employee, answerable to the CEO, and fireable at will in the US,[61] may not be total. Hackett argues that boards are far more willing to fire an external law firm than they would their own in-house lawyers,[62] but economic incentives, Jenoff suggests, 'may subtly or overtly coerce ... in hopes of personal recognition and reward',[63] or leave an in-house lawyer 'beholden to the company for his financial wellbeing'.[64]

---

[60] To be clear, we are not suggesting that independence issues are unique to those working in-house. For an account of how such issues play out in private practice, see Coe and Vaughan (n 22).
[61] Heineman (n 2).
[62] Susan Hackett, 'Corporate Counsel and the Evolution of Practical Ethical Navigation: An Overview of the Changing Dynamics of Professional Responsibility in In-House Practice' (2012) 25 Geo J Legal Ethics 317.
[63] Jenoff (n 1).
[64] ibid.

Bonuses may shape overtly and implicitly how lawyers perform their functions.[65] The evidence discussed above reinforces the importance of this point.

The nature of the job, and the management and reporting structures into which in-house lawyers fit, is thus only part of the story of lawyers' place in organisational networks. The way that employers see the role of their lawyers is clearly important. The literature tends to emphasise a scepticism of the in-house lawyer. Organisations can be mistrustful of their lawyers, seeing them as deal-blockers rather than deal-makers, or costs centres, rather than part of the profit-making enterprise.[66] In government, lawyers can be portrayed as inhibiting democratically legitimate policymaking through the overly cautious interpretations of the law.[67] Such a view is sometimes allied with a concern that lawyers are too conservative when it comes to taking risks or seen as legal perfectionists (wanting to eliminate risk rather than manage or accept some tolerance for legal problems with proposed courses of action). Equally and oppositely, overly aggressive appetite for risk may pose problems to the administration of justice, and for organisations seeking to promote a culture of full compliance.[68]

Our survey measured three components of the relationships between lawyer and the organisation, as follows.

(i) Component 1 – The Existence of Sometimes Negative Relationships with the Business

It was particularly common for the in-house legal function to sometimes be criticised for inhibiting or slowing decisions (80 per cent agreed that this happened); 57 per cent agreed that colleagues were sometimes reluctant to raise issues with legal; and close to 50 per cent agreed that actions were sometimes taken against their advice on legally important matters.

---

[65] See Morse, Wang and Wu (n 23) and the discussion above.

[66] For a discussion of the evolution of the role in this context, see: Jenoff (n 1) and Nabarro, 'From In house lawyer to business counsel' (Naborro LLP Report, 2010).

[67] Dame Ursula Brennan, former Permanent Secretary at the Ministry of Justice indicated there had been a change in approach within the Government Legal Service, in a recent interview: 'One of the things that has changed in the way we advise ministers is that we used to say: "You can do that, you can't do that." Now we more often say: "If you do that, there will be a legal challenge, and it's quite likely we'll lose." And some ministers in those circumstances will give up, and others will say: "No, actually, if there's a chance we might win, I want to try. And as democratically elected politicians that is their prerogative."' See Jess Bowie, 'Dame Ursula Brennan: The Former Ministry of Justice Permanent Secretary on Why She Left the MoJ, What She's Most Proud of – and Why It Can Be Tricky to Cut Senior Civil Service Roles Written' *Civil Service World* (London, 18 February 2016).

[68] This was a lesson we learnt from our risk work. See Richard Moorhead and Steven Vaughan, 'Legal Risk: Definition, Management and Ethics' (Social Science Research Network 2015, SSRN Scholarly Paper ID 2594228).

(ii) Component 2 – An Understanding of Independence and Role

Thirty-nine per cent of our survey respondents agreed that there was a clear and common understanding within their organisation of 'what the role of the legal function is' (31 per cent agreed somewhat) and 43 per cent agreed that the independence of the legal function within their organisation is 'strongly supported by the business functions' (20 per cent agreed somewhat). So, in contrast to *some* resistance or negativity towards the legal function being common, most of our respondents also felt supported by their organisations, albeit some felt this somewhat tentatively, and a substantial minority (over one in five) did not. A lack of understanding about role or support for independence is likely to lead to opportunities for pressure and unfair criticism potentially undermining the legal function.

(iii) Component 3 – The Existence of Uneven Relationships with the Organisation

Sixty-seven per cent of our survey respondents agreed that parts of the organisation are more challenging to in-house lawyers than others (22 per cent agreed somewhat) and 75 per cent agreed that parts of the organisation are more supportive of legal than others (18 per cent agreed somewhat). We see thus widespread agreement with the idea that support of, and challenges for, the legal function are unevenly distributed.

In broad terms, then, our respondents reported working in organisations where they felt supported, but where an unevenness of relationship was common, and where they were sometimes criticised for being obstructive. Importantly, about half agreed that action was sometimes taken against legal advice on important matters.

We explored these issues in more depth in the interviews, asking about in-houser relationships, and the relationships of the in-house team, with the wider organisation, and how our interviewees thought they (and legal) were perceived by the business. Unusually, the consistency of responses was very strong indeed. Almost everyone we talked with was wary of being seen as 'creating obstacles … being difficult' [IHL46], of being 'the checkers and the blockers and a silo' [IHL41]. Some acknowledged the scepticism of lawyers as something that was just a fact of life that needed to be ignored, 'I just get over it! … So do we block deals? That's their perception. However, I would say that we enable good deals.' [IHL47]

Everyone we spoke with wanted to be seen as a 'problem solver' [IHL41], as 'people who help them [the organisation] to achieve their objectives' [IHL31], 'on the right side of not being obstructive' [IHL36]. This was often, almost universally, framed in terms of being perceived to 'add value'. We explored with our interviewees what 'adding value' meant to them, and how their organisations perceived it. One in-houser thought those lower down the organisational chain saw value in the legal team, who were sometimes seen as a, 'life raft in an ocean ... where they say, 'Guys look I can't get my head out of all these issues. What do I do?' [IHL29], but the majority, countervailing view was:

> the big figures from top level management ... get it, because they've done the big deals and they've done the big cases and they realise that they absolutely need lawyers. It tends to be the middle layer and the procurement function way, there's this constant quest to show value ... but actually it's nigh on impossible because it's all about avoided costs and avoided losses ... legal value is intangible for a very large extent, I think. [IHL38]

Value could be demonstrated by a counterfactual or a 'bad apple' problem in the organisation's own past (which highlighted the need for a greater input from legal):

> if you can show where a company that people would otherwise respect has got it so badly wrong, General Motors for example ... that's the kind of example that really hits home. We're not talking about somebody you've never heard of in a country which has dubious ratings in Transparency International index. [IHL39]

The intangibility of legal value, and sceptical views of lawyers, meant that the common posture of our interviewees was to be seen as someone proactive, who added value (but was unsure what that meant) and who created solutions (not problems). Our in-housers could see that this risked sometimes running counter to a need to be independent and to give robust advice. We explore this in-depth in Chapter 4, but this interviewee puts the problem rather vividly:

> they're your employer ultimately and the concern [is] that you are ... you are poking a stick in the eye of the person who is potentially in control of your own destiny. [IHL24]

Unevenness of relationship often seemed to reflect different perceptions at strategic and operational levels, with management seeing the legal team as, 'incredibly important' but the 'the business per se, the local offices ... they tend to see us as sort of policemen, right?' [IHL52]. Relationships, for some interviewees at least, varied as a function of how 'helpful' that in-house lawyer was perceived as being. 'How much of a barrier I'm seen to be putting on that sales pipeline' (IHL25) was a particular issue. 'Culture and size' [IHL33] and the extent to which legal was involved proactively, to shape events, rather than being seen as someone brought in at the last minute as 'more of a rubber stamp' [IHL37], were also determinative. In this way, being more strategically engaged meant, 'feedback [from legal] before something gets underway' [IHL37] rather than having to consider saying 'No' if something had gone too far.

These cultural and structural variations suggest differences in pressure towards wrongdoing coming from employers. Nelson and Nielsen identify 'extremely aggressive business executives' who would do anything for their bonuses,[69] but the overall tenor of their work is of business people being ignorant of, rather than hostile to, the law. Moorhead and Hinchly note not business hostility to legality, but a willingness to minimise or ignore its significance in certain circumstances,[70] although *some* in-house lawyers are actively 'managed toward "thinking the unthinkable"'.[71] As Parker et al document, though, the pull towards illegality does not always, even generally, come from business: it can come from lawyers keen to promote creative compliance solutions.[72] Indeed, creative compliance can be part of the professional's modus operandi in, for example, tax.[73]

ETHICAL PRESSURE

These competing viewpoints show the importance of paying close attention to whether and when there are actual conflicts between in-house lawyers and their host organisations. Interestingly, while much of the socio-legal literature tends to suggest conflict is inherent in the in-house role, attempts to quantify conflict have often suggested its absence more than its presence. Gunz and Gunz looked for but did not find high levels of organisational-professional conflict ('OPC') amongst employed lawyers.[74] Chamblis and Remus also found 'surprisingly little conflict' in their study of government agency lawyers in the US,[75] and Rostain suggests there is no conflict because her in-house informants were robust and willing to be 'cops' (which we explore further in Chapter 6).[76] The 'absence of conflict' idea fits with how in-house lawyers often describe their work. One possible explanation for low levels of OPC is that in-house practice simply does not give rise to actual tensions between business and professional values. A claim not uncommonly made by in-house lawyers,[77] including those we spoke with, is that they work for ethical organisations. Individual values and corporate

---

[69] Nelson and Nielsen (n 2).
[70] Richard Moorhead and Victoria Hinchly, 'Professional Minimalism? The Ethical Consciousness of Commercial Lawyers' (2015) 42 *Journal of Law and Society* 387.
[71] ibid 401.
[72] Christine E Parker, Robert Eli Rosen and Vibeke Lehmann Nielsen, 'The Two Faces of Lawyers: Professional Ethics and Business Compliance with Regulation' [2007] *Yale Journal on Regulation* 202.
[73] Doreen McBarnet, 'Legal Creativity: Law, Capital and Legal Avoidance' in Maureen Cain and Christine Harrington (eds), *Lawyers in a Postmodern World: Translation and Transgression* (Open University Press, 1994); Doreen McBarnet and Christopher Whelan, 'The Elusive Spirit of the Law: Formalism and the Struggle for Legal Control' (1991) 54 *The Modern Law Review* 848.
[74] Hugh P Gunz and Sally P Gunz, 'The lawyer's response to organizational professional conflict: an empirical study of the ethical decision making of in-house counsel' (2002) 39(2) *American Business Law Journal* 241, 248.
[75] Elizabeth Chambliss and Dana Remus, 'Nothing Could Be Finer: The Role of Agency General Counsel in North and South Carolina' (2015) 84 *Fordham L Rev* 2039, 2058.
[76] Rostain (n 42).
[77] Such claims are made in Nelson and Nielsen (n 2) 471; Moorhead and Hinchly (n 70).

values may tend towards alignment.[78] If true, this would reduce the incidence of such tensions: conflict would be aberrant.[79] Yet, a review of corporate scandals, and data such as Nelson and Neilsen's, suggest instead that there *are* such conflicts.[80]

A second explanation is that professional values are overly adaptive, allowing in-house lawyers to turn a blind eye to ethical problems. Faced with the cognitive dissonance of helping an organisation behave unethically, the temptation is to reframe the situation as somehow permitted. Nelson and Nielsen noted in-house professionalism involved 'the practiced art of embracing their new clients' objectives as their own', enabling them to become 'enthusiastic partners'.[81] Gunz and Gunz note the 'primary identification' of in-house lawyers may be with their organisation rather than with their profession and its ethics and rules.[82] Indeed, one way of interpreting the professional rules is to say they mandate that primary identification through the idea of zealous advocacy.[83] Relatedly, a technician-like attitude to the lawyer's roles, advising on the legality of the organisation's goals, without thinking whether short-term goals are consistent with wider, long-term objectives, 'might cynically focus on the interests of the company at the expense of its broader legal obligations to society [in ways] ... subsequently deemed to be unethical.'[84] There is the further possibility that some organisations actively keep their in-house lawyers out of key decisions from which conflicts may arise.[85]

We thought it important to measure in our study both understandings of professionalism and perceptions of conflict, to understand whether high levels of professionalism were driven by low levels of conflict. As a result, we are able to examine whether an absence of conflict or weak professionalism explains the apparent comfort with which in-house lawyers perform their roles. We think the perception of conflict depends on the individual in-house lawyer and their context. Some do not perceive conflict, and some do but respond by engaging ethically, whilst others disengage. Some in-house lawyers may be able to switch self-assuredly between gatekeeping, counselling and entrepreneurial roles, by knowing when each role is important, and others seem likely to ignore, minimise or avoid conflicts to maintain their influence in the organisation. How they

---

[78] Kibeom Lee, Julie J Carswell and Natalie J Allen, 'A Meta-Analytic Review of Occupational Commitment: Relations with Person- and Work-Related Variables' (2000) 85 *Journal of Applied Psychology* 799.

[79] A kind of moral licensing effect, see, Anna C Merritt, Daniel A Effron and Benoît Monin, 'Moral Self-Licensing: When Being Good Frees Us to Be Bad' (2010) 4 *Social and Personality Psychology Compass* 344.

[80] Nelson and Nielsen (n 2) 483.

[81] Nelson and Nielsen (n 2) 489.

[82] Gunz and Gunz (n 74) 253, 256.

[83] Stephen L Pepper, 'The Lawyer's Amoral Ethical Role: A Defense, a Problem, and Some Possibilities' (1986) *American Bar Foundation Research Journal* 24.

[84] Gunz and Gunz (n 74) 256.

[85] ibid.

Table 3.2 Constituent Data for Ethical Pressure

	Strongly Disagree	Disagree	Somewhat Disagree	Neither Agree nor Disagree	Somewhat Agree	Agree	Strongly Agree	N
I'm sometimes asked to advise or assist on things that make me uncomfortable ethically	12.2%	23.4%	21.1%	10.9%	17.3%	13.0%	2.0%	393
There are tensions between the way I and the business respects obligations to uphold the law	14.2%	28.9%	18.0%	13.2%	14.4%	7.6%	3.8%	395

	Never	Rarely	Sometimes	Regularly	Very frequently	N
How often are you asked to advise on something where the legality of a proposed action by the organisation is debatable?	8.6%	51.9%	26.3%	9.4%	3.8%	395
How often are you asked to advise on something where the ethicality (as opposed to the legality) of a proposed action by the organisation is debatable?	6.8%	48.9%	34.3%	7.6%	2.5%	397

do so depends, in part, on their own models of professionalism, as we will see later in this book.

This leads us to our next reflection on the place of lawyers in their networks: the extent to which they come under ethical pressure. As we have seen earlier in this chapter, about half of our respondents agreed that action was sometimes taken against legal advice on important matters. Our survey also measured perceived ethical pressure more explicitly as a composite of responses to four questions. The constituent results are shown in Table 3.2.

About 15 per cent agreed or strongly agreed that they were asked to advise on things that made them uncomfortable ethically (about a third agreed somewhat with this proposition), and just over 10 per cent suggested that their organisation took a different view on whether and/or how to uphold the rule of law (about a quarter agreed at least somewhat with this). Around about 10 per cent of our respondents were asked to advise on ethically or legally debatable actions frequently or very frequently; and about 40 per cent were asked to so advise at least sometimes.

Interestingly, it might have been thought that those in small teams would be more vulnerable to ethical pressure and so experience more of it. We did not find this. There was no correlation between size of team and ethical pressure. Interestingly too, lawyers working in a public sector organisation showed significantly *higher* ratings of ethical pressure than those working in a business.[86] Statistically significant differences were also found according to the number of years working in-house, with those working in-house for 0–5 and 6–10 years reporting lower levels of ethical pressure than those working in-house for more than 15 years. Ethical pressure increased somewhat with seniority and/or experience, although the strength of the relationship was weak, emphasising that other factors may be at play.[87]

We explored these issues with our interviewees, who often talked about ethical pressure as part of the tournament of influence, deciding whether and when to say 'No' (or 'No, but …'). This is the core of the following chapter. Suffice it to say at this point, and in the context of organisational networks, that a number of our interviewees suffered from exposure to what the following interviewee termed the 'shouty man syndrome'. IHL24 wraps up, rather nicely, the desire to be seen to be adding value, to not being a deal blocker, as a 'helpful' part of the team:

> The problem we face is what I call the 'shouty man syndrome', which is it doesn't matter how much we agree this is the right way to go, if you've got a client, an internal stakeholder, shouting at you to get something done because it's urgent and you just don't understand why is legal being so difficult? You end up defaulting to all too often being helpful even though long-term that's the wrong answer. [IHL24]

---

[86] $p = .002$.
[87] Linear regression analysis: $\beta = .018$, $t = 3.16$, $p = .002$, $\eta 2 = .02$.

CONCLUSION

The status inferiority of working in-house is much diminished. Team sizes have expanded, the in-house legal role has become less narrow and more strategic, and governance and compliance roles have become stronger. In-house lawyers have become more embedded in organisational decision-making and influential in processes. That is not to say that a broader, stronger and earlier exercising of legal influence is always what happens, or that such a role is without its problems, but there does appear to have been a qualitative change in the nature and shape of in-house roles in at least some organisations. Where once the mantra about in-house lawyers may have been solely about being cheaper than external counsel, now there are plausible expectations that in-housers should be cheaper, better and (perhaps) more ethical, at least to the extent that they are expected to be more tuned in to the long term interests of their organisation posed by legal and reputational risk.

A more embedded role, closer to the organisation, and with more varied work, is part of the reason why many of our interviewees chose to go into, or stay, in-house. So too was an explicit rejection of elements of private practice: the 'moral bankruptcy' of time sheets and pyramid models of selling hours; avoiding over-specialisation; and the sense that a broader set of skills might be engaged by working in, rather than for, an organisation. Equally, with this embedding is an interesting question of balance: between not presuming a conflict between business and professionalism and not being ready for one; between giddy naivety and ascetic cynicism. Rather than choosing independence over partnership, we think it more important to understand the conditions under which a positive or negative approach is more likely.

In this chapter, we begin to see how the embedding of professional expertise takes place in a predominantly organisational context. The everyday grounding of this embedding is interesting. The increasing emphasis on 'value adding' (something lawyers had to demonstrate, but found hard to identify); the integration of lawyers into business development and planning functions; and the changing nature of the job (away from 'pure' legal advice towards risk management and commercial input) shifted the nature of in-house work and how in-housers thought about it.

Parallel to this shift, in-house lawyers continue to work from a presumption that colleagues see them through the lens of a stereotype: as deal-blockers and costly nit-pickers. Whilst senior executive colleagues understood the need for legal within their organisations, in-house teams were measured against organisational (usually commercial) imperatives that are incommensurate. As a result, understanding of the role of legal was seen often as tentative, and unevenness of relationships within the business was common, as was criticism for being obstructive. That such discomfort was important is suggested by almost half of our respondents who reported that their organisations acted against legal advice on important matters.

Conclusion 69

Furthermore, about 10 per cent of our respondents were asked to advise on ethically or legally debatable actions frequently or very frequently, and 40 per cent were asked to so advise on such actions at least sometimes. About 10–15 per cent agreed or strongly agreed that they were asked to advise on things that made them uncomfortable, or in ways which suggested their employer took a different view on whether and/or how to uphold the rule of law. About a quarter to a third agreed at least somewhat with these concerns.

In describing these points of difference we can see how engagements with the organisation are part of a tournament of influence which lawyers sometimes (often perhaps) expect to lose. There is a trading of helpfulness for acceptance. Lawyers adapt to organisational resistance by adopting a cultivated posture of helpfulness. In-housers suggest the need for independence and difficult advice is present but also camouflaged, restrained or diluted. The question is not whether to compromise, but how much, and in what circumstances.

One last finding from this chapter deserves a mention in this context. If governance and ethics is a key concern of a new model of in-house lawyer, we might also see this reflected in their line management and reporting arrangements. We would not criticise the desire for influence seen in the commonly expressed desirability of GCs reporting to CEOs: our data were inconclusive on whether this was likely to be a good or bad thing, with interviewees essentially rehearsing the arguments found elsewhere. Proponents of board representation were most interested in the in-house legal function having influence; and opponents were most interested in potential conflicts of interest, and in compromises to independence. What we think is particularly interesting is the relative absence of reporting lines to non-executive directors. Such reporting lines may help to reinforce (for the in-house lawyer, and the employer) that the organisation is the ultimate client and that its interests may, at times, conflict with senior executives, employees, and other internal constituencies. Often these reporting lines were absent.

The partnership model relies on the idea that in-house lawyers and their organisations strike a balance between competing interests. We have looked here at the way in which the role is structured and at the role of in-house lawyers in the organisational network. We have also seen that issues of objectivity and independence are contextualised by sensitivity to corporate hierarchies and networks of influence. It is to independence, and the willingness of in-housers to push back against their organisations, that we turn in the following chapter. We will come to show that the independence of in-house lawyers is relational, specific to the circumstances of each case, and (from the perspective of the in-house lawyers) best understood as having a temporal dimension and being part of a series of interventions and non-interventions on their part. A willingness to say 'No' is part of the picture, but there is a good deal more to it than that.

4

The Tournament of Influence
Saying 'No' and The Independent In-House Lawyer

THE TOURNAMENT OF INFLUENCE

Our discussions of embeddedness in Chapter 1 and in Chapter 3 pit binary paradigms (public interest versus commerce; profession versus organisation) against a networked or partnership paradigm of hybrid professionalism. Binary paradigms see risk as largely negative; hybrid professionalism sees risk as freighted with the possibility of harm and welfare gains. The binary paradigms ask if in-house lawyers are more like businesspeople and less like professionals, and if they are captured by their clients, rather than being independent. The networked paradigm points out that engagement between business and profession is inescapable, that we cannot imagine a workable professional utopia, and that such engagement creates benefits as well as tensions. Yet both paradigms must engage with the role of lawyers as gatekeepers.

Gatekeeping is a prevention or enforcement strategy designed to inhibit wrongdoing.[1] The idea is that in-house lawyers provide a barrier to wrongdoing: a gate through which illegality cannot pass. A subtler variant of gatekeeping is lawyers acting as reputational intermediaries: their involvement in legal matters signalling the veracity of information or the fitness of a decision or process.[2] A classic example of reputational intermediation is disclosures made to securities markets; but it can include the giving of advice ('Our lawyers say we can do this') as well as internal investigations of allegations of corporate wrongdoing ('We have looked into this and are confident we have done nothing wrong'). Perhaps because reputational intermediary work is more often associated with outside counsel, the literature on in-house lawyers tends to concentrate on gatekeeping in the first sense: namely, on the lawyer as blocker of the bad men of business.

---

[1] Reiner H Kraakman, 'Gatekeepers: the anatomy of a third-party enforcement strategy' (1986) 2(1) *Journal of Law, Economics & Organization* 53.
[2] John C Coffee Jr, 'Understanding Enron: "It's About the Gatekeepers, Stupid"' (2002) *The Business Lawyer* 1403.

Is there a need for gatekeeping? Executive surveys and other evidence often suggest ethical problems are entrenched within organisations.[3] Lawyers are rarely the primary focus but where they are, there are occasional indicators of concern. One such survey has claimed, 'General Counsel are more likely than other executives to justify backdating contracts in order to meet financial targets.'[4] Other work suggests that lawyers can inhibit compliance activity,[5] and can be more inclined to defend the chief executive than take a judicious position on right action.[6] Creative compliance (sanctions-busting through enforcement-proofing would be one such example) is evidently sometimes a problem.[7] In crude terms, the concern is that a creative or zealous lawyer may advise what an organisation can get away with, actively opening the gate for conduct which may be questionable. Large majorities of in-house lawyers appear to see reporting misconduct as part of their role,[8] but whistleblowing by in-house lawyers is rare.[9] And, as we saw in Chapter 3, the presence of senior lawyers in the upper reaches of companies has mixed effects on risk-signalling, risk-taking and compliance, that may depend on how their role or activities are structured.

Independence is the principal concept which ensures that in-housers step in as gatekeepers at the appropriate times. It is a matter of professional judgement whether the law requires the in-house lawyer to advise against, even sometimes work actively to prevent, unlawfulness; or whether they are required to litigate (or advise or act) in a certain way. And the classic way in which independence is tested, the acid test much employed in studies of in-house lawyers, is the willingness of in-housers to say 'No' to their employers.

Professional independence has broader professional resonance. It is seen as a hallmark and a bulwark of professionalism,[10] with collective independence (self-regulation) and individual independence (detached, unbiased judgement) being indelibly entwined. Mostly, independence at the professional level is framed as

---

[3] See, for example, Ernst & Young, '13th Global Fraud Survey Overcoming Compliance Fatigue Reinforcing the Commitment to Ethical Growth' (Ernst & Young Report, 2014), Sabrina Basran, 'Employee Views of Ethics at Work: 2012 Continental Europe Survey' (IBE, 2012), and a review of US evidence by Kim in: Sung Hui Kim, 'Inside Lawyers: Friends or Gatekeepers?' (2016) 84 *Fordham Law Review* 1867.

[4] Ernst & Young (2014) ibid.

[5] Mike Rosen, 'Tensions Rise Between Chief Compliance Officers and General Counsel' (Blog, 28 January 2014), http://blog.providertrust.com/blog/bid/333888/Tensions-Rise-Between-Chief-Compliance-Officers-and-General-Counsel, accessed 18 April 2018.

[6] David Wilkins, 'Team of Rivals? Toward a New Model of the Corporate Attorney-Client Relationship' (2010) 78 *Fordham Law Review* 2067.

[7] Richard Moorhead, 'On the Wire' (2012) *New Law Journal* 1080.

[8] Chad R Brown, 'In-House Counsel Responsibilities in the Post-Enron Environment' (2003) 21 ACC Docket 92, cited in Tanina Rostain, 'General Counsel in the Age of Compliance: Preliminary Findings and New Research Questions' (2008) 21 *Georgetown Journal of Legal Ethics* 465.

[9] Roger C Cramton, George M Cohen and Susan P Koniak, 'Legal and Ethical Duties of Lawyers after Sarbanes-Oxley' (2004) 49 *Vill L Rev* 725.

[10] Tanina Rostain, 'Self Regulatory Authority, Markets and the Ideology of Professionalism' in Robert Baldwin, Martin Cave and Martin Lodge (eds) *The Oxford Handbook of Regulation* (Oxford University Press, 2010) 169.

an issue between the profession and state; but at the individual level it is also an issue between professionals and their clients.

As we noted in the previous chapter, issues of objectivity and independence are contextualised by sensitivity to corporate hierarchies and networks of influence. That sensitivity sometimes involves a negotiation between the in-house lawyer's view of what is lawful and right, and their view of what is tolerable. That negotiation may be with colleagues but it may also be internal: there is a degree of self-censorship involved in needing to be seen as helpful. Embedded compromise contrasts with the analytic clarity of reducing independence to a 'Yes/No' question in which 'good' in-house lawyers are willing to say 'No' when faced with 'illegality'. We have three binaries in this idea: (i) 'good' lawyer; (ii) illegality; and (iii) saying 'Yes' or 'No'. These binaries are of course artificial. They are the endpoints of normative judgement, part of a thought experiment trying to test out whether in-house lawyers are 'really' independent.

One of the things we wish to tease out in this chapter is how this binary testing does not fit well with what actually happens. Independence is far more relational, specific to the circumstances of each case, and best understood as having a temporal dimension and as being part of a series of interventions and non-interventions on their part. A willingness to say 'No' is part of the picture, but there is a good deal more to it.

Independence also links to professional status and regulatory protections. As we have previously set out, in some European jurisdictions in-house lawyers are diminished by an obligation to relinquish local Bar membership because of concerns over a lack of independence.[11] The regulatory protection the client relinquishes is legal professional privilege.[12] In a competition law case, the European Court held that 'independent lawyers' were 'lawyers who are not bound to the client by a relationship of employment'.[13] In *Akzo Nobel*, the court commented that an in-house lawyer does not enjoy, 'the same *degree* of independence from his employer as a lawyer working in an external law firm does in relation to his client' and so, 'is *less able* to deal effectively with any conflicts between his professional obligations and the aims of his client' (our emphasis).[14]

We would challenge the assumption that private practice lawyers are automatically better placed than their in-house peers to provide independent legal advice. Indeed, recent work, in the context of large corporate finance law firms, has shown a series of independence challenges faced by those in private practice.[15] It is possible to imagine that significant competition, more precarious

---

[11] For an overview, see: Philippe Coen and Christophe Roquilly (eds), *Company Lawyer: Independent by Design* (LexisNexis, 2014).
[12] Case C-155/79 *AM & S Europe Ltd v Commission* [1982] ECR 157.
[13] ibid, para 21.
[14] C-550/07 *Akzo Nobel Chemicals and Akcros Chemicals v Commission* [2010] ECR 512, para 45.
[15] Steven Vaughan and Claire Coe, 'Independence, Representation and Risk: An Empirical Exploration of the Management of Client Relationships by Large Law Firms' (Solicitors Regulation Authority Report, October 2016).

relationships with clients, the way clients define law firm mandates, and the need to hit financial targets makes private practitioners as, or more, prone to independence problems.[16] The ECJ were rightly anxious about 'economic dependence' but private practitioners often have economic dependencies of their own.[17] Hackett also pushes back at the idea that in-house lawyers may be, or may feel, less independent than their private practice peers.[18] However, drawing attention to the issues faced by private practice lawyers does not detract from the independence issues in-house lawyers face. They both may be (and likely are) challenged. Yet in-house lawyers do have a different form of relationship with their employers than private practice lawyers do with their clients.

THE TOURNAMENT OF INFLUENCE

As a leading former GC has noted:

> Because of their unique 'positioning' within the client entity, in-house counsel face extreme pressures to be all things to all people – pressures that often place them in situations where they find that the professional rules meant to guide their practices are often inconsistent with or irrelevant to the practical requirements of their work.[19]

Our interviews show us in the strongest terms that this 'positioning' is something in-house lawyers see as having to work to maintain. The *way* they conduct their work is central to this positioning. They have to be overtly helpful to be influential. Influence cements their place in the network. It is this network positioning that we call the tournament of influence. We think it can have an important effect on how in-house lawyers view their role, how they see their professional obligations, and also in terms of how in-housers negotiate their position vis-à-vis others within their organisation.

Some of this influence is economic. Incentives 'may subtly or overtly coerce an attorney into acting in ways which they otherwise would not in hopes of personal recognition and reward.'[20] There are carrots (performance-related bonuses) and there are sticks ('dangling sword of being fired and losing one's financial security').[21] These are rather crude, but not inaccurate, views of what

---

[16] For an analogous discussion in relation to ABSs see Paul A Grout, 'The Clementi Report: Potential Risks of External Ownership and Regulatory Responses A Report to the Department of Constitutional Affairs' (Department of Constitutional Affairs, 2005).

[17] *Akzo Nobel* (n 14) para 49.

[18] See, for example, Susan Hackett, 'Corporate Counsel and the Evolution of Ethical Practical Navigation: An Overview of the Changing Dynamics of Professional Responsibility in In-House Practice' (2012) 25 *Georgetown Journal of Legal Ethics* 317, 319; Richard Moorhead and Victoria Hinchly, 'Professional Minimalism? The Ethical Consciousness of Commercial Lawyers' (2015) 42 *Journal of Law and Society* 387; and Coe and Vaughan (n 15).

[19] Hackett (n 18).

[20] Pam Jenoff, 'Going Native: Incentive, Identity, and the Inherent Ethical Problem of In-House Counsel' (2011) 114 *West Virginia Law Review* 725, 739.

[21] ibid, 740.

can sometimes influence in-house counsel.[22] Certainly, our interviewees were alive to these issues: 'if your own rewards, for example, are so closely connected to the way in which that business does things' [IHL 25]. However, it was often suggested that direct links between the remuneration and behaviour were unlikely: 'the chain of events between decisions, things that I do and the profit that the company makes [and impacts on my bonus] is lengthy and tortuous. It just doesn't – it doesn't figure' [IHL26].

Incentives may thus not be crudely determinative, but they are there to influence behaviour. Importantly, the bonuses of our interviewees were not purely profit-related. Some 'are not reliant on business performance [but are] … metrics … based on management or reduction of legal risk in all its myriad forms rather than volume number of transactions' [IHL 30]. But some were related to a direct 'reporting line' in a particular business unit, so that the profit of the unit directly correlated with the bonus of the in-house lawyer, so that in this situation there was 'potential for conflict. And issues' [IHL 27]. When it came to performance management of in-housers, 'the devil's in the detail' [IHL 27].

Incentives also contribute to a broader culture of signalling what is important. The general, sometimes frenetic, pace of in-house work and the general emphasis on financial targets could impact on an ability of our interviewees to stand back and provide independent counsel to their employer:

> But when you are … where I am now, you are so incredibly driven by the next three months, four months or even the next three hours that the opportunity to stop and reflect, or to consider, is extremely rare, extremely rare. [IHL25]

Influences are not purely economic; they are also relational in nature:

> I think that can happen sometimes, particularly if you're working on a major project with one department and it's over a long period of time, it's inevitable that you will go native to an extent, and sometimes, in those circumstances, it is difficult to maintain objectivity when you're dealing with the same people day in and day out. [IHL36]

Whilst it is important that some in-house lawyers recognised the problem, this lawyer said they could still 'step back' and advise objectively. The more important question is whether they actually step back in practice, or do so as often as they ought to.

Our interviewees were divided on whether they thought that their employers recognised and/or valued their independence as professionals. The majority thought that 'the business doesn't see the professional qualification' [IHL28]. This was despite 80 per cent of survey respondents agreeing that their organisation *needed* to understand their view was independent:

> literally nobody in – who I've ever worked with who isn't a lawyer, has any idea what our professional status means in terms of having an obligation independent of what management wants me to do. [IHL26]

---

[22] See the discussion of Morse and others in Chapter 3.

> I would be really surprised if you asked a CEO, 'Name me the top three criteria of why you want a general counsel,' I don't think because they will hold a higher ethical standard than anybody else in the business would be featuring, but I stand to be corrected. [IHL48]

A minority (who tended to come from sectors which had a history of corporate scandals or a loss of public confidence) thought that the 'culture' [IHL30] in their organisation was one that recognised, and valued, the independence of their in-house lawyers. This suggests professional independence can be reinforced by the host organisation. For example, our interviewees sometimes (although not often) reported a deliberate attempt to align the professional claim to independence with a leadership desire to do, and be seen to do, the right thing within their businesses. Changing regulation and redressing a history of non-compliance could support this.

> Because you ... you have the dual role. You're supposed to be independent of the business and advising the business. And I can see, you know, with tougher regulation, you know, potentially more corporate scandals, if, you know, that continues to be the way things develop, that there could be more pressure on lawyers to be more independent. Which I think would unwind some of the business partnering. [IHL27]

And interestingly some of our interviewees saw being too service-oriented as a potential problem for independence. Notice in the following quote how internal management of 'customer satisfaction' became a pro-independence point of resistance.

> I've just got a new Chief Executive here, and I was doing my budget and she said to me, have I done any survey to work out what my clients think of the service I'm providing. And I said, 'I'm not a service provider' ... if you start to think of yourself too much as a service provider and not that balance between service and assurance and governance I actually think you're missing the point of the point of having an in-house team. [IHL31]

For IHL46 (and for a number of others), it was his expertise as a solicitor that was really valued by the business (not his professional status, and not his independence):

> The fact that you operate and think independently, I suspect doesn't really cross their mind, to be honest. But they clearly do value your experience and knowledge and guidance in terms of what can and cannot be done. But I can't imagine that they're thinking that you're a solicitor at the Supreme Court and that you are completely independent and governed by the SRA and the Law Society and what have you. I just don't think it comes across their mind, they just get on with the business. [IHL46]

Sometimes a failure to appreciate professional obligations led to tension: 'it would be helpful for employers to understand ... we are employed by them but we are regulated by another body in terms of which we have to adhere to certain professional standards' [IHL49]. Our sense is that the employers of our interviewees see their in-house lawyers as (expert) technicians or business advisors, not as professionals, but with some isolated spots of difference if the employer is more interested in a culture of integrity.

Furthermore, most interviewees understood themselves as operating within a network of influence not founded on independence but on trust and commerciality. This is manifested in an ability to characterise legal issues and strategies in business terms and priorities, and in close working relationships and lines of communication with other parts of the organisation (especially with – or on – the board, as discussed in the previous chapter). Under this view, to be a successful in-house counsel you need the business to trust you enough to provide you with the relevant information, and involve you in the important decisions, but to gain that trust you may have to adjust your sense of tolerable and intolerable risk. As IHL13 put it:

> I'd seriously wonder now having worked 25 years as an in-house lawyer whether you can really be independent, and I seriously wonder how people who are in the senior management and GCs in multi-nationals, whether they can be independent or whether they have to align themselves to the direction of travel – is a nice way of putting it – or to the instructions of the Board. That's what I would say about the in-house role. It's a very difficult role.

This notion that in-house lawyers are dependent on others coming to them with the information is criticised by some.[23] Waiting to be asked to advise, or relying on what one is told, are reminders as to how independence is in tension with passive, reactive, and neutral advisor models of lawyering. Equally, professional claims to independence by our interviewees were subtle and not naïve. An alternative, more critical way of putting it, is that their contingent notions of independence were compromised but not without merit. Our interviewees understood that professional independence is (sometimes) in tension with their need to serve, and be seen to serve, the business.

> How would I describe the role – yes it's a very broad question, isn't it? There's a number of aspects to it. I see myself as a support function but also as having to be this conscience of the business so although you're employed by the business you still have to keep your distance in some respects and keep in mind your professional responsibilities and try and keep some distance. ... you're an employee but not at the same time. [IHL40]

In standing back, in not saying 'No', and in allowing their organisations to 'take the risk' (through the in-house lawyer merely advising and the client deciding) there is also a corporate discipline at work that protects the discretion of senior decision-makers and that disciplines in-house lawyers towards organisational norms. That discipline reminds in-house lawyers they are there to support their

---

[23] Sung Hui Kim, 'Gatekeepers Inside Out' (2008) 21 *Geo J Legal Ethics* 411.

employer organisation. The discipline is also, sometimes, disciplinary. We were told of CEOs 'calling out' in-house lawyers for being obstructive. Sometimes this is done very publicly in town-hall meetings; more often it is done subtly, but the result could be similar. And often, but with notable exceptions, in-house lawyers and the organisations they work within had an allergy to the word 'No' being exercised with finality by anyone other than the ultimate decision-maker. 'Soft noes' aside, the in-house lawyer's role as adviser generally precluded them from that decision-making function.

As a result, all sides avoid the posing of a question or reduction of an answer to 'no' where they can. The idea of risk (which we explore further in the following two chapters) facilitates the avoidance of that problem:

> What you mustn't do is say no to anyone, that's a big, big mistake ... But very rarely do you get a question, the question is more like what will happen if? The lawyer is probably guessing with huge experience and knowledge, and the guess might be in the right ballpark but it's still a guess. Much, much better to give options to a management team and to indicate the degree of risk with each one, and then let the management team form its own view about it, try and get the dialogue going. If you can form that kind of relationship then you will grow the legal service. [IHL19]

What we notice in this quote is how the seeking of legal influence involves a balancing of long-term aims (growing the credibility of and trust in the legal team and its influence within the company) and short term aims (influencing the immediate decision without damaging the long term aim of a stronger legal team). Pragmatism was an important part of getting comfortable, deploying influence, and challenging the organisation:

> I think you're less effective in my role if you've got your head in the sand and just aspire to eradicate all risk all of the time. That's just not realistic. [IHL17]

The need for influence was not simply, or mainly, about the job satisfaction and career trajectory of in-house lawyers (although it was partly that). It was also a battle for resources. Influence was a way of getting the needs of the legal team, and what it means to behave legally, or to minimise legal risk, understood within the organisation. That was a battle for resources which in-housers were sometimes felt to be losing:

> There is often lack of appreciation in the organisation of how much pressure the legal resource is under and what complex decisions they are trying to juggle ... [W]here General Counsel are concerned that they have not [been] able to do things which they would ordinarily anticipate being able to do and that that potentially compromises them or their business. I think that is a, if trend is the right word, that is something of a regular conversation. [IHL1]

Within the tournament of influence was a resistance from our respondents to legal being seen as an insurance policy through, for example, rubber-stamping dubious decisions with the imprimatur of legality. In the following example, the 'don't say no' approach is maintained, but the in-houser is resisting being blamed for taking a decision which appears to be bad in other than purely legal terms:

> [P]eople often come to me and say, 'Can we do this? And it's this and this, and I don't think it's that bad because of this.' And I'll say, 'I'm not going to say yes or no. What do you think?' [IHL14]

This lawyer was seeking to responsibilise a colleague in the organisation by not taking a legal view of a problem which could be decided without resort to legal advice:

> And invariably they go, 'Actually it's not right.' And they're coming to you for validation because they don't want to make that cost decision themselves, but if something isn't inherently right, morally or ethically or legally, people really do know. [IHL14]

This perhaps suggests some form of vicious circle in which 'bad' decisions are taken to in-house lawyers for rubber stamping which, when they are not rubber stamped, reinforces the view of legal as the 'Department of No' and makes people less likely to go their in-house lawyers for advice.

SAYING 'NO'

We turn now to the willingness of in-house lawyers to say 'No', especially in situations where potentially unlawful or unethical conduct is proposed. The willingness to say 'No' is part of the 'Cops' conception of the in-house lawyer that we discussed in Chapters 1 and 3: the idea that in-house lawyers can and should act as gatekeepers restraining illegality within the organisation.[24] Nelson and Nielsen describe the gatekeeping function in the following terms:

> When the corporate attorney acts as a gatekeeper, he or she monitors legal compliance and serves as a final hurdle or 'gate' through which business ideas must pass prior to implementation. The ability to 'trump' a business decision has been identified by researchers as a source of contention and confusion for both lawyers and their business clients …[25]

To be effective gatekeepers, in-house lawyers need to be sought out for their advice. This raises tensions between having a reputation as someone who says 'No' (someone who is a deal-stopper) and someone who can find legal solutions to problems or who can facilitate business. Equally, however, in-house lawyers can be seen as the voice of reason, to whom hard decisions should be brought before bear traps are sprung.

---

[24] Robert L Nelson and Laura Beth Nielsen, 'Cops, Counsel, and Entrepreneurs: Constructing the Role of inside Counsel in Large Corporations' [2000] *Law and Society Review* 457.
[25] ibid, 470.

Our interviewees were very alive to the perception that the legal team may be perceived in a negative light:

> I think a lot of people see legal and compliance as anti-commercial or as business blockers, and I think that's the fault probably of the in-house lawyer in not taking the right approach. Normally there is a way of approaching something that might not be exactly how the business had envisaged doing it, but allows them to do what they wanted to do in the right way. [IHL34]

It is easy to advocate in theory (and often, we are sure, in practice) that the dilemma of saying 'No' can be avoided by saying, 'Don't do it like that, but do it like this.' We are reminded, though, of the apocryphal story of the marketing spiel for one lawyer being 'We think "can't" is a misspelling of "can"'. Sometimes 'can't' is the right response. The in-house lawyers that Nelson and Nielsen interviewed indicated that, if they were faced with a serious ethical dilemma, they would do whatever was necessary to stop the deal going ahead: 'in a John Grisham-like tale of corporate intrigue, they would know how to get help.'[26] Yet Nelson and Nielsen sensed a reluctance to say 'No'. Rostain has a different, more positive view, although based on only 10 interviews in a pilot study of General Counsel in Fortune 1000 companies. Her interviewees 'articulated a robust account of their jurisdiction over questions of legal risk', and spoke 'with one voice' about their gatekeeping functions.[27] Rostain was confident that her lawyers were 'team players and cops',[28] who treated, and reacted, to different risks differently (some risks were not matters for the legal team and instead were left to business managers to decide on).

WHO SAYS 'NO' (AND WHEN AND HOW)?

The different emphases of Rostain and Nelson and Nielsen's analyses suggest the contextual sensitivities regarding who will say 'No', and when and how 'No' gets said. In the US, the Sarbanes-Oxley Act (SOX) may have strengthened the hand of those who say 'No' by including provisions for reporting wrongdoing within the company hierarchy to the board. The influence of SOX is seen in Rostain's study and is also central to work on in-house lawyers by Kim,[29] and that of Nicholson.[30] Kim argues that:

> In the long run, gatekeeping actually serves the legal profession's self-interest because lawyers are valuable to their clients to the extent, but only to the extent, that they

---

[26] ibid, 471.
[27] Rostain, 'Age of Compliance' (n 8) 473–74.
[28] ibid, 475.
[29] Sung Hui Kim, 'Naked Self-Interest? Why the Legal Profession Resists Gatekeeping' (2011) 63 *Florida Law Review* 129.
[30] Lisa H Nicholson, 'SarbOx 307's Impact on Subordinate In-House Counsel: Between a Rock and a Hard Place' (2004) *Michigan State Law Review* 559, 561.

can be trusted by constituents and third parties not to game the system in a way that damages the entity, the integrity of the capital markets, and the legal framework.[31]

In simple terms, when we asked our in-house survey respondents whether they are willing to say 'No', almost all recognise that they ought to do so. Ninety-seven per cent of our survey respondents agreed that insisting something cannot be done within the law is sometimes necessary (2 per cent disagreed). Eighty-eight per cent agreed that they might do more than just refuse to act if their organisation insisted on an illegal course of action (5 per cent disagreed).[32] Conversely, a significant minority, 9 per cent of our respondents, agreed that saying 'No' to the organisation is to be avoided, even when there is no legally acceptable alternative to suggest (86 per cent disagreed). This is an important piece of data: almost one in ten of those in-house lawyers we surveyed indicated an unwillingness to step up and advise against acts where they do not have the comfort of being able to advise on a legal Plan B. Recall, from the discussion in the previous chapter on ethical pressure, how about 15 per cent of our survey respondents agreed or strongly agreed that they were asked to advise on things that made them uncomfortable ethically (and where about a further third were agreeing somewhat with this proposition). Just over 10 per cent suggested that their organisation took a different view on whether and/or how to uphold the rule of law (about a quarter agreed at least somewhat with this). Around about 10 per cent of our respondents were asked to advise on ethically or legally debatable actions frequently or very frequently; and about 40 per cent were asked to so advise at least sometimes. Putting these two parts of our data together, a significant minority of our survey participants are routinely asked to advise on ethically or legally debatable actions and a significant minority would be unwilling to step up and say 'No'. Importantly, also about half agreed that action was sometimes taken against legal advice on important matters.

We were interested to explore with our interviewees how saying 'No' occurred. What became clear was a series of interplays between the in-house lawyer and the person inside the client organisation seeking advice which would lead to 'soft noes', 'hard noes', and various forms of 'No, buts' It was evident that, for most in-house lawyers that we interviewed, saying various forms of low-level or simple 'No' to something the business wanted to do was a common part of their professional lives.

> I And how often are you saying to the business, 'Look, you just can't do this. I'm saying no.' Is that something that happens frequently?
>
> R Daily.

---

[31] Kim (n 29) 160.
[32] We see this as implying escalation of the problem within the organisation and/or resignation, but it might also include whistleblowing or other responses.

> I And then it's a game of push-back, where they say, 'Actually could we do it like this?' Or are you saying, 'No, you can't do it like this but you can do it like this instead'?
>
> R Yeah, so we try and provide options, and I think that's a key thing to do, as counsel, is providing options ...
>
> I And how often are you just saying an absolute 'No, this can't be done and there aren't any other options or any other ways of doing it'?
>
> R I would say the maximum, maybe about once a month, but that's normally about something which is very cut and dried, like export to Iran or something like that. [IHL47]

It was the hard 'No' that was a rare thing:

> There are always times in your career – I think it would be unusual if an in-house lawyer didn't find themselves some time in their career where they are being pressurised to give advice on something they don't agree with – I would say I've only once in my career absolutely refused to do it. Most of the rest, even if I've had difficult conversations, ultimately people have come round to my way of thinking when I've gone through why I think it's not the right thing for the organisation to do long term. [IHL31]

Indeed, a common concern was about using 'No' selectively and wisely:

> It's important to know when to say 'No'. You want to avoid the legal department being the 'Department of No'. [IHL33]

Avoiding becoming the 'Department of No' was important so that those with problems in the organisation would come to legal for support, and because 'otherwise you just become the dog that always barks and after a while people ignore the dog' [IHL41]. As such, hard (or absolute) noes were to be used selectively: 'if you use that, not a veto, but that power [to say no] too often, it loses some potency' [IHL36]. The extent to which the person receiving the in-house lawyer's advice would accept or reject a 'No' depended on various factors: the 'relationship with the person' [IHL34]; explanatory legitimacy (that is, whether 'whoever it is you're saying no to understands why you're saying no' [IHL43]); a clear demonstration of helpful intentions, through 'trying to come up with alternative suggestions' [IHL49]; and (and perhaps most importantly for our interviewees) 'picking the right fights' [IHL48]. One very experienced General Counsel said that she would store up 'brownie points' to be used when she had 'nasty' and unpleasant, but necessary, jobs to perform (telling the business things they perhaps did not want to hear) [IHL35]. This was a relatively common strategy:

> I suppose the phrase I say to my team is 'you pick your battles' and the other cliché is 'keep your powder dry' so that you know when you've got something that is of such importance or if there is something that you genuinely feel you shouldn't be doing for whatever reasons then having that ability to actually say a hard 'No', really you can't do that. If you've got a reputation or a past record of just being the person who

says 'No' to everything then you lose credibility whereas one of the things my digital director said the other day in a meeting, which was quite flattering, he said, 'The thing I like about you, is that if you say "No" I know you mean it.' And that comes again from this relationship, from being there and trying to be helpful. [IHL51]

I guess it's the trusted advisor role that … you know, I've been able to build up. Whereas, you know, if I … if I then look the … you know, the head of the business in the eye and say, 'Look, no ifs, no buts, we need to do this', that is … that is accepted. [IHL28]

In-house lawyers, perhaps like all other senior management, have a 'credit bank' with their peers which gets topped up by being 'helpful' and which gets eroded when 'difficult' decisions or requests are made. Consequently, many in-house lawyers are outcomes-focused: if you can get to the legally preferable outcome because others have non-legal reasons for wanting that outcome too then, by catalysing and capitalising on this, it means that you get the right outcome and more credit in your credit bank by being perceived as commercially aware. This means that, on the rare occasions that there is no other way to achieve the legally right outcome, then those in the organisation will accept the hard (and absolute) 'No' offered up by the in-house lawyer.

Another perspective was that saying 'No' was not only difficult in and of itself, but it was a process which required political coalition-building within the business.

I've never been unfortunate enough to work for a CEO who, when confronted with a stark line like that, hasn't said, 'Okay fair enough.' If, for example, that hadn't happened in that situation, I would've had to resign. You really hope it doesn't come to that. I think the next step after that is you go to the rest of the board, go to the chairman, try and get it dealt with that way and actually it's not quite as simple as that because in a situation where you think you're going to need to apply pressure to somebody who's powerful like a CEO, the reality is actually the way you go about doing it is building a coalition for your viewpoint before you reach the line, right? I wouldn't want to be pulling a ripcord on my CEO just with no warning. I just don't think that's the way to build a relationship which is going to survive. [IHL21]

We can see then that saying 'No' was not impossible, but it was seen as a last resort, and many of our interviewees saw it as a mark of their skill that they avoided a situation where the need to do so arose. What we see is that saying 'No' is part and parcel of how the in-house lawyer is used and perceived by the organisation, and part and parcel of the how the relationship between the in-house lawyer and the rest of the organisation plays out. It is a bargaining chip in the tournament of influence. Lawyers need the power of 'No', but they also need to use it judiciously. A number of the interviewees were firm (very firm) on the importance of the in-house lawyer sometimes playing 'the bad cop' [IHL41] with their employers:

They're not going to respect you if you don't say no occasionally … I mean the lawyers who are disliked are not the lawyers who say, 'Actually, we shouldn't kill people,' they're the lawyers who go, 'Well, I'm going to give you six pages of closely written advice and I'm not going to tell you what I think or take any responsibility for it, but I am going to make it all down to you and you've got to understand it.' [IHL35]

Indeed, for a (small) number of interviewees, challenging the organisation was *the* reason organisations had in-house lawyers:

> Like without that we're just a complete waste of space and of time and desks and computers. We're just an overhead. We've got no role unless people are challenging the decisions of the business ... Because I think sometimes the great in-house lawyers and people I've really sought counsel from and seen as mentors over the years, are the people who are counsel in the most general sense of the word. And they're used as a sounding board before anybody does anything crazy. That's where you really want everybody to get to. And without that, and some in-house lawyers do this very successfully, you just say yes to everything and the business love you, you get great feedback at the end of the year. But really I'm much more interested in the circumstances in which people say 'No'. And if people never say 'No' then that's not right either. [IHL30]

An interesting complication is one of internal jurisdiction. It is possible to avoid saying 'No' by seeing a question as outside one's domain, although some saw the role of in-house lawyers in looking across such boundaries:

> I mean, one of the dangers of ... a large corporation is that people are used to sort of operating in very defined swim lanes. And, you know, that becomes habitual over time and people don't question it particularly ... a lot of my role in executive committee meetings would be to ask questions. Just to ask people if they've thought about this, if they've thought about that. And that's where I add in the most value, both from a legal perspective and commercially. [IHL27]

For these interviewees, in-house lawyers, 'instead of being facilitators ... become challengers' [IHL13], providing 'that voice and challenge' [IHL14].

In this way we can start to see how it is not just a willingness to say 'No' that is important. Other things matter, like a willingness to be proactive, to look beyond the way a problem presents itself. There are also issues of timing. Part of the tension in when and where and how to say 'No' also went to how those in the organisation outside of the legal team viewed and used their in-house lawyers. If the approach was one where 'we [the legal team] paper decisions that have already been made ... a common business view' [IHL26] (where lawyers were only brought in at the end of a process), then saying 'No' had greater importance (and difficulty) than a 'No' earlier on in the scheme of things.

> Because I think one of the problems we've had in the past is they've seen us very much as problem resolvers rather than the people who can help them avoid those problems in the first place. So once there is a problem they'll come to us and expect us to fix it but they won't necessarily engage with us in strategy conversations to avoid it happening in the first place. [IHL49]

> Lawyers find themselves arguing against decisions that have already been made, which is a losing battle and it's one of the reasons why people don't like lawyers. [IHL3]

This interviewee suggested that getting involved early on in decision-making meant he was less likely to say 'No' to what the deal team wanted to do:

> Where the tension arises is if someone has made quite a quick decision or an opportunity has presented itself and they want to take advantage, and you haven't been able to go through that process. So you're almost doing it backwards. They've already made the decision and you're then having to go back and fill in the gaps and advise them on how they might approach it differently. If time is a factor it can be quite difficult because they just want to get on with the business. So that tends to be when you get into those tensions. [IHL34]

In terms of getting 'No' taken seriously, everyone spoke about escalation of one form or another. There were situations in which the in-house lawyer would need to refer the advice to someone else in the organisation (above the head of the person asking for the advice); and situations in which those seeking advice attempted 'forum shopping' (either seeking out another lawyer to run the same issue past, or going above the head of the lawyer first asked). Escalation was rare, but like saying 'No', could be hard or soft:

> In terms of hard escalation, you know, probably, you know, probably maybe five times. But in terms of a sort of a soft escalation, you know, many multiples of that. I think a lot of it comes down to sort of how you do it. But ultimately, you know, things do fall off the chain. And it's about, you know, sort of making sure that happens in an appropriate way at an appropriate time. But I don't believe in sort of giving people ultimatums particularly. I think there are more effective ways to escalate and get the outcome you need. [IHL4]

Escalation was sometimes a means of effectively saying 'No' without actually saying 'No':

> I've had experience of people – you know, of people pushing the boundaries but I've never really felt that much pressure as a consequence because, you know, there's – you can push so far and then you stop. And I've not been in a position where I've ever been asked to push further than I'm comfortable with and if I'm uncomfortable with it, it stops and I escalate it to my boss or their boss and it usually stops that way. [IHL49]

For the in-house lawyer who acts as too much of a gatekeeper, there is the risk that those inside the organisation looking for legal advice may go elsewhere (to another in-house lawyer) for the answer they want. This is known as 'forum shopping':

> this absolutely gets my goat ... they don't like the answer that I've given and that's when they go and try and get another answer from somebody else, another lawyer from a different region, and they say, 'If [Country X] is doing it, why can't EMEA do it? Latin America is doing it, why can't EMEA do it?' In those situations I really, really want to punch them! It's just undermining of my people and it shows lack of respect of those channels. By all means talk about, 'Can we explore what other regions do and can we actually standardise?' by all means, but don't go behind my back. [IHL47]

As such, getting a 'No' can be avoided by the organisation through 'an attempt to re-litigate it ... to challenge the advice, challenge the conclusion if it's an unfavourable outcome' [IHL30]. Such shopping around for internal legal advice seemed relatively common in the bigger organisations our interviewees often hailed from.

A number of the interviewees had left previous employers because of concerns over how those organisations had been run or what those organisations proposed to do. This interviewee had left a job because she felt no one was taking her legal advice 'seriously':

> It was closer to the breaking the law end than it was just the 'I wouldn't do that if I were you' type stuff, where I eventually got to the point where I reckoned that there were arguably quite significant potential offences that may be being committed. [IHL48]

She was not alone in having resigned because of such concerns. There seems to come a point (often expressed as a clash between personal values and the employer's direction of travel) when enough is enough:

> I think the biggest question, the biggest issue that lawyers will have in an in house environment is to know what to do if your advice, you know, isn't heard. You know? What do you do with that? What is the correct chain of command? Ultimately I think, you know, you need to be prepared to resign. Which is, you know, something I did in the past. Because I didn't ... from a corporate governance perspective, I didn't like the direction of travel. But ultimately along the way you find a sort of ... you're trying to influence and counsel your client and get the right outcome, the ethical outcome, but, you know, the real judgement call is when is it enough? When is enough enough? [IHL27]

One way of interpreting that view is that even the neutral adviser role had broken down. Sometimes more specific, tangible attempts to influence the substance of legal advice were discussed:

> I was asked by [the CEO] to give him particular advice in relation to [Employee Y's] contract when [the CEO] and [Employee Y] fell out. He wanted me to say legally he was required to pay this amount of money by way of compensation; and I refused to give him that advice because it was wrong. I was prepared to give him the advice that legally he had the powers to do so if he wanted to do it; but I was not prepared to tell him he had to do it. And that caused a pretty big barney. But at the end of the day those are some of the things, I was very clear, I was mature enough in my career at that stage to know that my own personal values and my own personal credibility with my peers was actually more important than whether I fell out with [the CEO] or not. [IHL8]

Ultimately, resignation may be the last weapon in an in-houser's armoury when seeking to deal with ethical problems that were not being taken seriously. As with saying 'No', this was seen as something which needed handling with care and without unnecessarily damaging relationships or one's future employability:

> I suppose there are two ways to look at that: either you want to do it as part of blackmail and say, I'm going to resign if you do this, in the hope that I don't want to lose

you so I'm not going to do it. Or actually I think it's more about if you believe that you're so conflicted or your role is being so pushed to one side that you've got no voice in the business then I guess I'd not be happy to stay here so I probably would resign. I think actually the way that the regulators operate their approved persons regime there are a number of people around the business responsible for business activity that are also approved persons, so have accountability to the regulator, that actually it's not about me; it's me pointing out to them that they run their own risk that the regulator will be critical of their activities because it's outside of appetite or outside of regulatory expectations. And that usually does the trick. [Compliance 3]

Others found it difficult to comprehend how they would behave if faced with a black and white case of their saying 'No' being ignored by their employers:

I can't – I've never known – and I've known some really awful people in my time but I don't think I've ever known somebody who would tell me that I had to sign something off that I didn't agree with. They would just say, 'Fine, we'll do it without you signing it off.' And then – and then you get to the point of well should I be actively trying to prevent this? I'm genuinely not sure what I would do because I can tell you – I could sit here and tell you in the comfort of my office chair – yeah, of course I'd try and prevent it, like go to the top, I'd whistle-blow. I actually have no idea whether I would or not because it would depend. I'm sure that you take all sorts of things into account, including your financial circumstances and the job market and all of those other things before you would do something like that I am sure. [IHL49]

GETTING COMFORTABLE

We have averted to the fact that saying 'No' to a particular 'plan' is located in a series of previous and future requests for advice or legal assistance; that such is a central part of a broader positioning for influence in the organisation. What else influenced any individual decision to consider saying 'No', or to stop pushing a particular line of (unwelcome) advice, or to decide that the 'risk' is something for the business (and not legal) to decide, make a decision on or take forward? A number of interviewees spoke of being 'lucky', of working in organisations where such pinch points did not occur, or were very uncommon.

One interviewee discussed a feeling of occasional 'bullying' of in-house lawyers [IHL24]. We asked for an example of how this manifested and how that in-house lawyer knew when to stop pushing back against a course of conduct he thought was inadvisable. It provides an interesting counterpoint to refined discussions about willingness to say 'No', and independence:

R Excuse the vernacular but 'I don't care, just fucking do it.' Quote, unquote – to me.

I And at what point do you, you know … do you think you would have the backbone to push back? At what point do you have to stop pushing?

R When you – when you are confident the person making the statement has authority to make the – to take the risk that you are highlighting and you have appropriately

> appraised them of that risk and you do not feel that it is going to kill the company in the process. [IHL24]

Here, saying 'No' was a transfer of risk, rather than a step towards illegality. The in-house lawyer's view is that it is not necessary to go further. The lawyer has advised and the client has decided to reject that advice. In a number of interviews, we saw how this idea of the neutral adviser ultimately trumped independence and ethical orientations for some of our interviewees. We discussed these orientations in Chapters 1 and 2 and develop them further in Chapters 7 and 8. These interviewees clearly articulated that their employer organisation, and not the in-house lawyer, was the decision-maker such that, as long as their legal advice had been given (and often appropriately documented), then the organisation could ignore that advice and decide to take the alternate course of conduct:

> But that's the point then when we'd say okay, you've got my advice, it's down to you, that's what you're paid for, you take the executive decision … [IHL44]

> … in the role of General Counsel you don't have the power to say, 'No you can't do it.' You have the power to say, 'We shouldn't do this. We mustn't do this' but ultimately I think the board and generally the chief executive will make a call on whether or not they do it and then as a General Counsel you have to take your own view of, 'Well where do I stand on this?' [IHL17]

The 'Where do I stand?' question reflected a significant number of interviewees who referred to the decisions on legal risk matters being taken which those interviewees were, or might be, uncomfortable with. Interestingly, those interviewees who tended to say that there were not ethical problems in the work they did *also* tended to portray advice in binary terms: either something was lawful or not. In this way, advice clarified and made plain the law, and clients then decided to act. This was so even though, in characterising the matter as one of 'accepting some risk', our in-housers are praying in aid a sense of uncertainty rather than certain illegality.

An interesting question is the extent to which that ambiguity can be rationalised after the event, or used to stretch the envelope of what is permissible under law. Heineman is clear that where the law is clear, it cannot be broken and legal obligations cannot be ignored as some kind of cost benefit calculation.[33] Many of our interviewees did not seem to agree. Several of our interviewees talked about the concept of 'comfort' and, as we will see in Chapter 6, were rather vague about the red lines which they would not cross. Rarer, but important, was a more explicit acknowledgement of ambiguity as an explicit deviation from what is 'really' permitted:

> you're almost never [at] the absolute standard and the decisions are always a bit grey because nothing is ever entirely clear. The lawyer's job is to always measure

---

[33] Ben W Heineman Jr, *The Inside Counsel Revolution: Resolving the Partner-Guardian Tension* (Ankerwycke, 2016).

back to the absolute standard and make a decision: so are we three centimetres, five centimetres, ten centimetres from the absolute standard... [IHL35]

In this example, the in-houser was seen as triangulating between the requirements of the law (ambiguous but 'absolute') and the pragmatism (or relativism) of their organisation:

> the business will normally be measuring from a comparative standard, 'We're only two centimetres from our competitors, we're only two centimetres worse, or the historic standard, we're only three centimetres worse than last month.' [IHL12]

Here, IHL12 is suggesting deviance from a legal standard is permitted by the ambiguity of the law (or tolerated by the practice of any particular regulator), but there comes a point at which deviance shifts from tolerable to improper. The question shifts from 'how does one comply?' to 'how much does one tolerate?', and may shift further to 'how much can one get away with?' Business imperatives may push towards permitting a behaviour, but the in-house lawyer's role is to look more objectively or independently than the business does at what the law says about this. This is part and parcel of the lawyer's professional commitment to the rule of law and to protecting their own independence. IHL14 gave another hypothetical example:

> there's definitely a judgement call to be made ... [if] it's a criminal offence in Outer Mongolia ... the answer's always going to be no. But if it's, 'The regulation says this in Outer Mongolia and everyone does it and we're pretty sure they don't enforce it,' there will be times when I've had to get comfortable with that risk and it's an informed risk that we'll take, but it can easily stray into the boundaries of something that I don't feel comfortable with and I think the key as a good General Counsel is if you don't feel comfortable with something you have to articulate that, you don't just sit back and get carried along with it. That's your job, is to articulate where you think something just doesn't smell right.' [IHL14]

Here we see explicitly, albeit with a hypothetical case, that the lawyer sees that they do, or may have to, get comfortable with something explicitly in breach of law, or be willing to resist that breach in terms the business understands and accepts. Put another way, unlawfulness alone may not be enough. This appears to be the case even where the law is clear. In this way comfort with risk involves a hypothetical weakening of law's legitimacy. This may be associated with calling some law mere 'regulation' (albeit sanctions may attach) in contradistinction to law that is 'properly' criminal. One does not have to strain hard to imagine a newspaper front page reframing this decision as a deliberate decision to flout the law. Where then, in this situation, is the independent legal counsel that the SRA Handbook (and associated case law) requires of a lawyer?

Getting 'comfortable' was also contextualised within the broader role of in-house lawyer as business advisor. Each piece of advice was part of a broader series of interactions where the in-housers worked to persuade their colleagues of their utility, relevance and commitment to their employer. Thus the tournament of influence involved negatives (not saying 'No' too often) and positives (demonstrating 'value'). One of the terrors of in-house lawyers was being perceived as 'difficult', and colleagues not then coming to them for advice when they ought. But our in-housers also needed to show they were thinking commercially in the way they delivered advice and managed their legal function. As we shall see in the following two chapters, legal risk management is one way of aligning with a strategic-commercial approach in an organisation. In response to this kind of dynamic, IHL12 suggested a social model of independence which could be eroded across a series of decisions rather than being (usually) a matter to be considered for one decision in isolation. Comfort implicated an overall judgement on one's status and credibility:

> You've got a, 'Can I endorse this if the business has taken a formal decision about the level of risk, even if I'm very uncomfortable? Yes or no?' 'If no, if the business decides against me, my protest is on the file,[34] can I live with this in the organisation and deal with the consequences? Yes/no.' And then the third one is, 'If I have the first two [situations occurring] regularly recently, is my credibility as a counsel and advisor prejudiced? Yes/no.' [IHL12]

CONCLUSION

Independence is a regulatory objective under the Legal Services Act 2007,[35] and required of all 'authorised persons [who] should act with independence and integrity'.[36] The Legal Services Board (the overarching regulator of legal services in England & Wales) emphasises it.[37] The Solicitors' Code of Conduct prohibits in-house solicitors, and private practitioners,[38] from allowing their independence to be compromised (Principle 3 of the Solicitors Regulation Authority Handbook). Academic writing on independence is voluminous.[39] Advising

---

[34] Interestingly, registering a position on file was something which some senior lawyers we spoke to explicitly deprecated as likely to be unhelpful and detrimental to their long term influence. Others were equally vocal that such a paper trail was both important and necessary, and something they encouraged in junior members of their team.

[35] s 1(1)(f) requires legal services regulators to, 'encourage[e] an independent, strong, diverse and effective legal profession.'

[36] s 1(3)(a). The 'Joint Committee on the Draft Legal Services Bill' was responsible for the inclusion of the word 'independent' into the LSA. In its first report, the Committee commented at para 119: 'We heard much evidence on the need for independence – the independence of the legal profession from Government, the independence of the regulatory framework from the influence of the regulated professions and the independence of the legal profession from market or economic pressures' – see www.publications.parliament.uk/pa/jt/jtlegal.htm, accessed 18 April 2018.

[37] LSB, 'The Regulatory Objectives – Legal Services Act 2007' (undated) 11, available at www.legalservicesboard.org.uk/news_publications/publications/pdf/regulatory_objectives.pdf, accessed 18 April 2018.

[38] The SRA's Handbook applies, in certain contexts, somewhat different to in-house lawyers. For a review of these differences, see www.slaughterandmay.com/media/2445501/srahandbook2011howdoesitapplytoin-houselawyers.pdf, accessed 18 April 2018.

[39] See, for example, Bruce A Green, 'Lawyers' Professional Independence: Overrated or Undervalued' (2013) 46(3) *Akron Law Review* 599; and Eleanor W Myers, 'Examining Independence and Loyalty' (1999) 72(4) *Temple Law Review* 857.

'independently' can be seen as essential to organisational legality, with in-house lawyers regulating the organisation to ensure its actions are *intra vires*; as requiring (some) control over the conditions of work to protect standards of quality; and as an important freedom from improper interference by the State and its regulators.[40] The latter does not mean clients are sovereign,[41] because 'client capture',[42] or power imbalances,[43] can render lawyers unable 'to provide the advice their profession requires of them.'[44] For some, this may require more refraining from advising clients 'to break laws or otherwise behave unethically.'[45]

Such debates begin to illuminate the question: what are the standards expected of in-house lawyers? Yet few cases in England & Wales speak to, or comment on, the concept of lawyer independence.[46] And none of these cases speaks specifically to independence in the context of in-house lawyering. Despite this lack of specificity, the rulings in the cases suggest lawyer independence comprises at least four facets: first, being prepared to say 'No' to a client;[47] second, an acceptance that independence may, in some situations, mean taking decisions that have negative financial consequences for the solicitor; third, a need for a solicitor to avoid becoming overly reliant or overly close to any given client;[48] and, finally, a recognition that, in litigation, individual lawyers are professionally responsible for their the handling of cases (ie they cannot simply rely on acting in accordance with the client's instructions to justify questionable tactics).[49] On the third

---

[40] Robert Gordon, 'The Independence of Lawyers' (Yale Law School Faculty Scholarship Series Paper 1361, 1988).

[41] Kevin T Leicht and Mary L Fennell, *Professional Work: A Sociological Approach* (Blackwell, 2001) 105–06.

[42] Ronit Dinovitzer, Hugh Gunz and Sally Gunz, 'Unpacking Client Capture: Evidence from Corporate Law Firms' (2014) 1 *Journal of Professions and Organization* 99; Ronit Dinovitzer, Hugh Gunz and Sally Gunz, 'Reconsidering Lawyer Autonomy: The Nexus Between Firm, Lawyer, and Client in Large Commercial Practice' (2014) 51(3) *American Business Law Journal* 661.

[43] John Heinz, 'The Power of Lawyers' (1982) 17 *Georgia Law Review* 981.

[44] Dinovitzer, Gunz and Gunz, 'Unpacking Client Capture' (n 42) 100.

[45] ibid.

[46] *In the matter of Paul Francis Simms*, Lawyers Disciplinary Tribunal, 2 February 2004; *SRA v Brian Laurence Miller and David Joel Gore*, SDT Case Case No 10619-2010, 3 October 2011; *In the matter of David Peter Barber and Others*, SDT Case 9698-2007, 21 July 2009; *SRA v Tax and Legal Consultancy Limited*, SDT Case No 10722-2011, 11 October 2011; *Reed v George Marriott* [2009] EWHC 1183 (Admin); *Crown Dilmun v Sutton* [2004] 1 BCLC 468.

[47] This facet is by no means a modern phenomenon. In the 1960s Talcott Parsons argued that lawyers' 'function in relation to clients is by no means only to "give them what they want" but often to resist their pressures and get them to realise some of the hard facts of their situations, not only with reference to what they can, even with clever legal help, expect to "get away with" but with reference to what the law will permit them to do.' See Talcott Parsons, 'A Sociologist Looks at the Legal Profession' in Talcott Parsons (ed) *Essays in Sociological Theory* (Free Press, 1964).

[48] We accept that 'overly' may not be a particularly helpful term, but the case law does not allow for further, more specific delineation in this regard. In their work in this area, Dinovitzer, Gunz and Gunz ('Reconsidering Lawyer Autonomy' (n 42) 697) comment that, 'there exists the risk that the relationship between lawyer and corporate counsel might become of sufficient comfort or familiarity as to detract from the appropriate level of professional autonomy or skepticism on the part of lawyer'. This may be a better, and more nuanced, way of understanding closeness.

[49] *R v Farooqi & Ors* [2013] EWCA (Crim) 1649.

point, it might be said that, having but one employer, this aspect cannot apply to the in-house community. However, an alternative is to see this as putting an obligation on in-house lawyers to manage more carefully for independence given the risks of having a single employer/client: to ensure they do not forget or avoid their professional obligations. This is consistent with the SRA's recognition that the clients of large law firms pose specific risks to independence, such that they, 'must resist client pressure which may adversely compromise their professional independence.'[50] Only belatedly does the SRA add, though, that, 'Maintaining independence is also relevant to in-house lawyers, who may come under pressure from their employers.'[51]

The fourth point from the case law on independence is a salutary reminder that lawyers cannot always fall back on the nostrum that a lawyer advises and the client decides (what we describe as a neutral advisor approach): sometimes the lawyer decides or shares in the decision and cannot distance themselves from it. In this sense, they have independent professional agency recognised by the courts.

The willingness to say 'No', and the corollary need to pay a potential price for saying 'No' (in performance appraisals that then go badly; by getting fired or feeling the need to resign) is, in theory not controversial: it is recognised by our interviewees as coming with the territory. Yet there is a complexity to how independence is understood and operationalised in-house. Independence is as much a process, a series of events, as it is a test for individual decisions. Independence is not a binary, and yet it is seen as a judgement call. It does not exist or not exist, but operates along a continuum and may be found to be weaker or stronger, in the same person, at different times and in different contexts. It relates to the positioning of the in-house lawyer in the organisation and the need to work for influence.

For some (albeit a minority of our interviewees), independence was at the heart of how they conceived of their roles: 'I'm a lawyer first and foremost … that does, by its very nature, create a conflict' [IHL54]. Others accepted that 'you start to get a bit blind after a time' [IHL38]. Insofar as professional independence is concerned with the ability of a lawyer to stand back, properly serving the client's interests by considering independently (of self-serving or client-serving rationalisations) what the rule of law and the administration of justice really demands, then we have seen in this chapter that such standing back may be easier said than done. This is true for some, probably many, and perhaps most, in-house lawyers. Being employed, paid and otherwise rewarded by the organisation create incentives for in-house lawyers to align themselves with the organisation, rather than employing independent judgement.

---

[50] SRA, 'Risk Outlook 2014/2015' (Solicitors Regulation Authority 2015). See further Coe and Vaughan (n 15).
[51] SRA, ibid.

Our interviewees recognised themselves as sometimes having, 'cognitive biases and bias blind spots which can impede' the lawyer's independent judgment.[52]

Equally, our interviewees often made subtle and not naïve claims to professional independence. In Chapter 7 we examine the strength of the independence orientation relative to the other orientations we can see at work in the interviews. The idea that the lawyer advises and the client decides provides an alternative and legitimate (but also independence-weakening) escape route for in-house lawyers faced with challenges to their view of the law. It may explain why organisations sometimes take decisions that are at odds with the in-house lawyer's view of the law or the ethicality of the situation, and why in-house lawyers felt the pressure we discussed in Chapter 3. Thinking of oneself as a mere advisor may also be how in-house lawyers reconcile independence with continued service. Certainly, those we talked to understood professional independence as (sometimes) in tension with their need to serve, and be seen to serve, the business.

Conversely, professional independence can be reinforced by the organisation or by lawyer regulation; sometimes respondents reported a deliberate attempt to align the professional claim to independence with a leadership desire to do, and be seen to do, the right thing within their businesses. Independence, its importance, and how it manifests is part of a complex series of interactions between the in-house lawyer and their employer organisation. Many of our in-house lawyers recognised that how they provided advice and how the advice was used was contingent on a number of factors: how the legal team was perceived; the relationship between the lawyer and the person seeking advice; the point at which legal had been involved in the decision making process etc.

Issues of objectivity and independence are most clearly raised in the context of in-housers being very sensitive to their place in the corporate network of influence. That sensitivity sometimes involves a negotiation between the in-house lawyer's view of what is lawful and right, and their view of what is tolerable. When it becomes intolerable, then the lawyer must say 'No' or resign. Several had resigned in the past. Other research echoes our work which shows a range of responses to saying 'No'. Some say legal constraints are treated simply as a fact of life; others think, 'it's a no-no to say no'.[53] We would add an important emphasis: the *dominant* position for in-house lawyers is to work hard to avoid conflict with the organisation; only to say 'No' judiciously, and to defer to the organisation on the acceptability of risk. Indeed, a stated willingness to say 'No' may be a very soft commitment to legality. We disagree with Rostain's more optimistic reading of GCs' 'capacity to stop deals that they believed posed significant legal risks to the company'.[54] We do so for two reasons: one is that some of those we surveyed and spoke to plainly had a weak or non-existent willingness to say 'No'. The second reason is that it is the interpretation of what

---

[52] Jenoff (n 20) 751.
[53] Nelson and Nielsen (n 24) 471.
[54] Rostain, 'Age of Compliance' (n 8) 473–74.

is significant legal risk in Rostain's work quote that is more important than a professed willingness to say 'No'.

Perhaps as importantly, saying 'No' is only the tip of an iceberg, a continuum of context-specific responses to risk, and one requiring significant effort as well as internal human capital. An in-house lawyer may need to be both well-placed in the tournament of influence, but also resourceful and willing to organise alliances within the organisation, before they can say 'No'. 'No' is both decided and negotiated. It is also avoidable. That avoidance by in-house lawyers may be pragmatic – because certain legal risks are tolerable or because bigger priorities lurk, requiring the spending of political capital in the tournament of influence – or it may be for want of courage. In evidencing a cohort of in-house lawyers who said they would not say 'No' *even where no legal alternative presented itself*, we demonstrate that the saying of 'No' is both a problem for many, and an acute problem for some, and also that it is more than a decision or an event, but a set of processes within a network. Each piece of advice, each 'Yes', each 'No', each 'Maybe', was part of a broader series of interactions where the lawyers worked to persuade their colleagues of their utility, relevance and commitment to the organisation.

We are going to underline the importance of positioning with one last, long quotation. It sums up, we think rather well, the tournament of influence we have been talking about in this chapter, but also the need for an in-house lawyer to stand up and ask hard questions of their employer when the occasion calls for it:

> To put it rather broadly, you win people over by being sensible, by making money for the company, by making good calls, by negotiating well, by being a really good ally on commercial projects, by making things happen, by going away and saying, 'Yes, that's a horrible messy thing and I'll sort it out for you.' And then, when you're in the Board and you're doing the unpopular thing, because let's face it, when it's a horrible, nasty thing that's gone a bit wrong, if you like, the really horrible things that happen to companies tend to be things that people knew about but didn't confront, and the reason they didn't confront them was nobody had the moral courage to confront them. So it was easier just to stuff them under the carpet and keep them there. I'm willing to bet that people in Volkswagen, there were going to be a lot of people, not potentially the Board, not potentially even, I would guess, the general counsel, maybe, I don't know, but I bet people blew the whistle on that in the sort of gentle, pathetic way. And the general counsel's job is to go, 'Someone's making a fuss about that. I should find out what it is, and then, if it's a thing we should be looking at, I'll make sure we look at it.' And at that point, you are absolutely not going to win friends and influence people and they will say, 'For God's sake, why are you doing this? That's horrible, that's nasty, that's beastly and I don't want to know about it so just shut up.' And that's the point at which you use all the brownie points you've got by doing all the other things that they liked, and eventually, if it all works out, they may say, 'Actually, that was quite a good call, it's a good thing you did that.' But they may not, they may just go, 'Oh well, she's a bit difficult sometimes, but on the whole, she's quite useful to have around.' [IHL35]

The tournament of influence and pragmatism is reshaped here as a kind of quiet heroism. If it works, it can work well. Another interpretation is of independence rendered contingent not fundamental; it is but one idea at work within the tournament of influence, intermixed with the operational significance and social status of individual in-house lawyers. In this way, when in-housers become so uncomfortable with the organisation's ignoring of their advice, the concern may be for intrinsic values (such as justice) or it may be for extrinsic values ('How well am I thought of; how rewarding is my job?').

We do not think that independence is a trope for self-interested influence, but there is a danger that independence is a less useful concept if it is not allied with an intrinsic value. Professional rules are clear (lawyers must protect the rule of law and the administration of justice) and this provides an intrinsic value that in-house lawyers should be thinking about independently. Put another way, independence does not mean simply not being prone to influence, or being one's own person. It means independently and (insofar as it is possible) objectively assessing what the rule of law and the administration of justice really requires.

Our interviews suggest that the independence of in-house lawyers is routinely muted or muffled in the service of their organisations. Put another way, the organisation's agency, (in business, the commercial orientation), is always legitimate, but legal's influence has to be managed, protected, sometimes fought for. To an extent, this is inevitable, and pragmatic adaptation of law to business and business to law will have its benefits. Equally, pragmatism must operate within bounds. Independence, and in particular, independent consideration of what the rule of law and administration of justice requires, needs to have a significant influence on in-house lawyers. Whether such muted independence is a problem depends on how, when and where they draw their red lines. We turn to that issue now, in looking closely at legal risk and the logics that accompany it.

5
Competing Logics – A Look at Risk

WE HAVE SEEN in previous chapters how notions of independence and professionalism blend with notions of client centrism, being commercial, and also with organisational embeddedness. That organisational embeddedness works to make the in-house lawyer more relevant and useful to their employers but also, some worry, more compromised in terms of their ability to practise professionally, with suitable regard for the rule of law and for regulatory expectations. Yet theories of ethical partnership or of hybrid professionalism suggest that this process of compromise might be an efficient, effective, even virtuous, way of reconciling the needs of law with the needs of commerce, government and the other employers of in-house lawyers.

In our account to date, we have seen the ways in which the logics of professionalism and organisation are in tension. We have seen something of how individuals negotiate with others in their organisations, and how they seek to protect a notion of professionalism whilst doing so. Institutional theory suggests an intermediate tier of understanding, between individuals and their organisations, and intermediate logics which operate as guides for, and limits on, action.[1]

One such logic might be the logic of risk. We have certainly seen legal risk management grow as a phenomenon of interest in legal spheres. And the ability to engage in legal risk management provides one means by which senior in-house lawyers ascend the organisational hierarchy. As we will see, it is also a logic that draws on, or seeks to blend, different kinds of knowledge in the organisation to provide a decision-making and governance tool.

Legal risk management is also as an example of the ways in which professional logics are instantiated in the decision-making apparatus of organisations. We use it to examine how organisational imperatives, independence, and legality are manifest in more detailed and specific ways. We do so first by showing how organisational imperatives and the technical and professional skills of lawyers are used to construct the notion of legal risk management. In notions of risk appetite we see the balancing of commercial and organisational imperatives against more public-facing values. And in looking at how risk is defined and managed, we see instantiations of the legal role and the influence of in-house lawyers in their organisations.

---

[1] Patricia H Thornton, William Ocasio and Michael Lounsbury, *The Institutional Logics Perspective: A New Approach to Culture, Structure, and Process* (Oxford University Press, 2012).

This interplay between the professional and the organisational is rendered in more detail in a second, methodological sense. We draw on risk vignettes (case studies of specific, practical problems) to tease out how the in-house lawyers we interviewed would respond to concrete risk situations. This enables us to draw a richer picture of the different approaches to legal risk than the typical abstractions of independence and the willingness to say 'No'.

RISK AND RISK MANAGEMENT LOGICS: AN OVERVIEW

Let us begin by discussing briefly some contours of the concept of risk. Risk is typically defined as the likelihood of harm and the likely impact of that harm from a given hazard of set of hazards. Seen in negative terms, and associated with anxiety and undesirability,[2] Beck famously argued that risk went hand-in-hand with high technological innovation, scientific development, and the inability to fully know the dangers we face.[3] Risk is thus elided with uncertainty and randomness,[4] with rendering the future less uncertain whilst essentially unknown.[5] Equally, not taking risks itself poses risks. And progress often entails risk: faster travel, better health interventions, even better financial instruments, may all require the balancing of pros and cons, the weighing of risks and benefits, and the pondering of the known and unknown. Similarly, risk is now a core organising principle both of organisations and of governments; much, some argue all,[6] regulatory activity is being defined or reconstituted in terms of risk.

The nature and existence of a risk will depend on human behaviour, and the acceptability of risk is dependent upon cultural context.[7] One of the reasons some banks took significant risks with Iranian money was the perceived illegitimacy of US sanction regimes. *The News of the World* and *The Times* hacked phones and emails because they valued stories more than privacy. Car recall decisions may be read as business decisions even when human lives hang in the balance.[8] Risks may be difficult to compare or contrast: is the loss of a leg or personal bankruptcy more undesirable?[9] And whilst 'risk management' has

---

[2] Nikolas Rose, *Powers of Freedom* (Cambridge University Press, 1999) 160.
[3] Ulrich Beck, *Risk Society: Towards a New Modernity* (Sage, 1992).
[4] There are those who argue that true uncertainty is wholly separate from risk, as risk requires that the likelihood of harm be capable of assessment. This is a not a debate with which we need to concern ourselves here.
[5] Julia Black, 'The Role of Risk in Regulatory Processes' in Robert Baldwin, Martin Cave, and Martin Lodge (eds) *The Oxford Handbook of Regulation* (Oxford University Press, 2010) 317.
[6] Elizabeth Fisher, *Risk Regulation and Administrative Constitutionalism* (Hart Publishing, 2007).
[7] ibid 8.
[8] Dennis A Gioia, 'Pinto Fires and Personal Ethics: A Script Analysis of Missed Opportunities' (1992) 11(5) *Journal of Business Ethics* 379.
[9] Black (n 5) 309.

become largely synonymous with 'quantitative risk assessment', no approach to risk is purely scientific or numerical: rather, the quantification of risk goes hand-in-hand with values and preferences.[10] Certain risks are more amenable than others to statistical reduction and even theoretically 'measurable risks' may not in fact be capable of accurate measurement.[11] Challenges in linking cause and effect can also be significant. Despite this, a view that quantitative risk assessment is an objective, scientific approach to modelling the future prevails.

How organisations respond to and manage risk is becoming an important element of good governance.[12] The industry for risk management is now vast. Many organisations have a chief risk officer,[13] but do not agree on why they conduct enterprise risk management ('ERM'), or how wide the scope of that risk management should be.[14] Risk is 'important', but there are not shared meanings about what 'risk' is or how it should be dealt with. In spite of, or perhaps because of, this inherent uncertainty, a process-based approach to risk has emerged: a process of risk identification is followed by the processes of mitigation, reduction, and acceptance of risk. Communication and evaluation of the overall success of the process completes the cycle and begins a new one afresh. If risk is values-dependent, then who participates in that cycle of processes, what evidence is considered as relevant, and what decision rules are applied are vital.

Risk management is important too because it provides strategic focus. It enables, or purports to enable, managers to 'see' complex organisations and 'target' the risks that are revealed by focusing on the most 'material' risks.[15] In the tournament of influence that we have discussed so far, the ability to see and control legal risk is a key mechanism by which managerial attention, or managerial power, can be garnered. It is an opportunity that depends on 'the acquisition, analysis, and presentation of information' as a pre-condition of 'sound judgments about risk'.[16] It demands a process of prioritising and simplification that requires legal risk data in a form digestible by and intelligible to decision-makers without misleading them.[17] Dashboards, graphic and tabular presentations are *de* rigueur.[18]

We turn to the more detailed consideration of risk definition and management later in the chapter. Let us begin by looking at the concept that many

---

[10] Jenny Steele, *Risks and Legal Theory, Legal Theory Today* (Hart Publishing, 2004) 161.
[11] Giandomenico Majone, 'Foundations of Risk Regulation: Science, Decision Making, Policy Learning and Institutional Reform' (2010) 1 *European Journal of Risk Regulation 5*.
[12] Michael Power, *Organized Uncertainty* (Oxford University Press, 2007).
[13] Accenture, 'Risk Management for an Era of Greater Uncertainty' (Accenture Report, 2013).
[14] McKinsey, 'Enterprise-Risk-Management Practices: Where's the Evidence?: A Survey across Two European Industries' (McKinsey Working Papers on Risk, No 53, 2014).
[15] Geoffrey P Miller, *The Law of Governance, Risk Management and Compliance* (Wolters Kluwer Law & Business, 2014) 544.
[16] ibid 547.
[17] ibid 547.
[18] ibid 550.

in-house lawyers told us was a central mechanism governing how they saw their role. That concept was risk appetite.

RISK APPETITE

An ambitious part of organisational risk management involves an attempt to define a risk appetite for the whole organisation. Risk appetite is how the organisation conveys what risks are acceptable, or unacceptable, or what risks require more or less care in decision-making. Risk appetite can be a formal statement, or more likely a series of statements, and is typically regarded as being enterprise-wide and adopted at the highest corporate level by the board itself.[19] It reflects a core conceit of enterprise risk management: *some* risk appetite is necessary, because of 'the return that cannot be achieved without accepting a certain level of risk'.[20] And it reflects a corporate culture that, up to a point, welcomes risk: enterprise risk management is 'used in a positive sense, conveying an idea of progress.'[21]

Whilst the literature suggests risk appetite as something formal, when practitioners discuss risk appetite they may be discussing something formal or informal, articulated or unarticulated, operating business-wide or via smaller signals about risk from business units, individual teams, even individual employees. In some ways, when used informally, the concept of risk appetite acts as a synonym for culture, through which in-house lawyers subtly mark out an organisational conscience that lies beyond them and marks out a view of what is right or wrong, prohibited or acceptable, spoken and (importantly) unspoken.

As well as purporting to reduce or mitigate risk, risk management also normalises an increased acceptance of risk as both ubiquitous and 'manageable'. It raises interesting questions about the overall social value of risk management. McCormick notes evidence that, 'the adoption of risk management practices and institutional investment in the 1990s has increased, not reduced, volatility in financial markets.'[22] As traditional carriers of risk seek to hedge, offload or otherwise manage their risk, they may push risk into the shadows or onto those less able to understand and/or bear that risk. When in-house lawyers facilitate earnings management, or enforcement proofing, or de-risking, they may be making things worse rather than better. This system-wide sense that risk systems have effects beyond their intended purpose adds to the complexity of understanding and scrutinising risk, as do the psychological biases impacting on risk perception and decision-making (which we discuss below).

---

[19] ibid 551.
[20] ibid.
[21] ibid 538.
[22] Roger McCormick, *Legal Risk in the Financial Markets* (Oxford University Press, 2010) 19.

Risk Appetite: Defined and Undefined, Dependent or Independent

In our in-house interviewees' organisations, risk appetite was subject to varying levels of formal definition. IHL20's company did not have a defined appetite for legal risk, but:

> I obviously get my steer from the flow down that I get from the Group General Counsel and generally from the communication I get from the EC [Executive Committee], and I certainly see no indication that there's any willingness to change from where our current risk appetite is.

The indication is that risk appetite is known informally but not defined. How robust or predictable such an approach is must be open to question. Unarticulated assumptions and subjective assessments of risk may mask significant variation in decision-making. Others had similar broad-brush approaches: IHL21's company did not have a defined appetite for risk, but 'I would probably describe it as the same [as his own] and the company thinks of itself as a long term [business].' Others saw it as something discussed but not documented, a consensus arrived at between key individuals: 'It's ... you know it when you do it ... Probably me and the CFO and we also have a risk and audit department which is separate which also gets involved in those discussions.' [IHL22]

Some were beginning to move towards defined risk appetites where categories of legal risk were given different tolerances. Some, such as IHL11, had begun by defining some risks and moving towards a more comprehensive statement. Others rejected the idea that definition was possible or optimal, suggesting that risk appetites understated a desirable appetite for risk or became too general. Compliance1 stated of her company with over 80,000 employees:

> In a group of that size it's very difficult [to have a defined risk appetite]. The metrics for appetite would be that there wasn't any appetite to have certain things, so there would probably be no appetite for regulatory intervention or inquiry, but the reality is you want to get away from that.[23]

A related implication was that, unless identifiable risk was forbidden, variation in decision-making was inevitable. We can also see here how a fixed risk appetite may lead to defining what is tolerable or intolerable in ways which may lead to less room for manoeuvre 'on the ground'. IHL10 emphasised the process as one of control, but a process which is only partially successful: 'business is constantly changing and I think generally the firm has a view of itself as risk averse. There are pockets that push against that.'

Those that took explicit risk appetites more seriously saw them as a documented policy that required work to support dissemination, understanding, and

---

[23] By way of reminder, and as set out in Chapter 2, in the book, we use 'IHL' to signify quotations form in-houser interviewees, and 'Compliance' to signify quotes from compliance personnel interviewees.

100 *Competing Logics – A Look at Risk*

application. Compliance2 emphasised the processes necessary to make certain that risk appetite was understood and taken seriously to ensure that it influences behaviour.

> [Our] employees have now got more understanding as to where our risk appetite is … we formally documented [it] and we have reported since July of this year … [W]e currently have a rollout where the risk manager is attending all team meetings, talking to staff across the whole organisation about … the fact that we've got the risk appetite and what they think it means for their day to day business for them to start capturing that and understanding how it makes a difference to what they're doing.

Whether or not respondents had a defined risk appetite, it was clear they thought risk appetite emerged from commercial and social interactions. Individual teams or personnel could make a difference, as could leadership, geography and levels of growth. IHL8 reported regions of high growth in Asia and Africa having 'much more consistency and a lower risk appetite in that region than there was probably twelve months ago … because the leadership has changed.' Expectations regarding profitability and return on investment were highlighted as key drivers of this. IHL14 talked about a private equity company they had worked for that had a much higher risk appetite for legal risk and would say, 'Yeah, yeah, I know the contract's not buttoned up here but I'm prepared to go with it anyway'.

Risk appetite was also primarily seen as organisation-led, with in-house lawyers responding to, rather than shaping, risk appetite 'to some extent' (IHL14). The organisation influences in multiple ways, led by the Board and the executive committee:

> it's done through the development of the strategy, it's done through the budget, it's done through discussions, reviews, approvals of developments in board meetings, so reviewing of proposals and the terms around which the board is prepared to move forwards with a proposal and I think it develops as a culture within a business. [IHL17]

Three interviewees went further and were explicit that the legal function did not have a role in setting risk appetite, or whether a decision came within it. For example:

> at [our company] the Legal Function we would say is advisory, so it's not for us to take on risks, it's for us to make recommendations and point out any risks, and if people want to take the risk then that's a matter for their decision. [IHL15]

> … my profile needs to fit with what the organisation's profile is. I've worked in very acquisitive, new, fast growing companies and I've worked in very conservative charities. You have to fit the mould, that's what my job is. [IHL17]

In some ways, this is counter-intuitive: if the legal function has ownership of legal risk management, it should have (or at the very least, want) some input in the shaping of the organisation's risk appetite. But a contrary view was to emphasise that any endeavour within an organisation was a collective one. Legal input had to adapt in a collegiate manner:

> you have to develop a collective approach as a business and actually if you find people with a very different attitude then they tend to be quite difficult to work with and it takes negotiation and management to find a mid-path through. Sometimes it's good tension, it's good to have a debate, but at the end of the day the organisation will come to a point that it's comfortable with. [IHL17]

Under this kind of language, risk appetite is dependent not independent. However some (albeit rarely) suggested that the in-house legal team led the process of defining the organisation's legal risk appetite. Contrast the following position with what we have heard so far:

> The General Counsel define it and have socialised that with the key executives, so your CFO, your chief merchandising officer, your chief marketing officer, etcetera so that everybody understands why we're taking the position that we are … if you want to deviate from it, it's escalated and then ultimately to the CEO, but nothing very rarely gets there. [Compliance 7]

Having considered how the risk appetite is set, we move on to understand what the personal risk appetites of our interviewees looked like. If, as appears, risk appetite is something set implicitly rather than explicitly, then personal risk appetite may be particularly important. We divide our cohort into three: risk conservatives, risk accepters, and a smaller group of risk facilitators.

Risk Conservatives

The traditional, commercial view of in-house lawyers is, as we discussed in the previous chapter, as the nay-sayers or the 'sales prevention team'.[24] Some, especially those working in finance and compliance functions, were very likely to describe themselves as conservative in risk terms. IHL10 described himself as 'pretty risk averse'; IHL4 as 'quite risk averse' in a company that was 'extremely risk averse'. Whereas IHL6 saw himself as 'innately more conservative on legal risk and risk generally than the [owner] … or the CEO of the business.' Compliance3 saw themselves as embodying a double-whammy of risk conservatism: 'I don't like running much in the way of risk. I suppose that's probably why I'm a lawyer and a regulatory risk person.'

Indeed, for some this was the point of the risk and/or compliance functions: 'to provide a counterbalance to the commercial team' [IHL7]; or to look at more than the bottom line, which others (like sales) would typically concentrate on. Here, compliance/risk activity was seen as part of a group of risk conservatives,

---

[24] Paul Gilbert, 'Dissent: Platitudes and a Missed Debate – How GCs Are Pushed off Their Ethical Course,' *Legal Business* (London, 2 September 2014).

'all of whom are pretty much of the same mind when it comes to risk appetite ... legal compliance, ... a risk function of course, audit ... the Administration Department' [IHL3]. The 'risk conservatives' tended to see risk (ie the risk of regulatory investigation and sanction) as something they had been employed to resist. Their role was thus to manifest a deliberate tension within the business.

Risk Accepters

The next group of our interviewees accepted risk as something organisational imperatives created, which organisations had then to define and manage. If behaviour was consistent with furthering an organisational goal it might be permissible even if otherwise risky: 'we specifically say that we will take risks to achieve our business goals, but not if any of the following three circumstances would arise' [IHL8]. We discuss the contra-indicated risks below. A subtly different view was IHL7's, who saw risk as ubiquitous, given the uncertainty of law and the needs of business:

> the law is all about balancing the commercial reality against the legal risk, there will always be some level of legal risk in anything you do. The idea is to mitigate it as best possible and to ensure that you're taking a sensible commercial view.

Here, it seemed that risk appetite was explicitly tailored in the context of organisational objectives and defined risks: 'So for every risk probably there is a separate risk appetite.' (Compliance11) This was usually part of a broader, explicit framework of risk management, tending often to be seen in financial organisations where the regulatory drivers are stronger.

'Risk accepters' tended to concentrate on discussing what was sometimes referred to as 'commercial legal risks'. They were comfortable talking about dealing with counterparties, where risk was seen either as ubiquitous or tolerable. This was in contrast to risk arising between the organisation and either regulators or vulnerable stakeholders. Compliance5 suggested risk only really came into play where there was no choice but to accept some potential downsides to a transaction, 'in some of the commercial deals that we do, because if we didn't then you'd never do any business.' It was seen as part of being 'sensible'. Compliance2 similarly focused on bilateral transactions 'on a contract; I'm not so risk adverse that I won't accept a limit on liability.' Under this approach, risk is acceptable because the organisation is thought to understand it, and takes on the risk as part of the desire to do a deal. For acceptable risks, IHL12 stated that risk appetite is not about saying 'yes' or 'no', but about taking a decision that is both suitably informed and taken at the right level of the organisation. Thus, for him, risk appetite was partly about defining who takes a decision on risk, about notions of ownership and responsibility within the organisation.

Yet risk appetite was not simply about accepting risk on behalf of the corporation: it could also mean pushing risk onto others. Here, risk was portrayed as acceptable because it was part of a process of negotiation with savvy counterparties:

> Could I get a bit edgy where we might be getting close to infringing somebody else's rights and giving them a claim? I'm not in favour of doing it to old ladies, but if it's organisations who have got the means to defend themselves ... [IHL15]

Similarly, IHL23 suggested that 'risk is divided up' through negotiation and that risk appetite is something which can evolve with experience:

> we're more robust ... based on previous experiences where we've not had any big problems ... we're prepared to take on more risk in contracts for something like competition.

In general, 'risk accepters' took a more organisation-led view of risk. That view was either formally defined through written risk appetites, embedded through management processes and monitoring, or defined through everyday interactions with the organisation and the commercial pressures within. These interviewees tended to emphasise in a rather general way that risk was necessary, but also that high risk was unsustainable:

> I want that to be sustainable success rather than overnight success. As a result of which I think it is important to take risk because if one takes no risk in the end the ultimate conclusion is you'd have to stay in bed in the morning and never go into work, but I would describe myself as moderate and a medium to long term. [IHL21]

Risk Facilitators

Our third group stated they had a higher risk appetite than their employer or other lawyers. This was sometimes true even in what were said to be risk-averse organisations. IHL1 saw himself as 'a little bit less cautious ... a little bit more commercial ... [yet] in the "careful" bracket, not somebody who takes big risks or cuts corners'. IHL1 suggested lawyers tended to identify potential risks and not identify upsides or the likelihood or scale of their risks:

> a lot of lawyers ... they go, '... We've got a piece of marketing puff and we're going to say something rude about [a competitor], there is a risk that they could sue us for trade mark infringement.' And I would go, 'There is a risk, but actually it's not a big risk for these reasons and we've got this to gain, so I think it's valid to take it.'

These 'risk facilitators' saw their role as defining and better quantifying the costs and benefits of risk to their employer organisations to enable informed decisions. Although some risk facilitators saw themselves as leading more conservative colleagues, they too tended to emphasise the idea that risk appetite was driven by the organisation:

> Personally I'm more than comfortable with taking legal risk if that is the decision of the relevant department having been given careful analysis of why, if you like, the risk

104 *Competing Logics – A Look at Risk*

> is at the level it is perceived to be by me. If that's what they choose to do that's what we choose to do, and they will have their own reasons for that. [IHL19]

The contrast is with in-house lawyers who saw their role as leading against the stereotype of conservatism:

> Yes I take risk. I have to control myself personally otherwise I am likely to take too much risk. Because a key element of my leadership with my management team will be ... do what the department wants you to do, and if they want to take a risk it may be they can take it. I want you to encourage them. I rather suspect ... if I don't have that sort of gloss on it ... risk-taking would be very low. [IHL19]

The encouragement towards risk was described in quite subtle ways. Putting in place approaches to manage or reduce the consequences of risk and describing the acceptance of risk as 'mature' were techniques used by Compliance10. And Compliance9 described how performance management encouraged him towards risk-taking:

> I think that without putting too fine a point on it I don't think that I would have reached the point in my old company where I did had I not been prepared to take risks and demonstrate that ability.

WHO OWNS 'LEGAL' RISK?

In the discussion of risk appetite we can see a number of competing ideas. The language of risk is both bureaucratic and normative, to an extent that varies depending on the role attributed to lawyers and other risk professionals. Risk is neutralised: it is not inherently good or bad, it merely exists to be managed. We have also seen how risk acts as a lens through which the organisational or commercial imperative is implemented. Concerns about illegal or otherwise questionable conduct are tested against the legitimate aims of the organisation to make a profit or otherwise 'get things done'. Legality is contingent, because risk-free operation is a utopian ideal.

The bureaucratic management of legal risk demands a clear definition of legal risk consistent with the way the organisation manages risk generally. We have already seen that risk appetite is not often clearly defined and that it is relational; negotiated by key individuals in response to perceptions of risk appetite in the organisation. A relational approach suggests that a key part of that process is the allocation of responsibility for each kind of risk identified, to ensure there is a clear sense of who owns, or is responsible for, that risk. So if you cannot define risk perhaps you can instead define who owns it. How does this work with legal risk?

Our interviews, and review of relevant literature, suggest two main approaches to defining what is meant by *legal* risk: the first is a broad approach where legal risk is seen as any 'legal' consequence of operational risk (such as a claim or regulatory action); or, and second, a narrow approach that sees legal risk as a particular sub-category of operational risk (that is, risk deriving *from legal work* and changes in the law: such as faulty contracts or a surprising appeal court decision).

In risk management theory, this demarcation is essentially driven by defining legal risk on the basis of potential consequences or of potential causes. Taken forward logically, this demarcation separates out the management of risk (where one would want to have processes which dealt effectively with the causes of risk) and the monitoring and quantification of that risk (where one would want to be alive to the potential consequences of any risk manifesting). The narrow approach concentrates on risks that in-house legal departments should manage themselves, and leaves the management of broader risks to the rest of the organisation who manage those as the first line of defence. A bridge between narrow and broad approaches might be found by in-house lawyers contributing to advice on those broader risks and how to manage them.[25]

A theoretically well-organised and comprehensive approach would see in-house lawyers responsible for the legal risks that they manage (the narrow framing of legal risk) and a clear role in overseeing or contributing to risk management of broader risks. A more worrying approach would see the narrow approach confining the in-house lawyer's role to the risks the in-houser is directly engaged in, seeing risk as a siloed activity, and one where in-house legal teams need to be invited to participate or, in terms of Chapter 3, one where they need to work towards influence. What kind of approaches did we in fact see in our data?

The Broad Approach

As we set out above, the broad approach sees legal risk as involving any 'compliance failures or other violations of the law'[26] or the risk of an event which brings about any legal consequence.[27] From a public interest perspective, we want any organisation to have a good, proportionate grip on all its legal risks in this sense.

The vast majority of our interviewees saw legal risk in this way. Thus, they spoke of the risk of 'breach' [IHL4] or of sanctions, and penalties 'by reason of a law and the business that you are in' [IHL6]. These included contractual and other claims (such as professional negligence) as well as 'other litigation risks such as employment risk or debt recovery risk, et cetera' [IHL8] In this sense, anything with a potential for legal action by regulators, customers or counterparties is what dominated the understanding of legal risk for a large proportion of our respondents.

[25] Karen Anderson and Julia Black, 'Legal Risks and Risks for Lawyers' (Herbert Smith Freehills and London School of Economics Regulatory Reform Forum Paper, 2013).
[26] Miller (n 15) 542.
[27] Stuart Weinstein and Charles Wild, *Legal Risk Management, Governance and Compliance: A Guide to Best Practice from Leading Experts* (Globe Law and Business, 2013), 16 (citing Hatton).

Sanctions and penalties were uppermost in interviewees' minds as definers of the negative consequences of risk, suggesting that legal risk was infused with a more regulatory than civil liability view. There was also accentuated concern about the risk posed by criticism from regulators, perhaps reflecting the potential for these critiques to have more personal repercussions where regulators might identify individual failings. Several interviewees discussed employee behaviour as a driver of risk (either creating problems with regulators and other external stakeholders, or internally with other employees). It follows that the definition of legal risk was both wide and amorphous for many of our interviewees:

> legal risk is where a contractual or statutory or regulatory obligation may not be fulfilled with the consequence of a business impact. [IHL12]

The behaviour of the organisation, not the competence of the legal department, is what drives risk under this approach. The approach also suggests a degree of reactivity on the part of those defining it. In-house lawyers only typically became involved when asked:

> We give advice to our in-house clients and indicate to them in terms of either contract negotiations, or whatever, what the risks are of signing up to particular types of wording. [IHL3]

In general, whilst some appeared to have clearly conceptualised maps of what such legal risks looked like in their organisations, the more dominant position was that broadly defined legal risk was understood in an ad hoc manner. This pragmatic approach overlapped with an intuitive or experiential approach and, for a number of interviewees, it was apparent that our interview prompted them to focus on the notion of legal risk for the first time in a direct, concrete way.

The Narrower Approach

Interestingly, narrower approaches to legal risk have often come from lawyer-led initiatives. McCormick emphasises legal risk as defective documentation risks, claims risk and change in law risk,[28] whereas the Financial Law Panel (FLP) points to organisational legal risk, legal methodology risk and conduct of business legal risk.[29] A second form of narrow legal risk definition is to see legal risk as the potential for 'unexpected interpretation of the law or legal uncertainty',[30] where gaps in the law exist, where 'the applicable law does not fit the market reality', or where law 'unnecessarily complicates or burdens a transaction'.[31]

---

[28] McCormick (n 22) 264.
[29] McCormick (n 22) 274. See also the work of the Financial Law Panel, http://uk.practicallaw.com/2-100-5227, accessed 18 April 2018.
[30] Bank of England, 'Oversight of Payment Systems' (Bank of England Paper, 2010) (cited in McCormick (n 22) 272).
[31] McCormick (n 22) 276.

Here we see how legal risk reflects a degree of dissatisfaction with, even resistance to, law as decided by politicians and judges. A related idea is that legal risk management involves understanding, predicting and managing regulatory change by being ready to adapt to changes in the law, but also being ready, able and willing to influence the nature of regulatory change through lobbying and the like.[32]

A smaller group of our respondents sought to define legal risk in narrower terms. Narrowness took a number of forms: 'ensuring that within Legal Services the management of the cases is as efficient and effective as possible' [IHL19]; or how in-housers respond to documents as sources of risk (such as when reviewing contracts or sales material) [IHL2]. A handful expressly rejected the extension of legal risk to (any or most) legal consequences arising from business or other risk. For these, a claim being made or the occurrence of some other event which results in a liability for the institution or other loss were seen as too broad to usefully define legal risk.

For this group, risk defined not something on which they might advise, but something for which they were *accountable*. That is, it defined the risks the in-house lawyers were responsible for managing, or the risks they had a stronger role in managing (and reporting on). Let us focus on claims for a moment and think about sales contracts. Under a narrow conception of legal risk, the in-house lawyers might be responsible for ensuring those sales contracts were 'good' contracts (ie, that they documented the agreement that had been made and complied with the various formalities needed for a contract to be effective); and in-house lawyers might be responsible for managing claims that arose on those contracts, but the in-housers would not ordinarily be responsible or accountable for the behaviours that drove problems with those contracts (eg, the sales team ignoring the terms or failing to manage contracts). Sometimes, therefore, accountability for particular risks lay elsewhere. Here we can see how risk definitions and practices delineate spheres of responsibility and influence for the in-house lawyers.

A related theme was seeking to draw a distinction between the source of risk and its consequences. IHL12 stated that:

> most business risks are business risks which have legal consequences and people then think of them as legal risks, but they're not, it is simply a consequence of the business risk having crystallised that we have a legal problem.

While another interviewee referred to 'legal interactions' suggesting that legal risk manifested when the legal team got involved or when law changed. IHL14's organisation had a policy for managing risks, 'to do with legal interactions ... be that contracts, be that litigation, be that new legislation. And it's about governance and control and anticipation of change ...'.

---

[32] Weinstein and Wild, p 11, n 47, discussing Philip Bramwell Group, GC of BAE Systems.

The narrowly defined approach did not necessarily inhibit the legal team contributing to the management of risks with legal consequences, but that did not mean those in-house lawyers saw those risks as legal risk:

> contract risk is really owned by the business, they have to be liable, responsible for the contracts they manage. What we [the in-house lawyers] can do is design a contract governance process, we can provide advice to them and all that kind of stuff, but that's not our accountability. [IHL5]

Even so, where a narrower definition of legal risk was attempted it could still be very broad and defined simply in opposition to other risks (such as financial risk):

> legal risk is in a broader sense non-financial risk or, at the least, risk which is not overtly financial in nature, such as the reporting requirements in revenue regulation, which clearly fall into the controllership functions within finance. So potentially legal risk is everything outside that space. [IHL21]

Some of our interviewees defined risk somewhat narrowly by reference to problems that had manifested or crystallised (where there had been a rash of problems in a particular area or a particularly serious problem). Here, risk was a response to a backward look at recent organisational mishap. Legal risk was also regularly conceived of thematically (for example reviewing bribery risks across the organisation, where regulatory agendas would partly drive the consideration).

A Broader, Broad Approach

It was interesting to see the narrower definitions of legal risk often emanating from interviewees in financial organisations; especially as the Basel Committee on Banking Supervision has defined legal risk as including loss to reputation resulting from 'failure to comply with laws, regulations, rules, related self-regulatory organisation standards, and codes of conduct applicable to its banking activities.'[33] Consistent with a broader approach, losses include risks posed by not adhering to soft law. The Basel document also emphasises needing to 'strive to observe the spirit as well as the letter of the law' and the reputational harm that may flow from not doing so, 'even if no law has been broken'.[34] In this way, reputational legal risk broadens significantly to encompass the social interpretation of corporate behaviour where it touches on law. Where an organisation is *perceived* to have behaved illegally, this may create legal risk even where that behaviour is lawful and where the standards applied reputationally – by the press, activists, consumers and other stakeholders – may differ from laws, codes and standards.

---

[33] Basel Committee on Banking Supervision, Compliance and the Compliance Function in Banks (Basel, 2005), www.bis.org/publ/bcbs113.pdf.
[34] ibid.

For the most part, the risk definitions of our interviewees did not adopt this broader approach. They concentrated instead on the obligations created by law, or enforced by regulators, although reputational costs associated with legal breaches were often discussed. Nevertheless, a small group did draw upon broader definitions of legal risk referring to the need to comply with internal codes of practices or the need to adhere to the spirit of the law. Some suggested this was because codes of conduct and/or spirit of the law provisions helped organisations manage their compliance with legal obligations by reinforcement. Managing to the letter of the law was too complicated when there were several countries' laws to take account of and hard to manage at a human level:

> where you fail to meet the spirit or the letter of a statute of whichever country you're in ... there's a world of difference knowing what the statute says to how you make sure employees follow both the spirit and the letter of that statute. [Compliance9]

Those voicing support for a broader approach saw a need to reach beyond minimal standards,[35] and to build in respect for the spirit and the letter of the law in organisational settings:[36] 'when you try to keep to the letter of the law while undermining the spirit, you are likely to violate a letter in the end.'[37] Being demonstrably well motivated was more likely to promote regulator sympathy if things do go wrong, but it also had an inherent virtue:

> [i]t's also about ensuring that the business is a good corporate citizen, that it behaves appropriately, that it reaches decisions according to its own values and is seen to be acting in a compliant manner and not just trying to find the narrowest interpretation of a rule or regulation to be able to do what it wants to do. [IHL1]

Aside from potentially providing a better guarantee of compliance, a broader view of ethics, risk and compliance suggests that promoting the spirit of the law may make organisations better at managing the myriad social relationships they depend on to be successful.[38] This systems approach suggests an ethically and economically thicker reality than mere compliance; a reality in which organisations respond to the needs of their stakeholders (employees, customers, shareholders, public opinion).

Are More Focused Definitions of Risk Necessary?

We can see that many of the narrower definitions of risk focus on legal work and the accountabilities given to in-house legal departments. These were largely

---

[35] Constance E Bagley, *Managers and the Legal Environment: Strategies for the 21st Century*, 7th edn (Cengage Learning, 2012) 23.
[36] Bagley ibid, Ben W Heineman Jr, *The Inside Counsel Revolution: Resolving the Partner-Guardian Tension* (Ankerwycke, 2016), fn 73.
[37] Mark Gimein, 'Commentary: The Skilling Trap', *BusinessWeek: Magazine*, June 11, 2006, www.businessweek.com/stories/2006-06-11/commentary-the-skilling-trap.
[38] Bagley (n 35), p. 3, fn 74.

emanating from in-house lawyers in financial institutions. The definition of risk was driven by the organisational context. In particular, legal risk was likely to be more narrowly defined where there are other accountability and risk functions within the organisation (such as finance or compliance).

The narrower definitions of legal risk also suggest a separation of organisational problems into their components or drivers, and opens up the possibility of the organisation allocating those components to the most effective and relevant means of tackling those problems. A number of interviewees emphasised the benefits of the in-house legal team *not* owning all legal risks. Certain risks such as human resources problems, for instance, were seen as best being managed by other functions, and so they fell outside the normal purview of their legal risk definitions. A more general point was to emphasise the 'first line of defence' argument that it is the organisation that is responsible for the risk and it is the organisation, as the prime driver of risk, that needs to modify its approach:

> It meant that compliance with the law, in the round, wasn't just something that people in an ivory tower did and people on the ground didn't have to worry about; it brought it home to them that they'd got an individual organisational personal responsibility. [IHL14]

Similarly, a narrower definition may simply be a pragmatic response to the need to prioritise management resources. A good deal of the narrowing of legal risk definitions by our interviewees was related to managing their workloads and internal responsibilities. Keeping away from difficult or unmanageable problems might save in-housers pain in the tournament for influence. IHL5 stated that an in-houser can try and put their 'arms round everything which might have a legal consequence, but trying to apply that practically in a business ... is a lot more difficult.'

In one sense, this indicates the struggle necessary to take on a more strategic view as an in-house leader. There needs to be both day-to-day management of risk and a holistic view of what legal risk is/could be for the organisation. A second point raised with us was that where the organisation (and not the legal team) owned the risk then this could emphasise the need to collaborate and compromise: 'we're all trying to adjust ourselves to come up with the optimum risk profile across all the risks' [IHL13].

These negotiations are a reminder that definitions of risk and responsibility are not stable; they change. For IHL2 a narrower approach could reduce proactivity:

> I struggle with the compartmentalisation of legal risks from general business risk ... It allows people to say 'You don't need to get involved in this. You only need to get involved in legal risks'. And there's virtually nothing that happens in the organisation that doesn't eventually come back to being something that the legal team need to get involved in sorting out ... I roll up my sleeves and try and deal with the risks in totality. [IHL2]

An interesting question raised then is whether there is sufficient legal input into understanding operational risks which are not defined as 'legal risks'. Put another way, is the voice of legal downgraded or marginalised with narrower definitions of legal risk? Or does legal have sufficient input into operational risks with some legal content? We could not say based on these interviews, but those who took a broader view that legal risk and organisational (or operational) risk are frequently intertwined sought to suggest this was a way that legal's voice could be mainstreamed in discussions of risk. However, these interviewees also tended to have a more reactive, less organised approach to assessing and managing risk generally.

Such varied definitions of risk point to the freedom of organisations to adapt their definition of legal risk to, 'any allocation of responsibility within that institution'.[39] Where these choices have been more consciously made, narrower ideas about legal risk, fitting with a professional preference for narrower roles and responsibilities, appear to have been adopted.[40] We can also see that narrower definitions have the potential to exclude in-house lawyers, or narrow their influence in situations where their contributions may be important. A narrow approach raises the potential for risks to fall through the gaps, or for there to be a lack of overall ownership or integration of legal risk into the broader framework of enterprise risk management. Narrow approaches can act to reduce legal influence, increase dependence and decrease independence. Equally though, other parts of the organisation might take sensible views: it depends on their knowledge and their risk appetite.

LOOKING BEYOND RISK APPETITE AND RISK DEFINITION – A VIGNETTE

We knew we would only get so far discussing legal risk in the abstract. To get a better grip on how risk is dealt with, we would need to look deeper. As a result, we employed vignettes (or case studies) to examine attitudes and approaches to risk in a less abstract way. At the end of each interview, interviewees were given three hypothetical problems on which they were asked to give us their responses. This enabled us to provide more insight into how different approaches to risk can play out against specific fact patterns.

In relation to a supply chain vignette, interviewees were asked how they would respond to the setting up of supplier relationships in a country where

---

[39] Roger McCormick, 'The Management of Legal Risk by Financial Institutions', 2004, www.federalreserve.gov/SECRS/2005/August/20050818/OP-1189/OP-1189_2_1.pdf.
[40] Guernsey Financial Services Commission, Legal Risk Guidance Note for Banks, www.gfsc.gg/The-Commission/Policy%20and%20Legislation/Legal-Risk-Guidance-Note.pdf, accessed 26 September 2014.

there were thin governance structures (see Case Study 1: Supply Chain Problems). This threw up some issues about narrow versus broad framing of legal's role in relation to risk.

> **Case Study 1: Supply Chain Problems**
>
> You are the senior in-house lawyer for a multinational company which manufactures specialist engineering components. Your company wants to begin trading for the first time in Country Y. It will need hundreds of suppliers/contractors in a particular developing country that has a thin governance structure and little by way of business regulation. What are the priority legal risk issues and how would you respond to them?
>
> **How do ethical issues such as environmental pollution and working conditions affect your decisions?**
>
> It becomes clear that this country only allows 'authorised sellers' to sell goods to anyone within the country. Authorised sellers are defined by statute and includes conditions regarding the ethnic origin/nationality of all those involved in the company structure.
>
> After trading for some months, you become aware that one of your dealers has sold goods to an unauthorised seller who then sold the goods on. How do you respond?
>
> **You subsequently discover the sales were at an excessive mark up. What do you do? Do you inform the regulator of the country?**

One set of interviewees took a narrow view of this scenario, framing the problem as being about the company's primary legal needs: setting up supplier relationships; whether there needed to be a corporate vehicle; what the contracting requirements should be, etc. Most took a slightly broader view: seeing tax, money-laundering, and anti-bribery risks that would need addressing. Their responses would include greater proactivity, instigating some scrutiny/control around outsourced dealers. A handful of other legal risks were identified, such as the potential risk of trading goods in a country with a thin governance structure.

Another, perhaps the main, difference within this group of interviewees was whether they then went on to identify, from this scenario, broader notions of risk relevant to their role. In particular, some emphasised broader obligations to manage outsourcing with particular regard to employment and human rights obligations. There was particular emphasis on the reputational problems posed:

> Antennae also up for social responsibility issues … are you satisfied that this isn't engaging people … like the nine year old children working in Bangladesh working fourteen hours a day making shoes for Nike. We need to do some due diligence here to find out what's going on because a) it's moral and b) it's our reputation if we discover we are in some form of exploitation of child labour or whatever it happens to be. [IHL16]

Unlike the narrower view, as regards reputation, this group saw agents as standing in their company's shoes reputationally, whether they did so legally or not:

> your suppliers or agents, or whoever they may be, may be doing things in your name that would fall below the governance standards of Country X. [IHL14]
>
> ... you're ultimately responsible for what they do, and that you're not going to be embarrassed by any of those activities reputationally, but also that you bring the same protections on the human capital and that you might put on your human capital, within obviously the local parameters. [IHL10]

Yet some interviewees suggested local standards on (say) employment rights were a matter for local businesses and regulators, save for clear concerns like slave or child labour. More common was the suggestion that the interviewee's organisation had common standards across all their companies and agents, but also a margin of appreciation for 'local parameters' [IHL10]. A clearer articulation of a defensible position within this group was a 'best local' standard that came from Compliance5:

> You have to comply with local laws, you have to comply with your own policies and standards, which in a company like ours tend to be the highest ones that we can find where we operate ... you'd look at that not only from a legal point of view or a regulatory one, but a reputational one, because going into countries just because they're cheap and exploiting other people, a) it's shocking, but b) can that be a good reputation for your company? No.

This reported commitment to higher-than-local ethical standards was, either substantially or in part, driven by commercial considerations and the impact of reputation on the organisation which was seen as increasingly important: 'Public perception and the public's ability to follow that reputational risk in the media is far higher' [Compliance1]. Notably two drivers of better standards were reputational concerns and regulatory interventions: 'we effectively adopt the highest common denominator which is therefore driven mainly by the [US] FCPA and the UK Bribery Act' [IHL16].

Some interviewees suggested what mattered was not so much the substance of the position, but having a position which was thought-through for consistency, defensibility and the implications of having to defend that position:

> you have to have decided what your culture is ... You are then either going to stand up in an environmental and other context and nail your cross to the flag, or not. [IHL14]
>
> ... [you should have] a position ... and that might be, 'We only pay what the wage is in that country because that's the way we do business', but they have to have a position on it and they have to be able to respond to it if it goes wrong. [Compliance1]

LEGAL RISK MANAGEMENT PROCESSES

The risk management literature suggests a structured, cyclical approach to risk management that begins with: (1) the identification of hazards (ie things that can cause harms); and proceeds to (2) the assessment of those hazards, generally involving an understanding of the likelihood, nature and scale of any harms; followed (3) by understanding how the management of those hazards can reduce, mitigate or hedge those harms, via mitigation strategies to cope with risk after it materialises (eg insurance) and via reduction measures to prevent risk arising in the first place (such as education and training). The cycle is completed by: (4) a risk management evaluation that examines how effective the process of risk assessment and management is, and how that process can be improved before the process begins again.

As with legal definition we found a variety of formal and informal ad hoc approaches to the legal risk management process. In broad terms, the management of legal risk went through something like these four stages for the majority of our interviewees, but often in a less organised or deliberate manner. Although some had well-mapped and defined processes covering each step with a clear sense of how the whole picture fitted together, many approaches appeared to be ad hoc rather than systematic; that is, they often touched on some of these stages without having defined, interlocking processes for dealing with each. Some steps were missed out, or were assumed to be happening naturally in the course of our interviewees' day-to-day work. Similarly, interviewees conceived of these processes in a range of ways: broadly or narrowly.

EXPERIENTIAL vs SYSTEMS APPROACHES

One approach to managing legal risk is the experiential approach. This relies on experience as the touchstone of risk.[41] This seemed most common where risk frameworks and systems were less developed and amongst interviewees who adopted the idea that legal risk was anything to which legal consequences might attach. Legal risk assessment was 'more common sense and pragmatic and driven by local strands of overall legal risk' [IHL15]. Or:

> it's my own knowledge, just based on twenty-five years' experience in the industry and my knowledge of the rules, my knowledge of the laws ... I've designed our internal procedures so I know them extremely well. [IHL4]

So, whilst decisions on risk all tended to refer to the likelihood of the risk, the magnitude of any consequences of that risk crystallising, the organisation's

---

[41] Weinstein and Wild (n 27) 15.

appetite for risk (in a broad sense) and any uncertainties around those judgements, these interviewees tended not to see risk as formalised and then systemised.

Movement away from informal, ad hoc and judgement-based approaches to legal risk most often occurred in relation to risks arising from legal work (for example through specific policies for the review of contracts). Perhaps process-based approaches to legal work risks are the simplest for legal teams to introduce and, as such, may represent the first step on an evolutionary scale of legal risk management. Or perhaps they represent the peripheral place of legal in organisational risk management in these organisations.

The more systematic approach to managing risk was related to a more thought-through specific definition of legal risk and also an attitude which saw risk as a generic management problem within an organisation. Some thought 'about it thematically. So we look for risk trends' [IHL8]. With organisations built on more specific definitions and carving up of ownership of risk, approaches to defining and measuring risk emerged from the organisation and often returned to the organisation. So, for example, the organisation methodically defined its appetite for risk through overarching policies within which the in-house legal team had to establish its place. There also tended to be a wider, more clearly defined range of responses to risk. These organisations had established functions which could assist with legal (and other) risk problems, especially training, compliance, and audit. Individual units within the organisation might also be, and often were, we were told, better placed to respond to elements of a problem as the first line of defence.

In formal approaches, hazard assessment and identification often involves compiling a risk inventory/register of existing and emerging risks.[42] Thus some of our interviewees operated risk grades, such as traffic light systems, to label the level of attention and care that a particular risk merited.[43] Such grades were founded on assessments of the size and likelihood of harm manifesting from any risky activity, which are usually subjective assessments by key in-house legal staff.

These systemically organised approaches overlaid or organised multiple, sometimes diffuse, subjective decisions but did not replace those decisions. Informing assessments with hard data, and the testing of the consistency of risk assessments when different people contribute to that assessment, appeared rare. The literature on attitudes to risk and the impact of biases on risk assessment show some of the difficulties inherent in such an approach. Risk appetite may differ depending on whether personal or company money is at risk (and bonus

---

[42] Miller (n 15) 552ff.
[43] See Matthew Whalley and Chris Guzelian, *The Legal Risk Management Handbook: An International Guide to Protect Your Business from Legal Loss* (Kogan Page, 2016) for examples of such frameworks.

schemes may mean that both are) or when the risk is financial or of some other kind.[44] Personal risk appetite also depends on how those risks are framed.[45]

Formulating an institutional risk appetite may help articulate organisational positions on particular risks and restrain some subjectivities around what levels of risk are acceptable, but there is a more fundamental problem. Risk appetite is, in fact, bound up with risk assessment and communication. Some managers appear to have an optimistic *perception* of risk rather than a greater *preference* for risk as commonly believed. So, it is possible that payment protection insurance (PPI) was developed by so many banks not in spite of it being high-risk, but because it was perceived to be low-risk. Risk assessments may thus differ not because of personal (or organisational) attitudes towards risk but because of differing assessments of the underlying risk: if you and I were asked to estimate the outcome of a court decision we might give widely differing estimates of the risk of an adverse decision.[46] Such dispositions in lawyers have not been much studied, but there are a series of studies which show that lawyers' assessment of the merits of cases is significantly prone to subconscious bias.[47] A further interesting problem is that there is evidence that a sense of controllability and manageability reduces the perception of the riskiness of the situation.[48] Thus the availability of systems of risk management, mitigation and control may lead to an overconfidence which not only impacts on the assessment of the mitigation, but also impacts on the assessment of the underlying risk.

We asked our interviewees how legal risk assessment and mitigation might impact on appetite for risk within their organisation: would it make for a more conservative or aggressive approach? In one sense, the interviewees tended to feel that the answers to this question might lie elsewhere; that risk appetite was influenced by regulator behaviour, legislative volatility, and sensitivity to media coverage about the organisation. Large sanctions and a propensity to prosecute from regulators would make a difference to an organisation's risk appetite, and not to an individual lawyer's approach; the ubiquity of risk and the association of risk with opportunity were counterforces. Some of our interviewees did,

---

[44] Elke U Weber, Ann-Renee Blais and Nancy E Betz, 'A Domain-Specific Risk-Attitude Scale: Measuring Risk Perceptions and Risk Behaviors' (SSRN Scholarly Paper, 2002).

[45] Daniel Kahneman and Amos Tversky, 'Prospect Theory: An Analysis of Decision under Risk' (1979) *Econometrica: Journal of the Econometric Society* 263.

[46] Weber, Blais and Betz (n 44); Ann-Renée Blais and Elke U Weber, 'A Domain-Specific Risk-Taking (DOSPERT) Scale for Adult Populations' (2006) 1 *Judgment and Decision Making* 33. See further Daniel Martin Katz, 'Quantitative Legal Prediction-or-How I Learned to Stop Worrying and Start Preparing for the Data-Driven Future of the Legal Services Industry' (2012) 62 *Emory LJ* 909; and Theodore W Ruger and others, 'The Supreme Court Forecasting Project: Legal and Political Science Approaches to Predicting Supreme Court Decisionmaking' [2004] *Columbia Law Review* 1150.

[47] For a review and a recent study see Andrew M Perlman, 'A Behavioral Theory of Legal Ethics' (SSRN Scholarly Paper 2013); and Ian K Belton, Mary Thomson, and Mandeep K Dhami, 'Lawyer and Nonlawyer Susceptibility to Framing Effects in Out-of-Court Civil Litigation Settlement' (2014) 11(3) *Journal of Empirical Legal Studies* 578.

[48] Weber, Blais and Betz (n 44) 266.

however, see risk assessment and management as increasing confidence that the organisation both understood risk and could learn how to control it. In many ways, this mirrors the wider turn in society towards the 'science' of risk assessment and the quantification of risks, discussed earlier.

> A company that has every single process in place that it could possibly have to remove even any scintilla of risk, would be a company that would very quickly sail off the cliffs of prosperity because that kind of decision has to be made all the time. But I think legal risk management allows that decision to be made in the context of knowledge and awareness rather than accident, whether the risk's materialising by accident or without any awareness. [IHL20]

We can see here how high levels of confidence in the process of assessment and management of risk *might* subtly increase appetite for risk, but such a judgement depends on the impact of cost-benefit assessments and other values at play. It is up to the outside world, the world of regulators or massed claimants, to make those risks so serious or so intolerable that they must not be taken on. Bribery might be one area where this is being attempted.

A related question is whether risk management process makes those risks acceptable. So, for instance, let us say that an organisation considers an activity which involves health and safety risks, and they understand the level and impact of such risk: should it take on those risks because of the upside of commercial gain? Research elsewhere suggests that processes that frame human impacts in quantitative and commercial terms may squeeze out ethical judgement, with sometimes devastating effects.[49] Such questions are not wholly answered by having a process. Even if that process reduces the risk it does not totally eliminate it and yet the process might make the risk tolerable:

> For example, there could be a significant injury under our health and safety, the risk of serious injury happening, and then looking at what are the controls that we have in place to mitigate that. We have then assessed the effectiveness of those controls, and then determined whether the net risk, taking into account those controls, still fits within our appetite. [Compliance2]

Whilst we cannot generalise, we should also note that interviewees tended to point towards risk assessment and management increasing risk appetite:

> Well I think it means you're making more informed decisions, so I think it probably increases your risk appetite because you know more about where to draw the line. So my view is that risk awareness and risk education actually improves your decision making and probably makes you a little bit more of a risk taker because you know better where your appetite actually is. [IHL21]

---

[49] Maryam Kouchaki and others, 'Seeing Green: Mere Exposure to Money Triggers a Business Decision Frame and Unethical Outcomes' (2013) 121(1) *Organizational Behavior and Human Decision Processes* 53.

Thus we can see that risk assessment and management is somewhat double-edged. Risk is normalised, yet organisations may take more sensible, informed decisions about the costs and benefits of particular decisions. It may improve behavioural predictability (ensuring consistency of approach and reducing deviance from compliance norms) or it might insulate from regulatory action and reputational scrutiny decisions which are in fact harmful or substantively poor. The process of risk assessment and management is a nesting of judgements, and ultimately it is the quality of those judgements which is crucial. We also saw, from some interviewees, an emphasis on the behavioural and political elements to risk systems which showed an appreciation of the subjectivities within them. Whether or not approaches to the assessment and mitigation of risk worked depended not just on the rigour and quality of the processes and rules applied, but also on the spirit with which they were implemented.

RISK MITIGATION

Risk mitigation can work: to pass responsibility/liability onto a third party (such as an insurer or a counterparty); to protect property (via 'good' contracts, and IP protections); to discourage or prevent risky behaviour; and/or to restrict or ameliorate harm arising from risky behaviour. Risk mitigation could draw on behavioural and management expertise as well as legal. It can also be purely defensive, protecting an organisation from regulators through reducing the likelihood of criticism or sanction, without necessarily changing the underlying behaviours or harms which might drive regulator concern. So, a GC's role can be seen as 'controlling messaging' and the timing and nature of disclosure to regulators.[50] Risk mitigation is thus able to make risky conduct less risky or more tolerable, either because it *actually* reduces risk/harm or because it can shift that risk to others (counterparties or insurers). Equally, where some risk is inevitably associated with behaviour, risk mitigation enables the organisation to say it has done what it could to manage or ameliorate risk. The latter risks are interesting because the harms have not been reduced, but the blame for any 'risk' associated with those harms has been reduced.

Amongst our interviewees, approaches to legal risk mitigation ranged in sophistication. Mitigation could be narrowly conceived of as a set of purely legal responses (eg what in-housers put in a contract, or what those lawyers advise the client they can do), or more broadly as part of a suite of behavioural and managerial responses (such as training, communication, monitoring, process design and other work on organisational culture). We saw some of these differences in the discussion of the supply chain vignette above. In the mid-range

---

[50] Ernst & Young, 'Turn Risks and Opportunities into Results' (Global Report, 2012) 5.

of sophistication, approaches could be complex and detailed, whilst focused mainly on legal work product. IHL16 described risk mitigation as:

> change in business practices, introducing training, introducing policies, updating policies, changing policies, changing clauses in contracts, imposing new provisions, entering into indemnities/warranties, looking at extending insurance cover, extending the financial terms of the cover, the level of risk covered by the cover, changing the deductible on the policy, so yeah, all involved and much more.

The more traditional approaches to risk mitigation and prevention involved training and (less commonly) supervision. Slightly broader but quite basic approaches to risk mitigation might specify what could or could not be agreed when contracting with suppliers or customers; who had delegated authority to decide on such 'risky' matters; and by identifying escalation points for decisions to go higher within the organisational hierarchy. Escalation points used financial thresholds (eg contracts, litigation, or bribery risks over a certain value) or other triggers (such as whether a process involves the use of personal information in the context of data protection). For some, the ideal was to embed such processes so that requirements were built into colleagues' systems of work: eg through 'template contracts, templates checklists, template guides ... a contract assembly tool which automatically generates a contract [and] ... makes the consultant aware of legal risk as he or she is completing the template' [IHL8]. Registers of spending for bribery and conflict-of-interest risks, as well as registers of errors and omissions against particular policies, were also employed by some interviewees.

Interviewees differed as to the extent to which they employed the full range of these approaches, and the extent to which they emphasised steps beyond processes and training (such as looking at whether the training worked, testing whether supervision was actually carried out, evaluating the impact of revised processes on underlying behaviour, etc). This would suggest a failure to have evaluation processes as part of their risk assessment process. Or, as some acknowledged, it might be that what was being monitored was adherence to the procedure rather than whether the underlying risk is materialising or not.

The broader the process and the more systematic the approach generally within the organisation to risk, the more likely it appeared to be that our interviewees had identified elements of process or risk which they felt could be meaningfully measured. Reflective of wider trends (discussed above) towards quantification, one of the drivers was organisational frameworks which required any risk to be reported up to key executive committees and boards. Risk metrics were a way of:

> ensuring that we can take a holistic Group view of the risks that we face in the legal arena around the world and a lot of the frameworks that we have in place are designed to ensure that we have visibility at the Group Corporate Centre of what's going on in the far reaching corners of our business. [IHL14]

Monitoring could take place in a myriad of ways: staff surveys on compliance and culture; exception and error monitoring notification of complaints, claims and problems with contracts; the collation of patterns of legal advice requests (the kinds of problems colleagues were asking for advice on, and where in the organisation those requests originated); audit of contract processes or sales processes; internal customer feedback (on perceived quality of advice and documentation); reputational monitoring (ie tracking reputation with regulators, joint ventures and mentions in the media); registers (eg for gifts, potential conflicts of interest); ethics hotlines; and whistleblower reports.

A number of our interviewees emphasised, however, a tension between monitoring and purposeful data collection. There had to be a willingness to act upon information collected for these data to be taken seriously and become meaningful indicators of underlying risk or adherence to risk mitigation. The crucial question therefore was:

> Do we monitor it and have active plans to make sure [risk is] at the same level, no higher, no lower? If it moves [above what is acceptable] we've got to start actively managing it down and it has an impact on other things. [IHL12]

> ... there is no point in doing it unless a) you communicate the results and b) you do something about them. [IHL16]

One of our interviewees emphasised narratives were needed beyond data, talking about anecdotes that could be fed back to keep sending cultural messages about the importance of compliance. Another used stories of historic episodes where the organisation had suffered harms as a tool to teach staff about risk management. This may be an important point. Indeed, some of the current criticisms of risk management emphasise over reliance on quantitative over qualitative data, preferences for checklist systems, and the drive towards the quantification of everything potentially risk-related.[51] In general though, the story is also that legal risk is playing catch-up: our interviewees were generally a long way from having a suite of metrics which enabled them to better and understand the legal risks posed to their organisations.

RISK AS A SYSTEM OF UNDERSTANDING AND INFLUENCE WITHIN THE COMPANY

What we hope we have begun to convey is how approaches to legal risk reflected the idea that risk more broadly understood was one of the frameworks of understanding and influence within the employer organisation. To simplify a little, either risk appetite was diffuse and risk dealt with experientially (some might say intuitively), or it was more thoroughly organised, with legal risk more likely

---

[51] See, for example, Nassim Nicholas Taleb, *The Black Swan: The Impact of the Highly Improbable* (Random House, 2017).

confined to narrower definitions of legal risk. Under either approach, the organisation led on risk. Although under the latter approach the in-house lawyers led on narrow legal risk, within organised or, we might say, bureaucratic frameworks, the in-housers might advise on broader legal risks if asked.

Yet we also saw a strain of thought that was more positive. Legal risk managers could be seen as informing, influencing or managing a larger machine:

> you need to have leadership, you've got to have risk assessment processes, you've got to have the right standards and controls, you've got to have good communication, training and monitoring and response so that you build a programme. [Compliance6]

This led some to emphasise the totality of the organisation as a system, and the needs for those appraising or managing legal risk to fully understand legal risk on the ground:

> it's people, process, systems, and you've got to have all three of those for it to work efficiently ... getting [say] attestations at the end of the year, saying, 'This is being followed properly' isn't enough, it's got to come together with all three of those aspects to make sure that people are following the processes, the right advice is being given. [IHL5]

Operating within such a system was of course political: interviewees needed to win the trust of colleagues and the leadership:

> the most important thing is to ensure that the legal function is well placed and well-staffed with people who can communicate with management and get these messages across. You can have the best systems in the world but if the legal function has no respect from the management, then it is very difficult. [IHL22]

This meant the cost of tackling risk mitigation often had to be balanced alongside the difficulty of its elimination. Risk managers, particularly perhaps those working in compliance, had to prioritise practicality. This echoes with the pragmatic approaches we have already discussed earlier in this book as part of the tournament of influence:

> when you look at when things go wrong ... why they've gone wrong is because the process was never followed because it wasn't a process that was ever really practicable and doable. So you've got to drive simplicity, make it easy ... You've got to make it as easy as possible for the right thing to be the default. [Compliance6]

Similarly, part of our cohort emphasised the interdependencies within an organisation that made risk management challenging and which engaged a wider set of skills. For example, the skill of collaboration: 'it's about engagement of colleagues and working with colleagues and not in any way minimising the extraordinary pressure that people can be put under' [Compliance2]. Indeed many interviewees emphasised the human and systemic complexity of driving change:

> having communities and building up a network of people who take ownership ... It's not drafting a policy, it's not having a risk and control matrix, it's having people who take ownership and are accountable for it. [Compliance10]

NARROW AND BROAD FRAMING: SOME EXAMPLES FROM THE VIGNETTES

The distinctions between narrow and broad approaches to defining and managing legal risk become more tangible when considering some of the case studies we discussed with interviewees. In the supply chain problem discussed above, those taking a narrow approach to risk mitigation concentrated on having contracts that would be in place to ensure suppliers were legally obliged to adhere to relevant money-laundering and anti-bribery standards as defined by the UK-based company in the scenario. They emphasised counterparties and major suppliers having 'read, understood and … acknowledged' [Compliance11] corporate anti-bribery policy and signing up to adhere to anti-bribery arrangements by contract. Or supporting the contractual approach with training and discussion so that they understood UK corruption and bribery standards. A further broadening was to conduct due diligence on potential suppliers: looking at ownership and sometimes employees to check for prior problems, in particular corruption and bribery. A small number of interviewees suggested a positive assessment that went beyond looking for problems in the past, to assess the extent to which suppliers understood and managed for compliance: 'making sure that they were appropriate' by assessing their internal standards, that 'they had the same values … how they're treating their employees, health and safety, bribery and corruption' [IHL5]. Or, 'We wouldn't deal with them unless we'd be satisfied that they'd have a certain standard of compliance awareness' [IHL4].

It is worth emphasising what is going on here may involve looking beyond legal parameters:

> recognising there is limited legal control in the company, what you're trying to do here is to make sure that those suppliers regardless of what the legal processes are in their own country, support you both in spirit and letter in meeting the laws that your organisation is subject to. And that's about building a relationship with them and also understanding why they can't meet the standards that you're setting. [IHL9]

Occasionally, ongoing monitoring of agent relationships was mentioned. The ways in which this was done differed, but some of our interviewees suggested the use of 'mystery shopping', ongoing audit, the recording of sales conversations, and the like:

> When you've got the pressure of a profitable product resting on the ability for us to maintain a control framework that has been proved to be a problem in the past I would want to be absolutely certain that that framework is going to operate correctly. [Compliance9]

An example of a further broadening was a risk assessment of local conditions: 'In my world you have to assess countries before you do business' [IHL3]. And for some, assessments were multidisciplinary calling on a range of expertise (for example, political and human rights assessments). Their organisations needed to understand what obligations they were under; the extent to which their interests would be or could be protected within that host legal system; and, more broadly (we were told) human rights and similar concerns. Risks might be segmented by industry types (where child labour or corruption might be more likely).

Interestingly, this was also seen as indicating 'what level of assurance can you have around people?' [IHL12], as well as being relevant to reputation: 'how trading with that country might feed back into issues within your own other markets ... embargoes or licences, issues around wider reputation on brand risk' [IHL12]. This interviewee went on to suggest that:

> Any properly structured process for on-boarding suppliers should have a full political analysis around the source of supply, the regulatory framework, the quality of the employee environment, the business risk, the litigation risks, the environmental risks, the bribery risks of going into the country. [IHL12]

CONCLUSIONS

The pursuit of influence takes place within a network that is pyramidal. That pyramid shape determines which work is seen as most valuable. If the 'GC value pyramid' places reactive work on compliance or regulatory issues at the bottom, and the proactive making of strategic business plans and introducing commercial opportunities at the top,[52] then risk management is one way in which in-house lawyers can move up within the pyramid, by becoming more strategic, by quantifying and generalising, by speaking to the organisation clearly in its own terms, by saving or making money; and by being able to demonstrate general impact. We see in this chapter for some in-house lawyers a shift from reactivity to proactivity, a shift from a dyadic lawyer-adviser role to a multi-dimensional networked role: adviser, information gather, influencer and system-designer. Interestingly, these opportunities are most often apparent in organisations that narrowly define legal risk. Where risk is more broadly conceptualised, risk management is generally less organised; but the different approaches to risk management showed us that it was possible for broad and proactive approaches to legal risk to be taken, and that some of our respondents had experience of doing so. Put another way, how in-house lawyers thought about risk, and how they conceptualised risk appetite was always influenced, sometimes dominated, by their organisational employer. What is more, risk logics and frameworks could institutionalise these limits. Yet, we saw how through leadership and organisation, proactivity and resources, it was also possible for a strong hybrid of professional and organisational logics to develop. In the next chapter we turn to the role of professional ethics in shaping that balancing of logics.

---

[52] Nabarro, 'From In house lawyer to business counsel' (Naborro LLP Report 2010).

6
Ethics and Legal Risk Management

As we saw in the last chapter, from a legal perspective the adverse events that legal risk mangers seek to mitigate or avoid are breaches of the law (for example, a failure to comply with regulations or the creation of tortious claims) but also the failure to protect legal entitlements (including poor contracts or failures to protect IP). If we think in terms of the dominant, traditional literature on in-house lawyers, risk management could be thought of as an edifice designed to deal with the issues of independence and naysaying. Risk management structures and proceduralises independence and entrepreneurialism in a framework for decision-making organised socio-politically and, if the process is developed formally, bureaucratically.

In terms of professional rules, a number of principles in the professional codes of conduct are implicated in risk management. The lawyer's obligations to 'uphold the rule of law and the proper administration of justice'[1] and to ensure the client's best interests may be in tension. This is true if the organisation is willing to place organisational imperatives above legality, but also if opportunities are forgone because of too cautious a view of legal risk. Such judgements are mediated by the in-house lawyer's ability to identify and calibrate risk accurately within their organisations. Their ability to balance these obligations, as we discussed in Chapter 4 in particular, is habitually seen as protected by an obligation of independence. And in-house lawyers must also, of course, behave with integrity and honesty. Complicating this mix is an additional professional obligation, on solicitors,[2] to carry out their roles, 'in accordance with proper governance and sound financial and risk management principles.'[3] Risk is thus both an organising principle of in-housers' work and relevant to their regulatory requirements.

An interesting broader question can be raised: are there *inherent* ethical dimensions to risk management? Do some approaches to risk diminish the ethicality of decision-making in particular directions? In seeing the future as an inevitably risky place, one response is to behave with short-term self-interest and less regard for adverse consequences.[4] Where discrete actions

---

[1] Principle 1, SRA Handbook and Code of Conduct 2014. See www.sra.org.uk/solicitors/handbook/handbookprinciples/content.page, accessed 24 April 2018.
[2] There is no Core Duty on barristers in respect of risk.
[3] Principle 8, SRA Handbook.
[4] Zygmunt Bauman, *The Individualized Society* (John Wiley & Sons, 2013) 52.

(of employees individually or the organisation collectively) create harms bigger than the behaviour of individuals (climate change; bribery and corruption; the dynamics of the financial services market are all plausible examples), then there may be a tendency (or a temptation) to see these modern 'natural forces' as relieving individuals of responsibility. Highly flexible employment contracts or high-pressure working environments may create conditions where employees are 'unable to take the necessary decisions in a properly founded way, by considering interests, morality and consequences.'[5]

On the other hand, the management of risk may make recognising the interdependencies between an organisation, its stakeholders and the broader public stronger. If one manages risk, one might be inclined to reduce it. The concept of risk necessarily includes the idea that there is an opportunity to choose: 'Risk creates space for action as it opens the future for calculation, deliberation and decision making ... [It] "enrols" futures and shapes policy formations.'[6] An essential question then is whether enrolling the future in this way reduces, normalises or externalises harm, and whether the ethicality of the decision-maker means they should take some account of that.

Related to these issues is the question of the role of in-house counsel generally and of legal leadership in particular. Is that role as a 'moral compass', a 'trusted business advisor', a 'gatekeeper', a mere technician or a provider of 'commercial' advice needing to 'demonstrate value' to the business?[7] Each of these roles depends upon influence in the organisation and we have seen how the tournament of influence can, in certain circumstances, diminish conventionally *professional* values. As we will explore below, the confluence of influence and objectivity is fraught with significant ethical risk.

Similarly, the variety in risk definitions we saw in the last chapter echoes (or perhaps reflects) a concern that professional rules have not yet permeated in-house roles in a clear and consistent manner.[8] Are traditional professional values the right values for the in-house lawyer? Is independence an important or viable concept? None of our respondents' legal risk definitions took professional principles as a, let alone *the*, starting point. The ways in which the organisation defined managerial responsibilities for risk was one starting point; but a general sense of what the role of the in-house legal was is another. The latter might implicitly have been related to professional principles, but it was never done explicitly.

---

[5] Ulrich Beck and Elisabeth Beck-Gernsheim, *Individualization: Institutionalized Individualism and Its Social and Political Consequences* (Sage, 2001).
[6] Sabine Roeser and others, *Essentials of Risk Theory* (Springer, 2013) 92.
[7] See for example Nabarro, 'From In house lawyer to business counsel' (Naboro LLP Report, 2010); and KPMG, 'Beyond the Law, KPMG's Global Study of How General Counsel Are Turning Risk to Advantage' (General Counsel Survey, 2012) 8–14.
[8] Susan Hackett, 'Corporate Counsel and the Evolution of Practical Ethical Navigation: An Overview of the Changing Dynamics of Professional Responsibility in In-House Practice' (2012) 25 *Geo J Legal Ethics* 317.

A lawyer is their client's agent and is supposed to pursue their client's best interests,[9] and whilst an in-houser is an employee, they may also have greater agency than their status as 'mere' employee suggests. Depending on their place in the organisation's hierarchy, and indeed the way decisions are structured by organisational policies and practices, they can be part of the organisation's controlling mind, especially on matters of legal risk, strategy, and corporate governance.[10] A private practice lawyer in Moorhead and Hinchly's study claimed that 'companies aren't in a position to have morals, they haven't got a soul', and that 'once you are outside the area where this is straight dishonesty'[11] there are no ethical restraints on what lawyers can do for their clients, but this was not a view widely shared by in-house lawyers. Organisations are not morally neutered automatons, and in-house lawyers, in the main, recognise this.

There is another way of thinking about this: in-house lawyers cannot fully make the separation between lawyer and client that enables the displacing of ethical accountability seen from this private practitioner because they recognise that they are *part* of the client. Whilst the decisions of in-housers are shaped by hierarchy, personal and economic relationships, and a myriad of other factors, they cannot escape the fact that one of their fundamental loyalties is to an abstraction, an organisation for which they ultimately have to take some personal responsibility. Even if they do not ultimately take the decision on how to deal with an ethically dubious, arguably legal act, how they approach their own role may impact on that decision. Similarly, to act in the best interests of the client means to also understand the notion of the short- and long-term interests of the organisation; risk appetite is a factor here. Furthermore, an in-house lawyer can also carry responsibility for regulatory compliance, they owe the conventional obligations of confidentiality, and best interests representation, but also obligations of disclosure and fiduciary duties to that organisation and sometimes to regulators and others.[12]

ETHICS AND RISK

How did these different viewpoints play out in our interviews? We asked our interviewees whether the management and assessment of legal risk raised

---

[9] The idea that private practitioners are independent and in-house lawyers are not may be overplayed, and is criticised in the literature. See, for example, David B Wilkins, 'Team of Rivals? Toward a New Model of the Corporate Attorney-Client Relationship' (2010) 78 *Fordham Law Review* 2067.

[10] See, especially, Joan Loughrey, *Corporate Lawyers and Corporate Governance* (Cambridge University Press, 2011).

[11] Richard Moorhead and Victoria Hinchly, 'Professional Minimalism? The Ethical Consciousness of Commercial Lawyers' (2015) 42 *Journal of Law and Society* 387, 399.

[12] John B McNeece IV, 'The Ethical Conflicts of the Hybrid General Counsel and Chief Compliance Officer' (2012) 35 *Georgetown Journal of Legal Ethics* 677, 687.

professional ethics issues. The responses broke down into three broadly similar sized groups: first, those who considered that the management of legal risk did not raise ethical issues; second, those who considered that the management of legal risk might raise ethical issues in theory, but because they had ethical employers such conflicts did not in practice arise; and third, those who considered that professional ethical problems could and did arise. With the latter group, there was occasionally a suggestion that ethical problems were fairly frequent. The most prevalent frame given to these ethical concerns related to independence.

Interestingly, those interviewees who tended to say that there were not ethical problems tended to portray legal advice in binary terms: something was either lawful or not. Similarly, for these interviewees, legal advice clarified and made plain the law, and clients then decided to act. They advised and the client decided. Those who perceived ethical problems were more willing to acknowledge the relationship of the in-house lawyer with legal ambiguity; they saw that ambiguity could be rationalised after the event, or used to stretch the envelope of what was permissible under law. They understood how ambiguity could be manufactured, to enable deviation from what is 'really' permitted.

It seems also to be true that the language of risk provided some comfort to those who saw themselves as mere advisors. These in-housers could advise on quantification of risk and on mitigation, and then the organisation, implicitly through a risk appetite or explicitly through decisions elsewhere in the hierarchy, absorbs responsibility for the decision on risk. The problem of saying 'No' could also avoided by seeing risk as something ubiquitous, relative (low–medium–high), and managed through a process. As an extreme example, the Rolls-Royce deferred prosecution agreement reveals in-house lawyers advising on what, with hindsight at least, seem plainly to be transactions facilitating bribes. This they portrayed as high-risk rather than intolerable.[13]

As we set out above, where our interviewees saw ethics problems they tended to be expressed in terms of independence. They sometimes talked about 'discomfort', meaning interviewees felt that on occasion, unreasonable positions were taken on legal risk, perhaps sometimes untenable positions. These problems included conflicts of interest, disclosure/notification requirements (eg in relation to listed company requirements), and compliance with specific regulatory frameworks in areas such as advertising. However, there was a notable reluctance to discuss specifics, even amongst those expressing concerns.

---

[13] Richard Moorhead, 'Rolls Royce Service – Risk, Compliance, and Ethics: Where Were the Lawyers?' (Lawyerwatch, 24 January 2017). See https://lawyerwatch.wordpress.com/2017/01/24/rolls-royce-service-risk-compliance-and-ethics-where-were-the-lawyers/, accessed 24 April 2018.

RED LINES

We found that the most illuminating way of approaching the issue of risk and ethics was to ask lawyers about their ethical red lines. How did they define the ethical boundaries which they would not cross? In this way, along with our use of vignettes, we sought a more grounded and specific articulation of the balance being struck between organisational imperatives and the rule of law/administration of justice requirements in professional codes of conduct.

Interestingly, the ability of our interviewees to articulate specific red lines was limited. They were clearly thinking on their feet when asked to tell us what they were, and often sought to push responsibility for decisions back on their employer.

> Not prescribed. I only have my own red lines. I couldn't off the top of my head tell you what any of them are. There are sometimes things like my senses will say that is too big a risk for us to be taking. As I said before we're a relatively small company, we're very un-corporate in that sort of structured way, very entrepreneurial, move very quickly, and so there's no sort of set out red line as there has been in other places I've worked. [IHL6]

Note first in this quotation the absence of any principles underlying the yet-to-be-formulated red lines. There was no reliance on principles in the organisation's own internal code of conduct, nor was there reliance on external professional principles such as those in the SRA Handbook. Note second that the interviewee implicitly acknowledges the absence of relevant principles; the approach is said to be intuitive and pragmatic. The absence of frameworks for thinking professionally about risk extends to an absence of ethical frameworks. Interviewees tended to look to the organisation to provide ethical leadership here in the same way as they looked to the organisation for a sense of risk appetite:

> I'm not sure I can [give examples of red lines], because it wouldn't ultimately be me making that decision and it would be very much on a case-by-case basis. [IHL11]

Those who indicated they did not have red lines tended to be associated with a view that the client, not the in-house lawyer, took all ethical decisions, and that the law in such circumstances was always ambiguous. For these in-housers, risk and ambiguity (almost) always left the organisation with a choice and that choice excused the in-house lawyer's involvement as an adviser:

> I don't have any absolute no-no's, that's me taking a risk, isn't it? I don't have any no's. You'd have to give me an example … The fact that we, Queen's Counsel and a group of lawyers of the highest level of knowledge and distinction, think that the answer to this particular whatever it is, is X, doesn't mean anything other than that's their opinion. Until you get the European Court, the Supreme Court or whatever saying what the answer is, you're guessing. I can either have that view, or I can have one that says if I were you I'd go along with all this professional opinion. Then the lawyers run the show … it's not my decision. [IHL19]

Recall that earlier we saw that one way of denying that legal risk gave rise to professional ethical problems was to suggest that in-house lawyers just advised on the law, and that whether something was legal or not was relatively clear. Here, we see the opposite. It is implied that the law, legal questions on which in-house lawyers are needed to opine, are so often inherently uncertain as to allow the client legitimate space to take a position at odds with their in-house lawyer's advice, simply because of law's general uncertainty and the organisation's power to take decisions. Very few decisions will be subject to an exactly equivalent Supreme Court decision, and therefore ambiguity and room for manoeuvre is ever-present.

Even here, however, the in-house lawyer recognised there may be situations where a lawyer acts rather than advises which gives rise to difficulty:

> there may well be examples where the most senior lawyers are in great difficulty, but I would have thought that's because they need to do something or they don't do it, rather than, for example, I'm going to resign because no-one's taking my advice. [IHL5]

Although interviewees often started from a position of uncertainty about red lines, 'criminal' activity (or, for some, 'serious' or 'imprisonable' criminal activity) and risks with existentially large financial consequences were often seen as no-go areas:

> It's not the job of the lawyer to [make the decisions], beyond keeping us out of jail and making sure we don't go bust from a legally generated risk. The rest of the job as a lawyer is to make sure that the business has a calibration of the risk and takes an informed decision; we're advisors, not deciders, and that's the frame. [IHL12]

> I would [raise resigning] if it was something that I felt was criminal activity; I'd have to. [IHL9]

Whilst in-house lawyers and organisations like to project a belief in legality or working within the law, in reality this often meant something narrower. The elision of legality with 'not breaching criminal law' was common. In this passage we see how quietly the qualification can be introduced.

> Well no breaking the law. I think the foundation of any sustainable company has to be honest numbers and compliance with the law. So that's no breaking the criminal law. [IHL21]

In actuality, the difference between civil and criminal law is not always so clear.[14] Some in-housers suggested it was only a subset of criminal liability that they would not consider. IHL12 talked about 'anything involving someone going to prison' and 'litigation which involves criminal liability for directors.' IHL12 referred to, 'areas where our personnel may be exposed personally as a result of what they do for the company'.

---

[14] For a starting point, see Matthew Dyson, *Unravelling Tort and Crime* (Cambridge University Press, 2014).

Where breaches of civil law were discussed in contradistinction to criminal breaches, they were often couched within an assumption that a process would be established to make amends for that breach:

> the reality is that organisations take deliberate decisions to breach civil law reasonably frequently ... [eg] in the field of employment law, for example. Now there are plenty of situations where employers take the view, hopefully after a process where they've tried to reach a reconciliation with an individual employee, but actually it would be better for the organisation and perhaps even for the individual for them to leave and they will deliberately unfairly dismiss them, probably pay them off to make them content about it or at least not furious about it, and that kind of decision is made reasonably frequently. [IHL21]

The process of deliberate (civil) illegality is excused by a process of remediation which is portrayed as, but may or may not be, fair. Even those more confident that there was a wider range of ethical and legal no-go areas were reluctant or unable to articulate them:

> There's a whole load of what I would call moral ethical and legal areas where the answer's just no ... it's quite hard to say I have a list of things that, 'Here it is, here's my complete list of things I'm going to say no to', because it actually depends on the circumstances, but obviously anything criminal or involving deception to a regulator or lack of transparency would be an absolute no. [IHL14]

In broad terms, the boundaries of tolerable risk for our cohort were generally defined by an amalgam of: (i) how ambiguous a legal question was; (ii) whether it was a criminal matter; (iii) whether risk to person or life could be attributable to the company's actions; (iv) reputational risks (often probably reflecting criminality, environmental damage, and risk of injury or to life); and (v) the costs and benefits of proceeding in the face of legal ambiguity (such as the risk of sanctions or enforcement).

It is clear also that judgements about risk were heavily driven by the cost-benefit logic of risk assessment. There is also a question as to whether and when 'risks' are perceived as pertaining to risk to life or as being 'criminal' in nature. Several mentioned health and safety risks or, more specifically, a risk of death, as a risk which would not be tolerated (for instance in relation to health and safety compliance). Compliance10 said, 'I think there's a pure ethical decision ... it's less about risk appetite. I just think we think it's unacceptable.'

In many ways, this is unremarkable. It may however be rare for decisions to be painted in such black and white terms. In organisations that deal regularly with health and safety risks, life and death decisions may sometimes be implicit rather than explicit. Equally, would the purported failings of General Motors' (GM) in-house lawyers, for instance, be perceived as raising a life and death issue?[15] There, ignition problems, revealed by road traffic accident claims made

---

[15] Richard Zitrin, 'Secret Settlements Fueled GM's Latest Ethical Inferno' (Legal Ethics Forum, 14 June 2014) www.legalethicsforum.com/blog/2014/06/secret-settlements-fueled-gms-latest-ethical-inferno.html, accessed 24 April 2018.

against GM, were not reported up the hierarchy; this may have failed to prevent deaths. Conversely, developments in corporate social responsibility and business and human rights suggest a greater acceptance of a wider responsibility.[16] Where health and safety risks are part of the fabric of business, death and harm are normalised; they become more difficult to deal with. Compliance6 discussed how these risks could be managed down, but that full elimination might not be expected:

> there was also a sense if we ensured all our subcontractors adhered to our standards then there would be no deaths and we certainly have reduced them significantly because we've ceased to do business with some companies who failed to maintain our standards.

Similarly, perhaps, anything involving a significant, turnover-based fine was an indicator of something posing a risk to the potential livelihood of the company: 'we wouldn't participate in anything where a single loss event would be catastrophic for the business … which would dilute our capital [or] … cause us to fail as a business' [Compliance2]. Potentially in a similar vein, IHL12 suggested there were other prohibitions which might be described as 'fundamental': 'anything fundamental, so a corporate criminal ban on trading with government, for example, which is increasingly common.' This might have meant fundamental to an organisation's relations with a host state, or one likely to provoke a significant regulatory response if breached. Whereas Compliance5 suggested risk tolerance was low (though not zero) for anything that affected the reputation of the organisation, 'and anything to do with it acting responsibly'. Competition law was a marker of intolerable risk for another: 'we've really got zero tolerance of breaches of competition law' [IHL22].

Some articulated a firmer notion of legality and resistance to creative compliance: 'I personally wouldn't and didn't recommend constructs to get around things' [Compliance1]. Several of our interviewees suggested (in a manner that fitted with the general risk conservatism described above) a general intolerance of regulatory breach. Compliance2 would 'not take risks which would lead to a breach of regulatory responsibilities or poor end customer outcomes'. Again, these views tended to be expressed by compliance officers. Compliance8 suggested that, 'if it's a breach of law then my risk appetite is zero, in which case there is no appetite to break any laws or regulations'. Compliance3 stated:

> we have zero tolerance for any activities that might lead us towards regulatory censure. So, the way we operate that is if there's any risk that the regulator will be unhappy with the stance we take on something then we won't do it.

IHL11 stated a similar intolerance for 'regulator breach': 'if we come across a regulatory breach or somebody brings a proposal to me that would involve us

---

[16] John Gerard Ruggie, *Just Business: Multinational Corporations and Human Rights* (WW Norton & Company, 2013).

breaching regulation, the answer is no.' Though in fact it sometimes became apparent that this was not as clear cut as was implied: 'Now it's never quite as black and white as that, of course, because there are always areas which fall into the grey and ultimately it comes down to a question of judgement of the individual' [IHL11].

Compliance8's employer had global standards which it applied to level up beyond local standards. Compliance7 stated, 'I'm sure we adhere to the law in whichever country we operate in; and that's not up for debate or negotiation. We are a fairly conservative company when it comes to that kind of thing.' And unpredictable risks were ruled out by one of our interviewees as known unknowns: 'we wouldn't take risks if it was something that was not clearly understood and we couldn't manage it' [Compliance2].

Reputational risk was often discussed. Although this seemed to be most strongly linked to the risk of regulatory investigation or prosecution of the organisations or its directors, we occasionally saw more specific indications: 'We also have a definition of reputational risk whether it's national newspaper or local newspaper or international' [IHL8].

UTILITY, SOCIALISATION AND BIASES: THE NETWORK OF INFLUENCE

As we have seen repeatedly through this book, it is clear that the host organisation shapes in-houser approaches to advice and action in ways both problematic and helpful. Our respondents would say, with justification and almost without exception, that being 'commercial' or results-focused and being relevant (solving problems rather than merely advising on legal possibilities) are virtues. That this problem-solving approach involves some appetite for risk, a tolerance of the possibility of unlawfulness, and a level of comfort with law's ambiguity would also be commonly accepted amongst our interviewees. We have also seen that concern about independence was an area where tensions were most likely to manifest. Being 'commercial' could also mean being willing to cut corners, to engage in arguably legal but probably illegal acts, or other sharp practices.

Others have written as to how socialisation can undermine independence and that may impact on in-house assessment of legal risk.[17] Langevoort identifies a series of biases which he suggests are likely to impact decision-making.[18] A bias towards optimism over unpleasant and paralysing negativity; taking cues from those in the organisation who are 'visibly untroubled, committed and intense';[19] and seeing intensity, passion and commitment to the business as

[17] Pam Jenoff, 'Going Native: Incentive, Identity, and the Inherent Ethical Problem of In-House Counsel' (2011) 114 *West Virginia Law Review* 72.
[18] Donald C Langevoort, 'Getting (Too) Comfortable: In-House Lawyers, Enterprise Risk, and the Financial Crisis' (2012) *Wis L Rev* 495.
[19] ibid 512.

indicators of good faith (rather than over-confidence) are all consistent with, perhaps reinforced by, practitioner rhetoric around 'being commercial'. Interestingly, Langevoort suggests the elision of passion and good faith may be especially prevalent when situations relate to risk. There can also be 'groupthink' problems: the tendency for members of groups to 'ignore concerns or risks that are inconsistent with a group's preferred interpretation of the situation it faces'.[20] Such concerns suggest that demonstrating commitment to the organisation can be taken too far, and harm decision-making.

Another potential problem is in 'trial and error' approaches to legal risk. Ambiguity about the law when facts are complex and the environment changing can lead to, 'small steps that test the legal landscape, pulling back if there is negative feedback, but taking increasing steps forward if there is not.'[21] The more an organisation rewards aspiration over regulatory compliance, the greater the risks.[22] If the temptation is to push the envelope of what constitutes compliance with a particular law, then when that prompts no pushback from regulators or others, or if feedback is delayed because problems take years to manifest, a further stretching of the envelope may occur. The payment protection insurance (PPI) debacle in the UK may be a good example of such a problem.[23]

It follows that cognitive dissonance, the 'small steps'/envelope-pushing problem, and the delayed negative feedback loop noted above can combine to ratchet up risk without it necessarily being noticed: a problem we can think of as inching blindfolded through the grey zone. For example, the financial products that significantly contributed to the financial crisis in the beginning were initially moderate in their approach to risk but:

> [o]nce that schema takes root, then very small innovations in deal structure and how assets are identified are measured against the assumption of permissibility, even as these innovations gradually aggregate into significant changes over time. Put simply, these lawyers would never come upon a discrete point in time where what might have been appropriate before is palpably no longer appropriate.[24]

For Langevoort, such biases are magnified by organisational selection and promotion processes. The practices, incentives and ethos of the organisation may manage those who are naturally conservative away from key positions. Some of our 'risk facilitators' (discussed in Chapter 5) suggested that their promotion within their organisations was due, in part at least, to their approaches to risk.

---

[20] ibid 510.
[21] ibid 510–11.
[22] Francesca Gino and Joshua D Margolis, 'Bringing Ethics into Focus: How Regulatory Focus and Risk Preferences Influence (Un)Ethical Behavior' (2011) 115 *Organizational Behavior and Human Decision Processes* 145.
[23] For an account of this, see Ellis Ferran, 'Regulatory lessons from the payment protection insurance mis-selling scandal in the UK' (2012) 13(2) *European Business Organization Law Review* 247.
[24] Langevoort (n 18) 512.

Similarly, 'a 'flexible' cognitive style,' and high-risk appetite are survival traits, 'where corporate strategy and its surrounding culture are strongly attuned to competitive success.'[25]

The network influence we have described takes place against that backdrop. In-housers absorb the risk appetite of their hosts and respond accordingly, without, as we have seen, much mediation from professional concepts other than a rather pragmatic concern about independence. Often this may be subconscious or seen as inherent in the in-house lawyer as 'mere advisor' relationships:

> And some of that is just about you don't want to become so conditioned within an organisation that its risk appetite is seen as always acceptable. [Compliance2]

But sometimes it is more explicit. We saw one very detailed example of the kinds of problems that Langevoort discusses in our interviews. IHL13 is worth quoting at length:

> If there's a criminal matter [the business proposes] you'd hope they'd agree and if they didn't agree [you would] leave. It's often not as stark as that. What it is has been in my experience is that you're in a culture within a firm where you're constantly having to swim against the tide and being pressured. Senior management and the business people know amongst their group of lawyers who is nice and easy and compliant and who isn't. One of the very senior powerful guys at [a bank] they often operate little banks within the banks where they have their own dedicated credit person. They're very smart at getting their business interests put first, so they will try and pick off compliant people and have them dedicated ... [to] this bank within the bank ... They'd choose their lawyers that facilitate their business.

> So what happens ... if you don't accommodate the business needs and you question things and you highlight risk and you're objective and exercise judgement ... you're just not picked by those people and you end up not doing what some people might call the best work in the bank or the most high profile, you can get side-lined.

It is important to note that IHL13 was not talking speculatively or theoretically. It was a discussion which ended with a real example:

> I was involved in these tax trades where they had these incredible flowcharts with 50 entities to do one trade, and as a lawyer you would want to understand why do we need so many SPVs and where are these cash flows going back and forth, what is happening here? And I was put on one transaction and I started asking some questions, and I was never asked to do another transaction. Inconvenient questions. [IHL13]

Whilst this was the most extreme example, we saw similar if more muted forces at work on many of our interviewees. These were not indicative of a deliberate attempt to sail close to the wind, but as part of a desire to be as helpful or 'commercial' as possible.

---

[25] Langevoort (n 18) 505.

VIGNETTE – THE NETWORK INFLUENCE

One of our vignettes (set out in full below, Case Study 2) involved the introduction of a risky financial product where the in-house legal team had doubts about the potential for mis-selling. What is of note is that the responses discuss the risk before it crystallises and the vignette also engages the role of the CEO. In responses to this vignette, we saw a number of examples of how the desire to maintain the in-house lawyer's position in the tournament of influence shaped responses to those problems.

Case Study 2: A Questionable Financial Product

You are the senior in-house lawyer for a multinational company. The head of the financial service division includes in this month's briefing details of a new financial product. That product would make the company a significant amount of money if it was first on the market with it.

This product involves your company offering investment opportunities in Country X to individuals and companies that are not resident in Country X for tax purposes. Part of the profits from the product derives from preferential tax treatment on non-resident investments in Country X. Country X requires a legal opinion that your processes ensure those who invest in the product are non-residents in that country.

Compliance have reassured you that the process for establishing and checking investor status is adequate. You have some doubts as to whether your company has previously classified some significant investors with the correct residency status.

What would you do?

If it still proves that it is uncertain, do you provide the opinion to assert that it is compliant?

Your chief executive instructs you to seek an outside opinion on the product and your processes. You know that if a legal firm was presented with the product and asked for their opinion, they would assert that it was compliant if you did not refer to the concern you have about your company's procedures.

Would you seek such an opinion?

Whilst the transactions comply with the letter of the law, and sales teams will be required under the process to give appropriate advice on the potential for tax treatment to change, you have a strong belief that sales pressure and practice mean that this will de facto be ignored.

Does this change your approach?

In response to this problem a number of interviewees referred to the need to be 'active with the business, and if you're not active with them, they won't listen to you' [Compliance1] or to 'do a lot of internal advocacy' [IHL13]. As IHL13 put it:

> you'll have to do a huge relationship management piece with Compliance, with Tax, your Ops people, to find out where that information is, and, ultimately, the Board, because they'd need to be making a decision about that.

Similarly to Case Study 1, where there had been a breach of import regulations in a foreign jurisdiction (discussed in Chapter 5), many interviewees suggested that in response to breaches they would 'report up' within the company but would carefully manage the up-flow of information: 'It might actually be something that I had flagged as being an issue, but one that I was investigating and would report in due course' [IHL17]. Interestingly, a handful emphasised that this would be done verbally, and not in writing. A key part of the process of investigating prior to reporting up or out was in collecting and managing evidence, working out:

> the document trail that they'd created, because clearly that's going to create some quite significant issues for you ... you've got to collate the facts set and then work out how to report in a way which demonstrates the issue is closed and contained and seek to get whatever clemency you can out of the regulatory framework. [IHL12]

Here, the in-houser is not as concerned with the actual underlying behaviour as they are with the susceptibility of that behaviour to proof and perhaps then cooperating with a regulator. Part of this protective stance could be ensuring harmful information was not written down:

> I would also be advising the colleague that he should not be writing anything down either and give him some guidance on how to deal with this situation in terms of his files and emails etc.

> ... We will then instruct them as to what they need to write down, that will typically be a report to us that's legally privileged. We then may take a statement, in this case you might take a statement which will also be legally privileged but they will only be writing things down on our instructions. [IHL8]

The approach to privilege by IHL8 may be wrong,[26] and it shows an interesting interface between the duties to protect the client and the tactical advantage that can be sought from cooperating fully in investigations when dealing with a regulator. Another way of looking at it is that this vignette may show in-house lawyers thinking like lawyers, and not like risk managers. Or it may show the in-house lawyer trying not to leave evidence that might be misconstrued (by regulators or opponents) if it is disclosed later. We might be seeing a specific instance of how the difference between the in-house lawyer as zealous advocate of the organisation's (or senior executives') interests may be in tension with the broader notions of the public interest and the interests of the organisation in the long term. The News of the World hacking evidence revealed significant awareness and management of evidence relevant to hacking by in-house lawyers. Attempts to discover whether that knowledge percolated up to the executive level floundered, partly because of a lack of written evidence about

---

[26] *Serious Fraud Office (SFO) v Eurasian Natural Resources Corporation Ltd* [2017] EWHC 1017 (QB).

who knew what. Rupert Murdoch said this in his evidence to the Leveson Inquiry:[27]

> I think the senior executives were all informed, and I – were all misinformed and shielded from anything that was going on there, and I do blame one or two people for that, who perhaps I shouldn't name, because for all I know they may be arrested yet, but there's no question in my mind that maybe even the editor, but certainly beyond that someone took charge of a cover-up, which we were victim to …

It is at least possible that Mr Murdoch is referring to an in-house lawyer as the second person. In the US, the recent investigation concerning General Motors, which also related to inadequacies in reporting up information which might have led to product recalls (which in turn may have saved lives), led to several in-housers being fired.[28]

VIGNETTE – DEALING WITH BREACHES

It will be recalled that in the last chapter we suggested the potential for a more strategic, proactive and pre-emptive approach to legal risk. When faced with probable legal breaches in our vignettes, interviewees differed in the emphasis they gave to reacting to the event as an isolated incident and/or seeing it as indicative of a broader problem. It is worth noting that the vignettes, especially when conducted in the context of an interview about legal risk, were framed to be forward-looking, at least up to a point.

Interestingly, and contrary to that framing, for some interviewees an approach was adopted which we could categorise as focused on zealous defence, concentrating on defending the organisation from legal liability. This example comes from our third vignette (see Case Study 3 below), when the interviewee is told an employee has been selling dual-use technology (ie technology that can be used for weaponisation) to companies on a banned list.

Case Study 3: Export licensing problem

You are the senior in-house lawyer for a multinational company. John, your colleague and friend, comes into your office and asks for advice about how he can best position himself having done the following.

Under export regulations in place at the time, shipping goods into Libya required a licence, which delayed transactions by two months. A good client had expressed a need for the goods urgently and said if the delivery could not be arranged immediately they would take their business elsewhere. You know that John's team was under

---

[27] Rupert Murdoch, Transcript of Morning Hearing (26 April 2012). See http://webarchive.nationalarchives.gov.uk/20140122145147/http://www.levesoninquiry.org.uk/wp-content/uploads/2012/04/Transcript-of-Morning-Hearing-26-April-2012.txt, accessed 24 April 2018.
[28] Zitrin (n 15). See further: Robert Eli Rosen, 'The sociological imagination and legal ethics' (2016) 19(1) *Legal Ethics* 97.

significant pressure to increase sales. John's solution was to have the goods shipped to Tunisia for the client to collect them from there.

This happened several times over three months. Subsequently the export regulations have changed and the goods may now be shipped without delay (although the client no longer places orders for such goods).

How would you respond?

During the course of the discussion, we would then add this detail:

John mentions that the product has a dual-use – in that they can be altered to help build explosive devices.

Some took a defensive approach to this scenario:

> it would be what's the purpose of what we're doing and are there other things that the people are purchasing, is that their genuine business and how we ascertain that? Is there anything that we can do with this, shipping of whatever it is, which means it can't be used for that, is there any requirement on us to do that? [Compliance1]

Whereas others started to discuss a need to be more proactive in dealing with the circumstances of the particular offence and obligations on the organisation, but theirs is still essentially a defensive, incident-specific approach:

> Do they attract to our company, to the agent, is there any defence that you had adequate procedures in place to make sure that they knew they were only meant to use authorised sellers? What's the potential impact and for whom? And is there a reporting requirement? Those would be the questions that I would ask. [IHL14]

A smaller group concentrated on protective steps that could or should be taken to deal with the immediate problem and then look at whether this particular problem indicated a wider difficulty. They moved beyond zealous defence to proactive investigation. This group suggested stopping the inappropriate behaviour (often, but not always, terminating the supplier/contractor agreement) and then: 'Make sure it's not happening anywhere else ... Find out how endemic it is and whether you need to improve awareness of the issues' [IHL22]. As examples: Compliance2 spoke of investigating the governance implications; IHL4 of looking at 'failing in our culture'; Compliance9 of 'the danger is if it keeps getting repeated then this just isn't an accident or a one-off, this is a systemic issue', and ILH2 and IHL6 of making sure it does not happen again.

WHAT INFLUENCES REPORTING UP OR OUT

As well as saying 'No', a key dilemma for in-house lawyers is when and how to report wrongdoing up and/or out of the organisation.[29] In relation to the

---

[29] For some of our respondents, Sarbanes-Oxley obligations may apply. Equally, the Law Society has indicated in the past that there is an obligation to report. See Loughrey (n 10), 186ff for a discussion of where there may be obligations to report in England and Wales.

dual-use vignette we have just discussed, many of the respondents anticipated the hypothetical company having to report the matter to a regulator. For some, this required caution: a more careful judgement, with a closer look at whether any rules had been breached, and whether 'we have any reporting requirements' [IHL23]. Also, the potential consequences of the breach needed factoring in. Some were, however, more immediately in favour of reporting out:

> You need to notify HM Treasury without delay! [IHL5]

> The fact is what was done at the time was incorrect, that would be regarded as a breach and that should be reported. [IHL3]

Interestingly, reporting out was seen as an opportunity to regain some control over the situation by being proactive with the regulator.

> I would back my ability to bring it to the authorities and go, 'Look here, we've got this wrong and we're bringing it to you and we're asking you for leniency.' [IHL15]

But for some it was more of a cost-benefit calculation:

> there's a risk that this matter could result in a prosecution and then one would have to analyse where those risks were and whether or not this was a case where the group should consider self-reporting and whether that would be better than waiting for it inevitably to be discovered and finding a much tougher sanction … So, all those type of things will need to be considered. [IHL16]

Either on cost-benefit or instinctive grounds (the latter often based on experience and a pragmatic belief that 'coming clean' was better in the long run), overwhelmingly our interviewees suggested that they leaned toward disclosing up and then out of the organisation, although some suggested greater resistance: 'if we needed to make disclosures, we'd make disclosures and we'd get independent legal advice and follow it through them' [Compliance10].

AN ETHICAL SPACE IN LEGAL RISK ASSESSMENT?

The proactive, pre-emptive approach is one way in which legal risk management has the potential to improve standards of compliance and legality derived, perhaps, from a broader organisational focus on managing for legality. An interesting related question is whether our interviewees saw ethical dimensions as relevant to legal risk assessment and management beyond their legal professional obligations. Some of our interviewees took a more expansive than average view of the in-house lawyer's role in relation to risk:

> We wouldn't do anything illegal, but it's not just about that, because you can do lots of legal things and they could be unethical, and that way you end up with lots of very clever lawyering going on and everybody thinks you're a bunch of crooks, so you've got to be careful about whether or not it's the right thing to do, and it might be legal to do it, but is it the right thing to do? So we spend a lot of time worrying about things like that. [Compliance5]

It is often claimed there is a growing responsibility for a broader notion of ethics within legal functions (beyond the profession-specific sense of ethics). Indeed, many of our interviewees reported greater systemic recognition of ethics within their organisations. Organisational positions were defined and transmitted through codes of conduct and statements of values. CEOs and management committees were seen as being responsible for showing ethical leadership by communicating corporate ethical positions, by punishing wrongdoing, and through training. For some, structures of support and/or monitoring had developed to translate that 'tone from the top' into the organisation. Similarly, senior legal and/or compliance officers were often responsible for developing and implementing the organisation's code of conduct.

The kinds of issues which were seen as ethical in this sense included fair dealing, appropriate behaviour between colleagues, and, importantly for us, how the organisation responded to legal grey areas or conflicts. Many of our interviewees said it was their organisation's code of conduct that was the crucial indicator of what counted as ethical or not. Interestingly, beyond this, interviewees did not generally speak confidently about how risk and ethics interface. Similarly, some emphasised ethics as maintaining a 'bifocal' approach to balancing short- and long-term interests. Within this group, some focused on a broader notion of stakeholders' interests that needed to be considered (as required under s 172 of the Companies Act 2006), and some focused only on a narrower idea of shareholder value. Conversely, some saw no relationship at all between risk assessment and management and ethics.

We have seen that there is a degree of vagueness about red lines and an absence of clear principles around risk. A pragmatic approach is implemented in the context of a tournament for influence on which hinges individual careers, job satisfaction, professional effectiveness, and the resourcing of the in-house legal function. It seems to us that those choices are, however, influenced by inchoate senses of professional responsibility. Some take a view that the in-house lawyer advises and the client decides, and limit their role accordingly, but others see a more nuanced negotiation of organisational imperatives and professional judgements.

Keen to probe the significance of professional qualification and regulation, we asked interviewees whether being a member of a professional body helped or hindered them in the performance of their role and in obtaining an ethical outcome. Whilst specific professional principles other than independence did not generally play an explicit role in their own decision-making, professional status was said to create some expectations within the business:

> people know that as a lawyer you are always going to operate to a higher standard of integrity or you are going to be held to a higher standard of integrity than other members of staff, and you are coming from a position of higher knowledge. [IHL13]

> ... if you are General Counsel in an organisation, you have a certain standing within an organisation because of the role you have that you could say comes from the fact

that you are a member of a professional body, which I think amplifies the need for you to act properly in everything you do because the shadow you cast as a General Counsel is pretty material. [IHL2]

And it was possible for the corporation to emphasise a determination to behave with integrity and in accordance with the spirit of the law and in so doing reinforce, and be reinforced by, the role of the in-house lawyer with independent professional status:

> if you take those responsibilities seriously and you make it clear that you do, and I don't mean daily, I don't come in everyday saying to my CEO, 'Look, you know, I'm an officer of the court' or anything like that, but … where the commitment of the leadership team including me to making sure that the new programmes that have been put in place were strong and that there was a genuine desire of both the board and, not just the lawyers, but everybody to try and root that out, I do think it helps because I think it's a credibility thing. [IHL21]

Many of our interviewees felt professional status underlined the importance of independence; and – interestingly – it was also these interviewees who tended to say that this gives rise to professional ethics concerns. Similarly, they rarely if ever were able to identify ways in which their professional rules have helped them take more ethical decisions in practice. So, for example:

> I think it helps because it helps you to understand the importance of being professionally objective… [but] … I can't think of an example where I've had to point out that professionally I can't do this or that professionally what's been suggested of me is unethical. I've never had that conflict. [IHL16]

Some did point to a slightly more concrete influence:

> It gives you that backdrop to say, 'I can't do it.' … in other jobs I've had, I could always say, 'This is somewhere I can't go because of my background.' [IHL9]

> … I think it gives a measure of objectivity, because ultimately your professional obligation is to the court and not to the organisation. It helps with that perspective. [IHL20]

> … I think it helps because I have a measure of independence and I have a sense of public duty which I think goes beyond what I do in the firm … It helps me with setting my own standards … [IHL8]

One explanation for the rather inchoate influence of professional rules may be the inadequacy of codes of conduct and ethical training as regards in-house lawyers:

> if you were relying on a set of professional rules to achieve an ethical outcome you'd be struggling to have any ethics. [IHL7]

> … I think if you just take in-house lawyers as a very significant constituency of the legal profession; there is virtually no training for in-house lawyers, specifically which deals with these issues. [IHL1]

Professional status provided, for some, a level of independence within organisations, and a basis for making claims on that independence and on the public interest. It was also said to form the basis of a claim for higher objectivity. One should be a little cautious about accepting such claims. There is research which shows that 'thinking of oneself as a professional' can lead to a form of complacency that promotes greater unethicality.[30] A commitment to professionalism, over and above simply seeing oneself as a professional, however, may promote ethicality.[31]

Similarly, those with a greater belief in their own objectivity have also been shown to be more prone to bias.[32] The fact that such studies tend not to focus on lawyers per se, and that one might regard lawyer training as promoting analytical neutrality, may mean that lawyers have more plausible claims to objectivity and independence. However, there is research specifically on lawyers and law students which casts doubt on that supposition. Lawyers tend to assess cases depending on who the client is: that is, they have an apparently subconscious bias which makes it more likely they think a case will be successful if they are told they act for that client.[33]

The relationship between the role of in-house lawyer as interpreter of legal obligations and as a strategic advisor interpreting legal risk may have opened something of a space in which ethical considerations may operate. We see throughout the interviews an importance placed on reputational considerations which reinforce some legal obligations (particularly those backed up by a risk of criminal investigation) but sometimes additional to or separate from legal obligations (particularly where media or social activists are likely to focus): 'the biggest risks that we have to manage are reputational rather than legal, because the legal stuff is quite straightforward' [Compliance5].

Predominantly, reputation and ethics were framed in negative terms – as avoiding bear traps – but some were interested in a more positive sense of ethicality as creating value, rather than simply preventing problems:

> I think it is the difference between an organisation which wants to comply with legislation, regulation as a means of keeping the regulator at bay. On the other hand, using a regulatory framework as a platform on which to create a proposition which enables competitive advantage to be taken from the way that employees behave towards customers and suppliers, obviously regulators and the like. I think it's a

---

[30] Maryam Kouchaki, 'Professionalism and Moral Behavior: Does a Professional Self-Conception Make One More Unethical?' (Edmond J Safra Working Paper 2013), http://papers.ssrn.com/abstract=2243811,> accessed 19 May 2014.

[31] ibid.

[32] For a review applied to lawyers, see Andrew M Perlman, 'A Behavioral Theory of Legal Ethics' (2007) 90 *Indiana Law Journal* 1639.

[33] Some work suggests lawyers may be less prone to framing effects than others, but they are still prone to them. See Ian K Belton, Mary Thomson and Mandeep K Dhami, 'Lawyer and Nonlawyer Susceptibility to Framing Effects in Out-of-Court Civil Litigation Settlement' (2014) 11(3) *Journal of Empirical Legal Studies* 578.

really interesting idea that there could be competitive advantage and a more ethical way of trading. It's something which I would like to see a little more of, but I think it's also a road for in-house legal teams to become much more influential in their organisations as well. [IHl1]

There are a number of works claiming that this kind of view is growing within organisations.[34] The business case argument for ethicality is partly about persuading other stakeholders of the company's good faith and partly about maintaining healthy relationships with customers and regulators, and attracting and motivating the highest calibre employees. Indeed, some interviewees claimed to have chosen an ethical employer as a signal of their own ethicality:

> So I wouldn't fit very comfortably in an organisation that didn't want to do the right thing against the spirit of the regulatory framework within which we operated because I feel that you will always get caught out eventually if you try to sort of find smart legal arguments around areas. [IHL2]

VIGNETTE – MISUSE OF THE LEGAL FUNCTION

The financial products vignette provided an opportunity to think about the professional integrity of the legal function. We can probe more deeply into the management of ambiguity, in particular. Recall that interviewees were asked if they would seek an opinion about whether a financial product's processes to ensure proper selling and tax treatment were compliant with the law (see Case Study 2, above). An aspect of this was that they were told that the hypothetical in-house lawyer in the case study had doubts about whether the formally compliant system was being, or would be, properly executed on the ground.

Generally, the firm indication was that our in-houser interviewees would thoroughly investigate and understand the processes on which they were advising. Also, they would decline to exclude relevant matters from their instructions to external lawyers:

> I've been in that situation, not on the sort of scale you're talking about, and it's very difficult because you'll find that people are seeking to use the legal function as their insurance policy. They simply want the lawyer to say it was okay; and can often put the lawyer in a very difficult position. [Compliance2]

As IHL3 put it:

> I wouldn't be so stupid as not to give the legal firm everything I need to know, because you do not use an external legal firm to give you a clean bill of health by not instructing properly.

---

[34] See for example Chris Park and Dinah Koehler, 'The Responsible Enterprise: Where Citizenship and Commerce Meet' (Deloitee Insights, 19 March 2013), www2.deloitte.com/insights/us/en/focus/business-trends/2013/the-responsible-enterprise.html, accessed 24 April 2018; and LRN, 'Ethics and Compliance: 2018 Program Effectiveness Report', http://pages.lrn.com/2018-program-effectiveness-report, accessed 24 April 2018.

So here there was an appearance of a red line. However, there were some interviewees, but not many, who stated or implied that they would accept the compliance position as indicated by their colleagues. That is, if they were told that the compliance process was operating satisfactorily, even though they harboured doubts, they might be inclined to regard the risks as tolerable, even if they were not entirely comfortable:

> I've taken the view that if the organisation decides to manage that outside of my responsibility that's up to them; but I've fulfilled my own personal obligation. [Compliance7]

And unsurprisingly those who said they would check compliance quite thoroughly indicated they were not looking for perfection: 'I'd want to satisfy myself that what they're doing is reasonable, appropriate and so on' [Compliance9].

Conversely, we occasionally saw the problem placed in its fullest context, with the desire for a helpful opinion being seen as a broader question about who the in-house lawyer in fact worked for and requiring more robust push-back:

> I think as well that these are one of those rare moments potentially at least when the chief executive is not necessarily acting in the best interests of the company. That's my job so there would be a conversation to be had about the limitations of such opinion and its value to the organisation. And maybe even the culpability of individuals who were seeking to mask non-compliance and maybe that would reassure people that we needed to go and get the right opinions in the right way. [IHL1]

Whilst this challenge to the CEO is important, it is also worth noting that it is rather tentative and careful. The word 'maybe' stands out.

CONCLUSIONS

Risk assessment and management provides a new perspective on ethical questions about the role of in-house lawyers. Risk assessment requires professional objectivity for such assessment to be useful and accurate, yet the culture of 'being commercial' and the framing influences of a professional culture that emphasises putting the client first strains that objectivity. The professional obligation of independence is also sometimes called into question.

As well as professional obligations to protect their independence and promote the best interest of the client, there are obligations on in-housers to uphold the rule of law and the proper administration of justice. A solicitor's professional obligations give primacy to the public interest and the public interest in the administration of justice.[35] This raises the interesting question of how legal risk management, which tolerates, normalises, and sometimes promotes the *desirability* of taking risks in relation to law fits with these

---

[35] SRA Handbook (n 1).

broader professional obligations. This is complicated by a further professional obligation on solicitors to carry out their roles, 'in accordance with proper governance and sound financial and risk management principles.' Risk is thus both an organising and regulatory principle, potentially in tension with the public interest.

Issues of objectivity and independence are most clearly raised in the context of in-housers being very sensitive to their place in the corporate tournament of influence. That sensitivity sometimes involves a negotiation between the in-house lawyer's view of what is lawful and right, and their view of what is tolerable. Corporate codes and pleas to take a long-term sustainable view, rather than a short-term, narrowly commercial view, were stronger drivers in that negotiation than professional principles. Risk appetites were also influential and similarly tended to come from the employer organisation. Langevoort's work suggests that the kind of influences at work may be stronger than interviewees would recognise, let alone admit.[36]

Indeed, where professional principles were called upon, it was most usually the obligation of independence that was summoned by our interviewees. The obligation to promote the rule of law and protect the public interest in the administration of justice had limited, if any, purchase. It was not a concept that was well articulated in their professional consciousness. Some articulated a firmer notion of legality and resistance to creative compliance, whilst acknowledging that legality was stretched or breached in practice, and in general, risk red lines were only clearly drawn around serious criminality, explicit risks to life, and financially catastrophic problems (which might include reputational problems, such as those associated with serious environmental harm).

In broad terms, the higher the organisation's risk appetite, the more consequentialist and relativist legal risk judgements appeared likely to become. Then, decisions would be driven by understanding the cost-benefit of a position and a relative weighting of the ambiguity of the law, the management of facts (in ways that might not reflect underlying truths) and how important the organisational objective was that raised the legal problem.

The closest articulation of professional rule of law obligations came implicitly when interviewees talked about the concept of 'comfort'. Interviewees contextualised getting 'comfortable' with law's ambiguity, but not allowing that ambiguity to be abused within the broader role of the lawyer as business-advisor. Discomfort and concerns about independence effectively meant that on occasion our in-house lawyers felt that their organisations were taking unreasonable positions on legal risk or, perhaps, untenable positions on the legality of their actions.

---

[36] Langevoort (n 18); Donald C Langevoort, 'Selling Hope, Selling Risk: Some Lessons for Law from Behavioral Economics about Stockbrokers and Sophisticated Customers' [1996] *California Law Review* 627; Donald C Langevoort, 'Chasing the Greased Pig Down Wall Street: A Gatekeeper's Guide to the Psychology, Culture, and Ethics of Financial Risk Taking' (2010) 96 *Cornell Law Review* 1209.

Whilst professional principles were generally not called upon, professional *status* was perceived as useful. It helped establish a level of independence within the businesses and a basis for making claims on that independence and on the public interest. It was also said to form the basis of a claim for higher objectivity. One should be a little cautious about accepting such claims. There is research which shows that 'thinking of oneself as a professional' may, on its own, lead to a form of complacency that promotes greater unethicality.[37] Commitment to the principles of professionalism, however, may promote ethicality. Equally, we have seen earlier in this book how the majority of our interviewees told us they felt their employers did not understand their professional obligations. Thus, the importance of professional *status* may simply be a thin status-marker without much knowledge of what comes with that marker.

Finally, if we think of the interplay between professional and risk logics at work here, then we see an opportunity for professional assertion and leadership. If management of risk is a strategic imperative, then being better able to manage legal risk is a way of improving organisational legality and ethicality whilst also improving the strategic influence of the individual lawyers. Organisational and personal incentives have the potential to align, in theory. We saw this potential on occasion: in-housers can lead on broader notions of ethicality, and can develop proactive, rather than defensive, roles in promoting pre-emptive risk work. It is an open question as to whether the organisation needs to shape itself as being open to that role, or whether particularly talented and influential lawyers can make the case.

Our data suggest quite strongly that the organisation leads, often under the watchful eye of regulators and sometimes in the backwash of scandals, but that does not rule out the possibility that such leadership has been instigated by in-house lawyers themselves. The previous chapter suggested that legal risk management had not solidified into a meaningful, professionally recognised practice. Pragmatism and individual judgement still, perhaps necessarily, lie at the heart of much legal risk work. The influences on that judgement are varied but often come from the organisation. Our interviews suggest that professional notions of independence and legality play some, if muted, roles. But in broad terms, legality is subverted to consequentialism; context is elevated over principles; and ethics is left to be negotiated pragmatically within the tournament of influence. This remains true even sometimes when dealing with serious crime such as the bribery at Rolls-Royce. As we will see in the next chapter, it is nevertheless possible to begin to see how different strains of thinking influence actual ethicality. We turn now to consider more fully how role and professional orientations impact on ethical inclination.

---

[37] Maryam Kouchaki, 'Professionalism and Moral Behavior: Does a Professional Self-Conception Make One More Unethical?' (Social Science Research Network 2013) SSRN Scholarly Paper ID 2243811, http://papers.ssrn.com/abstract=2243811, accessed 2 June 2013.

7
Striking the Balance: Identity and Orientation

EARLIER IN THIS book we explored notions of embedded and networked professionalism, contrasting the agent-heavy models of independence so beloved of traditional professionalism with system-level, ecological understandings of institutional approaches deriving predominantly from management sociology. In examining in-house lawyer understandings of their work, we see how they manifest this ecological understanding. Independence is complicated within their organisational networks; it is de-binarised and contingent. Independence from employers is not total: the obligation to the client's best interests is ever-present and for some, overwhelms other obligations. Nor is independence simply, or usually, reflected in 'Yes' or 'No' responses. Independence is rather about reflecting on the authentic rather than the desired answer; it is about the timing and shaping of advice; and, it is about investigating and preparing advice. Here, independence might not be best understood only as a response to a particular decision, but also as a process, as a way of thinking and doing in-house practice. That understanding involves saying 'No' sometimes, but also positioning oneself to be ready to divert from and resist, but also sometimes accept, risky action within limits. The organisational embeddedness we have sketched out works to make the in-house lawyer more relevant and useful to their employers, but also, some worry, more compromised in terms of their ability to practise professionally, with suitable regard for the rule of law and regulatory expectations.

Against that background, we explored, in the preceding two chapters, legal risk management as an example of the ways in which professional logics, ideas of ethics and role, are instantiated in the decision-making apparatus of organisations. We thus began to make our discussion of organisational imperatives, independence and legality more detailed and specific. We come in this chapter to a more granular level: how individual in-housers conceive of themselves, their roles and their teams.

Through a process of internalisation, in-house counsel adopt a view of the world which is shaped by the organisation within which they work, by their relationships with colleagues, and by how they see their own role and purpose within that organisation. They might develop 'cognitive biases and blind spots which can impede an attorney's independent judgment',[1] or 'engage in motivated reasoning, justifying a directional goal by searching for and interpreting information in a way that is consistent with the sought outcome.'[2] It is not an idle concern. Even without economic incentives or employment relationships, client loyalty has its own subtle biasing effects on lawyers generally: team loyalty, for instance, encourages a subconscious biasing of legal assessments towards client preferences.[3] Nelson and Nielsen, Donnell, and Rosen all note a 'strong identification of corporate counsel with their employers' even when undertaking gatekeeping functions.[4] Conversely, practitioner-oriented texts identify the need to guard against too much closeness, and for having 'managerial courage' to protect independence.[5] The competing identities of in-house lawyers are important and are part of the balancing act that we have highlighted earlier in this book. It is to those identities that we now turn.

An issue crucial to our understanding of the in-house lawyer is how they conceive of themselves and their role. In the professional periodicals, ideas of commerciality, efficiency, status and strategic influence dominate. Much of the academic literature suggests in-house lawyers are paradigms of a new form of organisational professional, in that they have shifted towards business over professionalism and who represent a distinct professional group within the broader legal profession.[6] Somewhat more fine-grained analyses point to different kinds of role, framed, as we have previously set out, as a series of metaphorical archetypes: cops (policing the legality of their organisations), counsellors (advising independently, at one remove from the hurly burly of the organisation's business), or entrepreneurs (actively exploiting opportunities presented by uncertainty in the law for business ends).[7] While these archetypes are useful starting points, we think a more incisive way is to examine team and individual orientations (and the balance of those orientations) more specifically: to disentangle the ideas contained within, for example, entrepreneurialism. As we began to explain in Chapter 2, we can separate out distinct elements of the metaphors and more clearly examine their relationships to ethical inclination; examining whether there are better and worse balances of these orientations in normative terms. What we suggest is that the metaphors collapse: most in-housers have orientations which are somewhat cop-like, share some of the characteristics of

---

[1] Pam Jenoff, 'Going Native: Incentive, Identity, and the Inherent Ethical Problem of In-House Counsel' (2011) 114 *West Virginia Law Review* 725, 751.

[2] ibid 742.

[3] Andrew M Perlman, 'A Behavioral Theory of Legal Ethics' (2015) 90 *Indiana Law Journal* 1639.

[4] Robert L Nelson and Laura Beth Nielsen, 'Cops, Counsel, and Entrepreneurs: Constructing the Role of inside Counsel in Large Corporations' [2000] *Law and Society Review* 457, 486 who cite Donnell and Rosen.

[5] ACC, 'Skills for the 21st Century General Counsel' (Association of Corporate Counsel Survey, 2015) 29–30.

[6] See, for example, Mari Sako, 'Make or Buy Decisions In Legal Services: A Strategic Perspective' (Said Business School Working Paper 2010).

[7] Nelson and Nielsen (n 4).

what previous researchers have called entrepreneurs, and see themselves as counsellors not decision-makers, at least some of the time. However, many of the ideas within the metaphors remain, as repertoires of action that they can draw on in their daily work.[8] As we shall see, the relative strength of these ideas can be associated with ethical inclination.

THE DISTINCTIVENESS OF THE IN-HOUSE LAWYER

Given the growing numbers and status of in-house lawyers,[9] an interesting question is whether in-house lawyers identify themselves separately from the rest of the legal profession. To shed some light on this issue, our survey respondents were asked how they thought of their identity. The results are set out in Table 7.1.

We can see that there is a reasonably even split between respondents thinking of themselves in terms of their professional title, and those thinking of themselves as an in-house legal adviser or other organisational role. This begins to suggest that a sizeable group of in-house lawyers see themselves as *distinct* from solicitors or barristers. An interesting question is whether shifting identities change the way in-house lawyers execute their role. Does it, for example, strengthen or weaken their ethicality? Might it begin to suggest that in-house lawyers should be seen as a separate group of lawyers, with their own regulatory code, whatever their background qualification? Mere self-conceptualisation

Table 7.1 How do in-housers think of their identity?

	n	%
As a solicitor, barrister or advocate (or your own jurisdiction's equivalent, eg attorney)	184	45.8
As an in-house legal adviser (rather than, say, a solicitor or barrister)	161	40
As a business adviser	18	4.5
As a manager	10	2.5
As a subject specialist (eg as a trade mark lawyer or a competition lawyer or whatever your specialism is)	14	3.5
As a business person	14	3.5
Total	401	99.8

---

[8] The idea of repertoires of action also draws on Patricia H Thornton, William Ocasio and Michael Lounsbury, *The Institutional Logics Perspective: A New Approach to Culture, Structure, and Process* (Oxford University Press, 2012).
[9] On status, compare and contrast how in-house lawyers are spoken of in these two pieces: Karl Mackie, *Lawyers in Business: and the Business of Law* (Macmillan, 1989); and Ben W Heineman Jr, 'The General Counsel as Lawyer-Statesman' (Harvard Law School Program on the Legal Profession Blue Paper, 2010).

would not decide such questions, but it does provide an interesting pointer about occupational and therefore, perhaps, professional identity.

There was some evidence from our data that in-house lawyers further through their career were less likely to think of themselves as a solicitor, barrister, or subject specialist. Those seeing themselves as solicitors or barristers (or equivalent) averaged just short of 15 years in practice (private and in-house), whereas those who thought of themselves as an in-house legal adviser (mean, 17 years) business adviser (mean, 17 years) or a business person (mean, 22 years) were likely to have been in practice longer. Conversely, the length of time spent in-house did not suggest a similar relationship. The identity profiles of men and women were very similar.

There were significant differences regarding work identities in different types of organisation:[10] public-sector lawyers were more likely to think of themselves as 'a solicitor, barrister or advocate (or your own jurisdiction's equivalent, e.g. attorney)' or as 'a manager', and less likely to think of themselves as 'an in-house legal adviser (rather than, say, a solicitor or barrister)', in comparison to those in business or in charities/social enterprises (see Figure 7.1). One hypothesis that might be derived from this is that in-house lawyers within commercial organisations are more occupationally distinct. Another would be that the public sector more actively cultivates a traditional professional identity

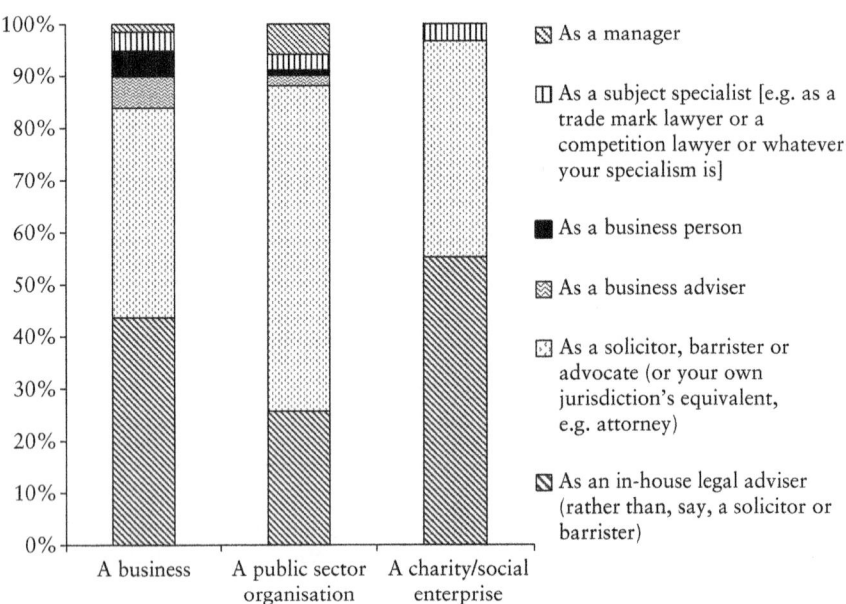

Figure 7.1 Occupational Identity by Sector

[10] Chi-square, $p = .019$.

(we certainly see this below, when we come to discuss whether in-housers see themselves as advisers and/or decision-makers in their organisations). It may also be that some public-sector lawyers spend more time in court/litigation-type activity and that this influences their identity. A further possibility is that those in the public sector spend more of their time working on national matters and with stakeholders in the UK (where 'solicitor or barrister' has greater purchase), compared with those working in commercial organisations (where 'solicitor or barrister' may have less meaning or relevance for large, international organisations, their employees and customers). Certainly, most of our interviewees called themselves 'lawyers', not necessarily because that was how they thought of themselves, but because jurisdiction-specific titles (solicitor, barrister etc) did not always translate well in large, global organisations. However, when we asked whether they still thought of themselves in terms of their underlying professional qualification, the interviewees, like our survey respondents, split.

For some interviewees, a minority, the professional title was important because of the professional obligations that title came with. One interviewee talked of how recalling that they were a solicitor was 'a useful reminder to kind of help navigate in the dark as to how to behave ... that I am an officer of the Court and I do hold that – take that seriously' [IHL24]. Such views, however, were not universally held. For some, the evolving nature of their day-to-day work had changed how they viewed themselves:

> The way that my role's moved and broadened out beyond legal, I now probably think myself as more of a business person and less of a lawyer ... I don't think I ever say I'm a barrister actually. [IHL34]

Part of this went to that lawyer becoming increasingly embedded within his organisation over time, and becoming more commercial. It is to that commercial orientation that we now turn.

ROLE CONCEPTION

As we have explored earlier in this book, in their work Nelson and Nielsen identify three 'ideal types' of in-house lawyer: cops, counsellors and entrepreneurs.[11] Whether one is a cop, counsellor or entrepreneur is determined by: (i) the extent to which an in-houser's work is 'limited to gatekeeping functions' (a major part of the cop's role, and part of the counsellor's role); (ii) the extent to which advice concentrates on legal advice (cops), contains ethical judgements (counsellors), or also develops business judgments (entrepreneurs); and (iii) 'the nature of the knowledge claims they employ' (cops primarily claim legal knowledge, counsellors claim legal and situational knowledge (experiential, common sense-type), and entrepreneurs claim economic, managerial and legal knowledge).[12]

---
[11] Nelson and Nielsen (n 4).
[12] ibid 462.

Nelson and Nielsen's tripartite division has been influential: the tendency is to suggest in-house lawyers are predominantly of one type.[13] In suggesting these types 'fit', work on in-house lawyers has also suggested that over the arc of recent history, in-housers have shifted from cops to a more entrepreneurial approach.[14] Nelson and Nielsen were uncertain, in fact, about the status of their three categories, although they attempted to put their respondents into one predominant role type. Most were counsellors and fewest cops, but entrepreneurs were seen as likely to grow in importance.[15] Yet Nelson and Nielsen also recognised the potential for role shifts: the same person could be a cop or an entrepreneur or counsellor depending on the situation. Counsellors, 'often speak in entrepreneurial terms'[16] and they thought ideal types could form part of a 'repertoire of approaches' for how in-house lawyers deal with their work, depending on the needs or pressures of their situation.[17]

This uncertainty points to some of the weaknesses of using metaphors governing a suite of concepts not necessarily strongly related to the essentials of the three types. As is attributed to Tversky,

> Because metaphors are vivid and memorable, and because they are not readily subjected to critical analysis, they can have considerable impact on human judgment even when they are inappropriate, useless, or misleading ... They replace genuine uncertainty about the world with semantic ambiguity. A metaphor is a cover-up.[18]

We do not imply Nelson and Nielson's excellent study should be criticised with such rhetorical force, but we do think that a more precise delineation of the concepts underlying their metaphors is worth exploring. The idea of entrepreneurialism, in particular, is a bundle of ideas, some more problematic than others. Entrepreneurialism is seen, in part, as dedication to managerial (or client) objectives. As we will see, this is probably better understood as something ubiquitous to service professionals and operating as a matter of degree. Certainly, all in-house lawyers are dedicated to this, up to a point. Serving the client is a central part of being a service provider and a professional. Nelson and Neilson sometimes, however, capture a qualitatively different *devotion* to the client, how the use of 'entrepreneurial discourse reflects the efforts of corporate counsel to use their legal knowledge to serve the ideology and prerogatives of corporate management.'[19] Echoing Cain's conceptive ideologist,[20]

---

[13] Oxera, 'The Role of In-House Solicitors' (Report for the Solicitors Regulation Authority 2014) 13. See Mackie (n 9); and Richard Woolfson, Joyce Plotnikoff and David Wilson, 'Solicitors in the Employed Sector' (The Law Society Research Study No 13, 1995).
[14] Sako (n 6).
[15] Nelson and Nielsen (n 4) 468.
[16] ibid 487.
[17] ibid 463.
[18] Michael Lewis, *The Undoing Project: A Friendship That Changed th World* (Penguin, 2016).
[19] Nelson and Nielsen (n 4) 469.
[20] Maureen Cain, 'The General Practice Lawyer and the Client: Towards a Radical Conception' [1979] *International Journal of the Sociology of Law* 331.

dedication speaks to motivation. Thus, Nelson and Nielsen have some entrepreneurial interviewees who see their first obligation as being to shareholders; others that reflect a desire to be doing 'popular' work (not litigation or gatekeeping); some that defer to managerial judgements on legal risk; and some that are distinguished by an interest 'in making money and growing the company ... Business objectives, rather than legal accomplishments, motivate his work.'[21]

Later in this chapter we will tease out other currents running within the cops, counsellor, and entrepreneur metaphors. Our original thinking was to test empirically whether the kinds of categories Nelson and Nielson saw, and other similar categorisations in the literature and in professional practice, were demonstrated in the in-housers we surveyed. We wanted to see if the existing metaphors and categories of in-house lawyers could be measured with more clarity and to examine more clearly some of the anxieties expressed about the different role types: Nelson and Neilson seem concerned, for example, about aspects of the entrepreneurial role. We supplemented the occupational identity question above (Figure 7.1) with a much more detailed investigation of how our respondents conceived of their role. They were asked, 'What is your attitude to the following statements about the in-house lawyer role?' and were given 28 attitudinal statements, based on our analysis of the literature, and the first set of interviews we conducted for this research.[22] We set out in Chapter 2 how five role orientations sufficiently reliable to be included in the analysis were developed. Our approach is to examine those as broad attitudes to role and professionalism, bearing in mind, the 'material practices and symbolic constructions', and the organising principles,[23] that organisations and individuals rely upon when taking decisions as we saw in the last chapters on risk.[24] Part of this involves thinking about how role orientations adopt logics from elsewhere.[25] Ideas such as commercial awareness, or risk, are invested with meaning from outside the legal professional domain. And some have suggested adopting such logics means abandoning civic-minded morality (or 'social trusteeship') in favour of a vision of professionalism as market-led, technical expertise.[26] Whereas Gunz and Gunz found problematic

---

[21] Nelson and Nielsen (n 4) 468.
[22] See Richard Moorhead and Steven Vaughan, 'Legal Risk: Definition, Management and Ethics' (Social Science Research Network 2015, SSRN Scholarly Paper ID 2594228).
[23] Richard W Scott, 'Lords of the dance: Professionals as institutional agents' (2008) 19(2) *Organization Studies* 219, 231–32; citing; Roger Friedland and Robert Alford, 'Bringing Society Back In: Symbols, Practices and Institutional Contradictions' in Walter Powell and Paul Dimaggio (eds), *The New Institutionalism in Organizational Analysis* (University of Chicago Press, 1991).
[24] See also, Patricia H Thornton and William Ocasio, 'Institutional Logics and the Historical Contingency of Power in Organizations: Executive Succession in the Higher Education Publishing Industry, 1958–1990' (1999) 105 *American Journal of Sociology* 801.
[25] Scott (n 23) 232.
[26] Steven Brint, *In an Age of Experts: The Changing Role of Professionals in Politics and Public Life* (Princeton University Press, 1996) 11, 103, 114.

decision-making styles related to how membership of organisational networks was structured.[27]

Commercial Orientation

The first idea defining the in-house role we called the commercial orientation. The idea that lawyers need to 'be commercial' or have 'commercial awareness' takes centre-stage in many discussions about commercial lawyers working in-house and in private practice.[28] Our respondents, whichever sector they worked in, almost always agreed this was a role they saw themselves as adopting. The constituent variables from our data of the commercial orientation can be seen in Figure 7.2.

Whilst usually seen as a virtue in professional discussions, academics often problematise a commercial orientation. Framing problems in business terms is suggested to lead to a less ethical approach to problems, for example.[29]

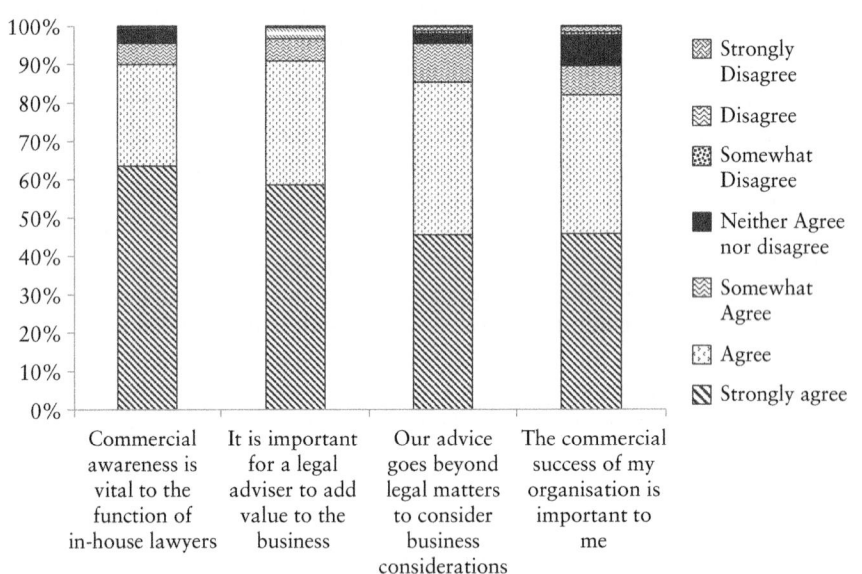

Figure 7.2 Dimensions of Commercial Orientation

---

[27] Hugh Gunz and Sally Gunz, 'Hired Professional to Hired Gun: An Identity Theory Approach to Understanding the Ethical Behaviour of Professionals in Non-Professional Organizations' (2007) 60 *Human Relations* 851.
[28] See, for example, Nelson and Nielsen (n 4) 477.
[29] Maryam Kouchaki and others, 'Seeing Green: Mere Exposure to Money Triggers a Business Decision Frame and Unethical Outcomes' (2013) 121 *Organizational Behavior and Human Decision Processes* 53.

Seeing product recall as a business decision not a health and safety decision is one example. Even subtly framing problems in aspirational, 'getting the job done' terms, rather than compliance terms, has been shown to increase unethical conduct.[30] And at the heart of most academic discussion of in-house lawyers is the belief that the needs of the organisation or its managers are sometimes in tension with the law or with ethicality, and that such tension can put a lawyer in an uncomfortable position.[31] We examine later whether there is evidence within our data to suggest a commercial orientation may sometimes lead to ethical problems. Interestingly, almost all of those we interviewed talked about a split between 'legal' and 'commercial' advice. Most see the former as the primary part of their role but the latter was also part of what they did. Some framed this in terms of both delivering 'efficient, effective, appropriately risk based legal products' [IHL24] and managing legal risk; others associated commerciality with 'grey areas', where a decision on the law was also necessarily a decision on what was a 'good deal' for the business [IHL47]. Finding the line between legal and commercial advice was not easy: 'the distinction between the law and general commercial advice and risk-averse advice, if you like, in-house does get very blurred' [IHL 46]. For many, the line between legal and commercial advice was also a function of where they worked, with some organisations (and some people in those organisations) more than others wanting their in-house lawyers involved in decision-making: 'I think it very much depends on the business and how the department has grown up.' [IHL43]

In discussing their roles, every interviewee spoke of the various 'hats' [IHL33] they wore as in-house lawyers. In this sense, 'being commercial' meant being more rounded in their approach, perhaps demonstrating a wider skill-set, and/or being more engaged in delivering work that was practically useful. In this vein, many of our interviewees sought to distance what they did from what lawyers in private practice did, some even speaking pejoratively of those in-house lawyers who take 'a very private practice approach', compared with those who are 'properly embedded in the business as a stakeholder with a voice' [IHL26]. This embedding also involves a blending of advice and decision-making which suggests a movement beyond being a mere advisor:

> It's a mixture of different roles. You're obviously a lawyer but, more than when I was in private practice, you're also a business adviser. [IHL39]
>
> I know that people want a view, they don't want me to play back external advice. [IHL30]

---

[30] Francesca Gino and Joshua D Margolis, 'Bringing Ethics into Focus: How Regulatory Focus and Risk Preferences Influence (Un)Ethical Behavior' (2011) 115 *Organizational Behavior and Human Decision Processes* 145.

[31] See, for example, Donald C Langevoort, 'Getting (Too) Comfortable: In-House Lawyers, Enterprise Risk, and the Financial Crisis' (2012) *Wis L Rev* 495.

Many of the interviewees spoke about new recruits to their teams who had been surprised on their arrival, concerned even, at the organisation looking to their in-house lawyers for decisions on what the organisation should do. In this way, the role of the in-house lawyer was far more embedded than they had expected. Some interviewees realised that that embeddedness, and the giving of 'commercial' advice, could go hand-in-hand with a lack of independence. As you embed, you become part of, not adviser to, the organisation. See, for example, how this lawyer talks about what he does:

> I felt at one point I wasn't really a legal adviser at all, I was just a business head. And it's quite nice, but you have to always try to retain some sort of neutrality in the business that you're a legal adviser. But it just happens, you get so immersed in the projects you're advising on that you feel you are something else, you're not just a legal adviser. I certainly feel like my advice would go beyond something that a private practitioner would tell me. [IHL29]

Embedding may also involve blunting technical specialisation: IHL29 spoke of himself as a 'GP' and accepted that 'You have to wear two hats really; you're seen to be immersed into the business, but also neutral enough to tell the business when they're doing something wrong' [IHL29]. For the following interviewee, what mattered was reflecting on the 'balance' between different approaches and different forms of risk:

> I think it's about achieving balance. That's not to say that you would ever do anything that's illegal or unethical, but you might accept a certain level of risk in doing something, and it's about achieving a balance between all those factors to do the right thing. [IHL34]

In his interview, IHL34 spoke of shifting from an idealised 'right way' of doing something that fitted with his professional ideals, to the eventual acceptance of something more risky. Being commercial seemed to represent the acceptance of that tension.

We could see also the commercial orientation being supported by an approach to the job which saw the legal function as a form of risk management. Eighty-one per cent of our survey respondents agreed with the idea that their job is to help set appetite for risk within legal bounds (10 per cent disagreed) and 77 per cent agreed that their job is to manage to a known risk appetite (11 per cent disagreed). Importantly though, whilst 65 per cent agreed that achieving what their organisation wants has to be their main priority, nearly a quarter (23 per cent) disagreed. As we might expect, the position is nuanced: 71 per cent agreed that it is sometimes necessary to think less about the organisation's needs and more about what the law requires; whereas 17 per cent disagreed. The body of evidence that points to the potential detriment of overly emphasising commercial ends is supported, to an extent, by 30 per cent agreeing that an emphasis on commercial awareness sometimes inhibits the in-house lawyer in performing his or her role, whilst 57 per cent disagreed.

Exploiting Uncertainties Orientation

In many ways the commercial orientation we have just described is uncontroversial. In-house lawyers exist to have closer, better understandings of what the organisational employer needs, and to be able to provide practically relevant solutions to their organisation's legal problems. In this way, if a common problem is that in-house lawyers offer impractical solutions (becoming the deal-blockers we discussed in Chapter 4), a more commercial approach may act as a synonym for more relevant and practical solutions. Yet under Nelson and Nielsen's metaphoric archetypes of the in-house lawyer, entrepreneurialism is further marked by creativity. This rather different dimension to 'being commercial' becomes important if it is related to creative compliance,[32] and the active promulgation, or exploitation, of loopholes in the law. It is the creativity within entrepreneurialism that seems to give Nelson and Nielsen most cause for concern. Whilst they see that 'highly creative applications of legal expertise to advance the economic interests of their employers'[33] might be a positive thing, it can go 'far beyond the Brandeisian ideal of counsel for the situation.'[34] For them, creative lawyering had 'a morally ambiguous edge' but was not always morally negative.[35] Creativity generated new sources of revenue, took advantage of loopholes, and created new forms of intellectual property and business entities.[36]

Attitudes towards uncertainty form the basis of our second idea defining the in-house role – an 'exploiting uncertainties' orientation. Here, we measure the extent to which lawyers said they oriented towards exploiting law's uncertainty for commercial ends, through the use of loopholes and the like. The constituent variables can be seen in Figure 7.3.

Nelson and Neilson's concern about moral ambiguity is not necessarily shared at a professional level. It is a signature of the zealous advocacy model of legal ethics that lawyers can, and perhaps should, take advantage of all opportunities available to their clients unless prohibited by law or their professional code of conduct.[37] Often referred to as the standard conception of lawyers, because it is claimed to be the dominant model, it posits lawyering as an amoral role.[38]

---

[32] Doreen McBarnet and Christopher Whelan, 'Creative Compliance and the Defeat of Legal Control: The Magic of the Orphan Subsidiary' in Keith Hawkins (ed) *The Human Face of Law* (Oxford University Press, 1997).
[33] Nelson and Nielsen (n 4) 474–76.
[34] ibid.
[35] ibid 487.
[36] ibid.
[37] For a recent discussion see Richard Moorhead and Rachel Cahill O'Callaghan, 'False Friends? Testing Commercial lawyers on the claim that Zealous Advocacy is Founded in Benevolence towards Clients rather than Lawyers Personal Interest' (2016) 19(1) *Legal Ethics* 30.
[38] Stephen L Pepper, 'The Lawyer's Amoral Ethical Role: A Defense, a Problem, and Some Possibilities' [1986] *American Bar Foundation Research Journal* 24; but see, for example, Daniel Markovits, *A Modern Legal Ethics: Adversary Advocacy in a Democratic Age* (Princeton University Press, 2009) for a defence of the morality of zeal.

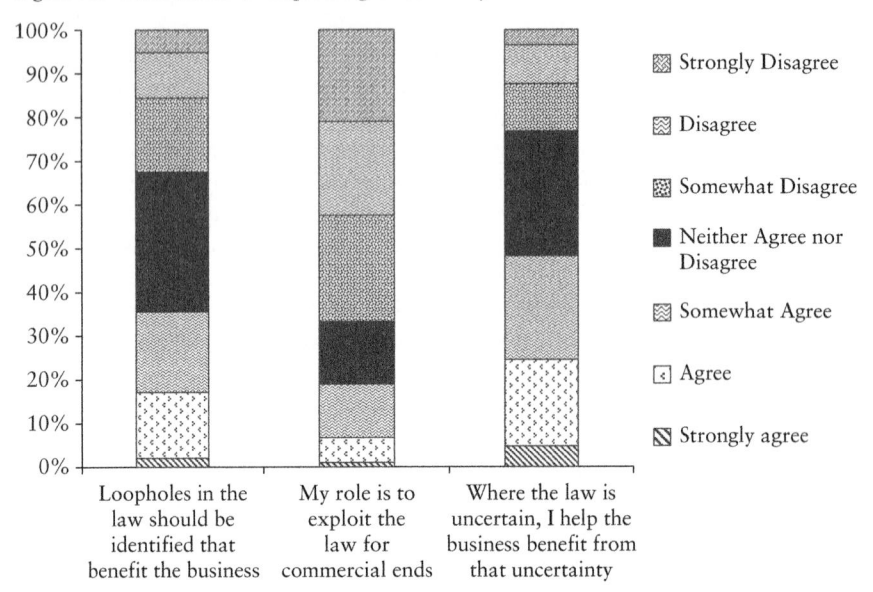

158 *Striking the Balance: Identity and Orientation*

Figure 7.3 Dimensions of Exploiting Uncertainty

If the standard conception of zeal is equated with taking advantage of uncertainty, we might see a stronger level of agreement with this orientation in the sample. In fact, our in-house lawyers were often resistant to this orientation. That said, over 30 per cent of respondents were willing to agree, at least somewhat, that loopholes should be identified that benefit the business. Just below 20 per cent similarly agreed that their role was to exploit the law for commercial ends, and almost half agreed that where the law is uncertain, they help the business benefit from that uncertainty.

The majority of the interviewees similarly resisted the idea that their role involved identifying loopholes or exploiting the law for commercial ends. The opposite was sometimes the case. This lawyer, for example, spoke of how his concerns (at the selling of particular PPI product) were pushed to one side:

> I was also saying, 'Look, it is really, really obvious where the FSA [Financial Services Authority] is going with this ... really obvious that you are not going to be able to go on selling single premium PPI in this way.' But all the lawyers and compliance people were shoved to one side on that because they were coining it; making ... I think the commission that they were making was about 85%, which is just a stunning amount. [IHL3]

Reflecting the survey data, the messages from interviewees were, however, more mixed when it came to allowing their organisations to benefit from grey areas in the law.

> I think because the law is grey you have to take a view or participate in a discussion which is a combination of what the law is and what the perception outside the law

of what you're doing might be. You can't always take the cautious view. Sometimes you have to realise that there are risks in what you are doing, but you have to analyse whether it's a reputational risk, which generally one seeks to avoid, or whether it might be a financial risk that can be quantified. [IHL42]

In this way, we see that the law's uncertainty (and how the uncertainty is used) is tied in with risk management and (and as offered up by a number of interviewees) goes to the heart of the organisation's reputation. As this interviewee put it, 'the fact that something may be perfectly legal doesn't necessarily mean, you know, people are just happy to crack on' [IHL27]. Nearly all (98 per cent) of our survey respondents agreed that their advice went beyond legal considerations to consider reputational aspects (1 per cent disagreed). Similarly, 97 per cent agreed that their advice encompassed both the letter and the spirit of the law (1 per cent disagreed). Interestingly, whilst agreement weakened when considering whether the organisation's decisions were determined by the purpose and not just the letter of the law, that agreement was still strong: 82 per cent agreed and 8 per cent disagreed that decisions were so determined.

For some of our interviewees, where the law was uncertain and the organisation wanted to press ahead with a course of action that offered up regulatory and reputational risks, the role of the in-houser was in 'managing all of those different sensitivities' [IHL30]. Only one of the interviewees discussed the law's (occasional) uncertainty as an opportunity to educate the organisation of the role of the in-house legal function (and questions of business ethics):

> We had a series of dialogue sessions where we would sit down with the managing director level people in pretty much all business units and functions and take them through eight to ten hard case hypothetical examples of business dilemmas with a grey legal position, so things like you're trying to do business in Indonesia and there's something that is lawful under Indonesian law but it's not lawful under US law or Swiss law and it's grey under English law and what's the right decision? And the main takeaway that we wanted people to have was, 'Look, there are decisions that are too hard, that there is no right answer.' [IHL38]

We were also given one specific example of one interviewee proactively pushing their organisation to use a particular interpretation of the law in a certain way to *take on* risk. Here, the in-houser pushed back against a 'legalistic view' [IHL28] in an opinion from an external (magic circle) law firm, to advise that his organisation should take more risk. It was based on his interpretation of a law on financial advice which was grey (and where others in the market had been somewhat reluctant to interpret the law in that riskier way):

> We just tried to give the business ... a steer of how they could come up with a ... solution. Taking an approach that we could intellectually ... we could sit down with the regulator ... if challenged by the regulator or in Court, we could sit down and explain ... at least explain our rationale. And explain, you know, the reasoning behind the considerations that we'd taken into account. And what we ... and why we felt that what we do was ... was permitted ... So that was an area where we took

legal risk. You know? No in-house ... no external counsel would give us an opinion that what we were doing was free of risk. And we felt it was the right thing to do for the end consumer. And that's been vindicated by subsequent actions at, you know, government regulator level. [IHL28]

What is striking is that IHL28, while pushing his organisation to take a particular course of action, still frames what he is doing in terms of 'a steer'. The idea that the lawyer advises, and someone else decides, was a common theme seen in both our survey and interview data, as we shall now come to discuss.

Neutral Advisor Orientation

The third idea defining how our survey respondents saw the in-house role can be described as a 'neutral advisor' orientation. The outlook being articulated here is that the in-house lawyer advises and then the employer organisation decides. Along with zeal, the neutral advisor orientation is often seen as part of the standard conception of lawyers' ethics.[39] Yet Nelson and Nielson identify a 'counsellor' in contrast to the more zealous 'entrepreneur'. In normative and behavioural terms the point worth emphasising is the premise of neutrality: lawyers, by reason of their advice or actions, are not thought to be 'supporting' their clients in a moral sense, and are thus able to advise clients unencumbered by ethical responsibility for the aims and actions of the client. Legal advice is for the lawyer, and any moral decisions about what advice is sought, and how that advice is used, are for the client. The implication is that neutrality involves a degree of moral prophylaxis.

It is claimed that neutral advisor non-accountability allows lawyers to distance themselves inappropriately from their own ethical agency.[40] A barrister representing a particularly unpopular criminal defendant has good reasons for being able to say they should not be associated with their client's misdeeds, but the issues become less clear with more transactional and forward-looking legal work, or with the kind of embedding we discuss above. To give an example, a lawyer who creates a tax device that is at the very borders of avoidance/evasion, and then encourages their client to use the device whilst also advising the client of the risks associated with this course of action, cannot in all honesty then claim that they bear no moral responsibility for the adoption of the device by the client.

We identified two statements which we associate with the neutral advisor orientation (Figure 7.4).[41] We can see that our sample of in-house lawyers often agreed with this orientation, although – interestingly – less strongly than with a commercial orientation.

---

[39] Pepper (n 38).

[40] See, for example, David Luban, *Lawyers and Justice: An Ethical Study* (Princeton University Press, 1988).

[41] α= .72.

Role Conception 161

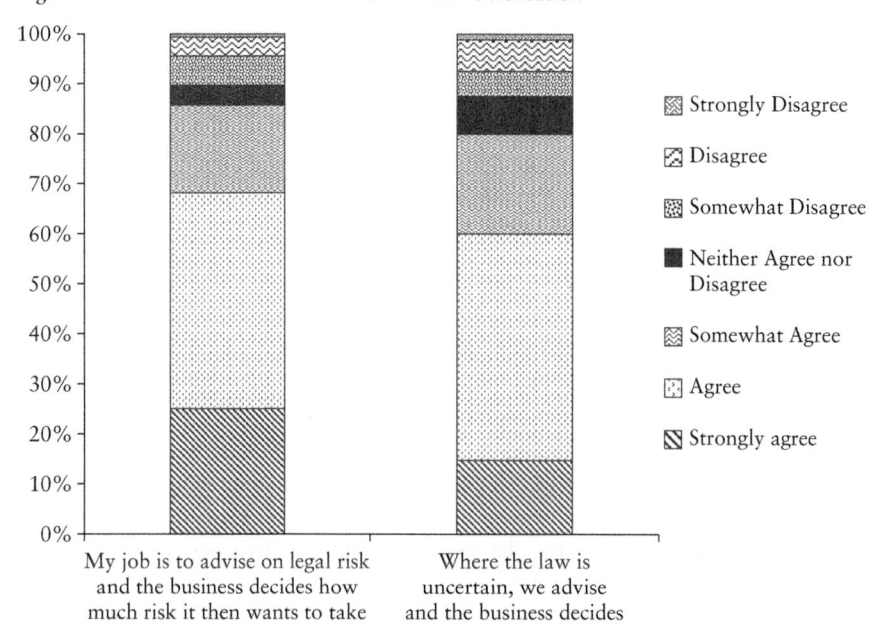

Figure 7.4 Dimensions of the Neutral Advisor Orientation

[Stacked bar chart showing two categories: "My job is to advise on legal risk and the business decides how much risk it then wants to take" and "Where the law is uncertain, we advise and the business decides". Legend: Strongly Disagree, Disagree, Somewhat Disagree, Neither Agree nor Disagree, Somewhat Agree, Agree, Strongly agree.]

From the interviews there was a rough, general consensus that in-house lawyers would (and should) only be decision-makers for matters within their specific remit and that in-housers otherwise generally gave advice on which the business acted or did not act: 'It depends entirely on what the decision is to be honest' [IHL45]. A number were reflective of their place in the organisation in this context – 'you are one of many voices' [IHL35]; 'legal isn't a decision-maker in most things within business, you're an influencer' [IHL39] – and that others in the organisation had been employed to be the decision-makers: 'that's his job, that's what he's been tasked to do, he's getting bonused on it. Get on with it' [IHL50]. Strikingly, it was often the in-house lawyers for public bodies who framed their role as one of advisor only (and not decision-maker): 'I've always made it my practice to say "No I give advice, you make the decisions" … we need to be clear who's taken the decision, who's giving the orders as it were' [IHL44]. For many, there was a subtlety about the word 'advice' that could be used as part of the tournament of influence:

> I've very rarely in my time in-house had to say, 'Ultimately my job is only to advise you'. I've probably used that three or four times just as a way of actually them stopping and thinking. Because once you separate yourself and say, 'Well it's up to you what you do with my advice' … it makes them think again about whether they should do something. [IHL41]

In that quote, we see the neutral advisor position being taken as a way of visibly emphasising the separation of roles. As we have seen already, a number of interviewees suggested that in-house lawyering was qualitatively different to private practice: that it was not possible in-house to simply give advice and walk away from how the operationalisation of that advice played out. Some framed this in strong terms:

> I think the hand-wringing Minnies, who say, 'The guys in Russia want to bribe someone and I advised them not to, therefore it's not my fault,' are a bunch of limp-wristed twits who should be sacked. [IHL35]

Equally, in-house life was said to be different to private practice because of the way in which work was approached, in how the in-houser sought balance:

> You can't go in there bible-bashing, fire and brimstone ... you have to be constructive. And there are ways and means of doing things, and that's what you learn. And I don't think I learned that in private practice; that's more something that's come with experience and from your background, you know, how do you influence people? [IHL39]

Standing back, a neutral advisor, or counselling, identity may seem less problematic than an entrepreneurial one and may better fit with how in-house lawyers report their day-to-day work (discussed in Chapter 3): company secretarial work; managing external counsel; acting as a 'cheap' alternative to external counsel; drafting and negotiating commercial terms; dealing with employment issues; giving compliance advice and training; identifying and avoiding risk; structuring deals; managing brands; and managing disputes.[42] The majority of these tasks appear to engage technical facilitation ('papering deals') and counselling (advising on risks), although within these, gatekeeping or entrepreneurialism may become relevant.

Whilst the counsellor-technician role may appear less controversial, there are normative questions about adopting this identity. In particular, there may be risks in taking a too narrow or too technical approach to problems, seeing oneself as a mere technician. One is a danger of atomisation, cutting off the lawyers from the broader picture.[43] Take for example the idea of a lawyer asked to opine on whether a Repo 105 was a true sale, rather than the fuller question to which it related: could the Repo 105 be used to take debt off the balance sheet?[44] The counsellor role can be a refuge from the gatekeeping role: rather than saying 'No', one can advise on risks 'neutrally' and shift responsibility to the organisation.

---

[42] Nabarro, 'From In house lawyer to business counsel' (Naborro LLP Report, 2010) 6.

[43] Ronit Dinovitzer, Sally Gunz and Hugh Gunz, 'Reconsidering Lawyer Autonomy: The Nexus Between Firm, Lawyer and Client in Large Commercial Practice' (2014) 51(3) *American Business Law Journal* 661, 679.

[44] David Kershaw and Richard Moorhead, 'Consequential Responsibility for Client Wrongs: Lehman Brothers and the Regulation of the Legal Profession' (2013) 76 *The Modern Law Review* 26.

Ethical Orientation

Gunz and Gunz, in a rare quantitative study of in-house lawyers, show some of the complexity to lawyers' decision-making and the ways in which technicians may abdicate from responsibility.[45] In experiments, lawyers were given problems and offered a choice of pre-coded actions in response to those problems designed to test their leanings towards what they called lawyer (cop-like), lawyer-technician (counsellor-like), and organisation (business-first) type approaches. Those more likely to select 'organisation' responses split into two subgroups: observers and advisers. Advisers would raise their head above the parapet when faced with potential ethical problems, but would not act as cops to stop the problem. Observers would simply adopt a watching brief, intervening only if absolutely necessary.[46] This emphasises the importance of proactivity and assertiveness that we have noted already in the chapters on risk, and suggests a continuum of approaches to the in-house role. Technicians 'may deliver clever but myopic solutions', while observers 'could well misjudge a situation and remain silent inappropriately.' Advisors avoid 'the "cop" aspect of the Lawyer role (in the sense that there is no implication that he or she intends to report the situation to the next level higher within the organisation, or to a regulator outside the organisation)', but at least raise the problematic issues.[47] And whereas Nelson and Nielsen emphasised 'cops' as dominated by legal mind-sets, Gunz and Gunz suggested the '"lawyers" lawyers' were more inclined to less ethical judgements: they saw their task as to 'do law' and the client's to 'do business', so ethics was left to someone else.[48] This approach is more consistent with the neutral advisor type of orientation we have just examined. The tendency of advisors and observers to 'sit back' underlines the importance of proactivity and reactions to uncertainty. We think this is important and relates to the fourth idea defining how our respondents saw the in-house role: an ethical orientation.[49] Its constituent dimensions are shown in Figure 7.5.

During the interviews we were struck by how few of the in-housers we spoke with framed (unprompted) their role in terms of ethics. Most spoke, at some point, about ethics and 'doing the right thing', but this was often only once the interview had proceeded to specific questions on ethics. Others framed these matters in terms of professionalism and how they were different to others in the organisation:

> You can just see it's human nature I think, that people like being liked. And because all you want to be [is] business partners, a lot of people just want to share in the

---

[45] Hugh P Gunz and Sally P. Gunz, 'The lawyer's response to organizational professional conflict: an empirical study of the ethical decision making of in-house counsel' (2002) 39(2) *American Business Law Journal* 241, 259: 'The methodology rests on the assumption that there is a connection between the person's response to the case and the way in which he or she would behave, were he or she to have experienced the situation in real life.'
[46] Gunz and Gunz (ibid) 272, 275, 276, 278.
[47] ibid 279–80.
[48] Dinovitzer, Gunz and Gunz (n 43) 695.
[49] $\alpha = .66$.

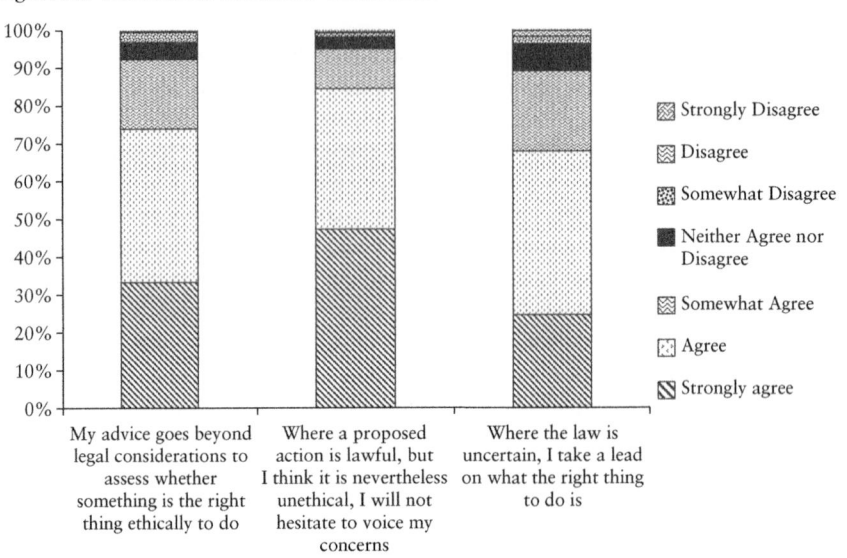

164 *Striking the Balance: Identity and Orientation*

Figure 7.5 Dimensions of Ethical Orientation

success and see it. Whereas sometimes success for me is stopping that deal and having a breather and looking at it and doing something else. Or pulling away from things that we'll do either deliberately or just not thinking it through. I sound really old now but I still focus on the fact that it is a profession and we do have those professional standards and that's what we should always be going back to. Otherwise I'm just a highly paid commercial person and what's the point of that? [IHL41]

Only three of the interviewees spoke unprompted of the 'ethical touch' that an in-house lawyer can add when giving advice, by being the 'moral compass' which prompted the organisation to have 'some of those more challenging conversations that they might not always have with each other, frankly' [IHL49]. This interviewee spoke of how his career in-house had developed: from giving legal advice, to better understanding the business, to giving reputational and moral steers, to becoming a 'rounded senior executive' who also has professional (ethical) obligations:

And then over time I think your career needs to develop so that you're more of a rounded senior executive who happens to have roots in law; but your prime obligation if you like to the business that you work for is to give them legal advice and actually when it comes down to [it] I will feel my way away from the business and stick to my practising certificate if push came to shove as well. So I say I'm an Officer of the Court and I just happen to work here. [IHL50]

The lack of discussion of ethics by our interviewees was striking but perhaps unsurprising. In other qualitative work, comparing in-house and private practice lawyers, Moorhead and Hinchly found five forms of 'ethical minimalism' among their research participants.[50] Understanding professional ethics is complex. Ethical questions being foundationally controversial and real problems rarely being public, they are difficult to capture empirically as 'fact'. While aspects of our interview data might point in various ways to broadly similar conclusions, our survey data paint a more nuanced picture. We will show in the next chapter how a stronger ethical role orientation did appear to have a positive impact for some, and that ethical minimalism is capable of being countered.

We should mention also that, consistent with the neutral advisor position, and somewhat inconsistent with the ethical orientation, 22 per cent of our survey respondents agreed that others in the organisation are responsible for considering the ethics of the organisation's decisions; their role is instead to advise on the law (a position rejected by 71 per cent). Our interviewees talked about this in terms of whether they saw themselves as the 'conscience' of the organisation. It is safe to say that views were polarised, with several interviewees talking of the idea of in-housers being the conscience of the organisation as being rather 'hackneyed' [IHL35]. Once again, a number of the interviewees framed this issue as part of what they did (as in-house lawyers) being qualitatively different to what private practice lawyers did:

> I can't see how you can do our job and not consider yourself as being there to be the conscience of the organisation or whatever you want to call it, because if you want to have that more detached role of well, I just give the advice and they can choose to follow it or not I think that's a very, very private practice attitude. [IHL53]

Despite this view, concerns were raised in seeing the in-house legal team as the sole conscience of the organisation when 'the business needs to have that conscience themselves' [IHL28]. This was because putting the 'badge' of the conscience of the organisation on the in-house lawyer 'allows everybody else to abdicate responsibility for being ethical and conscientious' [IHL48]. This might then lead to fewer problems down the line: 'if you get to the stage where we take that role [being the organisation's conscience] solely on ourselves then where's your backing? And to be successful it's got to permeate through the entire business.' [IHL39]

Independence Orientation

The fifth idea defining how our respondents saw the in-house role can be described as an independence orientation. In Chapter 4 we explored the concept of professional independence and saw that it is as much a process, a series of events, as it is a test for individual decisions. In our survey, our measure is based

---

[50] Richard Moorhead and Victoria Hinchly, 'Professional Minimalism? The Ethical Consciousness of Commercial Lawyers' (2015) 42 *Journal of Law and Society* 387.

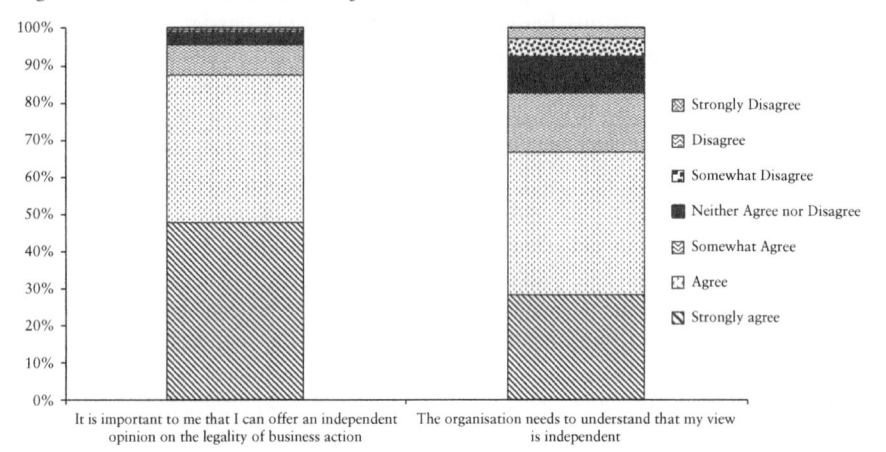

166 *Striking the Balance: Identity and Orientation*

Figure 7.6 Dimensions of the Independence Orientation

on two variables which confine an independence orientation to agreeing that: (i) there needs to be an understanding between the employer and the in-house lawyer, on the lawyer's independence; and (ii) independence is important to the in-house lawyer (Figure 7.6).[51]

Our respondents agreed quite strongly that an independence orientation is necessary and important. As we have seen earlier in this book, organisations sometimes take decisions that are at odds with the in-house lawyer's view of the ethicality of the situation or of the law on legally important matters. The neutral advisor orientation provides a rationale for justifying any snub to their independent view. The strength of the independence orientation is somewhat, but only somewhat, stronger than the strength of agreement with the neutral advisor orientation. Faced with a choice between asserting one's independence, and seeing the situation as one where the in-house lawyer merely advises and the client decides, may depend on context and a willingness – which we were all prone to – to engage in ethical fading.[52]

The weight given to opinions also appears to matter: 74 per cent of our respondents agreed that it is important to them that the business agrees with their opinion on the legality of proposed actions, whereas 14 per cent disagreed. Perhaps surprisingly, as many as 12 per cent agreed that where commercial desirability and legal professional judgement are in tension, commercial desirability is more important, suggesting independence was not strong within that 12 per cent. But 69 per cent disagreed with this view.

We have begun to see in the data a minority group that appeared to agree with a less independent or more subservient role. This was supported somewhat

---

[51] $\alpha = .61$.
[52] Ann E Tenbrunsel and David M Messick, 'Ethical Fading: The Role of Self-Deception in Unethical Behavior' (2004) 17 *Social Justice Research* 223.

by our principal components analysis which suggested that where respondents tended towards disagreeing with the idea that commercial awareness sometimes inhibits the in-house lawyer in performing his or her role, they tended to agree *more* with the ideas that: (i) others in the organisation are responsible for considering the ethics of its decisions, and that their role is to advise on the law; (ii) that saying 'No' to the organisation is to be avoided, even when there is no legally acceptable alternative to suggest; and (iii) where commercial desirability and legal professional judgement are in tension, commercial desirability is more important. The level of commonality was not strong enough for us to see these as measuring subservience as one underlying construct,[53] but it is illustrative of the potential difficulties with allowing a commercial and neutral advisor orientation to become too strong.

A CLOSER LOOK AT THE ORIENTATIONS

As discussed in Chapter 2, composite scales were developed so that we can step back from the detail and get a stronger sense of the overall picture. Here, we can get a comparison of how *strongly* in-house lawyers identified with each of the orientations by comparing the distributions of each scale. In Figure 7.7 the thin vertical lines represent the top and bottom 25 per cent of each distribution and the boxes represent the middle 50 per cent. Where there is no vertical line, the

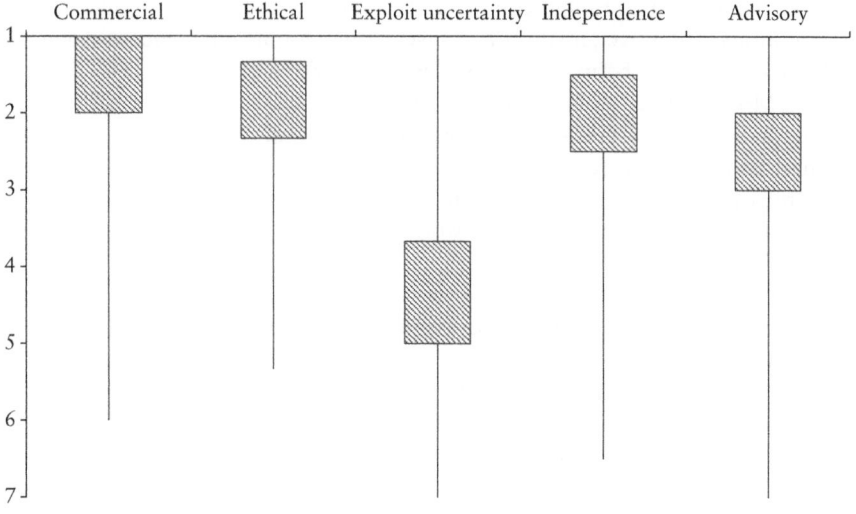

Figure 7.7 In-House Role Orientations

1 = strongly agree, 7 = strongly disagree

[53] See Chapter 2.

Table 7.2 Orientations by Organisation Type

	A business		Public-sector organisation		Charity/social enterprise		ANOVA	
	Mean	SD	Mean	SD	Mean	SD	F	p
Commercial	6.58	0.44	5.68	0.88	6.16	0.81	79.01	0.00
Ethical	6.08	0.74	5.73	0.84	5.97	0.89	7.63	0.00
Independence	5.94	0.93	6.08	0.91	5.86	1.16	0.99	0.37
Neutral advisor	5.39	1.29	5.70	0.93	5.57	1.23	2.42	0.09
Exploit uncertainty	3.90	1.19	3.52	1.18	3.62	1.18	4.10	0.02

box represents 75 per cent of respondents. So, we can see that 75 per cent have very high levels of agreement with a commercial orientation. Ethical orientation was the next strongest. Independence the third; and neutral advisor the fourth. The exploit uncertainty orientation prompted the widest spread of agreement-disagreement, with the centre of gravity of the group being just towards disagreeing with the idea that this was part of their role.

We can also compare the scores on these components by organisation type (Table 7.2). In the table a value of 7 = strongly agree and a value 1 = strongly disagree.

Our analysis of variance (ANOVA) found significant differences between in-house lawyers working in different organisation types (ie, business, public sector, charity) regarding commercial, ethical, and exploit uncertainty orientations.[54] However, no differences were found for independence and neutral advisor orientations between in-house lawyers working in different organisation types. More detailed comparisons showed statistically significant differences across a number of groups.[55] In-housers working in a business showed the highest commercial orientation, followed by those working in charities/social enterprises and then those working in the public sector. Ethical orientation was significantly higher amongst those working in business compared with those working in the public sector. Although most respondents did not have an exploit uncertainty orientation, those in-housers working in a business environment showed more agreement with the exploit uncertainty approach than those working in the public sector.

Whilst it is important to know in absolute terms whether someone agrees or disagrees with an orientation, it may be also be important to know the *relative* importance of each orientation to an individual. Someone might tend

---

[54] A statistical test used to determine whether there are any significant differences between the means of three or more independent (unrelated) groups.

[55] Post hoc comparisons were conducted; statistical significance is recorded at conventional levels of $p <= .05$.

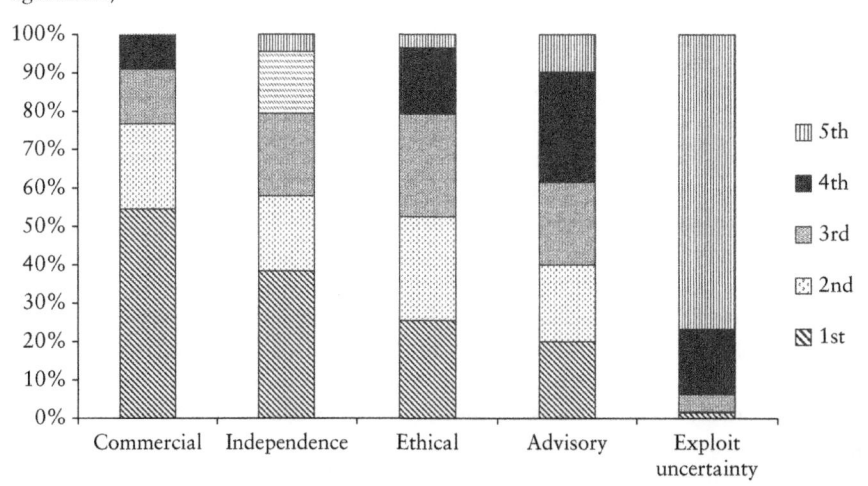

Figure 7.8 Ranking of Orientations (1st = strongest agreement, 5th = weakest agreement)

to rate both commerciality and ethicality highly, but which is most highly rated by them, for instance? Another way of thinking about this is: if a decision poses a conflict between one or more orientations, which is likely to be the most influential? If we look at the effective ranking of each orientation by each respondent (see Figure 7.8),[56] we can see that a commercial orientation was in the top two for almost three quarters of respondents. Independence was the next most highly ranked orientations, with it ranking in the top two for just over half of our respondents. An ethical orientation was similar but slightly less highly ranked.

We also analysed the rankings by organisation type. Nearly all in-house lawyers working in a business had commercial orientation as the first (66 per cent of them) or second (21 per cent of them) strongest orientation. In the third sector, 48 per cent ranked it first and 24 per cent second. In the public sector, 23 per cent ranked it first and 21 per cent second. An independence orientation was ranked as the top orientation for 53 per cent of public-sector in-house lawyers and second for 20 percent. The figures were 24 per cent and 25 per cent for those in the third sector, and 34 per cent and 14 per cent in the business sector. An ethical orientation was strongest in the third sector, where 35 per cent ranked it first and 21 per cent second. Twenty-five per cent ranked it first and 25 per cent second in the public sector, and 25 per cent first and 22 per cent second in the business sector. A neutral advisor orientation was first ranked for 28 per cent of third-sector lawyers, and second for 14 per cent.

---

[56] Respondents were not asked to rank each orientation. We have derived rankings from the strength of agreement they indicated with each of the statements making up our components.

The figures for public-sector lawyers were 23 per cent and 26 per cent respectively. Indeed, it was the third or higher orientation for three-quarters of public-sector in-house lawyers (but similarly rated for only 50 per cent of business lawyers and 48 per cent of third-sector lawyers). An exploit uncertainty orientation was generally lowly ranked, though slightly less so for business lawyers. For 67 per cent of business in-house lawyers, exploit uncertainty was ranked in their bottom two orientations. The figure was 83 per cent in the public sector and the third sector. Interestingly, for six in-house lawyers in business this was in the top two strongest orientations.

From the data we get a strong sense of the diversity of orientations within our sample of in-house lawyers. The strongest consensus was around a commercial orientation: most of the in-house lawyers working in businesses saw this as a strong orientation in absolute terms (they strongly agreed with it) and in relative terms (they tended to rank this orientation highly). Public-sector in-house lawyers tended to agree most strongly with an independence orientation. Third-sector in-house lawyers, consistent with their organisational mission presumably, put a somewhat greater relative emphasis on an ethical orientation.

It is interesting to see, too, the somewhat stronger level of agreement with commercial, ethical and independence orientations over a neutral advisor orientation. It is not that our sample did not generally agree that the in-house lawyer advises and the client decides (they did), but rather that they emphasised orientations which saw a stronger emphasis on their own agency. That is, they were more strongly in agreement with a role which saw themselves as influencers towards commerciality and/or ethicality, and for that influence to be exercised from a position of some independence, than they were to distance themselves from difficult decisions by saying the client (and not them) is responsible. This is an important signal of maturity in the majority of approaches and adds further weight to our conceptualisation of in-house lawyers engaged in on-going tournaments of influence. In-house lawyers, whilst they might sometimes call on the language and values of non-accountability, do not really see themselves as neutral, non-accountable advisors as strongly as they see themselves as commercial or ethical agents (that is, as people with some form of commercial or ethical role to play).

IN-HOUSE LAWYER TEAM ORIENTATIONS

As we have noted earlier in this book, context and culture are critical influences on ethicality. We have already considered relations with the business and ethical pressure. Here we look at team orientations. Our survey respondents were asked to 'Indicate the overall orientation of [their] team by rating the extent to which the following subjects are a topic of conversation for them'. This approach reflects how respondents assessed their teams, not what the teams themselves thought. A risk is that respondents saw teams through their own perspectives. So, an ethically oriented respondent might be more likely to see their teams as ethical (of course, the opposite is also possible, depending on how happy they were with their team). We guarded against this to a degree by asking the respondents to reflect on team behaviours rather than on something more nebulous.

Four distinct team orientations were identified using Principal Component Analysis. An ethical team orientation had three dimensions.[57] Here, most (70–75 per cent) of respondents indicated that their teams regularly or very frequently discussed: (i) 'doing the right thing'; (ii) 'treating people fairly'; and (iii) 'valuing integrity as much as profits'. Very few were willing to say they rarely or never discussed such matters.

A second component was a performance and productivity orientation.[58] This consisted of strategy and planning, and productivity and efficiency. The third, a financial performance orientation, was measured based on discussions about financial performance and shareholder/investor interests.[59] Our survey data show that strategy, productivity and finance were more frequently discussed within in-house lawyer teams than ethical matters, with the exception of shareholders and investor interests, which a substantial minority said they never discussed.[60] The fourth component, a 'societal orientation', was based on teams discussing two questions: (i) 'Seeking the good of society'; and (ii) 'the organisation's role in society'.[61] Here our respondents split more evenly between those who said they discussed this regularly and those who are more equivocal, doing so only sometimes or rarely.

When looking across the sectors at team orientation, significant differences were found between in-house lawyers working in different organisation types (ie, business, public sector, charity) regarding their ratings of the different team orientations (ethical, financial performance, productivity and strategy, and society). These are set out in Table 7.3.

We can see that teams working in commercial organisations were most oriented towards productivity and strategy. Public-sector in-house lawyer teams emphasised ethicality most strongly, followed by society and productivity/strategy. Charity/social enterprise in-house lawyers emphasised society most strongly. More detailed analysis showed several statistically significant differences. Here, those in-housers working in a charity/social enterprise rated their team as having greater ethical orientation than those working in a business. Perhaps unsurprisingly, those working in-house in a business rated their team

---

[57] $\alpha= .73$.
[58] $\alpha= .70$.
[59] $\alpha= .62$.
[60] Although these were often public or third-sector organisations, even in business organisations about 20% rarely or never discussed shareholder and investor interests.
[61] $\alpha= .82$.

172 *Striking the Balance: Identity and Orientation*

Table 7.3 Team Orientation by Sector

	A business		Public-sector organisation		Charity/social enterprise		ANOVA	
	Mean	SD	Mean	SD	Mean	SD	F	p
Ethical orientation	3.91	0.75	4.09	0.72	4.25	0.62	4.38	0.01
Financial performance	3.78	0.85	2.57	0.86	2.81	0.81	80.08	0.00
Society orientation	2.90	0.90	3.89	0.82	4.36	0.68	72.73	0.00
Productivity and strategy	4.13	0.70	3.87	0.79	3.88	0.68	5.56	0.00

as having a greater financial performance orientation than those working in either the public sector or in a charity/social enterprise. Equally, for those working in a charity/social enterprise, they showed higher ratings of their team's society orientation, followed by those working in the public sector, and finally those working in a business. Those in-housers working in a business rated their team as having greater productivity and strategy orientation than those working in the public sector. We consider the significance of team orientations in the next chapter.

CONCLUSIONS: IDENTITY, ORIENTATIONS AND THE TOURNAMENT OF INFLUENCE

The competing identities of in-house lawyers are important and are part of the balancing act of commercialism, independence, professionalism, and relevance, that we have highlighted earlier in this book. Much of the academic literature has concentrated on the extent to which in-house lawyers are paradigms of a new form of organisational professional who have shifted towards business over professionalism, and who represent a distinct professional group within the broader legal profession.[62] Our survey respondents split reasonably evenly between those thinking of themselves in terms of their professional title and those thinking of themselves as an in-house legal adviser or other organisational role. This begins to suggest that a sizeable group of in-house lawyers see themselves as somehow distinct from solicitors or barristers. This may have important knock-on consequences for how in-housers are trained and regulated. Public-sector in-house lawyers were more likely to think of themselves as a solicitor, barrister or advocate than those in business or those in charities/social enterprises. Given this, we might hypothesise that in-house lawyers within

---

[62] See, for example, Sako (n 6).

commercial organisations are more occupationally distinct, and/or that the public sector more actively cultivates a conventional professional identity. It may also be that the geographic spread of the organisation and the extent to which those in the organisation (and its customers) recognise the jurisdiction-specific titles of solicitor and barrister have purchase.

Our particular interest was in how in-house lawyers conceived of their role. From a range of questions, we isolated five orientations. The first is a commercial orientation: here our data supported the view that in-house lawyers frame their role strongly in terms of the needs of the organisation they work for. The second is an exploiting uncertainties orientation, supported by a significant minority of our respondents. The third and fourth orientations (ethical and independence) were both generally supported. The final orientation (a neutral advisor orientation) was agreed with by most of our respondents, if less strongly than the ethical and independence orientations. There were differences across sectors. In-house lawyers working in a business showed the highest commercial and ethical orientations in absolute terms. They also showed the highest exploit uncertainty orientation. If we look more at relative ranking of orientations we can see that in-housers working in a business were particularly likely to rank commercial orientation as the strongest orientations (in their top two); whereas, public-sector in-house lawyers emphasised an independence orientation more strongly, and third-sector in-house lawyers emphasised an ethical orientation.

It is interesting to see, too, the somewhat stronger level of agreement with commercial, ethical and independence orientations over a neutral advisor orientation. It is not that our sample did not generally agree that the in-house lawyer advises and the client decides (they did), but rather that they emphasised orientations which saw a stronger emphasis on their own agency. That is, they were more strongly in agreement with a role which saw themselves as influencers towards commerciality and/or ethicality, and for that influence to be exercised from a position of some independence, than they were to distance themselves from difficult decisions by saying the client (and not them) is responsible. We see this is an important signal of maturity in the majority of approaches adopted by our respondents.

The existing literature suggests the importance of commercial influences of varying types: some mundane (the desire to deliver practically useful work) and some more controversial (creativity through loopholing, in particular). The mixed attributes of entrepreneurialism are, as we have set out in this chapter, capable of more precise articulation. Some elements of role identity are controversial with in-house lawyers (the idea that lawyers should exploit uncertainty for their business, for example) and some are not (the idea that a client's interests should usually be dominant or that advice should be practical and client focused). Similarly, when we look at risk, we see how some of the non-legal knowledge-types that Nelson and Nielsen associate with entrepreneurialism are applied in the more proactive and holistic approaches to legal risk which seem more managerial than entrepreneurial. Thus, the idea of entrepreneurialism has distinct elements, the implications of which we think should be examined separately.

We have seen that technical counselling or 'lawyer's lawyer' approaches, whilst appropriate in some circumstances, may represent a relinquishing of gatekeeping functions and a narrowing of the professional frame that shuts out ethical considerations. And we have seen the significance of context: the nature of tasks; the nature of the business environment; even the particular preferences of the people involved. These may all have an impact.[63] The literature suggests to us how the shifting between different mind sets about the in-house role can be influenced by strategic choices made for intrinsic (economic and status) benefits but also, sometimes, for extrinsic reasons (judgements about what is 'best'). In-housers can go beyond simply saying 'No' to illegality, creating wider systems of scrutiny and control, and extending their roles to exercising influence over corporate culture and reputational matters.[64] This encompasses thinking proactively about legal risk, but also how legal departments contribute strategically to the organisation.[65] Our own data show how thinking and acting proactively may be an under-appreciated dimension of in-house ethicality which reaches beyond a passive, gatekeeper model. Our data also show that the strategic role is an evolving one: not as well developed across in-house lawyer teams or as well recognised by boards as might be understood from professional rhetoric on the matter.[66]

The academic literature on in-house lawyers presumes a tension between business and profession. It presents a zero-sum conflict of logics, whereas the self-image of in-house lawyers is premised on ideas of alignment of opportunity. Status, economic reward and influence but also, more rarely, ethical opportunity are presented by practitioner accounts of their work; compromise, venality and worse are the focus of academic accounts. The gatekeeping role of in-house lawyers has received the most attention, as the one most ethically fraught. It is performed within what we call a tournament for influence. That tournament takes place within a network of agents, ideas and tasks, and is impacted on by how the individual in-house lawyer sees their role and their purpose in the organisation. The principal analytical tool for understanding this tournament has tended to be independence, with the clearest test of that understanding being the in-house lawyer's willingness to say 'No' to their employer. Accounts of blended professionalism enrich our understanding of the role of in-house lawyer, reminding us that concentrating only on 'No' and on independence is overly reductive. We agree that they are reductive, but as we hope we have shown, they can be useful reductions when placed in context. Independence and

---

[63] Moorhead and Cahill-O'Callaghan (n 37).
[64] ibid.
[65] ACC (n 5) 15.
[66] ACC (n 5) 33.

a willingness and ability to say 'No' are important elements of in-house professionalism, alongside other dimensions. Those dimensions include a willingness to look beyond a narrow, technical approach to lawyering that risks ethical blindness. They also include the extent to which the practice of in-house lawyers is impacted by other external and internal factors (the organisation's ethical infrastructure; the extent and nature of regulation imposed on the organisation; the influence of professional codes of practice etc). It is to those factors that we turn in the following, penultimate chapter.

8

Mapping the Moral Compass
Orientations, Infrastructure and Ethical Inclination

THE LAST CHAPTER separated out constituent parts of in-house lawyer role and team identity. In this chapter, we explore our other measures of in-house lawyer practice not covered in the book so far, including professional orientation and ethical infrastructure. We look at what those measures tell us about the in-house lawyers in our sample, and we then bring all our indicators together to more comprehensively examine the network of influences at work on in-house professionalism. Firstly, given the debate around whether in-house lawyers should serve on corporate boards, we examine whether in-house lawyers who are members of, or attend, boards have different orientations to other lawyers. Secondly, and most importantly, we examine the relationships between our in-house lawyer metrics and a more explicitly normative measure of ethical inclination. Through that process we explore whether particular orientations, or environments, are associated with stronger or weaker ethical inclination. Put another way, it is in this chapter that we begin a process of mapping the moral compass of in-house lawyers.

PROFESSIONAL ORIENTATION

Our interview data suggest that the role of professional principles in the work of the in-house lawyer is muted. And whilst public interest principles appear to take a back seat to the idea of putting the client first, it is important to remember we saw a range of responses to risk and ethics that suggested a diversity of professional self-conception (see especially Chapters 3 and 7). As we discuss in Chapter 2, we sought to gain some further insight into in-house lawyer professional orientation by asking our survey respondents how frequently certain principles had an important influence on them in practice.

Our analysis suggests that professional principles can be considered in three distinct groups: (i) 'independence and legality' obligations, which concentrate on professional obligations in the broadest terms, beyond lawyer–client relationships; (ii) 'effective service and integrity' obligations, which can be seen as more limited to the lawyer–client relationship, mediated by notions of personal integrity; and (iii) a single criterion, focused on the best interest of the client. To our minds, the 'best interest of the client' principle, when emphasised on its own, concentrates on the narrowest framing of professional responsibilities. It is defended in theories of zealous lawyering as pre-eminent, whilst also tending to align with the commercial interests of lawyers as private practitioners or employees.[1]

The professional orientations of our survey respondents are profiled in Figure 8.1. Although marginally stronger on the composite indicator, the client orientation and the effectiveness and integrity component are very similar in

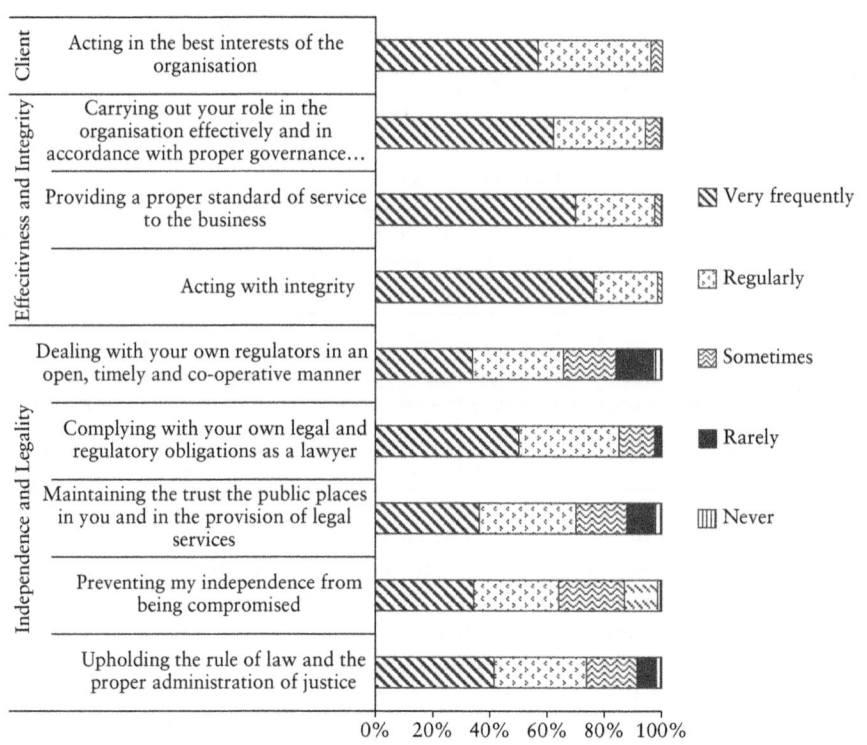

Figure 8.1 Professional Orientation

---

[1] See, for example, Stephen L Pepper, 'The Lawyer's Amoral Ethical Role: A Defense, a Problem, and Some Possibilities' [1986] *American Bar Foundation Research Journal* 24. Compare Pepper with Richard Moorhead and Rachel Cahill O'Callaghan, 'False Friends? Testing Commercial lawyers on the claim that Zealous Advocacy is Founded in Benevolence towards Clients rather than Lawyers Personal Interest' (2016) 19(1) *Legal Ethics* 30 and Donald C Langevoort, 'Getting (Too) Comfortable: In-House Lawyers, Enterprise Risk, and the Financial Crisis' (2012) *Wis L Rev* 495.

strength; with the independence and legality component third. Even so, legality and independence principles were at least frequently important for about 70 per cent of respondents.

It is worth emphasising that the 'best interest of the organisation' obligation is treated distinctly from the effectiveness and integrity orientations. Almost all in-house lawyers saw this as regularly or frequently important. But our respondents were also somewhat less likely to see the client's interests as being very frequently influential than they were for the effectiveness and integrity principles.

As set out in Table 8.1, significant differences were found between the in-house lawyers working in different organisation types (ie, business, public sector, charity) regarding their ratings of the professional principles of 'Independence and Legality'. A mean score of 4 in Table 8.1 would indicate that the particular set of principles was regularly important, and an average of 3 sometimes. A 5 would indicate that they were very frequently important. As we can see, 'Independence and Legality' was more important for in-house lawyers working in the public sector than by those working in a business. No significant differences were found regarding 'Effectiveness and Integrity' and 'Client Interests'.

Table 8.1 Professional Principles Usage by Sector

	A business		Public-sector organisation		Charity/social enterprise		ANOVA	
	Mean	SD	Mean	SD	Mean	SD	F	p
Independence and Legality	3.88	0.76	4.30	0.66	4.00	0.86	11.54	0.00
Effectiveness and Integrity	4.67	0.43	4.64	0.44	4.62	0.48	0.41	0.67
Client Interests	4.54	0.56	4.44	0.64	4.66	0.48	1.82	0.16

This takes us a bit further on the subtle view of in-house lawyer agency that we saw when looking at role orientations in Chapter 7. Effectiveness and integrity principles are apparently the most influential of the professional principles in decision-making, alongside client interests. One interpretation is that our survey respondents retain a sense of their own integrity, and the importance of that as part of an ethical orientation, but that the strongest contextual influences are about being effective and serving the client's needs. Another interpretation is that the ethical world is seen by in-house lawyers as giving the client what it wants, unless this poses a challenge to personal integrity. In this way, ethics is seen as a dyadic exchange between the in-house lawyer and the client's values. If the client's actions do not implicate the lawyer (perhaps if the in-houser can see themselves as a mere advisor), then all is felt to be well. Both views fit with the intuitive view of ethics of those of our interviewees who professed limited (or non-existent) knowledge or engagement with their professional code.

A more emphatic notion of independence, oriented towards the rule of law and notions of public trust, does not come through as strongly in our survey data, although independence and legality principles were stated to be regularly influential by many. Independence and legality principles were more influential for public-sector lawyers where ideas about the rule of law being in tension with the dictates of political masters may be stronger. This stronger emphasis may also reflect a particular culture of independence within the Government Legal Department, the wider culture of the civil service, and/or the need for civil servants to be impartial and objective in their work. There may also be a greater sensitivity to threats to that independence and/or a more pragmatic response to the risk that decisions for their employers would be scrutinised by judicial review.[2]

The stronger role of client/effectiveness principles is also interesting because, whilst the professional principles require acting in the best interests of the client, the codes of conduct in England & Wales for both solicitors and barristers show that where the best interest of the client principle conflicts with other principles then it is the principle which best serves the public interest, and especially the public interest in the administration of justice, that takes precedence.[3] Does the frequency with which client interests are emphasised in our survey data suggest a resistance to, or lack of awareness of, the pre-eminence of the public interest in the rule of law when dealing with difficult decisions? Certainly, our interviewees were hazy (sometimes very hazy) on the content of the SRA Handbook principles.[4] There are a number of ways of interpreting the data here: one is that rule-of-law type concerns simply surface less often for in-house lawyers. Another is that the rule of law and administration of justice principle is less well known, less well understood, and/or has less practical traction. A third is that any 'ethical orientation' is more likely to be seen through an integrity rather

---

[2] Shelagh Campbell, 'Exercising Discretion in the Context of Dependent Employment: Assessing the Impact of Workload on the Rule of Law' (2017) 37(2) *Legal Studies* 305. See also the interview referred to in Jess Bowie, 'Dame Ursula Brennan: The Former Ministry of Justice Permanent Secretary on Why She Left the MoJ, What She's Most Proud of – and Why It Can Be Tricky to Cut Senior Civil Service Roles Written', *Civil Service World* (18 February 2016), www.civilserviceworld.com/articles/interview/dame-ursula-brennan-former-ministry-justice-permanent-secretary-why-she-left-moj, accessed 28 April 2018.

[3] SRA, 'Handbook – The Principles' (Version 19) para 2.2. And the BSB Handbook (Version 3) gC1.

[4] Research on new advocates, including barristers working in-house, suggests that knowledge of ethical principles and rules is a problem in practice. See also, on barristers, Richard Moorhead and others, 'The Ethical Capacities of New Advocates' (Inns of Court College of Advocacy Report 2016), www.advocacytrainingcouncil.org/images/download/ethics/moorhead-et-al-2015-ethical-capacities-of-new-advocates-final-report.pdf, accessed 28 April 2018.

than a public interest/rule of law lens, with the ever-present need to serve the client's best interest given high priority.

Equally, what the data do not support is the view that in-house lawyers are not at all influenced by professional principles in their everyday decision-making.[5] Our respondents said they *were* influenced by these principles, although this may reflect a reaction to being presented with a list of obligations which are, in the abstract, uncontroversial. Our findings do support the view that client-facing obligations and notions of integrity tend to be prioritised over public interest considerations. The treatment of legality and public interest concerns as the least called-upon of the professional principles is evidence that the in-house legal community surveyed here may have a misapprehension of its professional obligations. Where there is a conflict between principles, barristers and solicitors are supposed to put the public interest in the administration of justice first, not last. Thus the principles which are, in general, prioritised by those we surveyed are emphasised in a way that is somewhat at odds with how the Solicitors Regulation Authority (and the Bar Standards Board) define solicitor (and barrister) obligations.

Given that our interviewees said that professional regulation felt disconnected from, or irrelevant to, their working lives (which we discuss further below), this is perhaps not surprising, but it also reflects their apparent lack of knowledge of the relevant codes of conduct. Equally, how in-housers prioritise particular principles may change in response to specific circumstances. What we have measured is a general sense of how, in terms of professional principles, in-housers may frame decision-making. The kind of framework we have used would benefit from being tested in detailed, context-specific ways to see if the emphasis we see here is maintained in more specifically problematic contexts.

We can see something of the nature of professional orientation from the data we collected on attitudes to regulation, as set out in Table 8.2. 'Net agreement' is calculated with a series of statements about regulation by subtracting disagreement or strong disagreement from agreement and strong agreement.

There was a surprisingly high level of disagreement among our survey respondents, as well as agnosticism, about whether there was too little or too much regulation of in-house lawyers. Perhaps asking about the *volume* of regulation is not the most helpful question unless, as seems unlikely given the other answers in this section, our survey respondents thought, like a lawyerly Goldilocks, the level of regulation was just right. That our in-housers wanted a more relevant code, with better guidance, suggests a view that in-houser lawyers see quality not quantity of regulation as the issue.

A majority of our survey respondents indicated that the codes of conduct have a material day-to-day impact. However, our interviews lead us to suspect

---

[5] Our qualitative work, here and elsewhere, tends to suggest such influence is modest. See further Richard Moorhead and Victoria Hinchly, 'Professional Minimalism? The Ethical Consciousness of Commercial Lawyers' (2015) 42 *Journal of Law and Society* 387.

Table 8.2 Attitudes to Regulation

	There is too much regulation of in-house lawyers	There is not enough regulation of in-house lawyers	The Solicitors' Code of Conduct addresses the needs of in house lawyers well	The professional codes of conduct should be made more relevant to the work of in-house lawyers	It would be helpful to have more rules/ guidance about the appropriate roles and responsibilities of in-house lawyers	Lawyers' professional codes of conduct have a material, day to day impact on the operations of me and/or my team
Strongly Agree	4%	2%	2%	15%	15%	11%
Agree	5%	6%	10%	33%	31%	28%
Somewhat Agree	10%	9%	19%	30%	28%	19%
Neither Agree nor Disagree	46%	44%	30%	17%	14%	15%
Somewhat Disagree	11%	15%	23%	3%	6%	10%
Disagree	20%	16%	12%	2%	5%	12%
Strongly Disagree	5%	8%	5%	1%	1%	5%
Net Agreement	−16%	−17%	−5%	45%	41%	21%
n	392	391	392	394	395	392

that the impact of the codes is not generally material day-to-day. We provide an example of one exchange:

> I   You've mentioned a couple of times professional regulation and the code of conduct. I'm not going to give you a test, but if I did give you a test on the 10 principles at the front of the SRA handbook, how well do you think you'd do on those 10?
> R   I'm quite confident I'd get probably nought out of 10.
> I   Nought out of 10?
> R   Yeah. I think if I was a betting man, that's probably the figure I'm going to get and anything above that is pure luck. [IHL29]

Our tentative view is that the survey respondents like to think that they are influenced by their professional code, but if pushed find this difficult to evidence. This was certainly the message from the interviews we conducted. We specifically asked our interviewees the last time they had looked at the SRA Handbook. The majority could not remember, and some indicated that they had never read it. Take this example:

> I   Do you think the business appreciates that distinction, that you as a solicitor have those professional obligations potentially over and above your employment relationship obligations?
> R   I don't know what those professional obligations are. What are they?
> I   What I'm mainly thinking of are the 10 principles at the front of the SRA Handbook.
> R   I've never read the SRA Handbook. [IHL42]

When we pushed our interviewees on the rarity of their recourse to the SRA Handbook, three themes were common. For some, the Handbook was simply not relevant to what they did as in-house lawyers, because the SRA did not understand in-house practice.

> The problem with an ethical and standards point of view, as soon as the SRA's become involved, they don't understand the in-house role at all. Their conduct rules are impenetrable because they were drafted by people who sort of understood private practice and stuck footnotes for in-house, which mostly are focused on local authority type work. So you get really no guidance there. [IHL41]

Here, and as set out in Table 8.2, we had asked our survey respondents whether they thought that the SRA Code of Conduct addresses the needs of in-house lawyers well. More disagreed (40 per cent) than agreed (31 per cent). For others among our interviewees, the Handbook was seen as a subconscious part of their practice – 'It is a bible in effect' [IHL66] – and so active reference to its contents was not needed.

> Once I'd qualified, and you go through your ethics and skills and all the rest of it – put it this way for the first however many years I've been in private practice I don't think I ever went back to the Handbook. It sounds a bit gung ho but you instinctively know. If something feels dodgy don't do it, and that's pretty much what the handbook can

be boiled down to. Yeah so I never looked at it in private practice and I've not looked at it since. [IHL51]

While an intuitive sense of right and wrong might seem like a reasonable starting point for considering the ethicality of decisions, it may underplay the formal obligations of being a professional and the different ways in which character, context, and capacities influence one's sense of right and wrong.[6] Keeping a subconscious eye out only for 'dodgy' acts might imply a concern only for criminal wrongdoing as unethical, a problem found in other research on commercial lawyers.[7] And such an approach ignores the potential for ethical blind spots: like drivers who think they are better drivers than average, we tend to think we are more ethical than we are in fact, and fail to notice, evaluate or act upon ethical problems as a result.[8] Similarly, professional regulation and codes are assumed to be static, simple and intuitive, when they are not. To give just one example, since the SRA Handbook was first published in September 2011, it has been updated 19 times. While most of these updates have had nothing specific to do with in-house practice, somehow expecting the relevant changes to drift into the subconscious of in-house lawyers by regulatory osmosis is rather wishful thinking. Indeed, many of our survey respondents and interviewees trained and qualified well before the SRA (and its Handbook) was created.

Finally, some of our interviewees sought solace in the idea that they were good people and so did not need the SRA Handbook to tell them how to behave: 'I think professional obligations are just a convenient manifestation of my personal position anyway, I would hope anyway' [IHL24]. We come back to this 'good people' argument below when we consider the relevance, and importance of ethical infrastructure.

DO EMPLOYERS UNDERSTAND PROFESSIONAL OBLIGATIONS?

We have so far been looking, in this chapter and the last, at how in-housers understand their own role and professional identity and at the orientations of in-house lawyer teams. The environment in which in-house lawyers work is also, however, likely to be an important predictor of their ethical inclination. Our interviewees split into two groups. Overall, most in-housers were of the view that their employers saw them as specialist technicians and/or business advisors and not as independent professionals. They were thus experts in the law, there to serve an execution function: facilitators of the business, getting the deal

---

[6] Moorhead and others, 'Designing Ethics Indicators for Legal Services Provision' (Legal Services Board Report, September 2012).
[7] Moorhead and Hinchly (n 6).
[8] Max H Bazerman and Ann E Tenbrunsel, *Blind Spots: Why We Fail to Do What's Right and What to Do about It* (Princeton University Press, 2011).

done and keeping regulatory problems at bay. A minority pushed back against this view, indicating that their employers employed in-house lawyers specifically because those lawyers were professionals willing to stand firm and offer robust independent challenge. Often it was said their employers were particularly interested in a culture of integrity.

This interviewee was unusual in offering up an example of a situation in which the professional obligations of someone in his team clashed with what the business was asking of them. Here, an employment lawyer had been asked by the organisation's HR team not to disclose certain documents in a tribunal claim (when disclosure was required):

> it's the only time we've had to force it to a real decision and it was really obvious and it has always been obvious to me that literally nobody in – who I've ever worked with who isn't a lawyer, has any idea what our professional status means in terms of having an obligation independent of what management wants me to do ... Somebody actually in that said, actually said to her in that conversation, 'You need to remember who you work for,' which I thought was – I think that kind of summed up the failure to understand the professional obligation. [IHL3]

Where our interviewees said that their employers did understand and value their professional obligations, this was often couched in terms of only certain people (normally those at the top) having that understanding, and normally on the basis of poor previous experiences and a current commitment to 'doing the right thing'.

The survey had put the following statement to our respondents: 'There is a clear and common understanding within the business of what the role of the legal function is'. It is worth dwelling momentarily on the important minority (40 per cent) of those that did not agree there was a clear and common understanding of the role of the legal within their organisation.

PROFESSIONAL ETHICAL INFRASTRUCTURE

With ethical pressure a feature of practice for a significant number of our respondents (see Chapter 3), the way in which ethical challenges are managed becomes more important. The business literature explores the value of an infrastructure which protects and promotes ethicality, but this is not something much explored within the legal field.[9] A question of some interest to us is therefore respondents' views on ethical infrastructure.

---

[9] Linda K Treviño, Gary R Weaver and Scott J Reynolds, 'Behavioral Ethics in Organizations: A Review' (2006) 32 *Journal of Management* 951; Francesca Gino and Joshua D Margolis, 'Bringing Ethics into Focus: How Regulatory Focus and Risk Preferences Influence (Un)Ethical Behavior' (2011) 115 *Organizational Behavior and Human Decision Processes* 145. For an exception in law, see Elizabeth Chambliss and David B Wilkins, 'Promoting Effective Ethical Infrastructure in Large Law Firms: A Call for Research and Reporting' (2001) 30 *Hofstra L Rev* 691.

Figure 8.2 Ethical Infrastructure

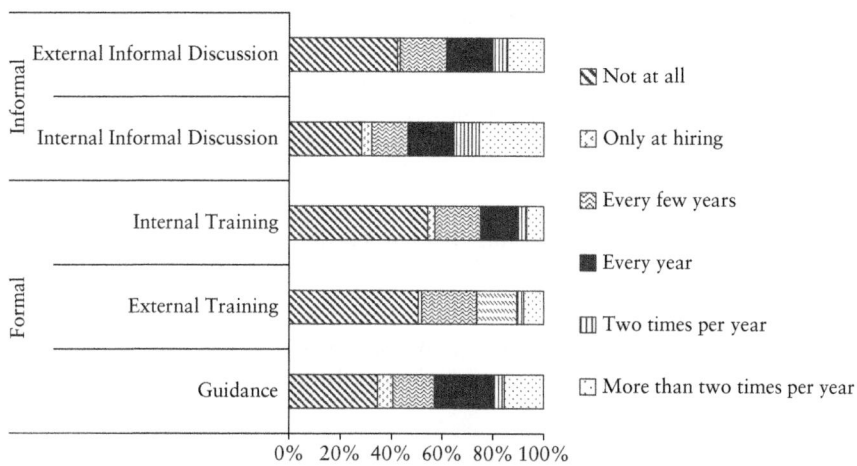

[Bar chart showing Informal (External Informal Discussion, Internal Informal Discussion) and Formal (Internal Training, External Training, Guidance) categories, with legend: Not at all, Only at hiring, Every few years, Every year, Two times per year, More than two times per year]

Ethical infrastructure reduced to two components summarising the questions in our survey: formal and informal.[10] 'Formal infrastructure' indicated how frequently professional legal obligations were implemented, through professional ethics training delivered by internal providers,[11] other written guidance from the organisation, and professional ethics training delivered by external providers. 'Informal infrastructure' was composed of two items, made up of how frequently our respondents communicated with other in-house lawyers about ethics and conduct issues through informal discussions of professional ethics, both with others outside the organisation and those within the organisation.[12] Figure 8.2 summarises the data.

Although 55 per cent of respondents indicated that corporate codes were also used to implement professional obligations, we see generally that a high proportion of respondents indicated that formal training or guidance either never took place or was only refreshed every few years. In these terms, professional ethics looks like a low priority, not much supported by these processes. The incidence of ethical pressure did not make a difference. In-house lawyers

---

[10] A principal component analysis was run for seven items related to ethical infrastructure. KMO was good (.80). However, the response scale used in one of the items was very different from the other ones – and communality of that item was very low. Thus, a subsequent principal component analysis was run without it. KMO was acceptable/good (.79). On the basis of the following criteria a) retaining components that have eigenvalues > 1, and b) scree test, two components were extracted. The two components explained 62.7% variance. Communalities were acceptable (above .50 except for one item that was .49). Given that some of the correlations between the components exceeded .32, oblique rotation (ie, Oblimin) was performed.
[11] α = .70 for this measure.
[12] α = .67 for this measure.

experiencing greater pressure to advise on unlawful or unethical activities did not receive more training and guidance to cope with these pressures.[13]

What was striking from our interviews was that while many in-housers were part of teams delivering various forms of training to the organisation (including on business ethics), few had dedicated programmes for themselves or their in-house teams: 'we have a code of conduct and we have a framework of training that people have to do every year, but that's not specific to the lawyers, that's everybody' [IHL30]. There was some sense, from a number of the interviews, that training on ethics is something that lawyers *do* (ie give to people inside the organisation who are outside the legal team), rather than something lawyers *receive*:

> We have regular trainings on things like bribery, side letters, ethical behaviour, decision-making, conflicts of interest, that the lawyers have to give to the wider community. [IHL39]

One interviewee raised with us the following concern about formal training:

> There's part of me that thinks shouldn't there still be some mandated training on ethics and professional conduct? And you think, well, if you mandate it, is it just going to be like health and safety training, where you don't really pay attention but you just click the buttons on the screen so that you get the certificate at the end to say you've done the training? [IHL36]

While we do not disagree that tick-box compliance could be the result of mandated ethics training, this strikes us as the wrong framing. Our interviewees were not asked whether training was mandatory, they were asked was there *any* training. Offering up the failings of mandatory training programmes is a rather straw-man argument which does not explain why there is so little training of any kind in this area. What was also notable from the interviews was that even for the in-house lawyers we spoke with who were adamant that their roles involved independent and robust push-back on the exercise of unwarranted organisational discretion, the underlying ethical infrastructure for in-housers in those organisations tended to be weak or non-existent. This was somewhat at odds with data from our survey (discussed above). This interviewee, for example, had spoken at length to us about her company and its ethics, and about her belief in the importance of in-house lawyers being able to stand back and question the business when appropriate:

> I   And as a team do you talk about ethics and professional conduct?
> R   No, I wouldn't say so.
> I   And is there regular training on professional ethics compared with business ethics?
> R   No. [IHL40]

---

[13] Similarly we found no correlation between levels of ethical pressure and formal ethical infrastructure. High pressure did not appear to prompt improved formal infrastructure.

Strikingly, few of those we interviewed included questions as to ethics or professionalism in interview rounds for new recruits to the team. This interviewee was a notable exception:

> In interviews I normally have at least one round where we're talking about how would you handle this situation, what would you do? If, for example, a sales person wants you to approve a contract that contains a clause that says this and you feel that that's inappropriate or whatever, how would you approach that? [IHL34]

Fifty-six per cent of our survey respondents indicated that assessment of an in-house lawyer's ethics forms an explicit and formal part of performance appraisals (14 per cent only somewhat). Twenty-two per cent disagreed (8 per cent somewhat). We followed up this information in interviews to see whether this was a genuinely significant part of appraisals and our view is that, in general, it is not. We think the survey finding here represented wishful thinking.

> I   And if you think about your own last appraisal, was ethics an item for discussion?
> R   No. I'm sure it would have been if somebody had said I'd acted unethically (laughs). [IHL3]

Even where we were told by our interviewees that appraisals did cover ethics-like issues, the term 'ethics' was often not used. As this interviewee sets out, this may be because appraisal forms are produced for the entire organisation and not just for its in-house lawyers:

> I don't know if it [the appraisal form] specifically says 'ethical', I can't really remember. But we have these five points that we need to deal with, I suppose every company has this sort of thing and one of them is about trust, integrity and doing the right thing by our customers and our colleagues. So I guess we do. It's not overly specific, but I guess that's because our appraisals are built for the whole company rather than just for lawyers. [IHL29]

If our data for this book, and our other work on lawyers, suggest that solicitors are happy that their firms and in-house teams are ethical because they contain 'the right sort of people' (and they do suggest that), then the lack of evaluation of this ethicality at the point of entry is both curious and concerning. Asking would-be in-house lawyers to demonstrate their commercial awareness in such contexts is, we think, more common. How do in-house lawyers satisfy themselves then that their teams and firms are ethical or that they can and do deal with the ethical pressures they face? It may, for example, be through dialogue. Let us turn then to informal ethical infrastructure.

One might expect informal interactions regarding ethics to be more frequent than formal interactions, and that is borne out by the data in Figure 8.2. However, it is again noticeable that communication, even informally, concerning professional ethical issues is infrequent, and for some does not occur at all, unless ethical discussions are taking place without the respondents framing those discussions in terms of 'ethics'. Indeed, 7 per cent of respondents indicated 'not at all' to all six questions, indicating that professional obligations were never instantiated internally or externally, formally or informally. However, we do see some signs of a relationship between ethical pressure and informal ethical infrastructure: pressure appears to sometimes prompt more informal discussion, but there is only a weak correlation, suggesting pressure does not prompt more informal discussion frequently.[14] Lawyers working in different organisation types (ie, business, public sector, charity) only showed near significant differences regarding their ratings of formal ethical structure but not with regards to informal ethical structure (the results suggested that charities had made less use of informal infrastructure).

What we learned from the survey on informal ethical infrastructures was matched in the interviews. We came away with the sense that 'ethics', as a term, was often not used by in-house teams in how they spoke with each other, and that other proxies would be used instead, with the now familiar emphasis on these discussions being focused on others not themselves:

> Can I honestly say in the four and a half years we've had a conversation around ethics? Well we've got a good policy on bribery, corruption and trading standards. We do compliance training on that to the sales team and we have a CEO and a board who are, I think, you know, trusted as it were and keen to promote the company as an ethical organisation. But we don't do much more than that I have to say. [IHL25]

We were told that issues would arise organically from on-the-ground conversations between members of the in-house team. Many set great store by the 'the value of conversations' [IHL49].

> We don't have this kind of, 'Oh let's have an ethical chat' situation. It's always we're sitting in an open plan office and we're all different ages and different abilities, all from different parts of the country. So we just sit there and we share. [IHL29]

We do not wish to doubt the useful role that such conversations can play, but we feel bound to note that the tenor of these comments reminds us of the claim that managers manage through 'my door is always open'. Furthermore, these sorts of ad hoc conversations might be more useful for those working and sitting in teams of in-house lawyers, but would perhaps be less easy for the many in-housers we spoke with who spend their day sitting with, embedded into, business units (and away from their in-house peers).

METRICS FOR THE MORAL COMPASS

The ultimate aim of developing measures for in-house orientations and context was to see what the normative dimensions to those measures might be. Ideally,

---

[14] $r(395) = .177, p < .001$.

one would examine orientations and context and look for causal links between those and unethical behaviour. Doing such work in real-life contexts is very difficult, if it can be done at all. Our approach was to use measures of ethical inclination and look for relationships between orientations, context, and that ethical inclination. In a sense we 'measure' the moral compass of individuals and look for relationships between that moral compass and how in-housers see their own role.

Of course, measuring the moral compass of an individual is fraught with difficulty. As one of us has argued elsewhere, a range of measures can be applied to context, character and capacity, and individual character and capacity interacts with systems beyond the individual.[15] And there is also the question of whether one can 'measure' ethicality at all.[16] Inevitably, measures of ethicality are blunt instruments – useful tools for examining differences – rather than the last word on what matters or on what ethics is. Rather than debate the merits of ethical metrics here, we explain the measures we have used, and what we think they tell us.

We rely upon two tools: one measures moral attentiveness, and the second moral disengagement. We are particularly interested in these as predictors of ethical misconduct. Importantly, as with most psychometrics employed in this field, the morality they concern themselves with is general, not professionally specific. One reaction to that is to say we are concerned with the professional ethics of in-house lawyers, and that is different to common morality. In a sense, our indicators of professional orientation and ethical pressure might be better measures of *professional* ethics. There is some truth in that, but the measures of common morality that we use concern themselves with core behaviours relevant to both common and professional morality: in essence, they can predict a propensity to lie and cheat (break rules). Even if one accepts that lawyers have some flexibility to bend both the truth and rules, lying and rule-breaking are forbidden.[17] So these general measures provide a test of the inclination of our respondents towards conduct which would be both socially and professionally flawed. In that sense, the measures *are* professionally relevant and enable us to go further than the measures we constructed ourselves because the evidence suggests these measures predict unethical behaviour.

---

[15] Moorhead and others (n 7).

[16] For our discussion on these matters see, for example, Richard Moorhead and others, 'The Ethical Identity of Law Students' (2016) 23 *International Journal of the Legal Profession* 235.

[17] rC9/.1 of the Bar's Code of Conduct, for example, prohibits barristers knowingly or recklessly misleading or attempt to mislead anyone. Similar requirements are included in the forthcoming draft Code for Solicitors. For a general discussion of truth-telling, and a specific discussion of negotiations, which – alongside advocacy – is the most interesting area of discussion in the academic literature, see W Bradley Wendel, 'Whose Truth? Objective and Subjective Perspectives on Truthfulness in Advocacy' (Cornell Legal Studies Research Paper, 3 February 2015); James J White, 'Machiavelli and the Bar: Ethical Limitations on Lying in Negotiation' (1980) 5 *Law & Social Inquiry* 926.

Moral Attentiveness

The first predictor of ethical inclination we use is moral attentiveness. This is examined across two dimensions: 'perceptual moral attentiveness, the extent to which the individual recognizes moral aspects in everyday experiences; and reflective moral attentiveness, the extent to which the individual regularly considers moral matters.'[18] Given that a failure to spot ethical problems is often a key precursor to ethical failure, this is really important.[19] A more morally attentive person is more likely to recall and report morally related behaviour, and moral attentiveness is associated with more moral behaviour.[20] Interestingly, this inclination may be influenced by the environment: positive forces – such as an improved ethical infrastructure – can induce more moral attentiveness, just as more negative experiences may have the opposite effect.[21]

In our analysis, we used Reynolds' moral attentiveness scale.[22] Moral attentiveness resolved into two components. First, *perceptual moral attentiveness* is an indicator of the extent to which an individual frequently recognises moral problems measured by the level of agreement with three statements in our survey: (i) 'In a typical day, I face several ethical dilemmas'; (ii) 'I regularly face decisions that have significant ethical implications';[23] and (iii) 'I frequently encounter ethical situations'. Second, *reflective moral attentiveness* is indicated by level of agreement with two statements:[24] (i) 'I regularly think about the ethical implications of my decisions'; and (ii) 'I often reflect on the moral aspects of my decisions'. We saw a fairly even split between those who perceive ethical problems in their work and those tending not to. In relation to *reflective moral attentiveness*, about a third agreed or strongly agreed that they thought about the moral aspects of problems or the ethical implications of their decisions often or regularly.

Moral Disengagement

Moral disengagement is our other indicator of ethical inclination. It is said to explain a significant proportion of in-work relevant behaviour.[25] The authors of the measure of moral disengagement 'cautiously' suggest it is 'the strongest

---

[18] Scott J Reynolds, 'Moral Attentiveness: Who pays attention to the moral aspects of life?' (2008) 93(5) *Journal of Applied Psychology* 1027.
[19] Bazerman and Tenbrunsel (n 9).
[20] ibid.
[21] Reynolds (n 19).
[22] ibid.
[23] $\alpha = .88$ for this measure.
[24] $\alpha = .80$ for this measure.
[25] Celia Moore and others, 'Why Employees Do Bad Things: Moral Disengagement and Unethical Organizational Behavior' (2012) 65 *Personnel Psychology* 1.

individual predictor of unethical behaviour identified to date,'[26] as well as being a practical test for adult respondents which is not generally prone to significant social desirability biases (ie respondents are not likely to answer in ways significantly influenced by the desire to look good). It is possible also that moral disengagement is particularly important in organisational contexts, as Moore notes:[27]

> The workplace provides ample opportunities for moral disengagement: organizations tend to be hierarchical, providing opportunities for the displacement of responsibility; work is often undertaken within teams, providing opportunities for the diffusion of responsibility; organizational membership automatically defines the boundaries of an in-group, providing opportunities for moral justification (to protect the organization) and the cognitive minimization of the consequences of one's actions for those who are outside the organization (and thus in an out-group). The propensity to morally disengage might also be particularly damaging in organizational life because work contexts have been documented as triggering amoral frames of judgment. As Jackall pointed out in Moral Mazes, organizations are particularly effective at assisting individuals in bracketing off moral schemas that guide behavior elsewhere. Thus, the propensity to morally disengage is likely to be particularly relevant in the prediction of unethical behavior in organizations.

Moore et al's scale proved reliable with our set of respondents.[28] Based on eight questions,[29] the scale provides a single measure of relative moral disengagement.[30] We do not use the measure to ascertain, in an absolute sense, that in-house lawyers display worrying levels of moral disengagement. Rather we use the scale to ascertain which in-house lawyers are more or less morally disengaged than others. The differences we report are statistically significant but usually modest in size. However, even small differences in moral disengagement

---

[26] ibid 40. Environmental/situational influences may for example be contrasted with influences deriving from the individual.

[27] Moore and others (n 25) 11.

[28] $\alpha = .84$.

[29] These were: (1) It is okay to spread rumours to defend those you care about. (2) Taking something without the owner's permission is okay as long as you're just borrowing it. (3) Considering the ways people grossly misrepresent themselves, it's hardly a sin to inflate your own accomplishments a bit. (4) People shouldn't be held accountable for doing questionable things when they were just doing what an authority figure told them to do. (5) People can't be blamed for doing things that are technically wrong when all their friends are doing it too. (6) Taking personal credit for ideas that were not your own is no big deal. (7) Some people have to be treated roughly because they lack feelings that can be hurt. (8) People who get mistreated have usually done something to bring it on themselves.

[30] Our analysis confirmed it was univariate when used here. A principal component analysis was run for item assessing moral disengagement. KMO was good (.84). On the basis of the following criteria – a) retaining components that have eigenvalues > 1 and b) Scree test – either one or two components could be extracted. Given that some of the correlations between the components exceeded .32, oblique rotation (ie, Oblimin) was performed. As can be observed from the two-components solution below, all items showed higher loadings on the first component, and thus we decided to retain only the first component, which also replicated the original measure of moral disengagement.

have been associated with a significant (but modest) increase in a propensity to behave unethically.[31]

Collectively, we refer to these measures of moral attentiveness and disengagement as indicators of ethical inclination. Lower levels of moral attentiveness and higher levels of moral disengagement predict unethical conduct but they do not guarantee it. As such, they are proxies for ethicality: we can examine our data on in-house lawyers for signs that environment, role conception, approach to professional rules, etc, have some relationships with ethical inclination, but we are *not* saying that our data 'prove' certain groups of in-house lawyers are unethical. Such proof is unavailable. What we are able to show instead is something more subtle: what is likely to influence or be associated with ethicality.

WHICH ORIENTATIONS ARE INDEPENDENTLY ASSOCIATED WITH ETHICALITY?

We look here at individual role orientations as potential predictors of each of the three indicators of ethicality in our data (ie, perceptual moral attentiveness, reflective moral attentiveness, and moral disengagement). Three linear regression models were deployed to estimate the independent contribution of each orientation to predict moral disengagement and the two measures of moral attentiveness.[32] So, in Table 8.3, by way of example, we can see **significant** associations between our measures of ethical inclination and (say) an ethical orientation separately from any association with independence orientation.

What this shows is that a stronger commercial orientation is associated with significantly lower perceptual moral attentiveness but significantly higher reflective moral attentiveness. Thus, the more commercially oriented in-house

Table 8.3 Associations between Orientations and Moral Attentiveness and Disengagement

Outcome variable	Predictors – orientation	ß	Sig.	η^2
	Commercial	−.264	.000	.06
	Ethical	.212	.000	.04
Perceptual moral attentiveness	Exploitation	.072	.153	.00
	Independence	.087	.085	.01
	Neutral advisor	−.032	.531	.00
	$R^2 =$	.09		

(continued)

---

[31] Moore and others (n 25).
[32] The five role orientations enabled explanation of 9% of variance in perceptual moral attentiveness, 9% of variance in reflective moral attentiveness and 15% variance in moral disengagement.

Table 8.3 *(Continued)*

Outcome variable	Predictors – orientation	ß	Sig.	η^2
Reflective moral attentiveness	Commercial	.269	.012	.01
	Ethical	.009	.000	.06
	Exploitation	.114	.863	.00
	Independence	.030	.025	.01
	Neutral advisor	−.133	.549	.00
	$R^2 =$	.09		
Moral disengagement	Commercial	−.065	.211	.00
	Ethical	−.219	.000	.04
	Exploitation	.249	.000	.06
	Independence	−.130	.008	.02
	Neutral advisor	−.059	.221	.00
	$R^2 =$	.15		

lawyers in our sample were less likely to perceive problems as moral ones but more likely to think about problems in moral terms, should such problems arise. Whilst the stronger impact of the two was for perceptual moral attentiveness, this is an intriguing but inconclusive combination of results suggesting some ethical ambiguity around a commercial orientation.

As one might expect, an ethical orientation predicted higher perceptual and reflective moral attentiveness and lower moral disengagement. An ethical orientation was thus positively associated with our externally validated measures of ethical inclination.

An independence orientation also predicted higher reflective attentiveness and lower moral disengagement, albeit more weakly. The exploitation of uncertainty orientation did not predict moral attentiveness, but did predict greater moral disengagement, indicating a positive association with this measure of concern. A neutral advisor orientation did not independently influence any indicators of ethical inclination. In broad terms, then, our data suggest predictable associations between the ethical and exploitation of uncertainty orientations, and a more complex but somewhat negative position in relation to commercial orientation. The strongest significant relationship was that those with a higher commercial orientation tended to be less likely to see ethical problems in their work; this may suggest a higher propensity to ethical blindspots. There was a weaker but positive impact suggesting, though, that the commercially oriented thought more often than the less commercially oriented about ethicality when taking decisions. There was no significant relationship between commercial orientation and moral disengagement.

Cluster Analysis – Inclination to Ethicality

A further, higher-level view of the data can be gained through cluster analysis, which allows us to examine whether different profiles of lawyers can be established in relation to their inclination to ethicality.

Cluster analysis is an exploratory multivariate data analysis technique which allows us to group our respondents into (broadly) homogeneous groups. Cases are classified according to their similarity in relation to a number of predefined attributes. We use it here to explore whether there are common groups or patterns or profiles of in-house lawyers in terms of their inclination to ethicality. As lower levels of moral attentiveness and higher levels of moral disengagement have been shown in other studies to predict a greater inclination to behave unethically, we classified our respondents on these indicators.

The analysis produced four clusters or groups. The clusters that emerged (using Ward's Method) showed significant differences for moral attentiveness (perceptual and reflective) and moral disengagement.[33] Statistically significant different levels of moral attentiveness and disengagement are shown in Table 8.4.

Group 1 we call the 'Troubled': these in-house lawyers experienced the second-highest levels of ethical pressure and had moderately high perceptual and reflective moral attentiveness, and yet also significantly higher levels of moral disengagement. They saw moral challenges and thought about moral challenges, but appeared to have begun to disengage in response. Eighty-nine respondents (22%) were in this group.

Group 2 we call the 'Coasters'. This was the largest group by some distance: 213 respondents (72%) were in it. They had moderately low levels of perceptual moral attentiveness but moderately high reflective moral attentiveness. Yet they also had lower levels of moral disengagement than Group 1 and Group 4. This position was seen in the context of the second-lowest levels of ethical pressure. Hence we speculate that this group is not yet being tested or testing itself in ethical terms.

Group 3 we call the 'Champions', as they had significantly higher perceptual and reflective moral attentiveness than the other groups and were also experiencing the greatest ethical pressure. They also (along with Group 2) had the lowest moral disengagement. This group had 48 respondents (12%).

Group 4 contained 47 respondents (12%). It was our smallest group and the one of most concern: we call them the 'Comfortably Numb'. They showed a significantly higher level of moral disengagement than Groups 2 and 3, and the lowest levels of moral attentiveness on both indicators.

---

[33] $p < .001$.

Table 8.4 Clusters – Moral Attentiveness and Moral Disengagement

	Troubled n = 89		Coasters n = 213		Champions n = 48		Comfortably Numb n = 43		ANOVA	
	Mean	SD	Mean	SD	Mean	SD	Mean	SD	F	p
Perceptual moral attentiveness	4.64	.61	2.94	.94	6.11	.55	1.87	.70	324.2	.00
Reflective moral attentiveness	5.13	.54	5.13	.96	6.57	.48	2.18	.65	261.0	.00
Moral disengagement	2.12	.68	1.58	.52	1.52	.64	2.03	.81	21.51	.00

Characterisation of the Clusters

A multivariate analysis of variance was conducted to examine the key characteristics of the clusters looking at types of lawyer and sector, individual and team orientations, use of professional principles, ethical infrastructure and relations with the business. This analysis tells us whether there are significant associations between each of the clusters and these variables. For example, are Champions more likely to be found in business or public sectors? Are they more likely to be male or female? Are the Comfortably Numb more likely to be commercially oriented? And so on.

Table 8.5 summarises the results of our analysis looking at the characteristics of our four clusters.[34] Interestingly, there were no significant differences across the clusters in terms of post-qualification experience, size of legal team, gender, use of professional principles, or work identity.

As previously described, our Champions are the most ethically vigilant and least morally disengaged, but also under the most ethical pressure. The analysis enables us to describe the characteristics associated with this cluster and so suggest (but not prove) that such characteristics are associated with greater ethicality (as measured by moral disengagement and attentiveness).

As a group, Champions had proportionately fewer business but more public-sector in-house lawyers and (possibly relatedly) more barristers than other groups. Thus, 8 per cent of business lawyers were classified as Champions, compared to 20 per cent of public-sector lawyers. Champions worked in teams with higher perceived ethical and societal orientations than the other groups. They also had higher individual ethical orientations than the other groups.

---

[34] For the full analysis on which this table is based, see Appendix B in Richard Moorhead and others, 'Mapping the Moral Compass: The Relationships between In-House Lawyers' Role, Professional Orientations, Team Cultures, Organisational Pressures, Ethical Infrastructure and Ethical Inclination' (2016) (Social Science Research Network, Scholarly Paper ID 2784758), https://papers.ssrn.com/abstract=2784758, accessed 24 April 2018.

196 *Mapping the Moral Compass*

Table 8.5 Summary of Cluster Analysis

1 Troubled ($n = 89$)	2 Coasters ($n = 213$)	3 Champions ($n = 48$)	4 Comfortably Numb ($n = 47$)
Mid/High Perception Mid Reflection Higher Disengagement	Low/Mid Perception Mid Reflection Lower Disengagement	Higher Perception High Reflection Lower Disengagement	Low Perception Low Reflection Higher Disengagement
More public-sector workers	Fewer public-sector workers	More years in house than Numb More barristers or advocates Fewer business, more public-sector workers	
In-House Role			
Lower ethical and independence orientation than Champions	Lower ethical orientation than Champions	Highest ethical orientation Higher independence rating than Troubled and Numb	Lower ethical and independence orientation than Champions
Relations with Business			
Higher resistant/negative relations with the business than Coasters and Numb. Lower uneven relations than Numb	Lower resistant/negative relations than Troubled Lower uneven relations than Numb	Higher resistant/negative relations with the business than Numb Lower uneven relations than Numb	Lower resistant/negative relations than Troubled and Champions Highest uneven relations

Which Orientations are Independently Associated with Ethicality? 197

1 Troubled (n = 89)	2 Coasters (n = 213)	3 Champions (n = 48)	4 Comfortably Numb (n = 47)
	**Team Orientation**		
Higher Integrity orientation than Numb	Higher integrity orientation than Numb	Highest integrity orientation	Lowest integrity orientation
Higher society orientation than Numb		Highest society orientation	Lower society orientation than Troubled and Champions
	**Professional Principles**		
Lower invocation of effectiveness and integrity than Champions	Lower invocation of independence and legality than Champions	Higher invocation of independence and legality than Coasters and Numb	Lower invocation of independence and legality than Champions
		Higher invocation of effectiveness and integrity than Troubled and Numb	Lower invocation of effectiveness and integrity than Champions
	**Ethical Infrastructure**		
Higher rating of formal and informal infrastructure than Numb	Lower rating of formal and informal infrastructure than Champions	Higher rating of formal and informal infrastructure than Coasters and Numb	Lower rating of formal and informal infrastructure than Troubled and Champions
	**Ethical Pressure**		
Second highest	Second lowest	Highest	Lowest

Champions had a higher independence orientation than the Troubled and the Comfortably Numb, suggesting a link between independent and ethical conceptions of the in-house role and inclination to behave ethically. Champions invoked independence and legality principles more than Coasters and the Comfortably Numb, and effectiveness and integrity principles more than Troubled and the Comfortably Numb. Champions also had stronger formal and informal ethical infrastructure than the Coasters and the Comfortably Numb. In comparison with the Comfortably Numb, Champions had a more negative relationship with the business and had weaker/less even relations with the business. Champions were also less likely to be inexperienced in-house lawyers than the Comfortably Numb.

The Troubled present an interesting contrast with the Champions. The Troubled's view of the in-house role was less emphatic on independence and an ethical orientation, and on effectiveness and integrity, but was in other ways similar, yet they were somewhat more morally disengaged.

The Comfortably Numb present a set of clearer differences. They had the highest level of uneven relations with their employer and the lowest ethical team orientation. The Comfortably Numb had lower resistant/negative relations with their organisations than the Troubled and the Champions. Their teams had a lower society orientation than the Troubled and the Champions. The Comfortably Numb had a lower rating for formal and informal ethical infrastructure than the Troubled and the Champions. Compared to the Champions, the Comfortably Numb had lower individual ethical and independence orientations and they were less likely to invoke professional principles of independence and legality and of effectiveness and integrity. The main difference between the Coasters and the Comfortably Numb was that the Coasters had a stronger ethical orientation.

CONCLUSIONS

The aim of these last two chapters has been to explore measures of in-house identity and context, and to explore relationships between those measures. In particular, we wanted to evaluate a normative dimension to those measures. We examine the normative dimension through measures of ethical inclination. These measures (moral attentiveness and moral disengagement) are drawn from other research where they have been shown, in particular, to act as predictors of ethical misconduct.

Previous work on in-house lawyers has tended to speculate on the normative dimension qualitatively. Our approach is simpler (cruder perhaps), but more specific. We demonstrate that: (i) there are distinctive but commonly present orientations to the in-house role (commercial, ethical, etc); (ii) individuals emphasise these orientations differently; and (iii) some of those differences are associated with different ethical inclinations. To give an example, whereas the entrepreneurial orientation is treated as a complex bundle of concepts by Nelson and Nielsen which may lead to ethical anxieties, we show that elements of the entrepreneurial orientation can be isolated (the commercial orientation and the exploitation of uncertainty orientation, in particular) and we can show quite specific impacts on ethical inclination. Thus our data show that thinking of the exploitation of uncertainty as part of the in-house role is associated with a weaker ethical inclination. The commercial orientation has a weaker influence and one which seems likely to make in-house lawyers somewhat more prone to ethical blind-spots, but also – interestingly – slightly more inclined to engage with ethical elements to problems if blind spots are avoided. As one would expect in research of this kind, neither effect is startlingly strong, but the influence of the exploitation orientation is stronger.

What we do not show is a causal direction: does a less ethically inclined lawyer adopt a more exploitative approach to uncertainty; or does an exploitative approach drive ethical disinclination? Testing that would require a research design of greater sophistication. On one level, this does not much matter: less ethically inclined in-house lawyers (as measured by moral attentiveness and disengagement) are more likely to see exploitation of legal uncertainty as part of the job; and more ethically inclined in-house lawyers are less likely to take that view. We get a strong sense of the importance of individual perceptions and environment (it is not very surprising that our more morally attentive respondents also tended to observe more ethical pressure) and some strong senses of difference (that some respond to pressure through disengagement is concerning, especially when we can see others that do not). The role of teams and ethical infrastructure is shown to be important. Stronger cultures of integrity and of thinking about the organisational role in society are associated with a stronger ethical inclination, but we cannot rule out the possibility that the ethically inclined perceive their teams as stronger, rather than the teams being objectively stronger. It seems unlikely to us that the ethically attentive would also be overly optimistic about the quality of their teams, but either way, the weaknesses in ethical infrastructure we have found in our research are concerning; especially when one considers the absent or weak relationships between ethical pressure and ethical infrastructure. It is a far from common response to ethical pressure to institute training, guidance and support to deal with it.

We see too that professional orientation is correlated with ethical inclination. All our in-housers tended to emphasise their obligations to the organisation (to the client) most often when taking decisions. This is a pragmatic approach but this is not how their relevant professional codes of conduct see professional obligations. Nonetheless, some practitioners emphasised independence and legality or integrity and effectiveness more strongly than others. Those that did so tended to be more ethically inclined. The importance of professional principles is thus seen, albeit in a way that is more muted than the codes of conduct might imply they should be.

We get a sense in this chapter of the importance of individual conceptions of in-house role, of specific ideas about professional obligations, and of other contextual factors. In our final chapter, we look at the concept of social trusteeship and at the likely importance of task instantiation, and we bring together our work to offer up our final thoughts on the tensions between organisational and professional logics and the tendency of our respondents to prioritise the former over the latter.

9
The Ecologies of In-House Ethicality

IN THIS CHAPTER, we examine our findings through a social trusteeship model of professionalism.[1] That model reminds us that professions are founded on the assumption that they apply and develop their knowledge in the public interest. It underlines why lawyers are obliged to protect the rule of law and the administration of justice, as well as the best interests of their clients. And, in certain areas of the law, lawyers are given specific gatekeeping responsibilities, either by requiring or encouraging their involvement in disclosure, or independent investigations, or as managers of litigation and advocacy.[2]

Our work recognises, too, that a discussion of professionalism must take proper account of its relational aspects;[3] and that professionals can be placed in hybrid roles which ask them to resolve tensions between competing value systems. Those value systems are typically those of the organisation (bureaucratic or commercial values) and the values that the profession is required to protect (such as health or justice).[4] When advising on or implementing a client's legal plans, lawyers perform a balancing of individual and collective rights. Lawyers ensure that a client is free to organise their affairs in the way that best suits the client; and the client properly takes account of what the law requires of them. And the lawyer, when working for the client, behaves with integrity and in accordance with their professional obligations. In this way, organisations are free to do business or implement policy in ways of their choosing, but with proper respect for the law.

---

[1] Steven Brint, *In an Age of Experts: The Changing Role of Professionals in Politics and Public Life* (Princeton University Press, 1996); Robert Dingwall and Paul Fenn, '"A Respectable Profession"? Sociological and Economic Perspectives on the Regulation of Professional Services' (1987) 7 *International Review of Law and Economics* 51.

[2] John C Coffee Jr, *The Acquiescent Gatekeeper: Reputational Intermediaries, Auditor Independence, the Governance of Accounting* (Columbia Law and Economics Working Paper No 191, 21 May 2001); John C Coffee Jr, 'The Attorney as Gatekeeper: An Agenda for the SEC' (2003) 103 *Colum L Rev* 1293; John C Coffee Jr, 'Gatekeeper Failure and Reform: The Challenge of Fashioning Relevant Reforms' (2004) 84 *BUL Rev* 301.

[3] Eli Wald and Russell G Pearce, 'Being Good Lawyers: A Relational Approach to Law Practice' (2016) 29 *Geo J Legal Ethics* 601.

[4] Maria Blomgren and Caroline Waks, 'Coping with Contradictions: Hybrid Professionals Managing Institutional Complexity' (2015) 2 *Journal of Professions and Organization* 78; Graeme Currie, Nicola Burgess and Penelope Tuck, 'The (Un)Desirability of Hybrid Managers as "Controlled" Professionals: Comparative Cases of Tax and Healthcare Professionals' [2016] *Journal of Professions and Organization* 142.

Our argument is that, under a hybrid trusteeship model, the application of law is not more extensive than intended, but nor is it less extensive. The application of law takes account of the contexts in which it is applied, such as the particular needs of the organisation. A hybrid model allows innovation and recognises the benefits of encouraging organisations to apply the law voluntarily, without the need to regularly coerce compliance. Professionals working for, or within, such organisations also have the benefit – over external regulators – of usually having better information about the real behaviours and intentions of those organisations.[5] Professional in-house lawyers are also part of the guiding mind of the client. They are in a peculiar position as adviser and agent: one of opportunity and responsibility, framed by an ecology of ideas and practices which are the focus of this book. In bringing the hybrid and trustee models together, *professional* lawyers are trusted intermediaries between the state, their client, and others affected by their client – this trust depends on them successfully resolving the tensions between organisational and professional values. They must strike the balance successfully with each value system: the instrumental values of commerce or policy; and the justice values of social trusteeship.

SOCIAL TRUSTEESHIP

Although there is plenty of argument about how one defines professions, or how one measures professionalism, there is not much doubt that professions are institutions granted status and privileges by the State to perform useful social functions.[6] Professions exist to protect quality and ethics, to advance the state of their art, and to provide an optimal means of regulating their members.[7] The granting of status and privilege to professional groups may allow for rent-seeking and social closure but, 'the meaning of their profession, both for themselves and for the public, is not that they make money, but that they make health, or safety, or knowledge, or good government, or good law.'[8] Such professional knowledge is esoteric but vital to the social fabric; its application uncertain, in law often contestable, and the consequences of being wrong socially significant. In this way, the application of law impacts on relationships between individuals and the state, but also on powerful organisations and their customers, employees, and environments. Relatedly, the rule of law demands

---

[5] Reinier H Kraakman, 'Corporate Liability Strategies and the Costs of Legal Controls' (1984) 93 *The Yale Law Journal* 857, 868.
[6] Alan A Paterson, 'Professionalism and the Legal Services Market' (1996) 3 *International Journal of the Legal Profession* 137.
[7] Richard Moorhead, 'Precarious Professionalism: Some Empirical and Behavioural Perspectives on Lawyers' (2014) 67 *Current Legal Problems* 447.
[8] Richard H Tawney, *The Acquisitive Society* (Palala Press, 2015) 94. On professionals as social mobility projects see Magali S Larson, *The Rise of Professionalism – A Sociological Analysis* (University of California Press, 1977).

that law is interpreted and applied on its merits; as independently as possible from such power relations.

Social trusteeship is vital to society. Investors and regulators rely on accurate disclosures often mediated by lawyers. Consumers rely on fair contracts, safe products, appropriate advertising, and balanced sales processes. Citizens rely on respect for privacy, human rights, the bearing down on bribery and terrorism, just taxation, and the upholding of environmental standards. Commercial and political organisations also rely on the predictabilities and protections provided by law, assurance that counterparties adhere to appropriate standards, and that competitors take regulatory restrictions on their operations seriously. Behaving lawfully is a critical part of an organisation's reputational mandate with employees, customers, and regulators.[9] Indeed, as we have seen in our discussions of risk, reputational mandates may extend beyond mere compliance to social and ethical ideas more onerous than baseline legality.

That said, there is no shortage of work suggesting professions do not live up to a social-trusteeship model. Some suggest professions are critically sustained and compromised by power relations;[10] others, that professions pursue self-interest over public interest and social closure over meritocracy.[11] Lawyers are associated with creative compliance rather than legality.[12] The interpenetration of business and professional values risks developing a managerial, inward-looking, narrowly technocratic view of professionalism. Commercial lawyers may be professional minimalists.[13] These critiques see professionalism dominantly defined by expertise, rather than 'social trusteeship'.[14] As such, expertise serves power rather than the public interest. Professions, on this account, are not sufficiently accountable for their individual actions or their collective governance.

In-house lawyers have been a particular focus of scepticism because they are employed by their clients, more economically dependent on their client-employer, and seen as more prone to the social influence of everyday relations with (non-lawyer) colleagues.[15] Some jurisdictions prohibit in-house lawyers

---

[9] Robert A Kagan, Neil Gunningham, and Dorothy Thornton, 'Explaining Corporate Environmental Performance: How Does Regulation Matter?' (2003) 37 *Law & Society Review* 51.

[10] Terence J Johnson, *Professions and Power* (Macmillan, 1972).

[11] See, for example, Richard L Abel, *The Legal Profession in England and Wales* (Basil Blackwell, 1988); Larson (n 8).

[12] Doreen McBarnet and Christopher Whelan, 'The Elusive Spirit of the Law: Formalism and the Struggle for Legal Control' (1991) 54 *The Modern Law Review* 848; Doreen McBarnet, 'Legal Creativity: Law, Capital and Legal Avoidance' in Maureen E Cain and Christine B Harrington (eds) *Lawyers in a Postmodern World – Translation and Transgression* (Open University Press, 1994).

[13] Richard Moorhead and Victoria Hinchly, 'Professional Minimalism? The Ethical Consciousness of Commercial Lawyers' (2015) 42 *Journal of Law and Society* 387. See also Kimberly Kirkland, 'Ethics in Large Law Firms: The Principle of Pragmatism' (2005) 35 *University of Memphis Law Review* 631; and Steven Vaughan and Emma Oakley, '"Gorilla Exceptions" and the Ethically Apathetic Corporate Lawyer' (2016) 19 *Legal Ethics* 50.

[14] Brint (n 1).

[15] Pam Jenoff, 'Going Native: Incentive, Identity, and the Inherent Ethical Problem of In-House Counsel' (2011) 114 *West Virginia Law Review* 725.

from bar membership and do not grant them the advantage of legal professional privilege. Yet the influences on in-house lawyers are not so different to the lawyer in a large professional services private practice law firm; these too are hybrids of business and profession.[16]

Some claim such hybridity is a means of managing institutional complexity.[17] Under this analysis, hybridity ensures regulation 'works', but in balance with competing values, such as economic growth in commercial organisations or the implementation of policy in governmental ones. Importantly though, the success of hybrids depends on them being successfully managed towards professionalism so that they balance organisational and public interests, rather than paying lip-service to one while promoting the other.[18] Accountability may be especially important.

Some evidence suggests that in-house lawyers *can* be successful hybrids, but the results are mixed. One study suggests in-housers improve corporate governance through their gate-keeping functions: they reduce problematic risk-taking.[19] Another suggests that share price reaction to adverse disclosures made by listed companies is stronger for companies when those companies have senior lawyers in top positions.[20] Are disclosures from companies with senior lawyers taken more seriously, or are market makers simply more worried when they see lawyers promoted up the corporate food chain? The latter view is supported by evidence that credit risk analysts react adversely to seeing lawyers promoted to senior in-house management positions.[21] Digging deeper, how roles are structured and incentivised seems to be important. Jagolinzer et al found corporate policies requiring General Counsel (GC) approval for potential insider trades produced 'a substantial reduction in informed trading by insiders'.[22] The Sarbanes-Oxley Act (discussed further below) amplified those positive effects. And requiring GC sign-off on SEC financial filings was an important factor driving SEC compliance in Morse et al's results.[23]

Perhaps the lesson is that GCs need good policies, eg defined responsibility for sign-offs and reporting up, and the right cultures and incentives to

---

[16] James Faulconbridge and Daniel Muzio, 'Organizational Professionalism in Globalizing Law Firms' (2008) 22 *Work, Employment & Society* 7; Aaron Cohen, *Multiple Commitments in the Workplace: An Integrative Approach* (Psychology Press, 2003); Crawford Spence and Chris Carter, 'An Exploration of the Professional Habitus in the Big 4 Accounting Firms' (2014) 28 *Work, Employment & Society* 946.
[17] Blomgren and Waks (n 4) 78.
[18] Currie, Burgess and Tuck (n 4).
[19] Adair Morse, Wei Wang and Serena Wu, 'Executive Lawyers: Gatekeepers or Strategic Officers?' (2016) 59(4) *The Journal of Law and Economics* 847.
[20] Byungjin Kwak, Byung T Ro and Inho Suk, 'The Composition of Top Management with General Counsel and Voluntary Information Disclosure' (2012) 54 *Journal of Accounting and Economics* 19, 19.
[21] Charles Ham and Kevin Koharki, 'The Association between Corporate General Counsel and Firm Credit Risk' (2016) 61 *Journal of Accounting and Economics* 274.
[22] Alan D Jagolinzer, David F Larcker and Daniel J Taylor, 'Corporate Governance and the Information Content of Insider Trades' (2011) 49 *Journal of Accounting Research* 1249, 1252.
[23] Morse, Wang and Wu (n 19).

perform the gatekeeper role. How the in-house lawyer is linked to the organisational environment matters. In one study, motivating the strategic alignment of in-house lawyers through equity incentives reduced gatekeeping dramatically (but not totally).[24] Another study showed that highly compensated GCs had 'lower financial reporting quality and more aggressive accounting practices', but nonetheless still played 'an important gatekeeping role in keeping the firm in compliance with generally accepted accounting principles.'[25]

A mixture of economic and reputational incentives appear to be at work, weakening or strengthening the inclination of GCs to monitor and inhibit specific types of risky or unlawful behaviour.[26] The complexity can be seen in Goh et al's work. They find that including GCs in top management increases tax avoidance.[27] Why might the results differ for tax and SEC work? One possibility is that GCs did not need to certify tax compliance, and therefore were not worried about being held accountable for it. They can also share responsibility for riskier tax decisions with external advisers.[28] There is also the opportunity for GCs on tax transactions to gain a reputation for being 'more commercial' in ways directly traceable to their legal work: tax advice can have an immediate and measurable impact on the bottom line.[29] Other factors were also influential in Goh et al's work. If a GC had tax-related expertise, this increased avoidance. The purchase of tax services from their external advisers also increased avoidance. The extent of the CEO's power over the GC was influential on GC behaviour too.[30] And certain GCs appeared to carry tax minimisation strategies with them as they moved from company to company.[31]

ECOLOGICAL APPROACH

The studies suggest complex influences on GC decision-making. They reinforce the idea that, 'professions are likely to be best understood as institutional actors

---

[24] ibid.

[25] Justin J Hopkins, Edward L Maydew and Mohan Venkatachalam, 'Corporate General Counsel and Financial Reporting Quality' (2015) 61 *Management Science* 129.

[26] These studies tend to be about GCs or in-house lawyers who are amongst the best paid in the organisation (who may or may not be GCs). For simplicity we refer to them in this section as GCs.

[27] Beng Wee Goh, Jimmy Lee and Jeffrey Ng, 'The Inclusion of General Counsel in Top Management and Tax Avoidance' (Social Science Research Network 2015, SSRN Scholarly Paper ID 2538292), https://papers.ssrn.com/abstract=2538292, accessed 25 April 2018.

[28] Another study claims the retention of 'top-tier' outside lawyers reduced the completeness of SEC mandatory disclosures. See Preeti Choudhary, Jason D Schloetzer and Jason D Sturgess, 'Do Corporate Attorneys Influence Financial Disclosure' (Working Paper, Georgetown University, 2012); Preeti Choudhary, Jason D Schloetzer and Jason D Sturgess, 'Boards, Auditors, Attorneys and Compliance with Mandatory SEC Disclosure Rules' (2013) 34 *Managerial and Decision Economics* 471.

[29] See, generally, Tanina Rostain and Milton C Regan, *Confidence Games: Lawyers, Accountants, and the Tax Shelter Industry* (MIT Press, 2014), although they are mainly concerned with tax practice by accountants and law firms.

[30] Goh, Lee and Ng (n 27).

[31] ibid.

embedded in a complex environment of related institutions.'[32] This view has the potential to fit with a relational understanding of professionalism as 'valued and trusted partnerships',[33] where virtue can be derived from ethical agency within webs of relationships.[34] As Wald and Pearce note, traditional notions of professionalism vs business may be too zero-sum. To their mind, professionalism is necessarily ideologically impure; professionals are both 'self-regarding and self-sacrificing', but balance self-interest through basic values, 'such as honesty, trust and cooperation, as well as consideration of the public good.'[35]

Ecological accounts of professionalism seek to explore the relations between individuals and social structures in ways that suggest that, 'individuals make their own histories, but ... in that making they produce larger structures that in turn render them unable to make those histories under conditions of their own choosing.'[36] Individuals are neither fully constrained nor fully free to act as they wish. They operate within ecologies. Professions compete to persuade relevant audiences that they should legitimately control the problems that those audiences want solved. Risk is one such problem. Is it a legal, compliance, or other kind of problem: who should decide how to solve it? For in-house lawyers, those audiences can include their colleagues, their organisation's leadership, regulators, and even the media. To succeed, the solution to the problem has to work in the ecology of the profession's own way of thinking, and in the ecology of the audience's ways of thinking. For in-house lawyers, their solutions have to be both legally acceptable *and* organisationally useful.

In this way, professionals facilitate 'exchanges between institutional spheres', whilst being in competition for influence within their organisations.[37] Different ecologies form alliances of mutual benefit.[38] Such alliances are not in and of themselves sinister, but essential. A lawyer and accountant may have to work together with a business to decide on financial disclosures, with evidence this can reduce risk,[39] as well as exacerbate it.[40] A risk manager, lawyer, and NGO may work together to understand human right risks in a country an organisation plans to do business in. A scandal around litigation may depend on reputational

---

[32] Roy Suddaby and Thierry Viale, 'Professionals and Field-Level Change: Institutional Work and the Professional Project' (2011) 59 *Current Sociology* 423.

[33] Omari Scott Simmons and James D Dinnage, 'Innkeepers: A Unifying Theory of the In-House Counsel Role' (2011) 41(1) *Seton Hall Law Review* 77, 85 and 90.

[34] Wald and Pearce (n 3).

[35] ibid.

[36] Andrew Abbott, 'Linked Ecologies: States and Universities as Environments for Professions' (2005) 23 *Sociological Theory* 245.

[37] Andrew Abbott, *The System of Professions: An Essay on the Division of Expert Labor* (University of Chicago Press, 1988).

[38] Abbott, 'Linked Ecologies' (n 36).

[39] Jayanthi Krishnan, Yuan Wen and Wanli Zhao, 'Legal Expertise on Corporate Audit Committees and Financial Reporting Quality' (2011) 86 *The Accounting Review* 2099.

[40] David Kershaw and Richard Moorhead, 'Consequential Responsibility for Client Wrongs: Lehman Brothers and the Regulation of the Legal Profession' (2013) 76 *The Modern Law Review* 26.

optics as much as law. Such alliances usually form around specific work tasks. They may be temporary or more permanent, but the framing and resolution of those tasks, and hence the nature of those alliances, is fluid and malleable. This framing and resolution is moulded by the logics at work in solving the problem and in the interests of those involved. In other words, our understanding of professions needs to account for the context, the fluidity, and the malleability of professional and institutional ecologies. A wide range of constituencies and ideas might influence the thinking and practices of professionals.

Yet, there is a good deal of fuzziness in this ecological approach: how is each ecology influencing the other? How can we make sense of the complexity? Work on institutional logics is helpful in unpicking this complexity. That work forges a middle path between structural determinism (the sense that economics and/or power dictates what happens in any given situation) and liberal agency (the sense that individuals are masters of their own destiny).[41] Influenced by many ideas, including Bourdieu's work on logics and Gidden's work on structuration,[42] '[p]erhaps the core assumption of the institutional logics approach is that the interests, identities, values, and assumptions of individuals and organizations are embedded within prevailing institutional logics.'[43] Institutional logics focus on the interrelationships between systems, organisations, and individuals.[44] Systems (such as the state, market, and profession) have:[45]

> unique organizing principles, practices, and symbols that influence individual and organizational behavior. Institutional logics represent frames of reference that condition actors' choices for sense-making, the vocabulary they use to motivate action, and their sense of self and identity. The principles, practices, and symbols of each institutional order differentially shape how reasoning takes place and how rationality is perceived and experienced.

Sense-making is thus vitally important. This sense-making constructs how a problem and its potential solutions are understood. It occurs with each interaction between the system, organisation, and individual. Sense-making contains material and symbolic or cultural elements; incentives and ideas.[46] In this way, ecological interactions are not purely instrumental or economic, but involve an exchange of ideas and information, status and reward. Ecological actors are not

---

[41] See, in particular, Patricia H Thornton, William Ocasio and Michael Lounsbury, *The Institutional Logics Perspective: A New Approach to Culture, Structure, and Process* (Oxford University Press, 2012).

[42] Pierre Bourdieu, *Outline of a Theory of Practice* (Cambridge University Press, 1977); Anthony Giddens, *The Constitution of Society: Outline of the Theory of Structuration* (University of California Press, 1986).

[43] Patricia H Thornton and William Ocasio, 'Institutional Logics' in Royston Greenwood, Christine Oliver, Kerstin Sahlin-Andersson, and Roy Suddaby (eds), *The SAGE Handbook of Organizational Institutionalism* (Sage, 2008).

[44] This paragraph draws on Thornton, Ocasio and Lounsbury 'Logics Perspective' (n 41).

[45] ibid 2.

[46] ibid 10.

purely rational economic actors but construct legitimacy from a raft of contradictory values, ideas, and influences available to them in any situation.[47]

Having sketched the theory, how might it apply to our data?

TEASING OUT INSTITUTIONAL LOGICS

The further teasing out of institutional logics involves identifying relatively stable ideas about in-house practice; and the ideas by which in-housers make sense of their role and the ideas which their institutions bring to bear on them. At the general level, our data suggest that in-house lawyers have a particular constellation of institutional logics. Many see themselves as a distinct professional group within, but different to, the broader legal profession. About half of our survey respondents thought of themselves as an in-house legal adviser or in some other organisational role, in preference to thinking of themselves as a solicitor or barrister.[48] At more detailed level, there is greater variation. At the individual level we focus on two types of logic, role orientation and professional orientation. As such, we are using ideas about institutional logics to explore the complexity of in-house practice, to better understand the values, ideas and practices that push and pull at in-house lawyering within organisations.

An ecological understanding fits with the generally contextual approach to socio-legal studies of lawyers. Work on in-house lawyers identifies the importance of context but *also* emphasises the agency of in-house lawyers: lawyers are said to adopt the role of cops, counsellor, or entrepreneur; this implies they choose how independent they are and whether to say 'No' to a legal risky course of conduct. Note also that the roles offered up elsewhere are metaphors, bundling together distinct characteristics or ideas about the in-house lawyer's role. We see value in more closely isolating the logics within metaphorical approaches and more clearly delineating the relationship between the logics and the ethicality of those logics. Our data on risk and independence show how one needs to go beyond singular events (the willingness to say 'No'), as a way of testing one core characteristic (independence) to more fully contextualise those characteristics and how they are manifested. For example, we think other dimensions – how widely or narrowly legal advice is framed; what is done when law is uncertain; how proactively in-house lawyers respond to risk; how they manage for independent decision-making, and so on – are important elements helping construct independence.

---

[47] Thornton and others draw heavily on the work of Paul DiMaggio, 'Culture and Cognition' (1997) 23 *Annual Review of Sociology* 263.

[48] See, also, Moorhead and Hinchly (n 13); Claire Coe and Steven Vaughan, 'Independence, Representation and Risk: An Empirical Exploration of the Management of Client Relationships by Large Law Firms' (Solicitors Regulation Authority Report, October 2016).

We show it is possible to identify and measure distinct elements of the institutional logics of in-house lawyers. We isolate five role orientations. We see a commercial orientation (being commercially aware; adding value; advising on business as well as legal considerations; and regarding the commercial success of their organisations as important) as being distinct from an ethical orientation (advising on what is right, as well as what is legal, including lawful but unethical actions; and taking the lead on what is right when law is uncertain). This is in turn distinct from an independence orientation (the desire that an in-houser's judgement is, and is seen to be, independent) and a neutral advisor orientation (the view that the in-house lawyer advises but the organisation decides). Almost all in-house lawyers recognise and agree that these orientations are part of their role, but they do so with differing emphases. In general, the commercial orientation is plainly the strongest, the ethical and independence orientations come next, and the advisory orientation is still strong, but less so. A final orientation, an exploiting uncertainties orientation, was more controversial. It split our respondents: some saw taking advantage of uncertainty in the law for their clients as part of their role, and some did not.

These five orientations are distinctive ways of seeing the role, but plainly they co-exist and most are strongly supported by in-house lawyers. In other words, most of our in-house lawyers saw their roles as drawing upon elements each of the cop, counsellor and, to a lesser degree, the entrepreneurial roles as defined by Nelson and Nielsen. A question Nelson and Nielsen posed was whether such roles represented ideal types or repertoires of action.[49] Our data point clearly towards the latter. In-housers have the commercial orientation of entrepreneurial lawyers (but not always the appetite for exploiting uncertainty), the advisory orientation of counsellors, and are independently oriented and ethically oriented (as arguably cops, and also perhaps counsellors, are). They have the potential to be cops, counsellors or entrepreneurs as the situation, or their organisation, demands. Though willing to be cops, they are reluctant to be so. Most, but not all, are (reluctantly) willing to say 'No' to their employers when there is no legal alternative to a proposed action, as we showed in Chapter 4.

It is interesting to see, too, the somewhat stronger level of agreement among our in-housers with the commercial, ethical and independence orientations over a neutral advisor orientation. It is not that our sample did not generally agree that the in-house lawyer advises and the client decides (they did), but rather that our in-housers emphasised orientations that placed a stronger emphasis on their own agency. That is, they were more strongly in agreement with a role as influencers towards commerciality and/or ethicality, with that influence to be exercised from a position of some independence, than they were with distancing themselves from difficult decisions by saying the client (and not them) is responsible. We see this as an important, if modest, signal of maturity in the approaches adopted by

---

[49] Robert L Nelson and Laura Beth Nielsen, 'Cops, Counsel, and Entrepreneurs: Constructing the Role of inside Counsel in Large Corporations' (2000) *Law and Society Review* 457, 463.

most respondents. Equally, however, they were often more comfortable expressing agency when being commercial than when being ethical.

We examined the normativity of different logics by looking for relationships between each orientation and ethical inclination. We do this by using measures of ethical inclination shown in other studies to relate to real behaviour, and less prone than some indicators to social response bias (Chapter 8). This provides a, but not the only, test of the ethical implications of each orientation. In general terms, our evidence supports a view that an orientation to exploit uncertainty is normatively problematic, and casts some doubt on the commercial orientation. In-house lawyers more inclined to take the view that their role is to exploit the law for the client's aims are on average less ethically inclined. In brute terms, the indicators suggest they are more inclined to lie and cheat. We surmise, but do not demonstrate, that they would be thus more likely to breach their professional obligations. Similarly, we might expect such in-housers to be less inclined to a social trusteeship model of professionalism. The commercial orientation was associated with mixed effects (see Chapter 8). If organisational imperatives really corrupt professionalism, this corruption would seem to be primarily achieved through an in-house lawyer's facility with uncertainty than commercialism per se.

The ecological approach also suggests environment is influential on ethicality. We identified in-house team orientations – which we label financial, delivery, societal, and integrity orientations – and consider organisational context by looking at the relationships between the in-house legal team and their organisation, as well as what ethical infrastructure is in place to protect against ethical pressure. Stronger team cultures of integrity, and of thinking about the organisation's role in society, are associated with a stronger ethical inclination in the lawyer members of the in-house team; so too, stronger ethical infrastructure (things like formal ethics training and guidance, and more informal conversations about conduct). We cannot rule out the possibility that the ethically inclined perceive their teams as stronger, rather than those teams being objectively stronger. However, it seems unlikely to us that the ethically attentive would also be overly optimistic about their teams. Either way, the weaknesses in ethical infrastructure we have found in the research are concerning. There is limited practice of training on, and of formal or informal discussions of, professional ethics issues. This is especially concerning, given absent or weak relationships between ethical pressure and ethical infrastructure. It is a far from common response to ethical pressure to institute training, guidance and support to deal with that pressure.

We also developed a measure of how professional principles influenced in-housers in practice through measures of professional orientation. Professional orientation had three distinct dimensions: an orientation towards the client's best interests; an orientation towards effectiveness and integrity; and an orientation towards independence and legality. In-house lawyers consistently emphasised the client's best interests and effectiveness and integrity interests most strongly when asked to think in terms of the principles having an important influence on them in practice. As with role orientation, distinct but subtle differences were found: some in-house lawyers emphasised legality and independence concerns more strongly than other in-housers. Similarly, some emphasised integrity and effectiveness principles more than others. In this way, it appears that some in-house lawyers may be more likely to draw upon, say, legality and independence frames for their problem-solving than others. Interestingly though, both the 'legality and independence' and 'integrity and effectiveness' orientations were more associated with stronger ethical inclinations.

This level of quantitative mapping of in-house lawyer orientations has not been carried out before. Quantitative analysis inevitably involves simplification, and through seeking to look as comprehensively as possible at environment and individuals we are forced to compromise on the depth with which certain concepts are examined. No doubt, the measures could be improved. Similarly, quantitative modelling might, in the future, more strongly draw out the importance of proactivity around risk; something which emerged in our interviews but was not as well captured by our survey.

Perhaps as importantly, many of the orientations can be seen to give rise to tensions. Is it possible to show ethical leadership *and* to be a mere adviser? If the law really is uncertain, is it wrong to take advantage of that? Or put another way, is it possible to respond to uncertainty neutrally rather than in an exploitative way? Our quantitative analysis cannot capture all these interactions, but it suggests the importance of emphasis and balance in weighing the logics at work.

We see the nature of the interaction as part of the sense-making that goes on in practice, being partly framed by an individual's preferences (some will start from a more client-centred approach; others more from an independence and legality approach), and partly by the exigencies of any situation (what the task demands; how it is framed, and so on). Thus the orientations we have mapped out provide a general starting point in understanding ethical inclination. Our interview data fill in some of these gaps, showing us how in-house lawyers shape their place in a network of organisational influences.

THE PLACE OF IN-HOUSERS IN THE NETWORK OF INFLUENCES

Traditionally, lawyers were brought in-house because they were cheaper, but as their status has risen, their role has broadened to include more strategic and managerial functions, such as the management of legal risk. In-house lawyers are no longer merely cheaper; they are different. Personal motivations for moving in-house reflect some of these differences. Our interviewees spoke of having a more embedded, varied role; less legally specialised, but involving a broader set of skills. Importantly, their in-house roles involved a closer engagement with organisational imperatives (be they business or policy). Elements of private practice were also rejected: the 'moral bankruptcy' of timesheets; hyper-specialisation; and the business model of big law, in particular.

In this way, lawyers who have moved in-house are cognitively and affectively open to being more business-like or policy-focused. Plausibly, they thought this enabled them to do a better job. Grady describes what happens when a client comes to a new in-house lawyer asking for a contract:[50]

> Those lawyers who had recently joined the law department from a law firm and those lawyers still in a law firm ... would jump into action, gathering data for the document and plotting the path to victory.
>
> A lawyer experienced with the in-house client and environment would take a different path. She would ask about the situation giving rise to the request. She would probe the context, the parties involved, the existence of other legal instruments, and the risks. A really good lawyer would ask questions trying to get at the situation from the client's perspective. By the time she was done, the client and lawyer might have concluded that no legal instrument was needed, a short amendment to an existing document would suffice, and that the client needed something different from what he first requested.

Here, the ecology of the organisation trains the in-house lawyer to better understand the organisation's needs. It strikes us as a good description of the pragmatic, results-oriented dimensions to what we call being commercially oriented. And as well as the better fitness for purpose that Grady describes, we saw ways in which greater cognitive openness to an organisation's needs might lead to more ethical approaches to practice: in-house lawyers could, through wider and earlier exposure to the organisation's decision-making, be more tuned into, and influential on, the long-term interests of their organisation that are shaped by legal and reputational risk. They could spot problems early and respond, at least in theory.

Embedding professional expertise in this way involves the everyday grounding of legal work in the organisation's values. The reason the job is being done, and the outcome that the job delivers, are influential on how the job is done. For many, this meant being asked to be 'value adding': integrating in-house lawyers into business development and planning functions, and away from 'pure' legal advice towards risk management and commercial input. Value-adding was a concept which sometimes unsettled, rather than worked with the grain of, the legal thinking of our in-housers. It destabilised professional norms. We would surmise they felt themselves rubbing up against a genuine incommensurability between legal and commercial ways of thinking. Value-adding very likely encourages cognitive dissonance which, by design or accident, encourages professional neuroticism. Imagine being faced with a legal question to which

---

[50] Ken Grady, 'What The 1,000 Floor Elevator Challenge And Professional Services Have In Common' (Medium, 27 August 2017), https://medium.com/the-algorithmic-society/what-the-1-000-floor-elevator-challenge-and-professional-services-have-in-common-5bf85e1d110, accessed 25 April 2018.

one is not sure of the legal answer, but to which the *commercial* answer is clear. Here, consciously or unconsciously, the incentive is to adjust one's view of the legal uncertainties to accommodate the organisational imperatives. In parallel, in-house lawyers worked within a negative stereotype: often, *very* often, assuming they were seen as deal-blockers or costly nit-pickers.

The extent of such dissonance was varied. A clear understanding of the in-house legal team's role in organisations was sometimes strong, but more often tentative or absent. It could also be hierarchical, with interviewees suggesting that understanding of the need for independent in-house legal functions was stronger at the apex of organisations. Unevenness of relationships within the business were common, as was criticism of in-house lawyers for being obstructive (see Chapter 3). That such dissonance was important is suggested by almost half of our respondents who reported that their organisations acted *against* legal advice on important matters. Furthermore, about 10 per cent of our respondents reported being asked to advise on ethically or legally debatable actions frequently or very frequently, and 40 per cent were asked to so advise on such actions at least sometimes. About 10–15 per cent agreed or strongly agreed that they were asked to advise on things that made them uncomfortable, or in ways which suggested the business took a different view on whether and/or how to uphold the rule of law. About a quarter to a third agreed at least somewhat with these concerns.

We can be depressed by such findings, but recognition of the problem may also be a healthy sign. Our work stands in contrast to other work on occupational professional conflict in law, which has tended to suggest that such conflict is muted, absent, or well-managed.[51] We see clearly here that conflict does arise. The key thing is whether it is recognised and how it is dealt with. As we saw in Chapter 8, our in-house lawyers varied in their moral attentiveness and engagement. To give two examples, those we called the 'Champions' were more morally engaged and attentive in the face of ethical pressure, whereas the 'Troubled' show signs of having succumbed to pressure through greater disengagement. Conversely, in describing the in-house lawyer's place in the organisational network, we can see how engagements with the organisation are part of a tournament of influence which in-house lawyers sometimes (perhaps often) expect to lose. There is a trading of helpfulness with any legal question or task for acceptance from their non-legal colleagues. Organisational scepticism, where it exists, is tackled by adopting a cultivated posture of flexibility. The need for independence and difficult advice is camouflaged, restrained, or diluted. The question is not whether to compromise, but how much, when, and in what circumstances.

---

[51] Hugh P Gunz and Sally P Gunz, 'The Lawyer's Response to Organizational Professional Conflict: An Empirical Study of the Ethical Decision Making of in-House Counsel' (2002) 39 *American Business Law Journal* 241; Tanina Rostain, 'General Counsel in the Age of Compliance: Preliminary Findings and New Research Questions' (2008) 21 *Geo J Legal Ethics* 465.

INDEPENDENCE

Independence is a signal professional logic and, as we have identified, it is viewed as an important role orientation by over 70 per cent of our in-house lawyers. In theory, our interviewees accepted a willingness to say 'No', and the need to pay a price for independence (negative performance appraisals, getting fired or needing to resign): they said it came with the territory. Yet only a minority of our interviewees placed independence at the heart of how they conceived of their roles. Others accepted that 'you start to get a bit blind after a time' [IHL38]. If the ability of an in-house lawyer to stand back consists of properly serving the client's interests by considering independently of self-serving or client-serving rationalisations what the law really demands, then our interviews suggested that standing back may be easier said than done. Being cognitively open to the needs of the organisation, with social and often economic incentives on in-housers towards aligning with their organisations, made standing back difficult.[52]

Equally, our interviewees often made subtle and not naïve claims to professional independence. Independence, its importance, and how it manifests are part of a complex series of interactions between the in-house lawyer and the organisation. Many of our in-housers recognised that how they provided advice, and how the advice was used, were contingent on a number of factors: how the legal team was perceived; the relationship between the in-houser and the person seeking advice; and the point at which legal had been involved in the decision-making process, for example. Issues of objectivity and independence are most clearly raised in the context of in-housers being very sensitive to their place in the corporate network of influence. That sensitivity sometimes involves a negotiation between the in-house lawyer's view of what is lawful and right, and their view of what is tolerable. Independence is as much a process, a series of events, as it is a test for individual decisions. In this way, independence is not a binary concept, but a judgement-call, often a series of judgement-calls. Independence operates along a continuum. It may be found to be weaker or stronger, in the same person, at different times and in different contexts. It relates to the positioning of the in-house lawyer in the organisation and the need to work for influence.

When independence becomes fatally compromised or intolerable, or when a proposed illegal action is clearly illegal, then the in-house lawyer must either say 'No' or resign. Several interviewees had resigned in the past, but our sense is that what is intolerable, or what is clearly illegal, varied. Some said legal constraints are treated as a fact of life: if the law clearly prohibits something then saying 'No' in such circumstances was straightforward; others seemed to believe 'it's a no-no to say no'.[53] We would add an important emphasis: the *dominant* position for in-house lawyers is to work hard to avoid conflict with their employer organisation, only saying 'No' judiciously, and to defer to the organisation on

---

[52] Jenoff (n 15).
[53] Nelson and Nielsen (n 50) 471.

the acceptability of risk. Indeed, a *stated* willingness to say 'No' may be a very soft commitment to legality. We thus disagree with Rostain's more optimistic reading of GC, 'capacity to stop deals that they believed posed significant legal risks to the company'.[54] We do so for two reasons. One is that some of those we surveyed and spoke to had a weak or non-existent willingness to say 'No' (see Chapter 4). The second reason is that it is the interpretation of what is *significant* risk in the Rostain quote that is as (or more) important than a professed willingness to say 'No'. Significance of risks circles us back to issues of uncertainty, as well as the consequences of any regulatory failure flowing from that risk. As we have noted already, one example is Rolls-Royce's prosecution for bribery. That involved the categorisation of contracts for bribes as high-risk rather than as impermissible.

Furthermore, saying 'No' requires significant effort as well as internal human capital. Where stakes are high, an in-house lawyer may need to be both well-placed in the tournament of influence, but also resourceful and willing to organise alliances within the organisation, before they can say 'No'. 'No' is both decided and negotiated. It is also avoidable: the relevant facts can be framed in helpful ways which make the legal tests easier to satisfy; the questions asked can be posed in ways which make it easier not to say 'No'; reservations can be expressed but not pressed. That avoidance by in-house lawyers may be pragmatic (because certain legal risks are tolerable), or it may be tactical (because bigger priorities requiring the use of 'No' lurk elsewhere, requiring the saving of political capital for later), or it may be self-protecting (because the in-houser wants to be seen as useful, helpful, and so on).

In this way, our evidence suggests that the saying of 'No' is both a problem for many, and an acute problem for some, and also that it is more than a decision or an event, but a set of processes within a network. Each piece of advice, each 'Yes', 'No' and 'Maybe', was part of a broader series of interactions where the in-house lawyers worked to persuade their colleagues of their utility, relevance and commitment to the organisation, part of the tournament of influence. Perhaps as importantly, saying 'No' is only the tip of an iceberg, a continuum of context-specific responses to risk, that require vigilance, proactivity, clear, strong communication, preparation and other virtues. To repeat the quote we used in Chapter 4:

> To put it rather broadly, you win people over by being sensible, by making money for the company, by making good calls, by negotiating well, by being a really good ally on commercial projects, by making things happen, by going away and saying, 'Yes, that's a horrible messy thing and I'll sort it out for you.' And then, when you're in the board and you're doing the unpopular thing, because let's face it, when it's a horrible, nasty thing that's gone a bit wrong, if you like, the really horrible things that happen to companies tend to be things that people knew about but didn't confront, and the reason they didn't confront them was nobody had the moral courage to confront

---

[54] Rostain (n 52) 473–74.

them. So it was easier just to stuff them under the carpet and keep them there. I'm willing to bet that people in Volkswagen, there were going to be a lot of people, not potentially the board, not potentially even, I would guess, the general counsel, maybe, I don't know, but I bet people blew the whistle on that in the sort of gentle, pathetic way. And the general counsel's job is to go, 'Someone's making a fuss about that. I should find out what it is, and then, if it's a thing we should be looking at, I'll make sure we look at it.' And at that point, you are absolutely not going to win friends and influence people and they will say, 'For God's sake, why are you doing this? That's horrible, that's nasty, that's beastly and I don't want to know about it so just shut up.' And that's the point at which you use all the brownie points you've got by doing all the other things that they liked, and eventually, if it all works out, they may say, 'Actually, that was quite a good call, it's a good thing you did that.' But they may not, they may just go, 'Oh well, she's a bit difficult sometimes, but on the whole, she's quite useful to have around.' [IHL35]

The tournament of influence and pragmatism is reshaped here as a kind of quiet heroism. If it works, it can work well. Another interpretation is of independence rendered contingent not fundamental. Independence is one idea at work within the tournament of influence, intermixed with the operational significance and social status of individual in-house lawyers. The organisation's agency (in business, the commercial orientation) is always legitimate, but legal's influence has to be managed, protected, and sometimes fought for.

To move on to another dimension of the problem, we do not think that independence is a trope, but there is a danger that independence is a less useful concept if it is not allied with an intrinsic value. Having influence when risk is mission-critical is not a sufficient test. Professional rules are clear that in-house lawyers (and those in private practice) must protect the rule of law and the administration of justice. This provides an intrinsic value that in-house lawyers should be thinking about explicitly. Another way of thinking about this is that the influence model of independence is prone to temporal and social vulnerability. If a GC has had to say 'No' in uncomfortable circumstances three times, the fourth time they will be less inclined to say 'No' simply as a result of three previous decisions rather than because of the actual risks posed by not saying 'No' to the fourth question. This is socially intelligible, but dangerous. Put another way, independence does not simply mean not being prone to influence, or being one's own person. It means independently and, insofar as it is possible, objectively assessing what the rule of law and the administration of justice really requires when one is advising or assisting an organisational client.

A BLEND OF COMMERCIAL AND LEGAL THINKING – RISK

The way risk is managed provides a more specific instantiation of professional, legal, and commercial logics. The pursuit of influence by in-housers takes place within a pyramid network that shapes which work is seen as most valuable. The making of strategic business decisions and facilitating commercial opportunities top the 'GC value pyramid'.[55] Risk management is one way in which in-house lawyers can move up within the pyramid by becoming more strategic, by quantifying and generalising, by speaking to the business most clearly in business terms, by saving or making money, and by being able to demonstrate general impact. In short, risk management provides, in theory at least, one means of overcoming the incommensurability of the commercial and professional views of the legal function which we discussed above.

Our interviews suggest risk is understood and managed in uneven and unpredictable ways. The strategic role of in-house lawyers is an evolving one: not as well developed across in-house lawyer teams or as well recognised by boards as might be understood from professional rhetoric on the matter.[56] A second point is that in-house lawyers' conceptualisation of risk and their understanding of risk appetite was always influenced and sometimes dominated by their organisation's approach. Risk logics and frameworks usually came from their organisations and from institutionalised ways of thinking about risk. Yet, through leadership, organisation, proactivity and resources, it was also possible for hybrids of professional and organisational logics to develop. When they do, we see some positive elements: the shift from reactivity to proactivity; a shift from a dyadic lawyer-adviser role to a multi-dimensional networked role; from adviser to information-gatherer and influencer to system-designer. In-house lawyer risk managers become more engaged in shaping behaviours than when they merely advise. Interestingly, though, this broader approach was more apparent in organisations that narrowly define legal risk around risks which the legal work of the organisation generates.

This leads us to ethical questions about in-house lawyers and risk management. Risk assessment requires professional objectivity for such assessment to be useful and accurate, yet the culture of 'being commercial' and the need to garner influence impact on that ability, as we have seen already. Professional orientations that emphasise putting the client first strain that objectivity further, as we will discuss below. A feature of legal risk management is that it formally tolerates, normalises, and sometimes promotes the inevitability, and sometimes the *desirability*, of taking risks in relation to law. If notions of risk were structured towards ideas of public interest, it was generally done by corporate codes and pleas to take a long-term sustainable view of an organisation's goals, rather than a short-term, narrowly commercial view. These were stronger drivers than professional principles.

Indeed, where professional principles were called upon, it was most usually the obligation of independence that was summoned by our interviewees. The obligation to promote the rule of law and protect the public interest in the administration of justice had limited, if any, purchase. It was not a concept that

---

[55] Nabarro, 'From In house lawyer to business counsel' (Naborro LLP Report, 2010).
[56] See also ACC, 'Skills for the 21st Century General Counsel' (Association of Corporate Counsel Survey, 2015) 33.

was well articulated in their professional consciousness. In broad terms, the higher the organisation's risk-appetite, the more consequentialist and relativist legal risk judgements appeared likely to become. In particular, decisions would be driven by understanding the cost-benefit of a position and a relative weighting of the ambiguity of the law, the management of facts (in ways that might not reflect underlying truths), and how important the organisational objective was that raised the legal problem. Some of our interviewees articulated a firmer notion of legality and resistance to creative compliance, whilst acknowledging that legality was sometimes stretched or breached in practice. When asked if there were risks which interviewees would not tolerate, risk red lines were only clearly drawn around serious criminality, explicit risk to life, and problems that would be financially or reputationally catastrophic either for the organisation or key individuals, including sometimes the in-house lawyers themselves.

Whilst professional principles were generally not called upon, professional *status* was perceived as useful. It helped establish a level of independence within the organisation and a basis for making claims on that independence and on the public interest. It was also said to form the basis of a claim for higher objectivity. One should be a little cautious about accepting such claims. There is research which shows that 'thinking of oneself as a professional' may (on its own) lead to a form of complacency that promotes greater unethicality.[57] Equally, we have seen earlier in this book how the majority of our interviewees told us they felt their employers did not understand their professional obligations. Thus, professional *status* being important may simply be that: a thin marker of status without much knowledge of what comes with that marker.

Finally, if we think of the interplay between professional and risk logics at work here, then we see an opportunity for professional assertion and leadership. If management of risk is a strategic imperative, then being better able to manage legal risk is a way of improving organisational legality and ethicality whilst also improving the strategic influence of individual in-house lawyers. We saw this potential on occasion, as we hope we have shown. In-housers can lead on broader notions of ethicality, and can develop proactive, rather than defensive, roles in promoting pre-emptive risk work. This was an important theme in some of the discussion with our interviewees. What influences some lawyers towards a broader, more ethical approach?

BROADER INFLUENCES

It is worth standing back and thinking in a broader sense about what influences the logics of lawyers working in-house. Different systems are at work: the organisation itself; the legal team within that organisation; the professional

---

[57] Maryam Kouchaki, 'Professionalism and Moral Behavior: Does a Professional Self-Conception Make One More Unethical?' (Edmond J Safra Working Paper, 2013).

bodies which regulate that legal team; and society more generally. There will be other systems which might be included, such as the field the organisation operates in (eg banking, or government, or the extractive industries), and it may be more accurate to think of society as a series of sub-systems (the press, the legislature, the public, regulators etc). Each influences the other. Society influences the field through law, the media, the purchasing decisions of customers, or the votes of citizens. The organisation is influenced through the nature of the markets in which they operate, the intensity and nature of competition, cultures of regulatory arbitrage, and so on. The organisation influences the legal team. The professions influence that in-house team too, through generally received ideas about lawyering amongst its members, through educational requirements, and through regulatory measures in particular. Those teams, the organisation, the profession, the field, and society more generally may all influence the individual professional.

We can think further about how the different systems interact formally within the organisations: we would emphasise task definition and delivery, and two levels of management.

Tasks might be cases or projects (such as delivery of a risk management process). How those tasks are framed,[58] what the scope of the task is (is an investigation narrow or wide-ranging, for instance), what the resources available are, whether legal is engaged early or late in any process, and what expectations all parties have of what constitutes delivery might all influence the how individual sees their role on that task (and over time on tasks more generally). It might also influence their willingness to draw on particular orientations: a task which is framed in strongly commercial terms might lead to an in-houser more strongly drawing upon commercial orientations.

Let us take an example, drawn from real life but embellished, to illustrate the way in which the logics from different systems interact.[59] In particular, let us consider again the values and ideas at work when in-house lawyers face uncertainty in the law. Imagine you are an in-house lawyer working for a lift-hailing app (let's call them Hike) and you are asked to advise on whether they can 'greyball' regulators. By this, we mean imagine that the plan is for Hike to alter its software application to avoid law enforcement or other government officials booking lifts using their service. The aim is to inhibit the regulator's ability to test Hike's compliance with the law.[60] Imagine your initial research suggests an imaginative prosecutor could say you were perverting the course of justice.

---

[58] Francesca Gino and Joshua D Margolis, 'Bringing Ethics into Focus: How Regulatory Focus and Risk Preferences Influence (Un)Ethical Behavior' (2011) 115 *Organizational Behavior and Human Decision Processes* 145.

[59] This example is only loosely based on the Uber example. It is a fiction and not meant to imply wrongdoing on the part of Uber or anyone associated with them.

[60] Richard L Cassin, 'Report: Uber Investigated for FCPA Offenses' (FCPA Blog, 30 August 2017), www.fcpablog.com/blog/2017/8/30/report-uber-investigated-for-fcpa-offenses.html, accessed 25 April 2018.

There is no analogous case, but you can see how the proposal fits the definition of the offence. If you had to advise on probabilities, you would say it was a 60:40 call that a criminal prosecution would not succeed. The regulators might also try to make life difficult in other ways. Recent history has shown regulators do not generally do so, because similar organisations are popular with the public and will fight tooth and nail if challenged.

The culture of Hike is to challenge regulation as 'anti-consumer'. How does one advise in that situation? Does one say: 'This is an extremely risky strategy with a whole of host of unpredictable and potentially serious regulatory risks that include the future of our operating licence and a risk of criminal prosecution'? Or does one say that whilst the situation is not clear, there are no obvious or clear legal impediments to the 'greyballing' strategy? Such responses may well be shaped, in part, by how the organisation framed the task. Say you give a measured response and the CEO says: 'I don't want to hear detail. I pay you to make decisions. I just want a "Yes" or "No" report that goes to the board saying whether we are acting within the law.' What then? Imagine the CEO had limited the scope of the advice sought ('We only want advice on clear legal barriers to doing this') in a context where legal's voice is usually ancillary to business decisions already taken 'in principle'. The extent to which such an approach will be acceptable within the organisation will depend in part on the routines established around legal risk decisions in the past: do non-executive directors feel that this is the kind of decision they should probe, for instance? And when you are asked to report to the board, do you simply say: 'There are no insuperable legal barriers to this action – in legal terms it is reasonable to go ahead'?

An in-house lawyer's actions here may be shaped by particular attitudes to risk in the organisation, by their attitude to exploiting uncertainty, by the extent to which they see themselves as a mere advisor or as someone used to leading through uncertainty. Is the in-house lawyer who says there are no insuperable barriers giving the appearance of leading through uncertainty here, whilst, in fact, following the lead of the CEO rather than giving an independent view? Who is the client, whose best interests are being advanced? An in-house lawyer comfortable with the idea that uncertainty is exploited, and who is especially motivated by their own success, might be more inclined to take the view that economy with the truth was simply part of the normal role of an in-house lawyer advocating a position for their client.[61] This might be especially true if the in-houser takes a narrow, shareholder value-led view of corporate governance.[62] The extent to which an in-house lawyer sees obligations to behave with integrity or to protect the rule of law as meaningful and important

---

[61] Richard Moorhead and Rachel Cahill-O'Callaghan, 'False Friends? Testing Commercial Lawyers on the Claim That Zealous Advocacy Is Founded in Benevolence towards Clients Rather than Lawyers' Personal Interest' (2016) 19 *Legal Ethics* 30.

[62] Robert W Gordon, 'The Return of the Lawyer-Statesman Essay' (2017) 69 *Stanford Law Review* 1731.

influences on decision-making here is also important. An in-houser accustomed to equate professional ethics with 'client first' may have a harder time seeing the risks in a zealous advocacy approach that allows himself to argue that the CEO might be right, rather than thinking about whether the CEO is really right.

It is this focus on the ideas that shape interactions between different systems that is most valuable from the institutional logics perspective, and which we think is crucial to understanding the embeddedness of in-house ethicality. Ways of thinking and speaking about problems are an essential component of the interaction between the different value systems: 'theorisation is a diffusion mechanism'.[63] Ideas such as 'commerciality' and 'client-first' dominate professional discourse, and some ideas (such as 'value') deliberately challenge the professional side of that discourse; but other notions are also important – integrity and independence for instance. We have begun to see in this book how a closer focus on other logics – especially the construction of uncertainty; but also ideas of independence and ethical leadership – are critical components too. There are, thus, counter-logics and tensions at work. In-house lawyers bring their ideas but must interact with their organisations. Individuals choose from, and are influenced subconsciously by, a wide range of competing ideas about how to frame a problem, see a solution, and act.

Task definition is important, but so too is the way the discussions are structured and shaped beyond the task. Organisational leadership approaches taken at the very top of the organisation around managing the legal function, and managers within legal teams, may develop and reinforce routines and norms around recognising and considering ethical challenges. We have seen in our data how ethical infrastructure can be important to ethical inclination, and our interviewees were very conscious of the ways in which in-house lawyers are talked about in their organisations. As discussed above, other work suggests the importance of incentives, and the structuring of gatekeeping decisions, on how in-housers balance gatekeeping and business facilitation roles.[64]

If the organisation is responsible for one set of management practices, the in-house legal team has at least some control over how it responds. They too can shape task definition, organisational leadership, and team management. If a task is defined too narrowly, such as when the CEO says 'we only want advice on clear barriers to this', the in-houser can seek to reframe it. If there is an absence of team infrastructure, they can try and build it. And if there is an absence of organisational leadership around legal matters, the in-houser can work to challenge and change that too. We do not trivialise the challenge: in-house leaders and individual in-house lawyers will have to negotiate this work with their teams and organisations, but increasing the extent to which in-house teams think about and support appropriate professional and role orientations is important.

---

[63] Thornton, Ocasio and Lounsbury, 'Logics Perspective' (n 41) 11.
[64] See nn 19 to 32 and associated text.

LAW AND OTHER INFLUENCES

Ecological theory reminds us that professionalisation is connected with 'the institutionalisation projects of other actors', nation states, corporations, and transnational governance regimes.[65] In-house lawyers' professional legitimacy, and utility to their organisations, comes from their ability to justify action as within the law, and to maintain the reputation of their organisations. They do so by anticipating not just illegality but allegations of illegality, and sharp or inappropriate practice. Some of that influence comes from the law itself (how far it really defines what is just and legal) and from the powers granted by regulators. Heightened regulatory (or litigation) activity raises the need for legal advice and action, in a general sense, but lawyers can also be specifically required or encouraged to act as gatekeepers by regulators, as well as by their host organisations (for example, calling in lawyers to act as independent investigators).[66]

If we look at the general weakness in ethical infrastructure in our data, and the general emphasis on a technical, client-driven model of service from our respondents, we can see how important task formulation and delivery is to understanding the ethicality of in-house practice. Task formulation is profoundly shaped by the law itself but is contingent on the certainty of the rules and the facts. Our interviewees displayed different levels of proactivity, curiosity, or scepticism around taking facts from their organisations as 'givens' when asked to advise. Task formulation and delivery – through attitudes to uncertainty – were also shaped by consequences (whether cases gave rise to criminal liability, or 'serious' criminal liability; or criminal liability *for directors*).

Some legal regimes have impacted on ecologies more profoundly than others by seeking to rebalance the way organisations and their in-house lawyers approach legal obligations. For lawyers practising before the United States' Securities and Exchange Commission, there are the reporting requirements under the Sarbanes-Oxley Act (SOX).[67] Prosecutor scrutiny of lawyers involved in corporate and tax scandals is stronger; Loughrey argues that higher levels of academic scrutiny in the US have had an impact too.[68] Lawyers working in-house for US-listed firms, or with US sister companies, are mindful that there may be SOX implications to their actions which they might be held

---

[65] Roy Suddaby and Daniel Muzio, 'Theoretical Perspectives on the Professions' in Laura Empson, Daniel Muzio, Joseph Broschak, and Bob Hinings (eds), *The Oxford Handbook of Professional Service Firms* (Oxfors University Press, 2015) 34.

[66] Coffee, 'Attorney as Gatekeeper' (n 2).

[67] Which mandates disclosure by in-housers in certain situations. See Roger C Cramton, George M Cohen and Susan P Koniak, 'Legal and Ethical Duties of Lawyers after Sarbanes-Oxley' (2004) 49 *Villanova Law Review* 725; Leonard M Baynes, 'Just Pucker and Blow: An Analysis of Corporate Whistleblowers, the Duty of Care, the Duty of Loyalty, and the Sarbanes-Oxley Act' (2002) 76 *St John's Law Review* 875.

[68] Joan Loughrey, *Corporate Lawyers and Corporate Governance* (Cambridge University Press, 2011) 26–27.

accountable for.[69] And the potential extra-territoriality of prosecution under the US Foreign and Corrupt Practices Act (FCPA),[70] or litigation under the US Alien Tort Claims Acts,[71] is also credited with adjusting the calculus of organisations about ethical problems which may give rise to prosecutions or civil suits.[72] FCPA practices around investigation and remedies are similarly credited with causing or influencing the creation of compliance teams, ethics leads, and so on. Also in the US, the Yates Memo signalled the importance of companies cooperating with investigators by providing evidence on individuals working within their organisations responsible for wrongdoing.[73] There is the increasingly prevalent practice (which began in the US, but has now been adopted by the UK's Serious Fraud Office) of prosecutors requiring the waiver of legal professional privilege to ensure an organisation is demonstrating full cooperation.[74] Seeking individuals to blame, and securing the cooperation of organisations against those individuals, may very well impact on the way in-house lawyers do their jobs. It serves as a reminder of who the client is for the in-houser (the organisation, not any particular manager, or even the board) and of the weaknesses that are inherent in legal professional privilege. In-house lawyers may fear greater scrutiny and a reluctance on the part of their client employers to seek advice if privilege is eroded, but other pressures (beyond privilege) drive the need for advice and the need to comply with it.[75]

Our purpose here is not to suggest that the external influences are perfect, or even effective. Some external influences may have minimal, or even retrograde, impacts. Yet we think it reasonably clear that trends in corporate governance regulation, and public (media) scrutiny of law-related activity, are towards in-housers taking their public interest obligations more seriously.

---

[69] Rostain (n 52).

[70] On which, see Daniel Ashe, 'The Lengthening Anti-Bribery Lasso of the United States: The Recent Extraterritorial Application of the U.S. Foreign Corrupt Practices Act' (2005) 73 *Fordham Law Review* 2897; David C Weiss, 'The Foreign Corrupt Practices Act, SEC Disgorgement of Profits, and the Evolving International Bribery Regime: Weighing Proportionality, Retribution, and Deterrence' (2008) 30 *Michigan Journal of International Law* 471.

[71] See Courtney Shaw, 'Uncertain Justice: Liability of Multinationals under the Alien Tort Claims Act' (2002) 54 *Stanford Law Review* 1359; David D Christensen, 'Corporate Liability for Overseas Human Rights Abuses: The Alien Tort Statute after *Sosa v. Alvarez-Machain*' (2005) 62 *Washington and Lee Law Review* 1219.

[72] John Gerard Ruggie, *Just Business: Multinational Corporations and Human Rights (Norton Global Ethics Series)* (WW Norton & Company, 2013).

[73] Sally Quillian Yates, 'Memorandum for the Assistant Attorney General [and Others]: Individual Accountability for Corporate Wrongdoing' (US Department of Justice Memorandum, 9 September 2015), www.justice.gov/archives/dag/file/769036/download, accessed 25 April 2018.

[74] *Serious Fraud Office (SFO) v Eurasian Natural Resources Corporation Ltd* [2017] EWHC 1017; Paul J Jr Larkin and John Michael Seibler, 'All Stick and No Carrot: The Yates Memorandum and Corporate Criminal Liability' (2016) 46 *Stetson Law Review* 7; Julie R O'Sullivan, 'How Prosecutors Apply the Federal Prosecutions of Corporations Charging Policy in the Era of Deferred Prosecutions, and What That Means for the Purposes of the Federal Criminal Sanction' (2014) 51 *American Criminal Law Review* 29.

[75] Andrew Higgins, 'Legal Advice Privilege and Its Relevance to Corporations' (2010) 73 *The Modern Law Review* 371.

Our interviewees indicated that consumer protection legislation, and personal liability for directors, meant 'companies started to see that the in-house role could be more supportive, give more direction' [IHL25]. Regulatory schemes for data privacy, bribery, and the FCPA had been influential and, 'lessons learned and hopefully still being learned' from poor behaviour uncovered after the financial crash, meant, 'there was the opportunity there to actually look at governance and compliance.' [IHL41]

We are aware of the need to be circumspect in any optimism this engenders. Interviewees are, 'engaged in public relations exercises' even when interviewed under the cloak of anonymity.[76] And, even against the background of such comments, our work on role and professional orientations shows that notions of public interest rarely trump, let alone replace, commercial and client-first orientations. For many in-housers there is room to strengthen integrity, independence, and ethical judgement. The external trend appears to be towards increasing roles for independence and ethicality, whilst 'being commercial' is emphasised internally and within practitioner associations and conferences. Shifts towards independence and ethicality may be superficial or genuine; motivated by a desire to 'regain trust' or to dampen down litigation or regulatory action against the corporate sector. The ideology of management may play a role in how orientations are emphasised. Taking to heart Welch's view that focusing too heavily on 'shareholder value is the dumbest idea in the world',[77] CEOs might encourage a more independent, challenging approach from legal colleagues as a bulwark against excessive commercial ingenuity in their organisation in the belief that this builds more sustainable organisations.[78] Gordon reminds us that the nature of corporate governance and in-house counsel leadership may be shaped by wider political currents and ideas about what constitutes good business that ebb and flow.[79]

The law has not generally sought to structure how in-house legal functions are managed, although regulators are taking a greater interest in how legal risk is managed. The UK Financial Conduct Authority suggests a senior manager, but not necessarily an in-house lawyer, needs to be identified who is responsible for legal risk.[80] Our data on whether appointment of an in-house lawyer to the Board led to a weaker or stronger ethical inclination were equivocal. In-house lawyers who sat on or attended board meetings had a different conception of their role from others, but it was not a conception that was shown to have a

---

[76] Robert E Rosen, *Lawyers in Corporate Decision-Making* (Quid Pro Quo Books, 2015).
[77] Franceso Guerrera, 'Welch Condemns Share Price Focus' (*Financial Times*, 12 March 2009), www.ft.com/content/294ff1f2-0f27-11de-ba10-0000779fd2ac, accessed 25 April 2018.
[78] Joseph L Bower and Lynn S Paine, 'The Error at the Heart of Corporate Leadership' (2017) 95 *Harvard Business Review* 50.
[79] Gordon (n 62).
[80] Financial Conduct Authority, 'Overall Responsibility and the Legal Function: DP16/4' (FCA Discussion Paper, 2016), https://www.fca.org.uk/publications/discussion-papers/overall-responsibility-and-legal-function, accessed 25 April 2018.

clear impact on ethical inclination. The importance of board appointment, as contra to or supportive of ethical in-house practice, depends on a wider constellation of features, including how the in-house lawyer is remunerated, but also – we are sure – on the kind of leadership that is shown by and expected from the board. In this light, it is interesting, and we think concerning, that reporting relationships are not more extensively established between in-house lawyers and non-executive directors.

Whilst it is conventionally thought that organisational influence is inimical to professionalism, it should also be acknowledged that some learning from organisational practices can be good.[81] The proactive responses to risk that we saw in some answers to our case studies came, at least in some respects, from an organisationally led approach which saw in-house lawyers as having a more strategic role and being better-resourced. The need for some managerial grip on risk is something that has prompted, for some in-housers, greater organisation, a stronger emphasis on process, and on more behavioural dimensions to their work (eg, does a bribery policy work, rather than simply looking good on paper?) Our interviews suggest this development is most likely to come where organisations have more developed, and specialised, management support functions. That is not to underplay some of the more worrying elements associated with such programmes: cost-benefit analysis of risk, particularly when the estimates of risk incidence and consequence are highly subjective, may provide a sense of managerial adequacy which could be characterised as over-confidence. Data are expected to play a stronger role in legal management, but there is some way to go before risk prediction is empirically robust. Furthermore, risk analysis is a value-laden endeavour: a cost-benefit space is not a principled space, other values must be brought into play.

As we have already noted, our in-houser red lines regarding risk do not give a great deal of confidence that in-house teams are generally inclined to challenge cost-benefit analysis approaches. And a more organised system of risk management is not necessarily a good system of risk management. That our most organised risk managers were found in financial services, with PPI and wire-stripping scandals clearly having a legal dimension, is a telling reminder that it is the nature and quality of judgements made during risk management that is as or more important than (perhaps) necessary but not sufficient systems.

PROFESSIONAL INFLUENCES

If we contrast external influences with professional influences, we sense the weakness of the latter. We see little, if any, evidence of professional rules and institutions having a strong influence on the ecology of in-house lawyers.

---

[81] Julia Evetts, 'A New Professionalism? Challenges and Opportunities' (2011) 59 *Current Sociology* 406.

In particular, the client-first orientation of our in-housers, shared with lawyers generally we believe,[82] is in tension with the profession's rules which see the rule of law as the first amongst equals of professional principles. Our in-house lawyers did not always show a basic awareness of their professional Codes of Conduct. Judged against the Solicitors Regulation Authority's (SRA) 'Competence Statement', we would have concerns about the abilities of in-housers in 'recognising ethical issues and exercising effective judgment in addressing them', and 'understanding and applying the ethical concepts which govern their role and behaviour as a lawyer.'[83] For those clearly willing to put commerce ahead of legality, there is the apparent reluctance to 'resist pressure to condone, ignore or commit unethical behavior.'[84]

In some ways, uncertainty about professional principles is reflective of the way in-house lawyers are treated in the Code. There, in-house lawyers are dealt with by way of specific riders at the end of each chapter, suggesting that regulation of in-house lawyers by the SRA was a bolt-on, or afterthought, to its 'core' regulation of private practice solicitors and law firms. Certainly, this is how it was perceived by our in-houser interviewees. Most considered that the SRA Handbook was 'historically a private practice driven document and therefore of little relevance' [IHL35] and/or were willing to admit to 'frankly being completely bemused by the regulatory framework' [IHL36].

A further way in which the SRA regulates legal services businesses is through entity (or 'firm-based') regulation. In particular, this requires the appointment of a senior individual inside law firms known as a COLP, a Compliance Officer for Legal Practice. The COLP has a key role in ensuring that suitable systems and controls are in place in recording breaches of professional rules, and in reporting material breaches to the SRA. Entity regulation is applicable only to law firms, Alternative Business Structures (including non-lawyer-owned multi-disciplinary practices) and those working inside the law firms. Whilst very large volumes of lawyers work in-house, neither their host organisations nor the in-house legal teams are regulated as entities by the SRA. Even where a business might employ more than 1,000 in-housers, each solicitor in that team is regulated as an individual and there is no entity-based regulation, by the SRA, of that in-house team. What this means is that that in-house legal teams are not required to have the same systems and processes in place as a law firm or ABSs for managing professional compliance and reporting breaches: in particular, they will not have a mandated COLP.

The lack of any entity-based regulation may have contributed to the disconnect between in-house solicitors and their regulator. The SRA would likely defend the approach by suggesting that, in the main, in-house lawyers are

---

[82] Moorhead and Hinchly (n 13); Vaughan and Oakley (n 13).
[83] SRA, 'Competence Statement' (Solicitors Regulation Authority, March 2015), rr A1(a) and A1(b).
[84] ibid r A1(d).

managed by their organisations, and that those organisations are better placed than distant regulators to ensure, for example, competence. Yet this misses the central problem: ethical challenges pose risks that organisations are poorly placed to deal with, where the organisations themselves are the source of that ethical risk. The SRA would also say that they regulate legal service businesses rather than other organisations, and so entity regulation for the diverse range of organisations that in-housers work in would not be inappropriate. That would not, however, prevent the SRA putting obligations on those leading teams of practising in-house solicitors in such organisations and, in any event, it is worth remembering that entity-level controls emerged on Alternative Business Structures partly because ABSs were likely to be more diverse, and sometimes multi-disciplinary, and so might require entity-level protections. It might also now be claimed that the benefits of entity-level regulation are in doubt,[85] although it is probably most accurate to say the distinctively different approach to in-house practice as represented in the current Code is as much historical accident as it is a clearly thought-through policy position.

A revised SRA Code promises a slightly different approach. In June 2016, the SRA, in a root-and-branch review of its Handbook,[86] indicated a desire to 'provide greater clarity around the individual responsibilities of in-house solicitors and the standards they must uphold.'[87] One of the ways in which this is likely to manifest is in the publication by the SRA of a 'compliance toolkit targeted particularly at in-house solicitors to support the proposed new code'.[88] The regulator has also proposed that there will, in future, be one code of conduct which applies to all solicitors (wherever they work and whatever they do: in-house or in private practice) and another which applies to the entities (eg law firms and Alternative Business Structures) that the SRA regulates. This, they claim, will 'put them [in-house lawyers] on an equal footing with other solicitors, bound by the same core standards.' The equal footing does not, however, require the regulation of in-house legal teams as entities or the appointment of Compliance Officers for Legal Practice.

A reminder of the need for regulation might be seen in banks holding out their own in-house legal departments as solicitors firms by using 'fake' letterheads designed to give debtors the impression they emanated from actual law firms.[89] If it looks like a law firm, and pretends it is a law firm, then should it be regulated as a law firm? But the arguments run deeper and more seriously than

---

[85] Sundeep Aulakh and Joan Loughrey, 'Regulating Law Firms from the Inside: The Role of Compliance Officers for Legal Practice in England and Wales' [2017] *Journal of Law and Society* 1.

[86] SRA, 'Handbook' (Version 19, Solicitors Regulation Authority 2018), https://www.sra.org.uk/solicitors/handbook/intro/content.page, last accessed 25 April 2018.

[87] SRA, 'Looking to the future – flexibility and public protection' (Solicitors Regulation Authority June 2016 Consultation Paper) 14.

[88] ibid para 54.

[89] Rupert Jones and Patrick Collinson, 'Revealed: the banks using "pseudo" solicitor firms to make debtors pay up' (*The Guardian*, 4 July 2014).

that. If we had to summarise the influence of the SRA on our interviewees, we would be hard-pushed to better disdain and indifference. SRA regulation does not matter in the same way as bribery law or FCA regulation does. Practitioner ecology is not much influenced by the SRA, or (the representative and lobbying body) the Law Society, or any similar practitioner group. Simply changing the Code of Conduct to appear more user-friendly is not likely to make much of a difference. A stronger interest in investigating potential in-house misconduct may however. The prosecutions of in-house lawyers Alistair Brett (convicted), for his work at The Times, and Jonathan Chapman at the News of the World (acquitted), may signal a more robust approach than hitherto. If we look at in-house conduct in terms of risk, the decision not to impose some form of entity regulation on legal teams does not make much sense either. Weigh the harms caused by SCB's wire-stripping, or Rolls-Royce's corruption, against the more standard fare of SRA enforcement (solicitors taking client money, misleading the court), and we are hard-pushed to see that in-house practice is low risk. Perhaps in-house behaviour is harder to police, or the SRA is simply less familiar with, and confident in dealing with it, something that was seen previously in relation to City law firms (and which 'relationship management' was used to tackle after the Smedley Review).[90]

SOME FINAL THOUGHTS

Our analysis repeatedly shows the tension between organisational and professional logics and the tendency of in-housers to prioritise the former over the latter. That is of a piece with most, but not all, work in this area. Importantly though, we identify what drives variation in ethical inclination. The collective effect of our survey and qualitative work suggests quite strongly the weaknesses of an approach to in-house lawyering which emphasises the non-accountability of the lawyer and which promotes the exploitation of uncertainty for an organisation's ends. Promoting independence and ethical orientations increases ethical inclination. As do conceptualisations of the professional role which strengthen the ideas of 'independence and legality' and 'integrity and effectiveness'. We should be clear that we are not saying that in-house lawyers are not advisors, and that others in the organisation often, legitimately, end up taking decisions. But in-house lawyers are not *mere* advisors; they have leadership roles and, if senior, constitute an important part of the client. As such, in-housers are both advisor and part of the client: dependent and constituent; servant and agent. Nor are we saying that uncertainty in the law should be cause for excessive timidity or risk aversion. There is a balance to be struck between the client's desires and

---

[90] Nick Smedley, 'Review of the Regulation of Corporate Legal Work' (Smedley Report, 31 March 2009), http://www.cigroup.org.uk/images/file/report_smedley_final_310309.pdf, accessed 28 April 2018.

an independent interpretation of the law. It is worth in-house lawyers reminding themselves every time they think that their professional obligations require them to put the client's interests first that this is not what their professional obligations in fact require. It is also worth them remembering that, psychologically, they are already likely to be interpreting the law through a lens of client loyalty.[91] Even if we put ethical issues to one side, in-house lawyers inputting high-quality assessments of legal risk need to work to protect the independence of their view from conscious and subconscious influence.[92] We do not identify a perfect end state, but our evidence points quite forcefully towards the benefits of a better balancing of these professional and role orientations which supports a stronger role for independence, legality, and integrity.

In this chapter we have also spent some time discussing the likely importance of task instantiation. Different tasks may demand, properly, different balances of orientation depending on what the law demands or what organisations can reasonably ask of their in-housers. Lawyers are dexterous in recharacterising facts and the legal tests that they apply for their organisations. Evaluating that dexterity requires getting down into the weeds of specific cases. The importance of attitudes to uncertainty often places this dexterity front and centre in any analysis of ethical conduct by lawyers. Regulators have started to make organisations, and individual gate-keepers, deal with this, by making those organisations and individuals more responsible for the risks they manage or create. Further research could, we think, draw out with greater certainty relations between orientations, tasks, and their instantiation: discovering how different ways of framing and managing tasks influence orientations could provide fruitful and practical insights into decision-making and practice. This is complicated, difficult work, but something which we think could advance our understanding of the interaction of professional and organisational logics.

In spite of our criticisms, our study also uncovers some in-house lawyers willing to identify and challenge occupational-professional conflict (what we call ethical pressure). That is not wholly consistent with the 'adaptation' theory that professions adapt to, rather than resist, institutional pressure.[93] Neither dominance nor adaptation is quite right: there is a kind of contingent professionalism at work here, as part of the tournament for influence. Independence is weaker or stronger. Resistance is context-specific; there is a general disinclination to take too robustly independent a line; but specific problems or alignments of ecological factors also nevertheless strengthen independence. As such, professionalism, in the public-spirited sense that Tawney et al meant for it,[94] remains an occupational value.[95] It is thus not completely true that 'professionalism

---

[91] Andrew M Perlman, 'A Behavioral Theory of Legal Ethics' (2015) 90 *Indiana Law Journal* 1639.
[92] See, for example, ibid and the work referred to therein on loyalty bias.
[93] Jean E Wallace, 'Organizational and Professional Commitment in Professional and Nonprofessional Organizations' (1995) 40 *Administrative Science Quarterly* 228.
[94] Tawney (n 8).
[95] Evetts (n 82).

is no longer a distinctive "third" logic since the exercise of professionalism is now organisationally defined and includes the logics of the organisation and the market: managerialism and commercialism.'[96] Also, professionalism is, even amongst those who scored more strongly on our independence and ethical orientations, a hybrid that balances organisational and professional logics. The ecology of in-house lawyers is permeated by non-legal ideas: value; influence; service; cost-benefit. Ideas about the public interest and legality are less strong, but they are present. The organisations themselves can recognise, affirm and develop their importance. In-house legal teams can be encouraged to interpret laws by the letter and in their spirit. The narrow framing of legal tasks can be discouraged. Proactivity can be resourced. There may be institutional protections to be stimulated through relationships with non-executive directors and careful management of incentives via appraisal processes and encouragement to discuss and sometimes escalate ethical issues. Similarly, in-house legal teams can seek to strengthen professional logics themselves: by taking tasks on the basis that they will look at them with a professional rather than instrumental mind-set; by defining and supporting a professional approach to work which attends to independence; through ethical leadership; and by their attitude to uncertainty. In-housers can strengthen debates about independence, what their role really entails, and how to be professional. We hope that some of the discussion in this book helps with that. We have been critical, but we remain optimistic.

[96] ibid 407.

Appendix A

Interview Schedules

As set out in Chapter 2, the interviews took place in two phases. The first set of interviews primarily covered matters to do with risk, and the second set of interviews were broader and concerned with ethics, in-houser role, identity, workplace relationships etc.

1. INTERVIEW SCHEDULE 1 – INTERVIEW QUESTIONNAIRE: IN-HOUSE COUNSEL LEGAL RISK STUDY

Introduction

1. Can you confirm your job title?
2. In outline, how would you describe your role?
3. What professional qualification(s) do you have?
4. How many years PQE [post qualification experience]? How long in-house? With this company?

Defining Legal Risk

1. What does legal risk mean to you and your colleagues?
2. Do you think other parts of the corporation have different understandings of what legal risk means?

Structural Issue on Reporting and Deciding

1. Who does legal report to on matters of legal risk?
2. Does the GC or equivalent sit on the board, the executive committee, audit committee, for example?
3. Does the GC/Head of legal risk have access to the CEO, exec board, senior non-execs for example?

4. Who is the final decision marker in relation to legal risk? Does it vary depending on risk types?
5. Does audit have any role relating to legal risk?
6. How do you assess legal risks?
7. Could you walk me through the processes?
8. Could you provide an example?
9. Do you use any kind of decision tools to assist in the evaluation of legal risk?
10. Is there a hierarchy of risk that makes some risks more important than others? For example, how does criminal liability compare to civil?
11. Do you consider the likelihood of breach, detection and sanction separately or together? Do you quantify them?
12. Is both quantitative and qualitative data used? How?
13. What information is used to evaluate legal risk? [Probe to see if they rely on information from colleagues or legal gathers its own info]
14. How do you make sure the information is reliable and representative of the situation?

Risk Appetite and Declining Risk

1. How would you describe your own risk appetite?
2. Does the company have a defined appetite for legal risk?
3. Do you consider there to be different risk appetites in the company?
4. What are your red-line issues?
5. How do you convey these red lines? (Get them taken seriously)
6. What legal risks have you said 'no' to?
7. Can you provide examples of legal risks you said should not be tolerated?
8. Have you ever resigned or raised the issue of resignation over a legal risk?

Managing Legal Risk

1. As well as assessing legal risk, do you manage risk?
2. What methods are used to reduce legal risk?
3. [Probe to understand whether they see risk as case by case or they take a broader more thematic view]
4. What are the elements of good case-by-case or thematic decision-making?
5. How are thematic issues, eg bribery or corruption dealt with?

6. What role does cost have in assessments?
7. Do you think legal risk management reduces or increases a tolerance for legal risk for the company or for others?
8. How is legal risk communicated?
9. Does it differ up or down the corporation?
10. Legal risk can involve quite nuanced judgments – does that present communication difficulties?
11. How are redlines communicated?
12. What skills and techniques are employed to get legal risk taken seriously?
13. Are legal risk strategies and decisions evaluated?
14. How? Using what information? Who is involved?
15. Are there general periodic reviews of strategy or individual decisions?
16. When a predicted (or unpredicted) risk manifests is any systematic review of the risk process conducted?

Relationship with Compliance

1. What is the relationship between legal risk, legal compliance and ethics functions within the corporation?
2. Do they influence or have a role in legal risk decisions or management of legal risk?

Ethics

1. Who is responsible for ethics within the corporation?
2. Does legal risk raise ethical issues for the corporation? When?
3. Does legal risk raise professional ethical issues for you? When?
4. Has being a member of a professional body helped or hindered you in the performance of your role?
5. In obtaining an ethical outcome?

Outcomes

1. What are the measures of success for legal risk or how does the company determine whether its approach to legal risk is a success?
2. Can you give an example of legal risk assessment gone wrong?

Appendix A

Vignettes

Please imagine that you are the person in these hypothetical companies, who has to respond to the issues raised as presented to you.

Study 1

You are the senior in-house lawyer for a multinational company. John, your colleague and friend, comes into your office and asks for advice about how he can best position himself having done the following.

Under export regulations in place at the time, shipping goods into Libya required a licence, which delayed transactions by two months. A good client had expressed a need for the goods urgently and said if the delivery could not be arranged immediately they would take their business elsewhere. You know that John's team was under significant pressure to increase sales. John's solution was to have the goods shipped to Tunisia for the client to collect them from there.

This happened several times over three months. Subsequently the export regulations have changed and the goods may now be shipped without delay (although the client no longer places orders for such goods).

How would you respond?

During the course of your discussion, John mentions that the product has a dual-use – in that they can be altered to help build explosive devices.

Study 2

You are the senior in-house lawyer for a multinational company. The head of the financial service division includes in this month's briefing details of a new financial product. That product would make the company a significant amount of money if it was first on the market with it.

This product involves your company offering investment opportunities in Country X to individuals and companies that are not resident in Country X for tax purposes. Part of the profits from the product derives from preferential tax treatment on non-resident investments in Country X. Country X requires a legal opinion that your processes ensure those who invest in the product are non-residents in that country.

Compliance have reassured you that the process for establishing and checking investor status is adequate. You have some doubts as to whether your company has previously classified some significant investors with the correct residency status.

What would you do?

If it still proves that it is uncertain, do you provide the opinion to assert that it is compliant?

Your chief executive instructs you to seek an outside opinion on the product and your processes. You know that if a legal firm was presented with the product and asked for their opinion, they would assert that it was compliant if you did not refer to the concern you have about your company's procedures.

Would you seek such an opinion?

Whilst the transactions comply with the letter of the law, and sales teams will be required under the process to give appropriate advice on the potential for tax treatment to change, you have a strong belief that sales pressure and practice mean that this will de facto be ignored. Does this change your approach?

Study 3

You are the senior in-house lawyer for a multinational company which manufactures specialist engineering components. Your company wants to begin trading for the first time in Country Y. It will needs hundreds of suppliers/contractors in a particular developing country that has a thin governance structure and little by way of business regulation. What are the priority legal risk issues and how would you respond to them?

How do ethical issues such as environmental pollution and working conditions affect your decisions?

It becomes clear that this country only allows 'authorised sellers' to sell goods to anyone within the country. Authorised sellers are defined by statute and includes conditions regarding the ethnic origin/nationality of all those involved in the company structure.

After trading for some months, you become aware that one of your dealers has sold goods to an unauthorised seller who then sold the goods on. How do you respond?

You subsequently discover the sales were at an excessive mark up. What do you do? Do you inform the regulator of the country?

Concluding Remarks

1. Do you have anything you would like to add?

2. INTERVIEW SCHEDULE 2 – ETHICAL LEADERSHIP FOR IN-HOUSE LAWYERS INITIATIVE: INTERVIEW QUESTIONNAIRE

Background

1. Can you run me through your career history and your current role?
    a. [Size of the in-house team, change in size and composition over time, and current spread of expertise/seniority/qualification type across that team]

2. What prompted your move into in-house practice?
3. Has working in-house been different to what you thought it would be like when you were in private practice?
4. Do you think that the role of lawyers has changed since you entered the profession? If so, how? Why do you think that might be? Has the nature of 'legal work' changed over time?
5. (How) do you see your work/the role of the in-house lawyer changing in the future? Why?

What Do IHLs Do?

1. How would you describe what you do?
   a. [tease out whether there's a wide variety or much the same]
   b. Do you see yourself as a professional? If so, what does that word mean to you? Is it important to you?
2. More generally, how would you frame the role of the in-house lawyer?
   a. How different is the work of an in-house lawyer compared to a lawyer in private practice?
3. How has your work and your role changed over the course of your time in-house?
   a. [If worked for different employers, ask re: different types of work in different fields]
4. Why do you think in-house teams are growing in frequency and in size?
5. In your business, what is the difference between the legal team and the compliance team?
   a. Do you see legal and compliance as separate? Do they serve different purposes?
6. How would you describe your relationship with the business? How do you think the legal team is perceived?
7. How would you describe the level of influence that the legal team has with the business?
8. Are you or another lawyer in the business on the board? What do you think are the pros and cons of a lawyer being on the board?
   a. How close are you to the business? To what extent is that closeness important for your role?
9. Do you see yourself as a legal adviser, as a business adviser or both?
   a. What is the difference between providing legal advice and commercial advice?

10. What sort of pressures do you face in your work?
    a. [where do they come from?; how do you respond to them?; different types of pressure?]
11. What principles underpin the work that you do?
12. How independent are you from the business? Do you think such independence is important?

Lawyer–Client Relationships

1. What sort of legal spend do you have? How do you appoint external legal advisers?
2. What are you looking for from the firms you engage?
    a. [= expertise? = capacity? = form of insurance? = sounding board?]
    b. Do you ever go to external counsel for advice on ethical issues as opposed to legal issues?
3. What, for you, are the most important elements of a good lawyer-client relationship?
4. Do you have different relationships with different sorts of law firms?
5. Who in the IHL team and in the organisation speaks with the external lawyers? To what extent do you filter contact with those lawyers?
6. What are your bugbears about the law firms you use? How could those lawyers do better for you?

Consequences

1. To what extent do you reflect on the consequences of decisions that the business takes?
2. Is it part of your job to act as a check on business decision-making?
    a. If not, should it be?
3. Can you think of situations in which you have challenged the business on its decisions? How often do you find yourself saying 'No' to something the business wants to do?
    a. Have you ever experienced negative consequences where the business didn't follow you're your advice, or negative consequences where they did? If so, how did you feel about this?
4. Do you see yourself a decision-maker for the business?
    a. [or is it your job simply to advise?]

5. Imagine you were faced with a piece of law whose meaning was uncertain. How do you see your role as regards the interpretation of that law for the business?
6. Do you think in-house lawyers should ever be held accountable for the consequences of decisions made by the business?
    a. Could you provide any examples?

Ethics

1. How would you describe an 'ethical lawyer'?
2. What ethical challenges do you think are faced by in-house lawyers?
3. To what extent do you reflect on the ethics of your work?
    a. And more widely on the ethics of the business?
4. Do you talk about ethical issues with the rest of the legal team? Do you undertake ethics training?
5. How much of your job is providing the business with ethical advice compared with legal advice? Do you think the two overlap?
    a. Do you feel that you are obliged to engage in moral dialogue with the C-suite/the business?
6. If you had serious concerns about the ethics of a proposed action by the business, what response would you take?

Regulation

1. Do you think the business understands that you have professional obligations as a solicitor/barrister?
2. When was the last time you looked something up in the SRA/BSB Handbook?
3. To what extent do you feel that regulation by the SRA/BSB impacts on your work?
4. Do you feel the SRA/BSB understands the worlds of in-house lawyers?
    a. Have you ever contacted the SRA/BSB for advice? If so, how would you rate the quality of that advice?
    b. Would you value more targeted guidance by the SRA/BSB?

Index

Abbott, Andrew 7
acceptance
   trading helpfulness for 69
accounting
   compliance 52
administration of justice
   objective assessment of requirements 216
   obligation to uphold 6, 39–40, 124, 128, 144, 177, 216
administrative burden
   generally 48
agent, in-house lawyer as 8, 23, 46, 113, 122, 126, 202, 208, 228
   risk management 23, 113, 122
Akzo Nobel Chemicals and Akcros Chemicals v Commission 72
Alien Tort Claims Act 19
ambiguity
   see also uncertainty
   moral 157–160
antitrust
   monitoring breaches 52
   risk management 52
Apple 4
appropriate behaviour between colleagues
   codes of conduct 140
Arthur Andersen 4
audit
   risk management 115
audit committee
   legal expertise 52
   reporting to 57

Barclays 4
Basel Committee on Banking Supervision 108
Beck, Ulrich 16, 96
best interests of client
   lawyers' obligation 12–14, 40, 124, 126, 136, 147, 176, 177–180, 199, 210–211, 221, 226
bias 92, 133–134, 147–148
   complacency leading to 142, 146, 183
   team loyalty 148

board
   in-house lawyer's attendance 58, 176
   in-house lawyers' membership 54–55, 58–60, 71, 176, 224–225
   non-executive directors 57–58
   reporting to 54–57
Bourdieu, Pierre 207
Brett, Alistair 228
bribery
   ethical conduct 125, 186
   legislation against 51
   register of spending 119
   risk management 122
   Rolls-Royce scandal 127, 146
bullying behaviour 86–87
bureaucratic-professional
   blended professionalism 46–47, 174
business strategy
   in-houser lawyer's role 3, 51
business-professional
   blended professionalism 46–47, 174

Cain, Maureen 152–153
case studies
   dealing with breaches 137–138
   export licensing problems 137–138
   questionable financial product 135–137, 143–144
   risk management 122–123
challenger
   in-house lawyer as 83–86
Chamblis, Elizabeth and Remus, Dana 64
change in law risk 106
Chapman, Jonathan 228
chief financial officer 56–57
chief operating officer 56–57
child labour
   supplier using 112–113, 123
civil law, breaches 129–130
claims risk 106
codes of conduct 13, 124, 128, 144–145, 176–182, 199, 226, 227–228
Coffee, John 55

240 Index

commercialism
  blended professionalism 50, 125
  creative compliance and 157–160, 203
  ethical orientation and 163
  generally 148, 151, 153, 154–156
  increasing unethical conduct 155
  independence and 156
  moral attentiveness and 192
  orientation towards 11, 21, 29, 36–38, 148, 151, 153, 154–156, 167–170, 173, 199, 209–210, 212
  perceived legal/commercial split 155
  prioritising client's wishes 156, 176
  public interest/commerce paradigm 6–7, 8–9, 70, 125, 176, 204
  risk management 216–218
competitive corporate culture 134
complacency 142, 146, 183, 187, 218
compliance
  accounting 52
  checklists 120
  commercial outlook and 155
  creative 10, 18, 36, 38, 64, 71, 131, 145, 157–160, 173, 203, 218
  effect of employing in-housers 52
  ethics and risk 127
  in-house lawyer's role 49, 51, 71
  incentives contributing to failures 54, 133–134
  insider training 53
  risk management 115, 120, 121
Compliance Officer 226–227
compromise
  compromised independence 10, 22, 39, 56, 59, 60, 69, 72, 76, 89–90, 91, 177, 213, 214
  cost benefit calculation 87–88
  ethically compromised role 3–4
  generally 95, 174, 211
  power relations and 203
  professionalism compromised 89–90, 91, 147, 203
  registering position on file 89, 89n
  risk-assessment and 20, 95, 110
  willingness to consider resignation 85–86, 214
conflict of interests
  board membership 54–55, 56, 58–60, 224–225
  ethical pressure 29, 64–67, 69, 229
  ethics and risk 127
  generally 145, 146, 174, 201–202

  in-house lawyer as part of client 126, 228
  organisational-professional conflict 8–9, 64–65, 85
  perceived legal/commercial split 155
  perceptions of conflict 65
  performance-related incentives 73–74
  professional codes of conduct 124–125, 128
  register of spending 119
  social trusteeship 22, 202
  training 186
consumer protection legislation
  effect 51, 224
contract
  backdating to meet financial target 71
  monitoring breaches 52
  negotiating 51
  risk management 52, 107–108, 119
  templates and checklists 119
corporate culture 134, 217–218, 225
corporate debt 53
corporate governance 51
corporate hierarchy
  independence and 72
  influence within 123, 211–213, 216–217
  role in 213
corporate responsibility 51
corruption
  ethical conduct 125
  register of spending 119
  risk management 122, 123
cost benefit calculation
  compromise 87–88
  reporting up and/or out 139
  risk management 87–88, 117, 121, 130, 218, 225
criminal and civil law 129–130
Crown Prosecution Service
  in-house lawyers 47

data protection
  legislation generally 51
decision-making
  escalating 84, 119
  in-house lawyers generally 155–156, 161
  risk appetite 102–103, 127, 145
  risk management 99, 102
  training 186
defective documentation risk 106
director
  see also board
  audit committee 52

conflicts of interest   54–55, 56, 58
  in-house lawyer as   54–55, 58–60, 71
  non-executive   57–58
  personal liability   51, 224
  primary obligation   60
  reporting directly to   54–56
disclosure
  controlled messaging   118
  in-house lawyers' role   204
  monitoring breaches   52
  risk management   52, 118, 127
  share price reactions to   53

earnings management   98
economic dependence   72–74, 91
  see also independence
effectiveness
  professional obligation   39–40, 177–179, 210–211
  emphasis on   74
employer-employee relationship
  bullying behaviour   86–87
  distrust of lawyer's role   61
  employers' understanding of professional obligations   74–76, 183–184
  ethical pressure   1, 29, 64–67, 69, 229
  generally   7–8, 23, 60–61
  identification with employer   148
  lawyers perceived as obstructive   62–63, 78–79, 81, 89, 101, 213
  negative   61
  professional obligations   176–183
  understanding of independence   62, 74–76
  uneven   62–63, 68, 213
employment criteria   75
Energy Solutions   4
enforcement proofing   98
Enron collapse   4
enterprise risk management   97
entrepreneurialism
  in-house lawyers' role   10–11, 27, 28, 41, 46, 65, 208, 209
  orientation towards   148–149, 151–153, 157, 160, 173–174, 199, 209–210
  problems arising from   28, 44–45
  risk management and   124, 128, 199
environmental issues
  ethical conduct   125
  generally   235
  risk management   130
  supplier causing pollution   112–113

equity incentives
  securities fraud and   53–54
escalating decision-making   84, 119
ethical inclination
  cluster analysis   40, 194–198
  environmental influences   210
  generally   1, 27, 29, 213
  increasing trend towards   224
  moral attentiveness   189, 190, 192–193, 194, 199
  moral disengagement and   189, 190–192, 193, 199
  organisation culture   221
  professional orientation and   199, 210
  team culture influencing   29, 210
ethical infrastructure   1, 29, 33, 176, 199, 221
  employers' understanding of professional obligations   74–76, 183–184
  professional   184–188
  recruitment interviews   187
  training   185–186, 210
ethical minimalism   164–165
ethical orientation   11, 13, 37–38, 163–165, 167–170, 172, 209–210
  moral attentiveness and   192–193, 199
ethical pressure   1, 29, 33, 64–67, 69, 229
  team size and   67
ethicality
  business case for   142–143
  compromised   3–4
  as construct   2
  defining organisational positions   140
  ethical leadership   128–129, 140, 146, 211, 221
  ethically debatable actions   213
  impact using in-housers   52–53
  in-housers' role   11–15, 49
  lawyers' ethics   11–15
  legal ambiguities   127, 128–129, 130, 133, 140, 145, 211, 218
  legal but unethical actions   139–143
  legal risk management and   124–127
  moral ambiguity   157–160
  recognition within organisations   140
  red lines   128–132, 140, 145, 218
  willingness to say no   9–10, 22–23, 72, 76–86, 92–93, 174–175, 214–216
explanatory legitimacy   81
exploiting uncertainties orientation   21, 38, 157–160, 167–179, 199, 209–210
  moral attentiveness and   192
export licensing problems   137–138

facilitator
  in-house lawyer as   83
fair dealing   140
Financial Conduct Authority   224
financial management   124
financial sector
  ethical conduct   125
  in-house lawyers working in   47
  questionable products   135–137, 143–144
  risk management   98
financial targets
  backdating contracts to meet   71
fine
  risking livelihood of firm   131
Foreign Corrupt Practices Act (FCPA)   19, 51, 223
forum shopping for legal advice   84–85

gatekeeping
  definition   70
  General Counsels   53
  incentives to   204
  insider trading   53
  lawyers as reputational intermediaries   70
  lawyers in senior management positions   53
  neutral adviser orientation   162
  professional independence and   71
  role generally   9–10, 65, 78, 125, 151, 174, 201, 204, 222
  willingness to say no   9–10, 78–86, 92–93, 174–175, 214–216
General Counsel (GC)
  gatekeeping role   53, 125, 204
  generally   3
  independence   76
  power   87
  SEC compliance   53
General Motors ignition-switch scandal   3–4, 63, 130–131, 137
Generally Accepted Accounting Principles
  General Counsel in management role   54
Gidden, Anthony   207
Goh, Beng Wee, et al   54, 205
Goldsmith, Lord   4
Gordon, Robert W   90, 220, 224
  governance-based role increasing   51
Government Legal Department
  distrust of lawyer's role   61
  in-house lawyers   3, 47
Grady, Ken   212

greyball technology   219–220
groupthink problems   133
Gunz, Hugh P and Gunz, Sally P   9, 11, 64, 65, 153–154, 163

Hackett, Susan   60
Hamermesh, Lawrence A   57
health and safety risk management   122, 130–131
Heineman, Ben W   1, 22, 54, 57, 87
holding out in-house team as independent   227–228
Hopkins, Justin J, et al   53
HSBC in-house legal team   47
hybrid-professional
  business and professional factors   46–47, 174
  compromise generally   3–4, 95
  generally   22, 201–202, 204, 217, 230
  risk-taking/management   22, 46–47, 70, 217

identity and orientation
  commercialism   11, 21, 29, 36–38, 148, 151, 153, 154–156, 167–170, 173, 199, 209–210, 212
  counselling role   28, 152–153, 160–162, 208, 209–210
  distinct from rest of legal profession   148, 149–151
  entrepreneurialism   10–11, 28, 41, 148–149, 151–153, 157, 160, 173–174, 199, 208, 209–210
  environmental influences   210
  ethical inclination   199, 210, 213
  ethical orientation   11, 13, 37–38, 163–165, 167–170, 172, 179–180, 209–210
  exploiting uncertainties   11, 14, 21, 36–38, 157–160, 167–179, 199, 209–210
  generally   1, 11, 33, 36–38, 147–149, 155–156, 167–170, 208–211
  identification with employer   148
  independence   11, 36–38, 148, 165–170, 209–210, 214–216
  influencer role   161
  legality orientation   37
  managerial   149, 150
  moral attentiveness and   192–193, 199
  moral disengagement and   193, 199
  neutral adviser   11, 37–38, 160–162, 165, 167–170, 209–210
  performance and productivity   171
  Principal Component Analysis   171

professional   1, 29, 33, 38–40, 176–183,
      199, 210–211
professional title   151
public-sector lawyers   150–151, 171
relative ranking   173
risk management   37
role conception   151–157
societal   171, 172
team orientation   33, 170–172, 199, 210
third-sector lawyers   150
tournament of influence and   172–175
troubled subservience   36–38
in-house lawyer
  administrative burden   48
  advantages of employment as   48–49, 51
  advantages to employers   47–48, 52, 83
  changing nature of job   50
  diversity of work   49–50, 52, 68, 211
  embeddedness   5, 15, 155–156, 211, 221
  evolution of in-house role   50–52, 211, 217
  financial rewards   20, 48–49
  financial services   47, 125
  growth of sector   3, 47–50, 149
  identity *see* identity and orientation
  influence *see* network of influence
  influences on   19–20, 218–228
  as insurance policy for dubious
    decisions   77–78
  legal leadership   125
  lines of reporting   54–57
  as moral compass   125
  number in England and Wales   47
  as part of client   126, 228
  perception of   62–63, 78–79, 81, 89, 101,
    203–204, 213
  place in legal profession   3, 47, 148,
    208, 211
  priorities   156
  professional codes of conduct   124–125,
    128, 227–228
  professional legitimacy   222
  reactive or proactive   123
  reasons for choosing employment as
    48–50
  role generally   3–5
  status *see* status of in-house lawyers
  supportive nature of role   76–77
incentives
  compliance failure and   54, 133–134
  equity incentives and securities fraud
    53–54
  incentivising gatekeeping   205

  performance-related   73–74
  tied towards risk-taking   20
indemnities
  risk management and   119
independence
  absence of independent professionals   55
  best interests of client and   124, 126, 136,
    147, 176
  blind spots   92, 133–134, 147–148
  board membership   59–60, 224–225
  collective   71
  commercial orientation and   156
  compromising   10, 22, 39, 56, 59, 60, 69,
    72, 76, 89–90, 91, 147, 177, 213, 214
  conflicts of interest   54–55, 56, 147
  corporate hierarchy and   72
  direct access to board   55, 56
  economic dependence   72–74
  employer supporting   62
  employers' understanding of   72, 74–76
  gatekeeping role and   71–72
  generally   1, 39–40, 48, 69, 71–72, 89–94,
    124, 147–148, 208, 229
  increasing trend towards   224
  individual   71–72
  moral attentiveness and   192
  network of influence and   71–76, 89–94,
    145, 214–216
  objectivity and   69, 72, 88, 92, 94, 144–145,
    214–216
  obligation of   124, 217–218
  orientation towards   11, 36–38, 165–170,
    209–210, 214–216
  passive lawyering   76
  performance-related incentives   73–74
  professional   7, 39–40, 71–72, 92, 140–142,
    146, 176–179, 199, 210–211,
    214–216
  public sector lawyers   179
  as regulatory objective   89–90, 92
  risk appetite and   100–101
  risk management and   124, 127, 147
  social trusteeship   202
  supportive nature of in-houser's role
    76–77
  trading helpfulness for acceptance   69
  willingness to say no   9–10, 72, 76–86,
    92–93, 147, 174–175, 214–216
influence *see* **network of influence**
insider trading
  gatekeeping   53
  generally   204

insider trading
  compliance 52
institutional logics 2, 19, 20–23, 206–211, 221
insurance
  risk mitigation 118–119
integrity
  professional obligation 12–13, 39–40, 177–178, 210–211
Iraq War 4

Jagolinzer, Alan D, et al 53, 204
Jenoff, Pam 9, 60

Kim, Sung Hui 9, 79–80
Kirkland, Kimberly 2

Langevoort, Donald C 132, 133–134, 145
leadership
  ethical 128–129, 140, 146, 211, 221
  in-house lawyers' role 3, 228
  legal 125
  organisation culture 221
  professional status and 146
legal advice
  action taken against 62, 213
  commercialism and 216–218
  perceived legal/commercial split 155
legal function
  misuse 143–144
legal profession
  see also regulation of legal profession
  in-house lawyers' status 47
legal risk management 1, 15–20, 102–103, 104–111
Legal Services Act 2007 89
Legal Services Board 89
legality
  contingent nature 104
  legally debatable actions 213
  orientation towards 38
  professional obligation as to 39–40, 176–180, 210–211
  uncertain 23, 29, 38, 127, 128–129, 130, 133, 140, 145, 157–160, 211, 218, 219–220, 222, 228–229
  willingness to say no 9–10, 22–23, 72, 76–86, 92–93, 214–216
Leveson Inquiry 137
line manager relationships 54–58
litigation
  risk management 105–106

local authority
  in-house lawyers 47
loophole exploitation 10, 23, 36, 38, 157–160, 173
Loughrey, Joan 138, 222, 227

McCormick, Roger 98, 106
management role
  business forecasts 52
  impact of appointing lawyers to 52–53
  in-house lawyers having 15–16, 46, 51–52, 71
  independence and 76
  lines of reporting 54–57
  monitoring breaches 52
  securities fraud and 53
  self-identification with 149, 150
  tax avoidance associated with 54
  work delegation 51
Mastenbroek, Ellen and Peeters Weem, Tanja 9
misconduct
  examples 4
  reporting 71
money-laundering 122
monitoring
  reputational 120
  risk management 52, 120
Moore, Celia, et al 190, 191, 192
Moorhead, Richard and Hinchly, Victoria 64, 126, 164–165
moral ambiguity 157–160
moral attentiveness
  generally 189, 190, 194–198, 199
  inclination to ethicality 192, 194
  orientations and 192–193
  perpetual 192, 193, 195
  reflective 193, 194, 195
moral compass
  generally 27, 176
  lawyers' role as 125
  measuring 188–192
  public interest/commerce paradigm 6–7, 70, 125, 176
moral disengagement
  generally 189, 190–192, 195, 199
  inclination to ethicality 190, 192, 199
  orientations and 193, 199
moral responsibility 160
Morse, Adair, et al 53, 204
motivated reasoning 148
Murdoch, Rupert 137

negligence   105
Nelson, Robert L and Nielsen, Laura Beth   9, 10–11, 28, 34, 38, 63–64, 65, 78, 79, 148, 151–153, 157, 160, 163, 173–174, 199, 209
network of influence *see* tournament of influence
neutral adviser
   moral attentiveness and   192
   orientation as   11, 37–38, 160–162, 165, 167–170, 209–210
News of the World case   136–137, 228

objectivity
   cognitive blind spots   92, 133–134, 147–148
   generally   216
   independence and   69, 72, 88, 92, 94, 144–145, 214–216
   professional status and   146, 218
   risk assessment   97, 134, 141, 144–145, 217
organisational-professional conflict
   bullying behaviour   86–87
   generally   8–9, 95, 126, 145, 201–202
   lawyer's advice ignored   85–86
   prioritising client's wishes   156, 176
   professional codes of conduct   13, 124, 128
   public interest   6–7, 8–9, 70, 125, 176, 204
orientation *see* identity and orientation

Parker, Christine E, et al   64
Parsons, Talcott   90
payment protection insurance (PPI) debacle   133, 158, 221
performance-related incentives   73–74
power relations
   professionalism compromised by   203
pragmatism
   generally   19, 77, 88, 93–94, 106, 110, 114, 199, 212, 215–216
   risk management   121, 140, 146, 216
privilege
   legal professional   5–6, 20, 223
product recall
   commercialist view   155
professional status
   expectations created by   5–6, 140–142
   generally   5–11
   objectivity and   146, 218
   usefulness   146, 151, 218

professionalism/professional principles
   see also regulation of legal profession
   administration of justice   6, 39–40, 124, 128, 144, 177, 216
   best interests of client   12–14, 40, 176, 177–179, 199, 210–211, 221, 226
   codes of conduct   13, 124, 128, 144–145, 179, 180–182, 199, 227–228
   compromised   89–90, 91, 147, 203
   conflicting principles   9, 180
   ecological accounts of   7, 205–208, 222
   effective service and integrity   12–13, 39–40, 177–179, 210–211
   employers' understanding of   74–76, 183–184
   generally   5–11, 39–40, 229–230
   importance of professional title   151
   independence   7, 39–40, 71–72, 92, 140–142, 176–179, 199, 210–211, 214–216, 217–218
   influence generally   225–228
   institutional logics   206–211
   legality, obligation as to   39–40, 176–180, 210–211
   misuse of legal function   143–144
   power relations compromising   203
   professional ethical infrastructure   1, 29, 184–188
   professional legitimacy   222
   professional orientation   1, 29, 33, 38–40, 176–183, 210–211
   promoting ethicality   142
   public interest   5–7, 11–12, 144–145, 177–180, 201, 204
   public trust in   39, 177, 179
   risk management   124, 204
   rule of law   6, 12, 39–40, 124, 128, 145, 177, 179, 216, 226
   self-interest   5, 203
   social trusteeship   22, 200–205, 210
   understandings of   65, 67
promotion and advancement   50, 133–134, 216–217
public interest
   generally   230
   lawyers' professional obligation   5–7, 11–12, 144–145, 177–180, 201, 204
   public interest/commerce paradigm   6–7, 8–9, 70, 125, 176, 204
   risk and   145

Index

public sector, in-house lawyers
  generally 3, 42, 47, 150–151, 171–173
  independence 179
  professional principles usage 178, 179
public trust 39, 177, 179

recruitment interviews 187
red lines 128–132, 140, 145, 218
register of spending 119
registering position on file 89, 89n
regulation of legal profession
  codes of conduct 13, 124, 128, 144–145, 179, 180–182, 199, 226, 227–228
  generally 19–23, 71, 75–76, 226–228
  impact 180–182, 210–211, 217–218, 226–228
  independence as objective 89–90, 92
  professional principles 2, 12–13, 27, 38–40, 124–126, 128, 140, 145–146, 176–183, 195–199, 210–211, 217–218, 226
  SRA Competence Statement 226
  SRA Handbook 38–40, 128, 182, 183, 227
regulatory breaches
  dealing with 131–132, 137–138
  preparation for regulatory changes 51
  reporting 136–139
relationship management 228
reporting
  arrangements generally 1
  cost benefit calculation 139
  lines of 54–57
  proactive approach 139
  reporting regulatory breaches 136–137
  up and/or out 138–139
  written 136–137
reputational issues
  advice on 159
  ethicality enhancing reputation 142–143
  gatekeeping role 70
  reputational monitoring 120
  risk management 108–109, 130, 131, 142–143
  supply chain problems 111–113
research methods used
  aim 1, 2
  case study vignettes 2, 27
  generally 1–2, 26–29, 44–45
  interviews 29–32; Appendix A
  mapping indicators 34–40
  response rate to survey 40–42

risk of bias 41
survey 32–44
resignation
  willingness to consider 85–86, 214
Reynolds, Scott J
  moral attentiveness scale 190
risk
  accountability 107
  advisory role as to 105–106, 127, 134, 142, 159–160
  appetite *see* risk appetite
  approach to generally 206
  assessment 77, 97, 115–117, 126–127, 144–145, 217
  contingent nature of legality 104
  corporate culture 217–218
  created by non-risk taking 96
  defining 1, 7, 16, 95, 96, 97, 115, 125
  desirability of taking 95, 96–97, 144–145, 217
  encouraged by lawyer 159–160
  fine, actions risking 131
  groupthink problems 133
  identifying 2, 115, 119–120
  insurance against 118–119
  legal, defining 102–103, 104–111
  logics 95, 96–97, 144–145, 146, 217
  management *see* risk management
  measuring 115
  mitigation 114, 118–121
  normalising 98, 118, 144–145
  objective assessment 97, 134, 141, 144–145, 217
  professional codes of conduct 124–125, 128, 144–145
  progress and 96
  remuneration and status tied towards 20, 73–74
  reporting method 136–137
  responsibility for 104–105, 127, 224
  significant 215
  small steps leading to 133–134
  source of 107–108
  toleration of 117, 144–145
  who owns legal risk 104–111
risk appetite
  balancing interests 95
  concept generally 98, 120–121, 123, 126
  corporate culture 134, 217–218
  decision-taking 102–103, 127, 145
  defined 99–100
  dependent or independent 100–101

factors affecting   115–116, 117, 134
organisation-led   100–101, 145
risk accepters   101, 102–103
risk conservatives   101–102
risk facilitators   101, 103–104
setting   98–101
risk committee
reporting to   57
risk management
accepting some risk   87–89, 97, 98, 102–103, 117
allocation of responsibility   104–105, 127, 224
allowing risk-taking   76–77
approach to generally   206
broad approach   105–106, 108–109, 122–123
case studies   122–123
changing business practices   119
commercial orientation and   21, 156
compliance   115, 120, 121
compromising risk-assessment   20, 71, 95, 110
as core organising principle   96
cost benefit calculation   87–88, 117, 121, 130, 218, 225
defining risk   95, 96, 97, 115, 121–122
enterprise risk management   97
entrepreneurialism and   10–11, 124, 128
ethical space in risk assessment   139–143
ethicality generally   124–127
experiential approach   114–115
facilitating risk-taking   46
generally   1, 15–20, 26–27
hybrid-professionals   22, 46–47, 70, 217
identifying   115
in-housers' role   49, 50, 52, 68, 204, 216–218
incentives towards risk-taking   20, 46, 133–134
increasing adoption by organisations   98
independence and   124, 127, 147
influence within company   97, 110, 120–121, 123
insurance against risk   118–119
legal risks   1, 15–20, 102–103, 104–111
litigation risks   105–106
management processes   114–118
monitoring breaches   52, 120
narrow approach   106–108, 109–111, 122–123

negative impact   98
network of influence   17, 97, 110, 120–121, 123
non-legal risks   102–103, 110–111
observing trends   115
organisational-professional conflict   95
orientation towards   37
passing risk to others   102–103, 118–120
pragmatic approach   121, 140, 146, 216
process-based approach   97
professional codes of conduct   124–125, 128, 144–145
red lines   128–132, 140, 145, 218
reputational issues   108–109, 111–113, 130, 131, 142
staff surveys   120
strategic focus   16, 97
supply chain problems   111–113, 122–123
systems approach   115–118
tax policy   54
templates and checklists   119
timing disclosures   118
trend awareness   115
trial and error approach   133
variation in decision-making   99
who makes the decisions   102
willingness to say no   9–10, 22–23, 72, 76–86, 92–93, 214–216
Rolls-Royce bribery scandal   127, 146, 215, 228
Rosen, Robert Eli   148
Rostain, Tanina   10, 57, 79, 92–93, 215
rule of law
objective assessment of requirements   216
obligation to uphold   6, 12, 39–40, 124, 128, 145, 177, 179, 216, 226

sanctions-busting
enforcement-proofing   71
Sarbanes-Oxley Act (SOX)   19, 53, 79, 204, 222–223
secondment
as gateway into in-house practice   49–50
securities fraud
equity incentives and   53–54
lawyer in management role   53–54
self-censorship   72
shareholders
director's primary obligation to   60
shareholder value   224
Siemens   4
Smedley Review   228

social responsibility
  societal orientation 171, 172
  supply chain problems 112–113
social trusteeship 22, 153
  professionalism 200–205, 210
Solicitors Regulation Authority *see* regulation of legal profession
staff surveys 120
status of in-house lawyers
  board membership 54–55, 58–59, 224–225
  employer status and 8
  expectations created by 140–142
  generally 8, 48–49, 68, 72, 148, 149, 204, 208
  increasing 8, 9
  independence and 146
  leadership role 146, 228
  leading to complacency 142, 146, 183, 187, 218
  perceived as obstructive 62–63, 78–79, 81, 89, 101, 213
  risk management 15
  tied towards risk-taking 20
supplier
  non-ethical behaviour by 111–113, 122–123

Tawney, Richard H, et al 229
tax avoidance
  creative compliance 18, 64, 71, 131, 145, 157, 203, 218
  General Counsel in management role 54
  risk management 54
team culture 29, 210
team loyalty 148
team orientation 29, 33, 170–172, 199, 210
team size
  ethical pressure and 67
  generally 47, 68
third sector
  in-house lawyers 42, 47, 150, 172–173
  professional principles usage 178
The Times case 228
tournament of influence
  case studies 135–137
  corporate hierarchy 72, 123, 213, 216–217
  'credit banks' 81–82
  explanatory legitimacy 81
  generally 51, 69, 70–78
  identity/orientation and 172–175
  independence and 71–76, 89–94, 145, 214–216
  lawyers as advisors 160–162
  lawyers as influencers 3, 7, 161
  network positioning generally 71–76

place of in-housers 211–213
pragmatism 77, 140, 146, 216
risk management 17, 97, 110, 120–121, 123
self-censorship 72
utility, socialisation and biases 132–137
willingness to say no 72, 76–86, 92–93, 174–175, 214–216
trade ban compliance 131
training
  professional ethical infrastructure 185–186, 210
  risk management 114, 115, 119, 120, 122
troubled subservience orientation 36–38
Tversky, Amos 152
Tyco 4

Uber 4
uncertainty
  attitudes towards 23, 29, 222
  exploiting 11, 14, 21, 36–38, 157–160, 167–179, 199, 209
  legal 38, 127, 128–129, 130, 133, 140, 145, 211, 219–220, 228–229
  risk management 218
United States
  Alien Tort Claims Act 19
  compliance regulation generally 19–20
  Foreign Corrupt Practices Act 19, 51, 223
  Sarbanes-Oxley Act 19, 53, 79, 204, 222–223
  SEC compliance 19, 53, 222–223
  Yates Memo 223

value-adding
  ethicality creating 142–143
  in-housers' role 3, 50, 51, 68, 212–213
  intangibility of legal value 63
  perception of 62–63
Volkswagen emissions scandal 216
voluntary sector *see* third sector

Wald, Eli and Pearce, Russell G 206
warranties
  risk management and 119
Weaver, Sally R 58
whistleblowing 71, 86
wire-stripping 225, 228
work delegation 51
working conditions
  supply chain problems 112–113, 122–123

Yates Memo 223
Yoo, John 4